TOURISM

Tourism: The Key Concepts offers a comprehensive collection of the most frequently used and studied concepts in the subject of tourism. Within the text, key terms, concepts, typologies and frameworks are examined in the context of the broader social sciences, blending together theory and practice to explore the scope of the subject. Terms covered include:

- authenticity
- destination management
- geographies of tourism
- hospitality
- LGBT tourism
- mobility
- planning for tourism
- society and culture
- sociology in tourism
- tourism strategy

Each entry contextualizes, defines and debates the concept discussed, providing an excellent starting point for those studying tourism for the first time, and a quick reference for those who are more experienced. With case studies, examples and further reading throughout, this text will be invaluable for all undergraduate and postgraduate tourism students.

Peter Robinson is Principal Lecturer and Head of Leisure at the University of Wolverhampton, UK. He has previously worked in senior management positions in the tourism industry, and has published internationally on the subjects of tourism and events management.

ALSO AVAILABLE FROM ROUTLEDGE

Tourism Management (Fourth Edition)
Stephen Page
978-0-08-096932-9

Worldwide Destinations: The Geography of Travel and Tourism (Sixth Edition)
Brian Boniface, Chris Cooper, Robyn Cooper
978-0-08-097040-0

Tourism and Climate Change: Impacts, Adaptation & Mitigation
Daniel Scott, C. Michael Hall, Stefan Gossling
978-0-415-66886-6

TOURISM

The Key Concepts

Edited by
Peter Robinson

Routledge
Taylor & Francis Group

LONDON AND NEW YORK

First published 2012
by Routledge
2 Park Square, Milton Park, Abingdon, Oxon OX14 4RN

Simultaneously published in the USA and Canada
by Routledge
711 Third Avenue, New York, NY 10017

Routledge is an imprint of the Taylor & Francis Group, an informa business

British Library Cataloguing in Publication Data
A catalogue record for this book is available from the British Library

Library of Congress Cataloging in Publication Data
Tourism : the key concepts / edited by Peter Robinson.
   p. cm. – (Routledge key guides)
   Includes bibliographical references and index.
   1. Tourism–Philosophy. I. Robinson, Peter.
   G155.A1T58925 2012
   338.4'791–dc23
         2012004159

ISBN: 978-0-415-67792-9 (hbk)
ISBN: 978-0-415-67793-6 (pbk)
ISBN: 978-0-203-10491-0 (ebk)

Typeset in Bembo
by Taylor & Francis Books

CONTENTS

LIST OF KEY CONCEPTS

accommodation providers
adventure tourism
agritourism (or farm tourism)
air transport
arts tourism
authenticity
backpacking
business tourism
carrying capacity
coastal and marine tourism
community-based tourism
consumer behaviour
corporate social responsibility
crisis management
cruise tourism
dark tourism (also thanatourism)
destination image
destination management
destination management organizations
destination marketing
domestic tourism
economics of tourism
ecotourism
education in tourism
entrepreneurship
ethnography
e-tourism
events and festivals
family tourism
film and TV tourism
gastronomy and food tourism
genealogical (or ancestral) tourism

geographies of tourism
geotourism
globalization
health and wellness tourism
heritage tourism
hospitality
human resources management
hyper-reality
independent travel
information technology
leisure
LGBT tourism
literary tourism
marketing for tourism
mass tourism
medical tourism
micro- and macro-environments
mobility
motivation
multiplier and leakage
nature tourism
neo-colonialism
niche tourism
operations management
planning for tourism
pro-poor tourism
public sector
recreation
regeneration
religious tourism
responsible tourism
rural tourism
self and other
semiotics
serious leisure
service quality
sex tourism
shopping and tourism
slow tourism
society and culture
sociology
spa tourism

special interest tourism
sport tourism
stakeholders
sustainable tourism
tour operations
tourism and the environment
tourism education
tourism ethics
tourism histories
tourism in developing countries
tourism lifecycle (and destination lifecycle)
tourism policy
tourism strategy
tourism supply and demand
tourism system
tourist experience
tourist gaze
transport
travel
urban tourism
virtual tourism
visitor attractions
visitor interpretation
voluntary (third) sector
wildlife tourism
wine tourism

LIST OF CONTRIBUTORS

Editor

Peter Robinson is Principal Lecturer and Head of the Leisure Department at University of Wolverhampton, UK. His responsibilities also extend to the management of the Arena Theatre, a university-owned arts venue. Peter has a background working in tourism and events management in the public, private and voluntary sectors, and his research interests include tourism management, events management, and visuality in tourism. Peter has published a number of edited textbooks, including *Operations Management in the Travel Industry* (CABI, 2009), *Events Management* (CABI, 2010) and *Research Themes for Tourism* (CABI, 2011), together with journal articles, industry publications and presentations at international research and industry conferences. Peter is the West Midlands Representative for the Tourism Management Institute and is also a member for the Executive Committee for the Association for Event Management Education.

Contributors

Dr. Marcjanna M. Augustyn is Senior Lecturer at Hull University Business School, UK. Her research interests include strategic management, strategic marketing and quality management within tourism and other service industries. She has published widely in these areas and also co-edited a volume, *Tourism in the New Europe: Perspectives on SME Policies and Practices* (Elsevier, 2006), within the Advances in Tourism Research Series. She is the Book Reviews Editor for *Tourism Analysis: An Interdisciplinary Journal*. She is also a member of the Editorial Review Board of *The Tourism Review* and a member of the Editorial Board of Advances in Hospitality and Leisure.

Dr. Iride Azara is a Lecturer in Tourism at the University of Derby, Buxton, UK. She is an active member of the university's Culture, Lifestyle and Landscape Research Group. Her research interests relate to heritage attractions, festivals, cultural tourism and the overall changing dynamics of these cultural practices. Recently she has begun researching in the area of spa and wellness tourism in conjunction with the move of the faculty to the Spa town of Buxton. Iride is a member of the ATLAS SIG Spa and Wellness Tourism, and in 2007 co-presented a research paper entitled 'Profiling day-spa visitors and motivations to experience wellness at home' at the ATLAS SIG meeting on Spa and Wellness Tourism: Historic Concept, Future Prospects in Budapest.

Dr. Sue Beeton is Associate Professor in Tourism and Director of the Tourism and Hospitality Research Unit at La Trobe University, Australia, where she specializes in film-induced tourism and tourism as a tool for community development. She has published over 25 articles in academic journals, as well as numerous book chapters, with her published books including *Ecotourism: A Practical Guide for Rural Communities* (Landlinks Press, 1998), which was also published in Japanese, *Film-Induced Tourism* (Channel View Publications, 2004) and *Community Development through Tourism* (Landlinks Press, 2006). She is currently working on a new publication on *Tourism, Film and the Moving Image*.

Harry Cameron is currently a Visiting Lecturer in the Department of Leisure at the University of Wolverhampton, UK. Harry has a background working in leisure, sport management, tourism planning, tourism transport studies and tourism destination management, and is currently undertaking doctoral research into power and politics at UK seaside resorts, with a particular focus on developments since 1945 at New Brighton in north-west England. He has contributed to the *Encyclopedia of Leisure and Outdoor Recreation* (Routledge, 2003) and has presented papers on seaside tourism history, investigating the 'maritime gaze', critical realism and seaside histories. Harry has worked on several overseas tourism destination management projects and has taught tourism in the Maldives, Hong Kong and Macau.

Dr. Jenny Cave is Senior Lecturer in Tourism and Hospitality Management at the University of Waikato in Hamilton, New Zealand. With a background in anthropology, museology and the management of cultural industries, her research interests include island tourism, cultural/heritage entrepreneurship, collaborative methods, rural tourism, events and migration. She has published in journals and research volumes on these topics, as well as on backpacker tourism and business macro-performance. She has guest edited three volumes on island tourism (marketing heritage, destinations and crisis response) and is a member of the Editorial Review Boards of the *International Journal of Culture, Tourism and Hospitality Research* and the *International Journal of Event and Festival Management*.

Dr. Glen Croy is a Senior Lecturer in Tourism at the Department of Management at Monash University, Australia. Glen's special areas of research interest are the role of media in tourism and tourism education. He also has an active research interest in tourism in natural and protected areas. A co-convenor of the International Tourism and Media (ITAM) conferences, Glen is also involved in the Research Skills Development framework projects and the innovative development and delivery of destination-partnered learning opportunities for students. Merging his interests in tourism, the media and natural and protected areas, Glen has been involved in a number of projects partnered with protected area agencies, including one on pre-visit communication for parks agencies.

Dr. Paul Fallon is a Senior Lecturer in the School of Sport, Performing Arts and Leisure at the University of Wolverhampton, UK, where he teaches tourism, hospitality, leisure, sport and events subject areas. His main research interests relate to consumer behaviour within the tourism sector (including visitor satisfaction, visitor perceptions, repeat visitation, student tourism, LGBT tourism and niche tourism). His work has been presented at international conferences and published in a variety of journals and books. He has carried out editorial and review work for a number of international journals and conferences, and has also completed research projects for a range of organizations, including the North West Development Agency, Marketing Manchester, Chester Civic Trust and the British Educational Travel Association.

Professor Alan Fyall is Professor in Tourism and Deputy Dean Research and Enterprise in the School of Tourism, Bournemouth University, Australia. He has published widely in his fields of expertise and is the author of over 100 articles, book chapters and conference papers, as well as 13 books, including co-author of *Tourism Principles and Practice* (Pearson Education Ltd, 1993, republished 2008), one of the leading international textbooks on the subject. Alan has organized a number of international conferences and workshops and sits on the editorial boards of the *Annals of Tourism Research*, the *Journal of Heritage Tourism* and the *International Journal of Tourism Research*. He is also Editor-in-Chief of Elsevier's new *Journal of Destination Marketing & Management*. His current research interests lie in destination management and emerging destination management structures, and the impact of generational change upon patterns of buying behaviour in the context of attractions and destinations. He is a former member of the Bournemouth Tourism Management Board and has conducted numerous consulting and applied research projects for clients across the UK and overseas. Alan currently serves on the ESRC Cluster Advisory Board for Exeter University Business School and is a reviewer for the Research Grants Commission in Hong Kong and the Department for Business, Innovation and Skills in the UK. Finally, Alan is a Fellow of the Tourism Society and a member of the Institute of Travel and Tourism.

Dr. Brian Garrod is Reader in Tourism Management at the School of Management and Business, Aberystwyth University, Wales. His specialisms cover sustainable tourism, ecotourism and heritage tourism. He has been a consultant to the United Nations World Tourism Organization and the Organization for Economic Co-operation and Development (OECD). He is Book Reviews Editor of the *Journal of Heritage Tourism* and currently sits on the editorial board of the *Journal of Ecotourism*, the *International Journal of Tourism Research*, *Tourism in Marine Environments* and the *International Journal of Sustainable Development*. His publishing output includes more than 20 papers in academic journals and four text books, among which is *Managing Visitor Attractions* (Elsevier, 2008), which he co-authored, now in its second edition. Along with Alan Fyall, he is joint editor of Goodfellow Publishers' *Contemporary Cases* book series. He is a member of the Tourism Society and a Fellow of the Higher Education Academy.

Dr. Gul Gunes is Assistant Professor and Department Head of Tourism and Hotel Management at Atilim University, Ankara, Turkey. Prior to her current position she was a research assistant in Ankara University, Department of Landscape Architecture, served with the Ministry of Environment and Forestry and was a part-time lecturer at Bilkent University, Department of Tourism and Hotel Management, and Ankara University, Department of Tourism Guidance. Her research interests are environmental management, sustainable tourism, nature conservation and participatory management planning in protected areas. She is the co-author of a book entitled *Sustainable Tourism Development Strategy for Protected Areas of Turkey* (2007). Some of her international papers are 'Identification of environmental threats in tourism destinations' (1998); 'Ecotourism in an old-growth forest of Turkey: The Kure Mountains experience' (2007); 'Tourism destination sustainability and NGOs: Beypazari Case' (2010); and 'World Heritage sites as tourism resources: The case of Safranbolu, Turkey' (2011).

Dr. Ebru Günlü is Associate Professor and Chair of the Department of Tourism Management, Faculty of Business, T. C. Dokuz Eylul University, Izmir, Turkey, where she completed her PhD thesis entitled *The Interaction between Conflict Management and Organizational Culture in the Hospitality Industry* in 2003. Dr. Günlü delivers undergraduate and postgraduate courses on Human Resources in Tourism, Human Resources Planning, Management of Tourism Operations, Organizational Change and Development, Convention Management and Tourism Sociology. Her main research interests lie in the application of managerial issues and behavioural sciences to the hospitality industry. Besides contributing numerous chapters to edited volumes, such as 'Crisis management in tourist destinations', which appeared in the 2005 edition of *Global Tourism* (Butterworth-Heinemann), as well as a conference paper, 'Concerning crisis management', presented at the International Congress on Marine Tourism, she has co-authored the book *Convention Management* (Educational Institute of the American Hotel and Motel Association).

Dr. Edward H. Huijbens is a geographer and scholar of tourism at the Icelandic Tourism Research Centre and the University of Akureyri, Iceland. His current research interests include health and wellness tourism, landscape experiences, tourism innovation and marketing strategies. Edward is the author of articles in several scholarly journals in Iceland and internationally, and has co-edited *Technology in Society/Society in Technology* (University of Iceland Press, 2005), *Sensi/able Spaces: Space, Art and the Environment* (Cambridge Scholars Press, 2007) and *The Illuminating Traveller* (University of Jyväskylä, 2008).

Dr. John S. Hull is Associate Professor of Tourism at Thompson Rivers University in British Columbia, Canada. He is also a Visiting Professor at the University of Trento, Italy, and a member of the Icelandic Tourism Research Centre and the New Zealand

Tourism Research Institute. His current research is focused on sustainable tourism in peripheral regions, strategic tourism planning and destination development, and community-based tourism development. John has worked on tourism planning projects in North America, Europe, the Middle East, Africa and Asia.

Dr. Lee Jolliffe is Professor of Hospitality and Tourism at the University of New Brunswick, Canada. With an academic background in museology, Lee has research interests in the intersection of culture and tourism, especially in the context of urban and rural settings, as well as of museums and arts events in North Atlantic Islands, South-East Asia and the Caribbean. Internationally, she has been a Visiting Professor at Hanoi University, Vietnam, and the Almond Chair in Tourism and Hospitality Management at the University of West Indies, Barbados. Her edited volumes include *Tea and Tourism: Tourists, Traditions and Transformations* (Channel View Publications, 2007) and *Coffee Culture, Destinations and Tourism* (Channel View Publications, 2010). Lee serves on the editorial boards of the *Annals of Tourism Research*, the *International Journal of Contemporary Hospitality Management*, *Tourism: An International Journal* and the *International Journal of Tourism Policy*.

Dr. Catheryn Khoo-Lattimore is an Associate Professor at the School of Hospitality, Tourism and Culinary Arts, Taylor's University, Malaysia. She holds a PhD in Marketing from the University of Otago, New Zealand. Her research interests lie mainly in the areas of tourism marketing, and include topics on tourist behaviour, tourist complaints and compliments, and tourist psychology. She is also ardently involved with helping doctoral students to complete the PhD successfully and has recently published *Secrets of Promising PhD Scholars Revealed* (2011). Wearing the PhD-mentor hat, Catheryn has been invited to speak at many international seminars and colloquiums for doctoral candidates.

Dr. Christine Lee is an Assistant Lecturer in the Department of Management at Monash University's only rural campus in Australia. Her research interests are in social inclusion, health and well-being, tourism, international business and management. She has published in international journals and presented her work at various international conferences. She is an Associate Editor of the *Higher Education Research and Development Journal*. In the local community, she is the Treasurer of the Latrobe City Business Tourism Association and Deputy Chairperson of the Gippsland Ethnic Communities' Council.

She also serves on the Latrobe City Tourism Advisory Board, Gippsland Heritage Park Committee of Management, Walhalla Tourist Railway Reserve Committee of Management, Latrobe City Disability Reference Committee and the Latrobe Cultural Diversity Reference Committee. For her community service, she has received the Government of Victoria's Multicultural Award for Meritorious Service to the Community (Individual).

Dr. Michael Lück is Associate Professor and Head of Department of Tourism and Events, and Associate Director with the New Zealand Tourism Research Institute (NZTRI), both at Auckland University of Technology in Auckland, New Zealand. He specializes in coastal and marine tourism, ecotourism, wildlife tourism, sustainable tourism, aviation and gay tourism. Michael published in various international journals, edited or co-edited two volumes on ecotourism, two on marine tourism, and two on polar tourism. He was also the overall editor of the *Encyclopedia of Tourism and Recreation in Marine Environments* (CABI, 2008). Michael is the founding Editor-in-Chief of the international academic journal *Tourism in Marine Environments* and Associate Editor of the *Journal of Ecotourism*.

Dr. Lisa Melsen is a Lecturer with the School of Management at La Trobe University, Victoria, Australia. Her research interests include tourism destination development, tourist motivations, tourist behaviour, value creation, food and wine tourism, festivals, events and regional/rural tourism. Lisa has completed a number of research projects in the areas of events and value creation for the tourism industry, the most recent one being her PhD. These projects have had a strong regional/rural focus, which continues to be the emphasis of her research. Lisa has also presented her work at Australian and international conferences and is in the process of publishing her research findings.

Dr. Vikneswaran Nair is an Associate Professor and Director of Research and Development at Taylor's University, Malaysia, where he specializes in the application of information and communication technology in hospitality and tourism, sustainable tourism, ecotourism management and environmental management, and is currently engaged in research in the field of responsible tourism and poverty alleviation via tourism. A seasoned and award-winning researcher and consultant for many government projects, he was honoured with the Outstanding Young Malaysian of the Year Award in 2006 and 2009. He has published extensively in major journals in tourism, environment and education, and served as editor and reviewer for the *Journal of Hospitality and Tourism Research*, the *Journal of Tourism Geography*, the *Asia Pacific Journal of Tourism*, *Tourism Review* and the *TEAM Journal of Hospitality and Tourism*.

Dr. Roselyne N. Okech is Assistant Professor and Head of Department for Tourism Studies at Grenfell Campus, Memorial University of Newfoundland, Canada, where she specializes in ecotourism and community and cultural issues in tourism, and is currently researching heritage tourism and spa tourism. Her key publications include *Managing Sustainable Events: Using Kenya as a Case Study* (CABI, 2009) and *Human Resources Perspectives on the Management of Events in Kenya* (CABI, 2009), together with journal articles, including 'Tourism impacts on local communities around coastal zones: Issues of sustainable development' (*Journal of Tourism Challenges and Trends*) and 'Socio-cultural impacts of tourism on World Heritage sites: Communities' perspectives of Lamu and Zanzibar Islands' (*Asia Pacific Journal*).

Ade Oriade is a Senior Lecturer in Tourism Management and Trans-National Education (TNE) Programmes Manager at the University of Wolverhampton, UK. Having worked in the industry in different capacities, Ade brings his service delivery experiences to bear in teaching services and operations management modules. Ade specializes in quality management in tourism, and also has a special interest in tourism/hospitality career analysis and sustainable tourism development. His current research focuses on the conceptualization of quality and its relationship with other service constructs, such as satisfaction, value, equity and behavioural intentions. Ade teaches across the leisure industries programme portfolio at Wolverhampton, which includes event and venue, hospitality and tourism management.

Linda Phillips is Principal Lecturer and Academic Group Leader for Management, Marketing and Services, Award Leader for Tourism Management and Events Management and International Programme Advisor for programmes delivered in Kosovo for Staffordshire University, UK. Linda has taught on a range of programmes at undergraduate, postgraduate and professional level. She specializes in marketing, tourism and events and has industry experience of marketing and corporate events. Linda's research interests include destination image and branding, and she is currently studying for a PhD focusing on the role of destination image in student decision-making. Linda has presented papers at conferences and published in academic journals and books. She is currently an external examiner for tourism and events and for business management, a chartered marketer, and a member of the Academy of Marketing and The Chartered Institute of Marketing.

Dr. Ige Pirnar is Professor and Chair of the Department of Tourism and Hotel Management, Yasar University, Turkey. Previously, Ige held job postings at Bilkent University and was Assistant Director of the School of Tourism and Hotel Management, Vice Chair of the Department of Computer Aided Accounting and Vice Chair of the Department of Commerce and Administration. He has also worked as a part-time lecturer at METU, Izmir University of Economics and Beykent University. Ige has written four books in Turkish: *Convention and Meetings Management*, *TQM in Tourism*, *Direct Marketing* and *PR in Tourism*, and is one of the editors of *Quality Management in Services*. He has published numerous articles on tourism management, international tourism studies, global marketing, alternative tourism applications, hospitality marketing and European Union tourism policy in national and international journals (e.g. *Tourism Analysis* and *Annals of Tourism Research*) and presented at national and international conferences.

Ghislaine Povey has been involved in the tourism and hospitality industry for most of her life, including restaurants, pubs and as a worldwide consultant. Since 1992 she has been an academic at the University of Wolverhampton, UK, where she has undertaken a range of teaching, consultancy and research roles. Ghislaine has authored a growing portfolio of articles and book chapters in the areas of events, culture, heritage and gastronomy. She is particularly interested in the links between food, culture, tourism and heritage, and is currently pursuing a PhD in this area.

Lisa Power is a Senior Lecturer in Tourism at Southampton Solent University, UK. Her professional tourism background is in tour operations, having worked overseas as a tour manager and courier. She also worked as a registered Green Badge tour guide for the Heart of England and Cotswolds. She is currently completing a PhD on the role of the tour guide in cross-cultural communication. In recent years, Lisa has been resident in the major British cruise port of Southampton and teaches on the cruise industry management undergraduate degree programme at Southampton Solent University.

Roya Rahimi is a PhD candidate of Tourism and Hospitality Management at Dokuz Eylul University, Izmir, Turkey. Roya completed an MSc in Tourism and Hospitality Management at Lulea University of Technology, Lulea, Sweden, and holds a BA in Industrial Management from Sheikhbahai University, Isfahan, Iran. While undertaking her PhD studies, she was a Research Assistant at the Management Department of Izmir University. In broadening her knowledge and academic experience, Roya became a PhD visiting student at the University of Wolverhampton, UK. Her research interests include customer relationship management (CRM) in the tourism and hospitality industry, the use of information technology (IT) in tourism, customer behaviour, the sociology of tourism and tourism economy. Her publishing outputs include a number of papers mainly in the area of CRM in tourism and the hotel industry. She has presented several papers at various conferences. Her industry experience comprises seven years of working experience in the hotel industry in a number of international hotels.

Dr. Dirk Reiser is a Lecturer of Business and Tourism at the Cologne Business School, Germany, and the University of Tasmania, Hobart, Australia. He is a social scientist who studied and worked in Germany, Nicaragua, New Zealand and Australia. Dirk also works at the European Overseas Campus of the University of Flensburg in Bali. His research interests include sustainable tourism, tourism and zoos/wildlife parks, climate change and tourism, event tourism, the history of tourism, World Heritage and tourism, and globalization and tourism. He has contributed to a number of books, including *Food and Wine Festivals and Events around the World* (Elsevier, 2008), *Contemporary Management* (McGraw-Hill, 2010) and *Facing Climate Change and the Global Economic Crisis: Challenges for the Future of Tourism* (2011).

Volker Rundshagen is Lecturer of Business and Tourism at Cologne Business School, Germany. In his early career stages he completed an apprenticeship and worked as a travel agent. He earned his first tourism degree at Angell Akademie Freiburg, and then held sales support positions with tour operators and in the airline industry. In 2001, he completed his MA in Tourism Management at the University of Brighton, UK, followed by tourism consultancy assignments for a German tourist destination and a Swiss travel intermediary start-up. In 2006, Volker joined his current employer, transferring his industry experience and his passion for the field into a new career in higher education. Upon the successful pursuit of part-time studies, he received his MBA from the University of Louisville, Kentucky, US, in 2007, and currently Volker is studying, once again part time, towards the DBA degree in Higher Education Management at the University of Bath, UK.

Geoff Shirt is a Senior Lecturer at the School of Culture and Lifestyle, University of Derby, Buxton, UK, where he specializes in tourism and business management, and is currently researching the motivation for rural recreation by ethnic groups, dark tourism and access to accessible higher education. He has contributed to several books, including *Tourism and National Parks: International Perspectives on Development, Histories and Change* (Routledge, 2009) and *Research Themes for Tourism* (CABI, 2010), and contributes to the LSA series of journals and the Dark Tourism Forum.

Carol Southall is a Lecturer in Tourism and Event Management at Staffordshire University, UK. With over 20 years of tourism industry experience in contract and operations management, and 16 years of further and higher education teaching experience, much of which was gained alongside industry experience, Carol continues to apply the practical elements of her operational role in an academic context. Research interests include the relationship between cultural awareness and service quality perception in tourism, as well as LGBT tourism and family tourism. She is a member of the European Regions Research and Innovation Network (ERRIN) Tourism Working Group in Brussels. Alongside teaching and research, Carol continues to work as a tour manager and driver, escorting tours to diverse destinations in the UK and Europe.

Isobel Stockdale is the Programme Leader for Beauty, Hair and Spa at the University of Derby, Buxton, UK. Having qualified and worked as a spa and beauty therapist in the UK, Isobel decided to enter education and has worked for the last 20 years in both the further and higher education sectors. Her research interests relate to spa, wellness and tourism, which informs programme development and teaching. In 2007, she co-presented a research paper entitled 'Profiling day-spa visitors and motivations to experience wellness at home' at the ATLAS SIG meeting on Spa and Wellness Tourism: Historic Concept, Future Prospects in Budapest.

Dr. Philip R. Stone is Executive Director of The Institute for Dark Tourism Research (*i*DTR) at the University of Central Lancashire (UCLan), UK. A former management consultant and general manager, Philip has an extensive commercial background within the UK private sector, which he now combines with social science perspectives to deliver undergraduate and postgraduate education within UCLan's School of Sport, Tourism and the Outdoors. Philip has a PhD in Thanatology – society's reactions to, and perceptions of, mortality. His thesis appraised the consumption of dark tourism (travel to sites of death, disaster or the seemingly macabre) and its fundamental interrelationship with death and dying in society. Philip also acts as a media consultant on dark tourism; his clients include the BBC, History Television, *The New York Times*, *The New Scientist*, the *Guardian*, and a host of other UK and international press and broadcast outlets. Philip has also presented at numerous international conferences, including delivering keynote addresses in the UK, the US, Taiwan, Estonia and Germany. Philip has published extensively in the area of dark tourism, and co-authored *The Darker Side of Travel: The Theory and Practice of Dark Tourism* (Channel View Publications, 2009) and *Tourist Experience: Contemporary Perspectives* (Routledge, 2011). His forthcoming book (with Richard Sharpley), *The Contemporary Tourist Experience: Concepts and Consequences*, is due to be published by Routledge in 2012.

Dr. Carsten Wergin is Senior Research Fellow at the Institute for Social Anthropology, Martin Luther University, Halle-Wittenberg, Germany, and Visiting Fellow at the Social Policy Research Centre, University of New South Wales, Sydney, Australia. He specializes in the anthropology of music and tourism in broad sociocultural and historical perspectives. Apart from extensive fieldwork phases in the Mascarene Archipelago in the south-west Indian Ocean, more recent research on tourism development, culture and heritage has brought him to the Kimberley region of Western Australia. Among his numerous publications are the journal article 'Re-scaling the anthropology of tourism" (2009), the monograph 'Kréol Blouz: Musical enactments of identity and culture' (2010) and the edited volume, with Fabian Holt, *Musical Performance and the Changing City* (Routledge, 2012).

Peter Wiltshier's interest in regeneration comes from a concern for the role of the resident and host in local communities. His role as senior lecturer and programme leader for travel and tourism management at the University of Derby in Buxton, UK, is to ensure that the public and private sector work together to develop resources and skills for communities to take charge of their own destinies. Building social capital by using learning in communities creates resource banks for the long-term benefit of all. Peter's focus is on embedding knowledge of 'when, where, how and who' to make everyone's lives easier where funds have allowed learning through experiences already obtained.

Caroline Ann Wiscombe is a Senior Lecturer in Hospitality and Retailing at Leeds Metropolitan University, UK. She specializes in financial and management accounting for hospitality and retailing, as well as small business development, strategic management and entrepreneurship at both undergraduate and postgraduate level. Caroline has been involved in higher education for over ten years and is currently undertaking doctoral research into the need for emotional literacy in the management of change. Key publications and conference papers reflect her pedagogic and teaching-related interests, including chapters on finance and funding in *Operations Management in the Travel Industry* (CABI, 2000) and *Learning Matters: Sport Management* (Sage Publications, 2009), as well as conference papers discussing the cruise industry, coastal communities and Foundation degrees. Her current entrepreneurial interests are based in West Cumbria, where she is developing a tourism and hospitality project, while her current research interests are in rural and wildlife tourism sustainability and corporate social responsibility (CSR) business strategies.

LIST OF ABBREVIATIONS

AA	Automobile Association
AAA	American Automobile Association
ACE	Association of Cruise Experts
ACR	Association of Consumer Research
AI	all inclusive
ANT	Actor Network Theory
B&B	bed-and-breakfast
B2B	business-to-business
BOAC	British Overseas Airways Corporation
CBT	community-based tourism
CCB	community capacity-building
CPD	continuing professional development
CRM	customer relationship management
CRS	Central Reservation System/Computer Reservations System
CSP	corporate social performance
CSR	corporate social responsibility
CVB	convention and visitor bureau
3DVT	three-dimensional virtual tourism
DEPICTS	demographic, economic, political, infrastructural, competitor, technological and sociocultural factors
DIY	do-it-yourself
DMC	destination management company
DMO	destination management/marketing organization
DMP	destination management/marketing partnership
ECC	effective carrying capacity
EIU	Economic Intelligence Unit
ETC	European Travel Commission
FID	free independent traveller
FIFA	Fédération Internationale de Football Association
GDP	gross domestic product
GDS	Global Distribution System

GIS	geographic information systems
HR	human resources
HRM	human resource management
HRP	human resource planning
IATA	International Air Transport Association
ICAO	International Civil Aviation Organization
ICRT	International Centre for Responsible Tourism
ICT	information communication technology
*i*DTR	The Institute for Dark Tourism Research
IFEA	International Festivals and Events Association
IGLTA	International Gay and Lesbian Travel Association
IIED	International Institute for Environment and Development
IT	information technology
ITT	Institute of Travel and Tourism (UK)
JCR	*Journal of Consumer Research*
LAC	limits of acceptable change
LCC	low-cost carrier
LGBT	lesbian, gay, bisexual and transgender
MICE	meeting, incentive, conference/convention/congress, exhibition/event
MPI	Meeting Professionals International
NEC	National Exhibition Centre
NGO	non-governmental organization
NTA	National Tour Association
NTO	National Tourism Organization
ODI	Overseas Development Institute
OECD	Organization for Economic Co-operation and Development
PATA	Pacific Asia Travel Association
PEST	political, economic, sociocultural and technological factors
PESTEL	political, economic, sociocultural, technological, environmental and legal factors
PPP	public–private partnership
PPT	pro-poor tourism
QAS	Quality Assurance Scheme
RAC	Royal Automobile Club
RCC	real carrying capacity
REP	recreation experience preference
RTP	Regional Tourism Partnership
RV	recreational vehicle

3S	sun, sand and sea
SARS	severe acute respiratory syndrome
SIDS	small island developing states
SIT	special interest tourism
SME	small- and medium-sized enterprise
STEEPLE	sociocultural, technological, environmental, economic, political, legal and ethical factors
SWOT	strengths, weaknesses, opportunities, threats
TALC	tourism area lifecycle
TIC	tourist information centre
TIES	The International Ecotourism Society
TMI	Tourism Management Institute (UK)
TOMM	Tourism Optimization Management Modelling
TQM	total quality management
TTRA	Travel and Tourism Research Association
UK	United Kingdom
UNCED	United Nations Conference on Environment and Development
UNEP	United Nations Environment Programme
UNESCO	United Nations Educational, Scientific and Cultural Organization
UNWTO	United Nations World Tourism Organization
US	United States
VAMP	Visitor Area Management Plan
VAQAS	Visitor Attraction Quality Assurance Scheme
VFR	visiting friends and relatives
VIC	Visitor Information Centre
WCED	World Commission on Environment and Development
WES	World Ecotourism Summit
WTB	Wales Tourist Board
WTM	world travel market
WTO	World Trade Organization
WTTC	World Travel and Tourism Council
YHA	Youth Hostel Association

LIST OF FIGURES AND TABLES

Figures

Tables

INTRODUCTION

Tourism

Tourism can be divided into two themes: tourism management and tourism studies. The difference is in the application of tourism. As a management discipline, tourism has relevance on a regional, national and global stage; is represented in the public, private and third sectors; and is seen as a major economic contributor. As an area of study, or research, tourism enables us to better understand the world around us, the way in which we travel within it, and the relationship between social mobility, regional cultures and the different places where these interactions occur. It has emerged from many different subject areas, and so many of the ideas, concepts and models which underpin tourism find their origins in different areas of research and study. Geography, for example, is essential to our understanding of spatial patterns, resources and movement; economics is closely linked to geography as it is tied to the use and capitalization of resources. History is equally important to define the development of travel and also as a central pillar of tourism destinations, with heritage and culture often acting as the focus for visitors. Sociology is a third area of interest as this defines the way in which societies and individuals behave, and explores the factors that influence decision-making and create demand for tourism, together with providing a foundation for studying the social impacts of tourism. Business studies, marketing and management theory are essential in order to understand the different organizations in tourism and the methods and modalities for the management of tourism businesses. Other topics include law, environmental science, psychology, anthropology, agriculture, politics, education and many more.

The composite nature of the construction of tourism is a key factor in understanding how the subject area has developed. It does, of course, claim rightful ownership of some specific frameworks (e.g. the Tourism System by Leiper); but it is also still a developing area of research. Since the 1970s, much has been discussed and debated in tourism; but the nature of the subject is such that, as quickly as the ground rules are established, other developments, such as new technologies, change the nature of our understanding of tourism and its relationship with people and places.

Tourism is often discussed as leisure, or as hospitality, and sometimes as recreation, although in truth it is none of these things, yet includes all of them, but within a framework where time and location are key variables. There is a general agreement that 'leisure' can be treated as an overarching title for the activities that we engage in during our free time, and that recreation is an activity that takes place close to home and for a limited amount of time. A walk or playing at the park are forms of recreation, but a walking holiday would be tourism and the use of tourism within a leisure spectrum is also problematic, because it does not recognize travel for business, despite the fact that this form of activity is a vital tourism product for many destinations.

Although tourism and tourists were discussed much earlier, and some definitions were attempted, the first definition to fully encompass the breadth of tourism emerged in 1941, when it was described as 'the sum of the phenomena and relationships arising from the travel and stay of non-residents, insofar as they do not lead to permanent residence and are not connected with any earning activity' (Hunziker and Krapf, 1942). In 1976, the Tourism Society suggested that 'Tourism is the temporary, short-term movement of people to destinations outside the places where they normally live and work and their activities during the stay at each destination. It includes movements for all purposes', and in 1981 Burkart and Medlik identified the key characteristics of the tourism industry as:

- Tourism describes the movement of people to a destination and their stay within that destination.
- All tourism activity comprises two elements: the journey to the destination and the stay within the destination.
- The journey and stay take place outside of the usual place of residence and work, so that activities are distinct and different from the everyday experiences of the traveller and the people who work in the destination.
- This movement is usually defined by a period of time for the stay – measured in days, weeks or months.
- The purpose for the visit is not to take up permanent residence or any form of employment within the destination.

In 1995 the United Nations World Tourism Organization (UNWTO) provided a categorization of tourists:

- domestic tourism: residents of a country travelling within their country;
- inbound tourism: explaining tourists arriving in one country from another;
- outbound tourism: describing tourists leaving to go to another country for tourism purposes.

Tourism, then, defines the activity, but not the people taking part. UNWTO (1995) defines tourists as people who are 'traveling to and staying in places outside their usual environment for not more than one consecutive year for leisure, business and other purposes'.

The final consideration in shaping our scope and understanding of tourism is the tourists' own perspective of being a tourist. Medlik and Middleton (1973; cf Middleton, 1988) noted that 'as far as the tourist is concerned, the product covers the whole experience from the time he leaves home to the time he returns from it … the tourist product is not an airline seat or a hotel bed or relaxing on a sunny beach … but rather an amalgam of many components … Airline seats and hotel beds are merely elements or components of a total tourist product which is a composite product.' This is important because it illustrates clearly the fact that tourism can mean different things to different people, and it is built upon an entirely intangible set of service values. While a tourist may take photographs and buy souvenirs, they never own anything of the experience, nor is it something that can be picked up and touched in the way any other product is. The tourist's judgement of satisfaction and value is based upon his or her own previous experiences, and the actual experience will be different for each individual, influenced by factors which may include the weather, the people in the destination, the time of year and the motivations of the tourists themselves.

The fact that tourism is comprised of many different industries and is closely related to economic, environmental and social issues leads to potential disagreement as a result of the different perspectives through which it is understood by tourists, businesses, communities and other actors within the tourism product. As Cooper et al (2000) observed: it is 'a multidimensional, multifaceted activity which touches many lives and many different economic activities'.

Bound to all of these discussions is the need to understand the shape and scope of the tourism industry, and it is because of this that the following pages define, explain, exemplify and illustrate the breadth and depth of this exciting, continually evolving and always challenging industry.

This book provides the reader with an accurate and insightful view of tourism, offering research and industry perspectives across the breadth of tourism studies. It is written to be a key companion for the study of tourism, and provides accessible explanations provided by leading tourism scholars. A list of abbreviations is presented, and the entries are then presented in alphabetical order. Where new ideas and concepts are introduced within an entry, those ideas are featured in the book and are highlighted in bold.

The entries featured in the book provide a comprehensive overview of the tourism industry, from early concepts through to contemporary tourism activity; each entry includes an overview of the chronology or development of a theory, concept or typology, supported with definitions. Where these definitions are contested, this will be explained in the entry, and where appropriate the explanation of each entry is supported with examples. At the end of each entry some sources are highlighted for further reading, and additional sources mentioned in the text can be found in the Bibliography.

At the time of publication this book provides a thorough introduction to the study of tourism and is a suitable text to read at all levels of tourism studies, and to keep as a source of reference for future research and management. Of course, new ideas and concepts are continually developing; but where these are untested, they may disappear as quickly as they emerged, and so some selection of ideas has been necessary to ensure that this book provides a narrative of the globally accepted language of tourism.

HOW TO USE THIS BOOK

This book is designed to be a valuable point of reference for the study of tourism. Entries provide an overview of the principal ideas, concepts and theories which are crucial to understanding tourism and are presented in alphabetical order so that they can be located easily. Each entry gives an explanation and discussion of a specific topic and includes a list for further reading. Terms that are explained elsewhere in the book are highlighted in emboldened text.

While the book is comprehensive in its coverage, there are terms which may not be included. It provides a function as an introductory text to the breadth of tourism – entries are selected based upon the topics that appear most commonly amongst the books and journals of tourism studies. Entries can be categorized as:

- Theory: the principles by which something can be explained, that has been tested through rigorous research and therefore can be used to justify and interpret new research in relation to existing knowledge.
- Concept: a theoretical construct which characterizes a particular theme or idea. Concepts include motivation, sustainability and globalization.
- Model: a diagram or formula which illustrates or demonstrates how a process occurs. An example in tourism is the Operations Management Model.
- Typology: a classification of a type of tourism. Examples include dark tourism and film tourism.

The entries provide a synopsis to introduce the background and key debates around each topic. It is an invaluable companion to refer to when reading other texts, provides an excellent introduction to tourism and offers a valuable starting point for further research, introducing the reader to seminal texts and contemporary research.

TOURISM

The Key Concepts

ACCOMMODATION PROVIDERS

The accommodation sector, usually known as the lodging sector in the US, is a significant component of the global tourism industry. By definition, tourism must include an overnight stay away from the tourist's normal place of residence. The accommodation sector therefore plays a crucial role in helping to define, explain and understand how tourism operates. Such knowledge is vital if tourism is to be developed, planned and managed successfully. Accommodation not only provides the tourist with a place to stay overnight but also somewhere to eat and drink, a base to explore the surrounding area, a source of local tourist information, and various ancillary services such as laundry, telephone services and Internet connection. Many also provide business services, including meeting facilities and conference centres, as well as overnight rooms for delegates. Such providers often specialize in business tourism.

The accommodation sector is also significant in that it often accounts for the largest part of the tourist's spending in the tourism destination. Of course, not all tourists stay in paid accommodation in the destination. Many stay in the homes of friends and family: a type of tourism known as 'visiting friends and relatives' (VFR) tourism. VFR tourism is difficult both to define and to measure, but is generally considered to represent a substantial element of tourism accommodation in terms of the number of tourist nights (the nights spent in accommodation away from home). For example, Taylor Nelson Sofres Research International Travel and Tourism (2010) report that almost one in six domestic tourism trips in the UK were for VFR purposes in 2009, representing more than one in eight domestic tourist nights. Research has also found that some VFR tourists spend more than tourists staying in paid accommodation (Lee et al, 2005).

It is possible, therefore, to include private homes in a list of categories of accommodation provider. Other major categories include:

- *Hotels, motels, apartment hotels, inns, lodges:* generally these take the form of serviced accommodation, where one or more meal is provided by the establishment.
- *Guest houses, bed-and-breakfasts, farm stays, youth hostels, backpacker hostels:* these also tend to be serviced accommodation but usually only breakfast is provided.
- *Holiday cottages, gîtes, camping barns, static caravans:* these forms of accommodation are usually offered on a non-serviced (self-catering) basis.

- *Timeshare apartments, touring caravans, mobile homes, recreational vehicles (RVs), tents:* these are usually owned by the tourist, but can also be hired. Most are mobile and as such are not fixed to a specific destination, although some may be 'sited' at a caravan park or holiday home complex. They are usually non-serviced, although many campsites will provide services such as electricity hook-ups, water supply and bathroom facilities.

The distinction between serviced and non-serviced types of accommodation is by no means rigid. Indeed, many accommodation styles offer room-only tariffs, while others serve meals to residents for a separate charge. Many hotels also offer room service, where meals and refreshments are served in the guests' bedrooms.

A further characteristic of the accommodation sector is the wide array of providers involved, ranging from large multinational business organizations with hundreds of thousands of rooms worldwide, through to micro-businesses with just one guest bedroom in the family home. The latter are often seasonal businesses, opening for the peak tourist season and then closing down for the rest of the year. For some tourism accommodation providers the season may be very short – for example, some residents of the Wimbledon area in London rent their homes to visitors to the annual tennis tournament, which lasts for just two weeks. Many hotels are part of global chains. The world's five largest hotel chains as of 2009 were the Intercontinental Hotels Group, with 619,851 rooms worldwide, followed by the Wyndham Hotel Group, with 592,880 rooms, Marriott International, with 545,705 rooms, Hilton Hotels Corporation, with around 500,000 rooms, and Accor, with 478,975 rooms (Hospitalitynet, 2011).

The distinction between the accommodation sector and other tourism sectors has always been somewhat blurred and has become more so in recent times. Thus, for example, transport companies often provide accommodation for their travellers in the form of sleeping compartments on trains and cabins on ferries. Airlines technically provide accommodation for travellers on long-haul flights and there has been a growing trend towards providing flat beds in first-class cabins. Many airports also provide hotel accommodation for travellers next to or even within the terminal building. A new breed of in-airport hotels now provides basic budget accommodation for those waiting for flight connections. These offer rooms that are larger than capsule hotels of Japan but are still much smaller than standard hotel rooms. Yotel, for example, already has branches at London Heathrow, London Gatwick and Amsterdam Schiphol airports, and has plans under way to expand its operations to New York and Abu Dhabi. Yotel's rooms are compact but comfortable, each featuring a flat-screen television, free Wi-Fi connection and 24-hour room service.

Further blurring of the boundaries between the accommodation and transport sectors exists in the cruise industry, which has experienced a significant consumer boom in recent years. The Florida-Caribbean Cruise Association (2011) estimates that a record 13.45 million passengers took a cruise holiday in 2009, an increase of 440,000 passengers over 2008. Of these guests, 10.3 million originated in North America. Meanwhile the Caribbean continues to be the dominant cruise destination, accounting for 37 per cent of all holidays in 2009. These figures represent a 3.4 per cent increase in worldwide cruise passengers on 2008: a significant increase given the effect of the worldwide recession on international tourism spending generally. There are also accommodation establishments that are visitor attractions in their own right. An example is the Gleneagles Hotel in Scotland, which is renowned worldwide for its golf course. Famous train services, such as the Orient Express, clearly occupy conceptual ground that crosses over between the transport, accommodation and visitor attraction sectors.

Another way in which distinctions between accommodation providers and the rest of the tourism industry are being blurred is through the development of destination resorts. These are tourist resorts that contain all the necessary components of the service product – including accommodation, hospitality, attractions, leisure shopping and entertainment facilities – so that it does not have to be located near an existing destination in order to operate. Examples include Atlantis in the Bahamas and Sun City in South Africa. Some are so large that they are termed 'mega-resorts'. Many operate on an 'all-inclusive' (AI) basis, meaning that guests pay a fixed price that is inclusive of meals, most drinks, entertainments, and so on. Examples include Club Med in the Mediterranean and Sandals resorts in the Caribbean. Resort destinations effectively integrate various elements of the tourism product that would, under other circumstances, be provided by a range of different organizations.

Another significant development in recent times has been the stretching of the hotel market at both the luxury and budget ends into what are known as the boutique hotel and budget hotel sectors. A boutique hotel is an upmarket hotel, usually small in size, where the rooms have been individually designed and furnished to a high standard. Most aim to provide exceptional standards of service and make this their selling proposition. Boutique hotels are often based in a distinctive, possibly restored, building. The term is said to have originated in 1981 with the opening of Blake's Hotel in London, UK. Budget hotels, in contrast, emphasize low cost. This means that many have no public rooms, except perhaps for a breakfast room. They also tend to offer few, if any, additional services, with food and drink perhaps provided through vending machines in the lobby. The most modern budget hotels even have computerized booking and checking-in facilities, with guests using their credit cards as room keys. Budget hotels typically aim for the short-stay market and high-occupancy rates. The market for budget hotels has grown significantly in recent times, following the rising trend of budget tourism. Examples of budget hotel chains include Accor's Formule 1, Travelodge and Travel Inn in the UK, and Motel 6 in the US. Another example of the stretching of the tourist accommodation market is the phenomenon known as 'glamping', which involves camping in high-specification accommodation, such as yurts, tipis, safari tents and airstream caravans.

Marketing tourist accommodation has traditionally been difficult because of the general lack of benchmarks available to guide the consumer about the quality of the accommodation that they can expect, especially when they are first-time guests and are buying the room unseen. Websites such as Tripadvisor are nowadays playing an increasingly important role in tourist decision-making. Before the existence of the Internet, however, the solution adopted by accommodation providers was to subscribe to one or more of the grading schemes that had been set up for that purpose. These remain important marketing tools in the accommodation sector today. Accommodation quality schemes are usually administered at the national or regional level, often through the country's National Tourism Organization (NTO), although in some parts of the world there are systems that operate either alongside or instead of the national system, such as that operated by the American Automobile Association (AAA) in the US. Such systems may either be voluntary or compulsory. Many have emerged from classification schemes, which tend to rate accommodation according to easily quantifiable variables such as size of rooms, room facilities (e.g. whether rooms are en suite) and amenities offered, thereby making no explicit reference to quality. Many of these have later been converted into grading schemes by the addition of an additional element to reflect various aspects of service quality. A grading scheme typically awards a number of stars to applicants, usually ranging from zero to five. This accounts for the term 'five-star' hotel. Some very large hotels advertise themselves as six star or even seven, but this grading is entirely unofficial. No formal grading scheme anywhere in the world currently awards more than five stars.

A good example of an accommodation grading scheme is the star-based system operated across Great Britain by Visit Britain, Visit Scotland, Visit Wales and the Automobile Association (AA). Previously, each organization operated its own grading system, with its own unique set of grading criteria. This led to some accommodation providers applying to more than one grading system, allowing them then to advertise the one that gave them the most stars. In 2006, however, the four organizations collaborated on the development of a harmonized system that uses a single set of criteria to grade properties. It covers the breadth of the accommodation sector and also includes the attractions sector (where it is known as the Visitor Attraction Quality Assurance Scheme). The scheme is voluntary and combines both quantitative and qualitative considerations into a unified set of grades, both of which have met with some criticism. The voluntary nature of the scheme means that guests cannot be sure whether accommodation that does not display grading is simply of too low a standard to reach one star or is actually of a high standard but has chosen not to join the scheme. The combination of both quantitative and qualitative information has been criticized because it can obscure high quality. For example, a hotel that has very high standards of service quality may not be able to achieve more than a three-star grading simply because it does not have a customer lift. Grading systems are also widely accused of encouraging standardization rather than the pursuit of individual excellence.

Further reading

Cooper, C., Fletcher, J., Gilbert, D., Fyall, A. and Wanhill, S. (2008) *Tourism: Principles and Practice*, 4th edition, Prentice Hall, Harlow, UK

Lee, G., Morrison, A. A., Lheto, X. Y., Webb, J. and Reid, J. (2005) 'VFR: Is it really marginal? A financial consideration of French overseas travellers', *Journal of Vacation Marketing*, vol 11, no 4, pp340–356

Page, S. J. (2007) *Tourism Management: Managing for Change*, 2nd edition, Butterworth-Heinemann, Oxford and Burlington

Dr. Brian Garrod

ADVENTURE TOURISM

Tourism and the notion of 'adventure' have always been inextricably linked; from the days of the early explorers to modern times, the idea of adventure in whatever capacity is never far from the concept of tourism. There is also a link between sport and adventure in terms of the categorization of activities; however, what separates sport from adventure is the idea of risk-taking, with the inherent risks involved in adventure tourism not generally perceived as being significant within the concept of sport.

Adventure tourism has grown rapidly in recent years (Buckley, 2006a). This is a growing segment of the tourism industry and growth is predicted to continue as consumers demand authentic and inspirational experiences. As with all sectors of the economy, expenditure fell during the recession; but the market is expected to be resilient in the long term. Studies differ on the exact profile of an adventure traveller; but the group tends to include those in professional/managerial occupations (often referred to as the AB social group), usually well educated with reasonable disposable income. The average age is disputed but tends to be around 40+, with an increasing number of fitter third-age participants. Both males and females participate in such trips (Page and Connell, 2009; George Washington University School of Business et al, 2010).

Often categorized as 'soft' and 'hard' activity, adventure tourism means different things to different people; but it is generally defined as a type of tourism that requires significant physical or mental effort, may involve real or perceived risk, involves generating a certain level of excitement, and engages a person in physical, natural or cultural excursions that take the individual outside their comfort zone. According to Beedie and Hudson (2003, p625): 'Adventure tourism brings together travel, sport and outdoor recreation.'

Buckley (2006b, p1428) defines adventure tourism as encompassing 'guided commercial tours, where the principal attraction is an outdoor activity that relies on features of the natural terrain, generally requires specialist equipment, and is exciting for the tour clients. The clients may operate the equipment themselves or they may simply be passengers.' Adventure tourism may therefore be defined as tourism that combines physical activity, cultural exchange or interaction and an engagement with nature. Indeed, for many people living in urban areas, natural locations such as mountains, lakes, rivers, jungles and oceans represent an opportunity for escapism, offering 'excitement, stimulation and potential adventure' (Beedie and Hudson, 2003, p625). According to Beedie and Hudson (2003), the natural environment is becoming increasingly co-modified in the search for the tailor-made adventure experience.

Adventure tourism may also be defined as the act of 'strenuous physical exertion with risk to life and limb' (Hudson, S., 2003, pxviii), although this definition is perhaps extreme in its reference to both the level of physical activity and the level of danger involved. Soft adventure, such as snorkelling and hiking, is the most popular form of adventure tourism because there is less requirement for physical effort, the participant requires little or no experience, the activity can generally be easily adapted depending on those participating, and risks are lower than those with hard adventure. It therefore appeals to a wider range of people who seek pleasure by escaping from routine. 'Hard' adventure, such as white-water rafting and bungee jumping, involves more demanding physical challenges and has a higher element of risk and, as with soft, may be spiritually rewarding. The inherent danger in extreme or 'hard' adventure tourism ensures that it is often referred to as adrenaline sport, further evidence of the link between adventure tourism and sport.

Access to new technology and the emergence of an increasing number of specialist operators have increased worldwide interest in adventure tourism. Better exploitation of adventure tourism requires travel retail professionals who understand both the market offering and the adventure tourism customer. The typical profile of the adventure tourist includes those with limited time and high disposable income who seek to use smart technology to package their adventure requirements at a time to suit their busy lifestyle, with 24-hour access to information and booking capability within a restricted time frame.

Other key developments in the adventure tourism market include the growing number of mixed-use resort destination developments in key tourist areas worldwide. Such developments combine hotels, entertainment, leisure and sporting activities, retail outlets and attractions. As short breaks replace or supplement longer holidays, multigenerational family holidays become more popular and adventure sports become more mainstream; such mixed-use resorts offer, for many people, an appealing combination of sport and adventure activity within a specific and demarcated setting.

Further reading

Beedie, P. and Hudson, S. (2003) 'Emergence of mountain-based adventure tourism', *Annals of Tourism Research*, vol 30, no 3, pp625–643

Buckley, R. (2006) *Adventure Tourism*, CABI, Wallingford, UK

Roberts, C. (2011) 'Sport and adventure tourism', in P. Robinson, S. Heitmann and P. U. Dieke (eds) *Research Themes for Tourism*, CABI, Wallingford, UK

Carol Southall and Linda Phillips

AGRITOURISM (OR FARM TOURISM)

A form of **rural tourism**, agritourism (or farm tourism) describes tourist activities with a focus upon farm accommodation, farmed landscapes and agricultural processes. Weaver and Fennell (1997, p357) define this as 'rural enterprises which incorporate both a working farm environment and a commercial tourism component'. Activities that fall into this category are diverse, and the terminology is used to represent different activities in different countries, but essentially can include:

- pick-your-own farms;
- farm shops;
- children's farms and attractions;
- farm-based accommodation;
- working holidays (see **Serious leisure**).

Agritourism is recognized as a niche growth area in parts of the world with a large farming economy, including the US, Australia and Canada, and may overlap with **food tourism** (see **Gastronomy** and **Food Tourism**), **wine tourism** and occasionally **ecotourism**. It is considered to be an important educational tool, raising consumer awareness of ethical production and the origins of food, and many farms have diversified into agritourism to boost their income. Examples may include cheese-making, where visitors can see the processes involved in producing cheese, before having an opportunity to taste the end product; or a honey farm – a major change from traditional farming; however, visitors are again able to test the produce, learn about production methods, and purchase honey and related items.

Farm tourism has been described as 'agritainment' and is often seen as a form of sustainable agriculture. During recent years there has been an increased emphasis placed on agriculture within existing tourist attractions, and in many places historic sites have reconstructed walled gardens to sell produce to an increasingly interested consumer base. In the UK, Open Farm Schemes offer opportunities for visitors to experience a working farm for a day, and Farm Stay UK has over 1200 working farm members where visitors can stay on holiday. In the US, an increased interest has been seen in guest-ranches, where visitors can try their hand working on a ranch, riding horses and contributing to the farming process (see **Authenticity**).

Further reading

Roberts, L. and Hall, D. (2001) *Rural Tourism and Recreation: Principles to Practice,* CABI Publishing, Wallingford, UK

Weaver, D. and Fennell, D. (1997) 'Rural tourism in Canada: The Saskatchewan vacation farm operator as entrepreneur', in S. Page and D. Getz (1997) *The Business of Rural Tourism: International Perspectives*, Series in Tourism and Hospitality Management, Cengage Learning EMEA, Andover

Peter Robinson

AIR TRANSPORT

Since the invention of the aircraft just over 100 years ago, air transport has become one of the most important sectors of the tourism industry. Aviation grew particularly after World War II, when many obsolete military aircraft were converted into passenger aircraft. While initially air travel was a costly adventure for affluent people only, some milestones helped to make air travel more affordable to the general public (Howell et al, 2003).

These milestones include the introduction of the first passenger jet aircraft (the DeHavilland *Comet*) in 1952, which allowed airlines to reach destinations faster and without stopping. The twin-aisle, wide-body Boeing B747 'Jumbo Jet' entered service in 1970, and made it possible for airlines to serve far away destinations much more economically. In 1976, the first supersonic passenger jet 'Concorde' entered service with Air France and British Airways, and brought air travel to a new level. A transatlantic crossing from Paris or London to New York took just over three hours. However, after the drastic increase of oil prices, it became increasingly important that passenger aircraft became economically viable to operate, and thus developments such as improved engines, wings and construction materials have been at the forefront of the latest aircraft designs. The introduction of the double-decker Airbus A380 has been another major milestone reflecting this development, offering costs per seat lower than any other passenger aircraft. Similarly, the Boeing B787 *Dreamliner*, a new design made mostly of composite materials, entered service in late 2011 (Cooper et al, 2000).

The importance of fuel efficiency became evident when the world saw large orders for modern aircraft, placed many years before their first flight. For example, in June 2011, Malaysian low-cost airline AirAsia placed a record order for 200 Airbus A320NEO (new engine option) during the Paris Air Show, and topped this order up with another 100 aircraft less than a month later. The A320NEO will not enter service until 2016, five years after these orders. In just seven months since the announcement of the A320NEO, Airbus secured over 1000 orders, underlining the growth of the airline industry and the emphasis on economy.

Modern passenger airlines can be categorized as scheduled airlines (also known as 'legacy' or 'network' carrier), as charter airlines (including air taxi services) and as low-cost carrier (or low-frills airlines) (Gross, 2011):

- Scheduled airlines offer air links according to a clearly defined and published schedule, regardless of the load factors for these flights.
- Charter airlines are usually flying regular services on behalf of large package tour operators, or *ad hoc* services for large groups and/or events.
- Low-cost carriers (LCCs) offer regular scheduled services at very low prices. Their operation is based on the lowest possible cost, and many services that are complimentary on network carriers are charged as extras by LCCs (e.g. checked luggage, catering, paper tickets).

Today's air traffic is highly regulated by a number of governmental and private bodies. Regulations span navigation, landing rights, air traffic control, safety and security measures, and passenger compensation (in the case of delays, lost baggage or accidents), to name but a few. Among the most important organizations are the International Civil Aviation Organization (ICAO) and the International Air Transport Association (IATA).

The ICAO was founded at the Chicago Convention on Civil Aviation (1944), where representatives of 80 governments agreed on the use of international air space. The second important outcome of that conference was the introduction of the five so-called *Freedoms of the Air* (in subsequent years, three more freedoms have been added to the initial five). The ICAO is a United Nations agency, ensuring safe and orderly air transport. In effect, the ICAO is responsible for the organization of international conferences, the mediation of conflicts between member states, and setting international standards for equipment and operations. This includes the strengthening of the legal framework of international aviation, an efficient and adequate navigation system, timely responses to safety and security concerns, and general assistance for civil aviation facilities and services (IATA, 2011).

One year after the inception of the ICAO, in 1945, the IATA was formed in Havana, Cuba. It is a modern-day successor to the International Air Traffic Association founded in The Hague in 1919. Its 230 members comprise virtually all international air carriers (passenger and freight). The IATA's goal is to facilitate the safe and smooth transport of passengers and cargo. The main task of the IATA is to standardize documents, such as tickets, waybills, baggage checks and similar documents (ICAO, 2011).

Further reading

Duval, D. T. (2007) *Tourism and Transport: Modes, Networks and Flows*, Channel View Publications, Clevedon, UK

Gross, S. and Schroeder, A. (eds) (2007) *Handbook of Low Cost Airlines: Strategies, Business Processes and Market Environment*, Erich Schmidt Verlag, Goettingen, Germany

Hanlon, P. (1999) *Global Airlines*, 2nd edition, Butterworth-Heinemann, Oxford, UK

Page, S. J. (2009) *Transport and Tourism: Global Perspectives*, 3rd edition, Pearson Prentice Hall, Harlow, UK

Page, S. J. (ed) (2004) *Tourism and Transport: Issues and Agenda for the New Millennium*, Elsevier, Amsterdam, The Netherlands

Dr. Michael Lück

ARTS TOURISM

The arts, including theatre and dance, music and the visual arts, are acknowledged as being an important part of tourism within a destination. They indicate that places for performing arts, museums and galleries are quite important to a great many travellers. Arts participation can thus be considered to be tourism where the tourist experiences forms of the visual and performing arts, including ethnic and minority art forms – for example, by visiting performing arts venues or art galleries, participating in arts events such as music festivals, and visiting traditional handicraft villages. While the arts are important to destinations, the tourism industry is also important to the arts as it can generate income that supports the arts and has the potential to broaden the market for the arts (Smith, 2003).

Zeppel and Hall (1992) divided cultural tourism into the subsets of heritage and arts tourism, considering the latter to be more contemporary and in the present. Hughes (2000) used the term arts-related tourism instead of arts tourism in his work on arts, entertainment and tourism. Richards (2001) concurs that cultural tourism includes both heritage tourism (related to the artefacts of the past) and arts tourism (related to contemporary cultural production). However, Timothy and Boyd (2003) consider that the terms 'cultural tourism', 'heritage tourism', 'ethnic tourism' and 'arts tourism' are almost interchangeable in their usage.

The role of the arts in the tourism experience can be encapsulated in a typology of arts tourists based upon participation intent. For example, Hughes (2000) classifies these tourists as arts-core (subdivided into primary and multi-primary) and arts-peripheral (subdivided into accidental and incidental). For the arts-core tourists, the arts are the main attraction for the visit; for the arts-peripheral tourists there is less interest in the arts as attraction. Smith (2003) notes that the profile of arts tourists is similar to that of general cultural tourists, and that they have relatively high levels of education, income and cultural awareness.

Performers and artisans using traditional methods or modes of cultural expression are of great interest to tourists. In traditional cultural areas, arts-and-crafts co-operatives often rely on tourism for their success – for example, the tribal arts-and-crafts co-operative Qualla Arts and Crafts Mutual, Inc. discussed by Duggan (1997). Arts-and-crafts centres, institutes, museums and galleries can thus be established to protect traditional arts. As McKercher and du Cros (2002) note, such centres provide a focal point not only for the artisans, but also for the travelling public, doubling as tourist attractions. These venues can also generate revenues, through admission fees and the sale of arts and crafts, to support the arts (Hughes, 2000).

Arts attractions do not need to be permanent, as in the case of arts **events and festivals**. However art, like other forms of cultural expression, needs to be bundled into a product, as indicated by McKercher and du Cros (2002), in order to be consumed by tourists. Methods of bundling can include performances, art tours (guided and self-guided), as well as gallery and studio tours.

In terms of urban revitalization, the arts are very often found clustered in specific arts districts, as highlighted in studies by Ali-Knight and Robertson (2003) of Barcelona, Edinburgh and Glasgow. Arts festivals are noted as a mainstay of urban renewal and regeneration efforts in cities, and as such are linked to tourism destination efforts (Quinn, 2010). Arts events can also encourage regional and even cross-border forms of arts tourism, as in the case of the annual Two Countries One Bay Studio Art Tour that links and opens art studios in Maine, US, and New Brunswick, Canada (Wallace, 2010).

Smith (2003) notes that arts tourism has developed more slowly than **heritage tourism** due to the apparent reluctance of both the arts and tourism sectors to embrace joint initiatives. Nonetheless, in contemporary **arts tourism**, tourism serves a valuable function in linking the arts to tourism and artists to tourists, while contributing to economic development, and to the revitalization of both urban and peripheral areas. As such, it plays a role as a facilitator in the creation of both destinations and experiences that resonate with a unique sense of place and authenticity that only the arts organizations and artists indigenous to that place can deliver.

Further reading

Ali-Knight, J. and Robertson, M. M. (2003) 'Introduction to arts, culture and leisure', in I. Yeoman (ed) *Festivals and Events Management: An International Arts and Culture Perspective*, Butterworth-Heinemann Ltd, Jordan Hill, UK, pp3–28

Hughes, H. (2000) *Arts, Entertainment and Tourism*, Butterworth-Heinemann, Oxford, UK

Dr. Lee Jolliffe and Dr. Jenny Cave

AUTHENTICITY

Authenticity explains the notion that an item or activity is original and genuine. Authenticity tends to be used in the context of heritage, where it refers to the traditional items and customs that define ways of life or origins of culture. Often, authentic items have a certificate of authenticity, and there are many souvenirs that are considered to be authentic. Such examples include 'a piece of the Berlin Wall' and 'original oak from HMS *Victory*'.

In a tourism context, authenticity more commonly refers to intangible authentic experiences such as traditional local festivals and tribal rituals, but these are often reproduced for public consumption and defined as authentic by the community. Similarly, tangible items such as locally produced traditional food and crafts are also considered authentic; but it may be the producer of the item who defines its authenticity.

Boorstin (1961) and MacCannell (1999) both discuss authenticity at some length and base their discussions on the inauthenticity of modern society and, therefore, the desire of tourists to seek true experiences, although Boorstin suggests that as many traditions are preserved, perhaps with some moderation, for modern consumers, what are experienced are pseudo-events. MacCannell, by contrast, suggests that tourists are, in effect, pilgrims, seeking real experiences to fill the gap between their sense of inauthenticity and their desire to find true authenticity.

This alternative may be a commodified or commoditized version of the original activity or item, understood in terms of its exchange value – or what it is worth as a tourist transaction (Cohen, 1988).

There are problems inherent in the commodification of cultural activities, generally in response to demand from travel operators, which may denigrate the meaning of cultural or religious heritage; but it may also contribute to the preservation of traditional ways of life.

MacCannell (1999) suggests that the concept of staged authenticity where bite-sized and accessible elements of culture are performed for tourists (the front stage) and the living of the true and full culture protected for the community (the back stage), which may be exemplified as local guides providing tours of the region, or wearing traditional costumes in order to be able to visit a religious site.

Cohen (1988) proposes the notion of negotiated authenticity, suggesting that different people have different interpretations of authenticity and recognizing that authenticity can change over time.

Authenticity is an essential concept in tourism, as much of the global tourism industry is reliant on the cultural heritage of each destination, and therefore its presentation, marketing and representation, together with the traditional values of the community, must be understood and articulated within academic discussion and by planners and managers in industry.

Further reading

Baudrillard, J. (1988) 'Simulacra and simulations', in M. Poster (ed) *Jean Baudrillard: Selected Writings*, Blackwell, Cambridge, USA

Cohen, E. (1972) 'Towards a sociology of international tourism', *Social Research*, vol 39, no 1, pp64–82

Cohen, E. (1988) 'Authenticity and commoditisation in tourism', *Annals of Tourism Research*, vol 15, no 3, pp371–386

Heitmann, S. (2011) 'Authenticity in tourism', in P. Robinson, S. Heitmann and P. Dieke (eds) *Research Themes for Tourism*, CABI, Wallingford, UK

MacCannell, D. (1999) *The Tourist: A New Theory of the Leisure Class*, second edition, University of California Press, Berkeley, CA

Uriely, N. (1997) 'Theories of modern and post-modern tourism', *Annals of Tourism Research*, vol 24, no 4, pp982–984

Urry, J. (2002) *The Tourist Gaze*, second edition, Sage Publications, London

Peter Robinson

BACKPACKING

Backpacking (and the number of backpackers) is a 'rapidly expanding phenomenon' (Cohen, 2003, p95; see also Paris, 2009), with the backpacking industry developing from a marginal tourism activity to a global aspect of the tourism industry (Richards and Wilson, 2004), especially in countries such as Australia and New Zealand (Godfrey, 2011).

The term 'backpacker' has been identified as being used in a commercial context as early as 1982 (Pearce, 1990), while as an activity its earlier labels include Cohen's (1972, 1973) 'non-institutionalised traveller' and 'nomads', Teas's (1974) 'youthful traveller', Vogt's (1976) 'wanderer', Mukerji's (1978) 'hitchhiker', Adler's (1985) 'tramping youth' or Riley's (1988) 'long-term budget traveller' (see also Uriely et al, 2002, pp520–521; Sørensen, 2003, p849; Teo and Leong, 2006, p109). Today, alternative terms such as 'budget traveller' or 'independent traveller' are sometimes used, especially in the US, where a backpacker is sometimes misunderstood to be a bushwalker (Tourism New South Wales, 2011). Its definition has therefore been widely debated.

There are generally two different definitions: governmental and social (Richards and Wilson, 2004). The Australian government, for example, uses a very simple governmental definition for statistical purposes. It defines a backpacker as 'a person who spends at least one night in either backpacker or hostel accommodation' (Tourism Research Australia, 2010, p1). However, one of the most commonly accepted and more detailed social definition of backpacker is by Pearce (1990), who defines backpackers as travellers who:

- are predominantly young (under 40 years old) and independent;
- stay for a longer period of time;
- focus on participatory and informal holidays;
- have a flexible travel plan;
- mostly stay in budget accommodation; and
- emphasize meeting other travellers.

Historically, the origins of backpacking are possibly one of the oldest forms of travelling. Adler (1985), for example, argues that youth nomadism was widespread in the pre-modern West, while Loker-Murphy and Pearce (1995) trace the origins of backpacking back to historic traditions such as the Grand Tour during the seventeenth and eighteenth centuries, when young English noblemen were sent to continental Europe to learn about culture, to connect with local business operators and to become independent.

The Youth Hostel movement that began in 1909 is another example of the early history of backpacking (Deutsches Jugendherbergswerk, 2011). Yet, Welk (2004) argues that the roots of modern backpacking came from the late 1960s and early 1970s when the Western

European and the American hippie culture hit the roads to Eastern Asia. Accordingly, Cohen (1972) was one of the first academics writing about this 'new' class of traveller. He used the term 'drifter', a tourist who 'immerses himself in the life of the host society ... the complete opposite of the mass tourist' (Cohen, 2004, pp44–45). Since then, academic research into the phenomenon of backpacking has developed through three different phases:

1 an exploratory phase during the 1970s (commentaries on the emerging groups of young budget travellers – e.g. hippies, drifters and road travellers);
2 a managerial phase during the 1980s and 1990s (backpacking is described as a mainstream institutionalized phenomenon);
3 a meaning-oriented phase during the last decade (understanding the consequences of backpacking for the individual and societies) (Pearce et al, 2009).

Backpacking is an important concept in tourism and tourism research (e.g. Richards and Wilson, 2004; Hannam and Ateljevic, 2007; Hannam and Diekmann, 2010). Organizationally, its development reflects the changes in tourism, in general, from an unorganized, independent (exploratory) movement of travellers to an organized, institutionalized (meaning-oriented) one. Cohen (2004) describes this as the change from a quest for authenticity to hedonistic enjoyment and fun.

Further reading

Hannam, K. and Ateljevic, I. (eds) (2007) *Backpacker Tourism: Concepts and Profiles*, Channel View Publications, Clevedon, UK
Hannam, K. and Diekmann, A. (eds) (2010) *Beyond Backpacker Tourism*, Channel View Publications, Clevedon, UK
Richards, G. and Wilson, J. (eds) (2004) *The Global Nomad: Backpacker Travel in Theory and Practice*, Channel View Publications, Clevedon, UK

Dr. Dirk Reiser

BUSINESS TOURISM

The term 'business tourism' may sound like an oxymoron. Tourists are conventionally defined as people who are taking time off work to have a holiday, spending at least one night away from home. Surely one can hardly be a tourist and be working at the same time? In many ways this view is correct. However, it tends to overlook the blurring of the distinction in today's society between leisure and work. With this blurring comes a new hybrid category: someone who is travelling and staying away from home for work purposes. Such individuals are known as business tourists (or business travellers).

While there is no agreed definition, business tourists can be thought of as people who are undertaking a trip away from their usual place of residence and work and spending at least one night away from home. The acronym 'MICE' is often used to categorize business tourists according to the purpose of their trip, whether it is a meeting, incentive, conference (or convention or congress) or exhibition (or event):

- *Meetings.* In an increasingly globalized business world, those attending face-to-face meetings need more and more to travel in order to participate. While such meetings can often be conducted by teleconference or videoconference, many business people still prefer to meet face to face. Such meetings are sometimes not even conducted in the home country of any of the participants, but in a 'third' country chosen as mutually convenient (or inconvenient). For the same reason, airports are often chosen as the venue of international business meetings and many airports have developed meetings facilities to cater to this need.

- *Incentives.* This term describes tourism that is undertaken by employees who have been awarded the prize of a holiday by their company. The style is usually luxurious and the destination exotic. This is often a reward for a job well done and is intended to incentivize employees to work hard.

- *Conferences (conventions or congresses).* This is tourism that is under-taken in order to attend conferences or conventions: meetings that are designed for discussion, fact-finding, problem-solving and/or consultation. These can be on any scale, from a few delegates to several thousand (the larger ones often being called congresses rather than conferences). Conference centres are often located near airports and train stations in order to maximize their accessibility to delegates. Such venues are often multipurpose facilities that can host a wide range of events and activities.

- *Exhibitions (or events).* These are a special type of event at which goods and services are on display for an audience to view. They may be restricted to trade buyers or may be public events. They are principally used in business-to-business (B2B) selling contexts and, hence, involve travel by business people to see them. This category includes product launches. There are, of course, many public events and exhibitions that attract general leisure visitors and tourists. Business tourists may also attend these but they are not generally considered to be part of the business tourism sector.

It is also possible to add training courses to this list, which may be internal in that only company employees are entitled to attend, or external in that they are intended for employees from a number of different companies.

In all the above cases, except that of incentive travel, the participant is working away from their home and usual place of work. As such, they may be identified as business tourists. The case of incentive travel is different insofar as the participant is not expected to work but to have a pleasurable leisure experience. Like all the other instances of business tourism, however, the incentive trip is not paid for by the participant but by the company he or she works for.

Business tourism can, of course, be undertaken by employees of public-sector and voluntary-sector organizations, which would not normally be described as businesses. It should also be noted that none of these definitions are intended to imply that the business tourist has no leisure time while at the destination, even though this might be true in some cases. Rather, the intention is to indicate that the business tourist is travelling for work purposes: if they were not working for that organization in that position, they would not be travelling.

The business tourism market is widely recognized to be highly significant. The United Nations World Tourism Organization (UNWTO) statistics, for example, suggest that the business and professional tourism market accounted for 15 per cent of world international tourism trips in 2009 (UNWTO, 2010b). Meanwhile, Taylor Nelson Sofres Research International Travel and Tourism (2010) found that business tourism accounted for over 14 per cent of all UK domestic tourism trips in 2009. This was equivalent to just over 10 per cent of all domestic tourism nights in that year. Furthermore, in 2009 domestic business tourists in the UK were found to spend UK£102 per night on average, compared to UK£55 per night for all UK domestic tourists (Taylor Nelson Sofres Research International Travel and Tourism, 2010). The sector has also been growing rapidly in recent times. The Business Tourism Partnership (2007) argues that there was a 53 per cent increase in business tourism in the UK from 1995 to 2005, the sector being responsible for generating some 28 per cent of all overseas visits and 27 per cent of all UK inbound tourism earnings.

Swarbrooke and Horner (2001, pxiv) further point out the following points in recognition of the growing importance of the business tourism market:

- Business tourism generally involves a higher level of spending per head than any other type of tourism.
- The business tourist is the core customer for many airlines and hotels.
- Business tourists are frequently served by their own suppliers and market intermediaries, which parallel those used in leisure tourism.
- Business tourism is the predominant form of tourism in many urban locations.
- Business tourism has its own physical infrastructure, such as conference and exhibition centres.

Of course, business tourism shares the infrastructure needed to meet the needs of leisure tourists, such as airports, train services, foodservice providers, accommodation, entertainment, and so on. Recognizing these essential compatibilities, many tourism destinations have diversified into business tourism. Some have also found the counter-seasonal nature of business tourism to be valuable. Business tourism tends to take place largely outside of the main leisure tourism season, providing a useful extension to the tourism season for destinations where it is limited by other factors such as climate. For this reason, business tourism is often identified as a core component of economic regeneration schemes.

In terms of air travel, the business tourism market has traditionally been the province of the flag-carrying national airlines, which can provide the high levels of flexibility and quality that business travellers expect. As such, the leisure and business tourism markets have traditionally been segmented, with different marketing propositions aimed at each one. Yet the situation now appears to be changing, particularly in view of the effect that the worldwide recession is having on companies' travel budgets. Indeed, easyJet, a low-cost airline with little or no experience of serving the business traveller, chose to enter the business tourism market, having seen a growing trend among business travellers to use its services (by 2011 business travellers comprised 18 per cent of their market by passenger numbers). While not introducing business class as such, easyJet offers business travellers a 'flexible fare', which includes preferential boarding, one piece of checked-in hold luggage at no extra cost, unlimited free date changes within a four-week period, and the ability to alter the ticketed flight time or transfer the existing ticket to a colleague for a small additional fee (plus any fare difference). As a low-cost carrier, easyJet is keen to maintain its commitment to the budget leisure traveller while also successfully serving the business traveller market.

Further reading

Davidson, R. and Cope, B. (2003) *Business Travel: Conferences, Incentive Travel, Exhibitions, Corporate Hospitality and Corporate Travel*, Prentice Hall, Harlow, UK
Swarbrooke, J. and Horner, S. (2001) *Business Travel and Tourism*, Butterworth-Heinemann, Oxford and Woburn

Dr. Brian Garrod

CARRYING CAPACITY

During the early 1980s, environmentalists defined carrying capacity as the maximum numbers of tourists that can be supported without causing excessive environmental deterioration and without leading to a decline in visitor satisfaction (Beaver, 2002, p287). While early definitions are now often perceived as being crude and simplistic, carrying capacity remains one of the main tools by which maximum visitor numbers are assessed. However, if it is to be fully understood, it must be viewed in relation to two other generic concepts, neither of which is exclusive to tourism.

The notion of **sustainable tourism** involves tourism development that preserves and harmonizes with the pre-existing economic, sociocultural and ecological situation (Goodall and Stabler, cited in Stabler, 1997; Beaver, 2002). Carrying capacity is seen as the threshold up to which sustainable tourism can develop.

Carrying capacity is a simple principle, and one of the oldest by which any market economy flourishes or declines. The customer can only take up a service that is present and it will only exist if there is a need for it. There is no need for a maximum limit to be enforced if the demand is low; only when demand threatens to exceed supply is carrying capacity really relevant.

Originally, the concept of carrying capacity was considered to be a fixed and exact number, derived by managers on a site-by-site basis. Later, however, the 'capacity' is invariably considered with an element of flexibility where, with the help of zoning techniques, certain areas under consideration may be allowed to exceed capacity or be brought below this given maximum (Weaver, 2008).

Those who advocate sustainable tourism seem to place great faith in the concept of carrying capacity, and numerous studies have been conducted around the world. Swarbooke (1997, p261) suggests that most use the term too simplistically, believing there to be six types of carrying capacity:

1 *Physical*: the number of people who can be physically accommodated on a given site. This is the most common interpretation of the term.
2 *Environmental*: the number after which irreparable physical damage begins to occur.
3 *Economic*: the number before local communities become adversely affected. This may be evidenced by property prices raised to such an extent that local people can no longer afford to purchase.
4 *Sociocultural*: the number before the host community begins to be irreversibly damaged by the tourist activity.
5 *Infrastructural*: the number before the receiving infrastructure cannot cope. This may show itself as congestion, rationing of water or public transport threshold becoming overstretched.
6 *Perceptual*: the number before the tourist experience is adversely affected. Unlike the first five, this is demand orientated, rather than supply driven. This is also the one that is most subjective!

These different thresholds may be linked together or may be in tension with one another. It may be the case, for instance, that one may be deemed to have 'exceeded' the level set, while another is considered within acceptable limits. For example, it is possible that an increased number of walkers on a mountain may have an adverse effect upon the environment, yet have no impact upon the levels of visitor satisfaction experienced by all those in attendance (Beech and Chadwick, 2006).

In some cases, the nature of the destination may have an impact upon carrying capacity. An urban setting is likely to be more resistant to damage than a soft area, such as the countryside. As a result, it may be considered to have a higher carrying capacity. A site that was originally constructed for large crowds, such as an amusement park, would allow a much higher perceptual level than perhaps a stately home in a more rural setting. Indeed, visitor satisfaction might be reduced in the former if it were not busy, as that might give the perception of being low quality or poor value.

The tourism manager has several ways of managing capacity. This is initially approached from the perspective of the mode of transport employed:

- *Private motor vehicles and coaches:* the simplest way of managing maximum numbers is in terms of car and coach park availability. It could be that temporary additional areas of grassland become available dependent upon the prevailing weather conditions. The Peak District's Dovedale in the UK is one of many examples where this occurs (Shirt, 2011, p170). Conversely, and following and during periods of prolonged rain, car parks may be reduced in size to minimize damage done to the natural environment.
- *Rail stations and airports:* similarly, access to the site may be restricted, in this case by the number and time of arrivals. The length of the train may be a subtle way of manipulating the number of arrivals, although in recessionary times it could be that the train operator may make that decision on the basis of yield – that is, the number of travellers in relation to available seats, rather than out of any discussion with the resort or destination managers!

As numbers approach the upper limits of carrying capacity, so the opportunity for customer dissatisfaction levels rises. What could be worse than a long drive to find that there was nowhere to park? A number of alternative and additional strategies and tactics, therefore, can be employed

It may be that the peaks of maximum demand may be deflected to less busy periods. This may be done by pre-payment and booking of tickets. One such proponent of this approach is the Wieliczka Salt Mine, located on the outskirts of Krakow in Poland. This UNESCO World Heritage Site employs an 'army' of tour guides and has achieved high satisfaction responses, despite welcoming over 1 million visitors in 2010 into the thirteenth-century workings (Cracow Tours, 2011). An attraction quite close to Wieliczka takes a slightly different strategy. Having witnessed a dramatic increase in visitor numbers over the past decade, the Auschwitz Death camp received 1.42 million visitors in 2010. The museum has two sites located 1.5 kilometres apart. Auschwitz 1, a series of ex-army barracks, is set within a compact built environment, while Auschwitz Birkenhau is an extensive area of mainly grassland, interspersed with timber sheds and concrete remains. Such is the pressure to visit the former site between 10am and 3pm that only pre-booked guided tours are allowed to enter, these having paid at least two weeks in advance. There are no visiting restrictions placed upon the latter site whatsoever, so individuals are encouraged to visit Auschwitz Birkenhau first, returning to Auschwitz 1 later in the day.

Another device employed to manage carrying capacity is de-marketing; this is used when demand exceeds supply and can take several forms, but essentially removes the promotion that normally accompanies the site. Tourism sites that often advertise widely through the year may elect on certain peak periods (e.g. Easter or public holidays) to remove or modify the promotion. This relates to the temporary suspension of normal media activity but rarely involves the removal of signposts for the weekend! De-marketing is often used with 'dispersion' where, in discussion with local government and other destination marketers (Page, 2009, p323), demand is diverted away from 'honey-pot sites' to alternative, less visited areas.

Although there are many supporters of the conceptual theory, that is all it is! The reality and practicalities for its use are fraught with pragmatic problems and have no shortage of critics. There are two main challenges facing its application; these are both simple and complex. The first surrounds the issue of precise measurement. This issue is made more difficult where the facility or area under consideration is of an outdoor nature and/or has an element of seasonality. The second questions who should do the measuring. There is often tension between the views of the professional environmentalist, the tourism manager and the host community; members of the latter often perceive themselves as the real experts and are the ones who have to live with it.

Although the threshold measurement is likely to be subjective and is considered simplistic, there is little doubt that the concept provides a starting point for discussion and debate between the various stakeholders.

Four journal articles have been identified that use and develop the concept of carrying capacity in a variety of settings (see 'Further reading' for full references):

- the consideration of the urban environment – in particular, *infrastructural carrying capacity*, written by Oh et al (2003);
- a questioning as to the validity of the generic concept and development of a more flexible approach by Garrigós et al (2004);
- the adaptation of the concept within a wildlife setting where *environmental carrying capacity* is the focus (Carpenter et al, 2000);
- the development of what is referred to as *real carrying capacity* (RCC) and *effective carrying capacity* (ECC) by Maldonado and Montagnini (2005).

Further reading

Carpenter, I., Decker, D. and Lipscomb, J. (2000) 'Stakeholder acceptance of capacity in wildlife management', *Human Dimensions of Wildlife*, vol 5, no 3, pp5–19

Garrigós, F., Simón Narangajavana, Y. and Palacios Marqués, D. (2004) 'Carrying capacity in the tourism industry: A case study of Hengistbury Head', *Tourism Management*, vol 25, issue 2, April, pp275–288

Maldonado, E. and Montagnini, F. (2005) 'Carrying capacity of La Tigra National Park, Honduras: Can the park be self-sustainable?', *Journal of Sustainable Forestry*, vol 19, no 4, pp29–48

Oh, K., Jeong, Y., Lee, D., Lee, W. and Choi, J. (2003) 'Determining development density using the urban carrying capacity assessment system', *Landscape and Urban Planning*, vol 73, issue 1, pp1–15

Stabler, M. (1997) *Environmental Standards for Sustainable Tourism in Tourism and Sustainability: Principles to Practice*, CABI, Wallingford, UK

Geoff Shirt

COASTAL AND MARINE TOURISM

One of the most enduring and popular of tourism trends has been the fascination with visiting coastal areas to partake in a multitude of different activities. Coastal and marine tourism activity is increasing globally, in both volume and diversity, with tourism and recreation-related development being one of the main contributory factors shaping development patterns in coastal zones. While it is difficult to estimate exactly the specific data for coastal and marine tourism, it is nevertheless evident that a high proportion of the 1.6 billion arrivals that the United Nations World Tourism Organization (UNWTO) predicts by 2020 will be involved in some form of coastal tourism experience. Although this development and growth in numbers of visitors may seem positive for economic growth, benefitting many sectors of the tourism industry, it nevertheless creates pressures on coastlines as environmental protection and coastal development become increasingly difficult to reconcile. The final part of this examination of coastal and marine tourism will consider some of these issues.

The concept of coastal and marine tourism encompasses a multitude of different tourism, leisure, sport and recreational activities that take place in coastal landscapes, rivers, estuaries, seas and oceans throughout the world. Orams (1999, p9) differentiates marine tourism from other forms of water-based tourism (freshwater zones, rivers, inland waterways, lakes) by designating it as 'those waters which are saline and tide affected'. At the coast there will be a combination of day visitors, long-stay visitors and residents who either will be involved in these activities or may work in leisure and tourism. Developing Laffoley's (1991) maritime recreation divisions, tourism, sports and recreation can be categorized into individual tourism, sports and recreation pursuits.

The coastal zone spectrum varies in the degree of development, from highly urbanized, industrialized areas, cities by the sea, seaside resorts and towns with a high level of coastal protection, to remote coastal deserts far off the beaten track. To support and capitalize on the tourism possibilities, many coastal tourism zones experience development in many different styles and forms, such as accommodation, hotels, caravan parks, houses, apartments (leased or owned), holiday camps (enclaves), and food and retail establishments. Specific and non-specific

Table 1 Typologies of coastal and marine tourism

Aquatic	Shore based	Air based
Ferries (platform for viewing the cityscapes and industrial heritage – e.g. *Star Ferry Hong Kong*, New York to Staten Island and Mersey ferries from Liverpool)	Shore based: can overlap with sea pageants, marine festivals, Tall Ship events (going on board moored vessels)	Events/ organized activities (e.g. air shows, balloon rides, helicopter rides)
Cruise ships: sea- and land-based tourism. Heritage cruising: sail (vintage sailing boats) and power (paddle steamer trips). Nature-based trips (e.g. seal and whale watching)		
Main land-based activities (e.g. bird watching, golf, land yachting, 4x4, fishing, bait digging, horse riding, cycling, photography, walking, promenading, marine gazing, dining, entertainment, painting, kite flying, beach activity, sun bathing)	Individual sports and recreation (e.g. hang gliding, flying light aircraft)	
Individual and organized activities (e.g. glass-bottom boats, jet skiing, sailing, snorkelling, diving, swimming, coast-steering, surfing, kite surfing, banana boats, leisure boat trips, power boating, kayaking, sea fishing)	Some of these are intertidal activities that take place on the beach between the high- and low-tide waterlines or on the foreshore	

infrastructure will be developed to support and facilitate this activity, transport links (roads, rail, airports, ferry terminals and marinas, sea defences, piers) and new innovations, such as artificial reefs that push existing waves upwards and shape them into better-quality surfing waves (e.g. the surf reef constructed at Boscombe near Bournemouth, UK) (Holloway, 2006).

The characteristics of each coastal area vary: shorelines range from vast expanses of sandy beaches or bays, rocky shores, mud flats and steep cliffs, to higher-density areas with theme parks, promenades and signage, with each of these characteristics determining the suitability of the coast for different tourism and recreational pursuits.

Having established the scale and scope of coastal and marine activity, it is important to trace early influences and trends that link to the coast becoming a popular destination for visitors, identifying early coastal activity, whether in the form of tourism or recreation activity. However, this is fraught with difficulties since the origins are lost in time. For example, when did people first observe and admire aquatic wildlife, or swim and sail for pleasure (Orams, 1999)? However, early trends and relationship with the sea and coast are useful for informing current fashions. The new fashion for spa tourism and health tourism, for instance, have their origins in natural springs at religious sites and the fashion for partaking medicinal properties, taking the waters at spa resorts such as Scarborough when a spring was found on the beach in 1662.

Another important theme is how romanticism, which developed through art and literature, helps to redefine the coast, altering perceptions of a place that was once viewed as hostile and dangerous (Hassan, 2003). The historical background to seaside resorts includes many popular and important themes, such as analysing how these resorts became places of mass pleasure; the holiday crowd; the profiles of holiday-makers; the influence of private and public policy on resort development; transport to the coast; and the changing fortunes of these destinations as new competition challenged their supremacy (see **Tourism histories**).

However, an important challenge for coastal resorts and coastal management is how to reconcile tourism activity and attempt to maintain sustainable coastal systems. This is becoming difficult to control as issues of industrial pollution, oil exploration, sewage and increased marine activity in the form of cruise ships and leisure craft are affecting many coastal regions in the world. Pressures to develop the coast have seen encroachment in the form of golf courses, marinas and new resorts, which impact upon coastal ecosystems, threatening existing and new sustainable coastal management strategies. Consequently, policy coordination is difficult to achieve between the various agencies that promote tourism and those that manage coastal and marine zones.

Finally, the threat of rising sea levels connected with global environmental change is now forcing many coastal regions to reassess their relationship with the sea. The Asian Tsunami disaster in 2004 and the effect of Hurricane Katrina in 2005 on New Orleans clearly highlighted the vulnerability of many coastal resorts in these regions and elsewhere to the problems of natural phenomenon. Pacific Asia Travel Association (PATA)'s website (www.pata.org) is a useful resource for information on the issues connected with tourism and the 2004 tsunami. A final example of changing perspectives on coastal management is the concept of managed retreat or managed realignment, which acknowledges that it is too expensive and almost impossible to control continual flooding in low-lying estuarine and vulnerable coastal areas. This type of policy approach to modernist thinking on coastal development and protection (that we can construct barriers and defences and build close to the coast) is also part of an important challenge for many vulnerable coastal tourism destinations worldwide as they face up to the threat of rising sea levels.

Further reading

Agarwal, S. and Shaw, G. (eds) (2007) *Managing Coastal Tourism: A Global Perspective*, Channel View Publications, Clevedon, UK

Dickinson, B. and Vladimir, A. (2007) *Selling the Sea: An Inside Look at the Cruise Industry*, John Wiley and Sons, Hoboken, NJ

Jennings, G. (ed) (2007) *Water-Based Tourism, Sport, Leisure, and Recreation Experiences*, Elsevier, Burlington, MA

Luck, M. (2007) *Nautical Tourism: Concepts and Issues*, Cognizant Communication, Elmsford, NY

Orams, M. (1999) *Marine Tourism: Developments, Impacts and Management*, Routledge, Abingdon, Oxon, UK

Harry Cameron

COMMUNITY-BASED TOURISM

Community-based tourism (or CBT) describes a bottom-up approach to tourism planning and development, and, although not a new concept, is increasingly relevant for many smaller destinations, although the level of true community involvement and leadership is open to debate. The concept of CBT was first mooted in the 1950s as a method for rural development, but it was overtly top down in nature. The 1960s and 1970s saw CBT promoted by the United Nations and various aid agencies on the basis that it was able to empower communities, remove the notion of charitable support and enhance local education. By the 1990s, CBT had become embedded within the study of tourism and centred on the involvement of communities in local tourism issues.

Defining CBT effectively is not a straightforward task, however, because there are many contested issues, and issues around ownership and power relations. Manyara and Jones (2007, p637) suggested an updated definition for the concept of CBT 'that it is a sustainable, community-owned and community-based tourism initiative that enhances conservation and in which the local community is fully involved throughout its development and management and are the main beneficiaries through community development'.

By the early 2000s, CBT had emerged as a management philosophy, and was closely aligned to other approaches towards **sustainable tourism**. For CBT to be successful, it must fully engage community members and leadership should come from within the community. However, community members frequently have different perceptions and attitudes, and may act out of self-interest rather than towards a shared objective. This is where many of the challenges for CBT are found. Shaw and Williams (2004, p178) state that 'communities are defined in various ways, but usually in geographical terms … communities are complex entities and far from homogenous, thus presenting significant measurement difficulties' and therefore 'may resist or embrace, or simply be overwhelmed by, the influences of the tourists. These host–guest relationships are central to tourism experiences and tourism impacts' (Shaw and Williams, 2004, p23).

Some of these problems are manifested in the self-interest of some community groups, an unwillingness to participate or the perception of the barriers that exist and that limit the ability of the community to share a sense of empowerment. These include the:

- nature of politics;
- nature of tourism;
- local understanding of politics;
- negative issues associated with tourism (litter, congestion, overcrowding);
- attitude of local media;
- apathy amongst citizens;
- cost in terms of both time and money;
- lengthy decision-making processes;

- failure to engage the whole community;
- lack of understanding around planning and policy.

There are, however, approaches to overcome many of these challenges, and these are underpinned by the concepts of social capital and community capacity-building (CCB). Social capital describes the skills and knowledge that can be shared between the members of a community and used to support CBT. CCB describes a way of working which engages the entire community and, as a result, equips them with a set of shared skills and knowledge. A CCB framework should consider the composition of the community, the individuals, organizations and businesses within it, and the supporting infrastructure.

CBT is best explained using examples of small villages where there may be a mixture of small businesses providing tourism services or products – for example, a gift shop, museum, bed-and-breakfast and guest house. Independently, these businesses have limited funds and capabilities, but work well in harmony with each other when they share marketing, contribute to overall promotion of the destination, and share best practice.

It is assumed that through the development of CBT a community will benefit from economic growth, greater political recognition and value, greater ability to determine the future of the community, environmental benefits, sociocultural gains, inward investment and a better quality of life. It should be noted, though, that not all research points to CBT as the method to achieve all of these benefits. While there are many examples of excellent CBT projects, it is not a one-size-fits-all solution, and some communities may find tourism is only a small part of the overall plan.

There are other criticisms of CBT as well, not least the fact that all too often CBT is delivered through top-down approaches almost by default because the suggestion or support for development is often made by an outside party with a vested interest, who then ignores the true sense of community development.

Where community tourism projects have worked, there is plenty of evidence to show that this is a result of effective stakeholder management, shared vision and an understanding of the policies, processes and responsibilities of a wide range of stakeholders, together with financial incentives to manage and maintain the project, often providing new employment and development opportunities for local communities, and allowing the community to be able to influence the types of business and employment that develop.

Further reading

Blackstock, K. (2005) 'A critical look at community based tourism', *Community Development Journal*, vol 40, no 1, pp39–49

Haywood, K. (1988) 'Responsible and responsive tourism planning in the community', *Tourism Management*, vol 9, no 2, pp105–118

Wiltshier, P. and Robinson, P. (2011) 'Community based tourism', in P. Robinson, S. Heitmann and P. Dieke (2011) *Research Themes for Tourism*, CABI, Wallingford, UK

Peter Robinson

CONSUMER BEHAVIOUR

Consumer behaviour is the study of why people buy and/or consume the products (or services) they do. It is the study of how consumers make decisions on their purchases, how and when they arrive at their consumption choices and, more importantly, what influences their choices. The history of consumer behaviour has evolved from the humble beginnings of the buyer behaviour school in the 1940s; but theoretical models of how consumers make purchase decisions have evolved from the economic paradigm. Early models were developed to explain consumer choice in terms of economic calculations such as demand theory and utility theory.

However, the 1950s saw scholars borrowing concepts and theories from behavioural science in areas such as psychology, sociology and social psychology. Consumer behaviour began to grow as a school of marketing thought in the 1960s. More and more researchers from different academic backgrounds began to develop their own theories of consumer behaviour. Consumer behaviour began incorporating a variety of concepts from different disciplines. Sheth et al (1988, p116) refer to this period as the 'sunrise of the buyer behaviour school' while Jones and Shaw (2002, p43) refer to it as the period of differentiation. As consumer behaviour continued to borrow from a vast discipline, it resulted in numerous theories of brand loyalty, buying behaviour, attitude research and family, as well as organizational buying behaviour. The 1960s is also the period that student textbooks on consumer behaviour were first published.

In 1968, Engel, Kollat and Blackwell published their first textbook on consumer behaviour and, even more importantly, this introduced the model they had developed (now known as the EKB model). The EKB model (Engel at al, 1995) focuses on the consumer decision-making process and is still very much advocated in the twenty-first century (Linquist and Sirgy, 2003). Like the EKB model, the Howard-Sheth model (1969) is another one of the most carefully constructed models of consumer behaviour. It was the first to be based on empirical data and to be tested in the real world (Shaw and Jones, 2005). Both the EKB and Howard-Sheth models of consumer behaviour introduced a turning point in the history of marketing theory and research. Since their conceptualization, they have provided a basic interpretive framework and become the fundamental knowledge for understanding consumer behaviour for many marketing students for years to come (Linquist and Sirgy, 2003).

Moving into the 1970s, research on consumer behaviour quickly saw phenomenal growth, with two major developments in the history of marketing that continue to make a contribution to current marketing practice:

- The Association of Consumer Research (ACR) was established in 1969 and held its first conference.
- In 1974 the publication of *Journal of Consumer Research* (JCR) commenced.

Both events are important in the history of consumer behaviour as it was a step further towards the establishment of consumer behaviour as a field of study. To the present day, the JCR has always maintained its subtitle, *An Interdisciplinary Quarterly*, reiterating how consumer behaviour is influenced by economics, psychology, sociology, anthropology and other disciplines and so it is important to know and trace its different roots.

Within tourism, consumer behaviour is translated into understanding tourist behaviours, attitudes, values, motivations, perceptions, expectations, preferences and choices from pre-purchases to post-purchases. Most consumer studies in tourism fall into one of the three broad categories:

- motivation;
- the buying process;
- integral models.

During motivational studies, scholars have looked into why people participate in tourism, and to a greater extent why certain groups of people participate in a specific type of tourism. These scholars attempt to explain not only economical but also cultural, psychological and socio-psychological factors that influence tourist purchasing behaviour. These factors, in tourism, are commonly known as push-and-pull factors. First espoused in tourism marketing, Dann (1977) described push motives as the specific forces in our lives that lead to the decision to take a vacation, while pull factors refer to those that lead an individual to select one destination over another once the decision to travel has been made.

Push-and-pull motives have generally been characterized as relating to two separate decisions made at two separate points in time – one focusing on whether to go, the other on where to go. Push motives, therefore, are viewed as relating to the needs of the traveller while pull motives have been characterized in terms of the features of the attractions, or attributes of the destination itself. For example, a person wants to get away from the mundane routine of life. This is a factor that will push the individual towards thinking of taking a vacation. This individual now chooses to go to Bali because of its beaches and because he thinks the people are friendly. The beaches and the people are factors that draw this tourist to Bali, and are therefore pull motivations.

The second category of consumer studies in tourism is the buying process. Work in this category revolves around the stages of the tourist buying process and how factors internal and external to the tourist influence this decision-making process. The consumer buying process in tourism is often regarded as being comparable to the purchase of other products and services – that is, the tourist is assumed to move through six different stages:

1 need recognition or awareness;
2 information search;
3 attitude formation;
4 evaluation of alternatives;
5 purchase;
6 post-purchase.

These discussions will lead the tourist to form an attitude about certain destinations. The next stage of the consumer decision process is to consider, compare and contrast the attributes of different products. Attributes such as price, reliability and availability are compared with the objective of gaining what is perceived to be the ideal holiday. The choice stage is where the tourist actually decides on where to go and makes a purchase. From the flow of the decision-making process model, the act of purchase is a cognitive effort based on an extensive information search and information processing in the preceding stages. After a choice is made, the tourist then consumes the tourism product – for example, hotel accommodation or a complete holiday package. In the final stage, the tourist evaluates whether the experience has been satisfactory. This evaluation will, in turn, influence all stages of the buying process in the future.

The third category of consumer studies in tourism is concerned with integrating models from disciplines such as economics, psychology and sociology. The aim is to explain how factors are inter-related to influence choice. These factors are commonly categorized as either internal versus external or personal versus social. The key internal or personal factors are motivation and values, perception, memory, personality, lifestyles and attitudes. On the other hand, external or social factors refer to influences such as cultures and sub-cultures, age, gender, income, social class, family lifecycle, and reference groups. These factors first appear in the EKB and Howard-Sheth models discussed earlier, and provided the building blocks from which consumer behaviour models in tourism are built. Some of the more popular consumer behaviour models that have been adapted to tourist behaviour include those of Schmoll (1977), Mathieson and Wall (1982) and Moutinho (1987). All the models vary in their approaches and emphasize significance to diverse aspects of travel decision. The Mathieson and Wall (1982) model is the most comprehensive as it considers destination and trip characteristics as important determinants of purchases and adds a geographical perspective to travel buying.

In summary, many of the consumer behaviour theories and models discussed in tourism are relatively similar to the topics covered in general consumer behaviour studies. However, it is acknowledged that the tourist buying decision does differ from that of general consumers. This is because when a tourist spends money, the core investment is often one without a tangible return value. The emergence of new trends continues to influence tourism marketing. For example, there is an increasing concern for the environment, a healthier lifestyle and

Figure 1 A model of consumer behaviour (Source: adapted from Mathieson and Wall, 1982)

spiritual development. Consumers today also demand experience, convenience, speed and customization. As consumers, in general, become more marketing savvy, tourists, too, are becoming more sophisticated in their travel behaviour. As such, the study of consumer behaviour in tourism is indispensable for businesses and organizations who want to respond and adapt to these changes.

Further reading

Jones, D. G. B. and Shaw, E. H. (2002) 'A history of marketing thought', in A. W. Barton and R. Wenslet (eds) *Handbook of Marketing*, Sage Publications, London, pp39–65

Moutinho, L. (1987) 'Consumer behaviour in tourism', *European Journal of Marketing*, vol 21, no 10, pp5–44

Pizam, A. and Mansfeld, Y. (1999) *Consumer Behavior in Travel and Tourism*, Haworth Hospitality Press, New York, NY

Dr. Catheryn Khoo-Lattimore

CORPORATE SOCIAL RESPONSIBILITY

Dahlsrud (2006) identified 37 different definitions of corporate social responsibility (CSR), a concept based on the idea that business organizations have a responsibility to society that encompasses more than just complying with the law and making profit. Rowntree's (founded in York, UK) and Cadbury (originating in Birmingham, UK) confectionery firms whose originators were Quakers were forerunners in developing this concept when, during the late 1890s and early 1900s, they built social housing for their factory workers, and provided schools and health services. Since then, and in response to historical developments such as World War II, the advent of consumer rights and the huge growth in the environmental lobby, this very local, and largely internal, business issue has become a worldwide topic of discussion in both developed and emerging nations. It is now seen to encompass many corresponding concepts; these can be termed 'corporate citizenship, business ethics, stakeholder management, and sustainability' (Carroll and Shabana, 2010). This last concept is particularly important to tourism businesses.

CSR has been defined as 'actions that appear to further some social good, beyond the interests of the firm and that which is required by law' (McWilliams and Siegel, 2001, p117). There is an underlying principle that CSR is a voluntary activity undertaken by the largesse of the company, or its founders; however, there are 'societal expectations of corporate behaviour; a behaviour that is alleged by stakeholders to be expected by society or morally required and is therefore justifiably demanded of a business' (Whetton et al, 2002). As this expectation has grown, various sectors of the tourism industry have responded by taking collective, or individual, actions. In hotels, for instance, there is now a worldwide effort to reduce the effects of the business on water usage and pollution by asking guests to reuse towels; many tourism organizations use fair trade coffee; and recycling has become the norm for most companies. In Kenya, domestic tourism has been enhanced by the CSR actions of the Bamburi Cement Company who, even before the environmental movement was founded, turned a quarried wasteland into a nature park that has an enhanced natural habitat and created improved biodiversity for the use of the community. It now receives over 150,000 visitors per year (Haller and Baer, 1994).

Carroll (1979) argued that 'the social responsibility of the business encompasses the economic, legal, ethical and discretionary expectations that society has of organizations at a given point in time'. The notion of 'social good' or society benefiting from specific actions is important in pursuing CSR strategies, particularly if the environment will change as a result of the adoption of tourism *per se*. The idea of societal expectations and, indeed, legal compliance *changing over time* is also important to understand as CSR cannot just be 'done'; it is, instead, an on-going management process which demands a clear standard of evaluation, hence the use of the 'corporate social performance' (CSP) measurement. CSP should be adopted in order to measure the corporate social responsiveness of actions taken by companies, their processes and, in some areas, their compliance (Frederick, 1994). Nevertheless, compliance with the economic and legal responsibilities of an organization is usually taken as a 'given' – a requirement that has to be met. Ethical responsibilities are not legislated for but would be expected, and that, which Carroll by 1991 had changed in definition from 'discretionary' to 'philanthropic', would be a desired state. Measurement, therefore, could be of how far a 'commitment to improve community well-being through discretionary business practices and contributions of corporate resources' (Kotler and Lee, 2005) had taken place.

The Economic Intelligence Unit (EIU, 2008) reports that within the tourism sector airlines have a high regard for CSR initiatives, while fast-food restaurants and alcoholic beverage companies are also heavily involved in ensuring philanthropic and ethical practices; but this survey requires critical thought: airlines are by their very nature creating problems with pollution (both noise and carbon) – the explosion of fast-food outlets provides a large amount of waste and alcohol and is, to all intents and purposes, 'licensed drug peddling'. The role of further investigation is essential to unpick these findings; but, nevertheless, CSR research has been discussed in academic peer-reviewed papers since the 1950s. De Bakker et al (2005) found that the number of papers focusing on CSR has increased since the 1990s, which is important if study of the empirical evidence or theoretical constructs shapes organizational behaviour; this could seem doubtful as many of the CSR papers are descriptive, commenting on what is rather than what should be. Nevertheless, they prove illuminating into practices currently undertaken in the tourism industry.

CSR takes many forms: philanthropic examples include donations to charitable causes while ethical considerations include providing employees with continuous employment even when the business is closed for refurbishment (Bohdanowicz and Zientara, 2009). Large hotel organizations seem to have inculcated more environmental and social measures as part of their corporate strategies under sustainability programmes (Kasim, 2004), whereas Sheldon and Park (2011) found that in travel organizations there is a strong link between CSR and the environment, rather than with the social community so distinctly targeted by the Quaker confectioners. This perhaps is concomitant to the idea of 'tourism and the environment' as being inextricably linked. Environmental or 'green practices' are a common theme in tourism literature on CSR (further examples include Ball and Taleb, 2011); but Sheldon and Park (2011) found that there is a need for these to be adopted much more sincerely. Traditionally, green practices use standards of recycling, reusing and reduction of usage, particularly of water and energy; but there is undoubtedly a financial payback, rather than just a philosophical decision, from this green theme as less use of resources impacts directly upon the bottom line.

Crook (2005) argues that businesses ought to justify their existence in terms of service to the community, rather than profit or employment; the tourism developments on the island of Corfu during the 1970s enhanced both employment in local businesses and a reinvigoration of interior villages whose core agri-business, olive groves, had fallen into disrepair due to competition with Italy. The building of completely self-sufficient tourist 'villages' along the coast in the 2000s, where the supplier provided 'all-inclusive' packages, has reduced the number of visitors to the island's hospitality provision, creating animosity and ill-feeling. In order to support the island, more CSR-orientated organizations, such as TrailFinders and Explore have now created walking tours of the Corfu Trail that bring some financial reward to the 'real

Corfu'. Van De Merwe and Wöcke (2007) argue that foreign customer bases should persuade hotel management to adopt responsible tourism practices, which they link to purchasing behaviour; but they also point to the differences between internationally owned businesses and those who may be small- or medium-sized enterprises.

Whatever the size of the tourism business, there is no doubt that to be truly effective CSR needs leadership, not just strategic intent. It needs direction, objectives and measurement in order to change habits (Sheldon and Park, 2011). For tourism organizations, this has been slow to emerge (Gordon, 2001) and, increasingly, legal requirements have been set by government (regional, national and international) in order to focus on essential tourism sustainability requirements. These range from planning legislation in Lanzarote, Canary Islands (which limits builders to one storey in order to avoid the overdevelopment experienced by its neighbouring island of Tenerife), to regulations on energy consumption in hotels adopted by both the Swiss and Dutch governments. Further growth in public concern over the consumption of resources by tourists and their impact upon environments will require organizations and countries to seek more responsible solutions: in the Maldives the regional government has legislated on both planning, design and biodiversity, while two airlines issued visitors with bags in order to collect their waste and transport this (for free) back to Europe in order to alleviate the impact upon the islands (Saeed, 1998).

Social responsibility for tourism organizations is no longer a 'corporate' issue and affects all sizes of business; therefore, CSR is a growing management issue. Providing strategic intent on CSR is applaudable; but unless a resourced infrastructure is in place that reports at board level, which instils changed mind-sets, such as that adopted by Scandic, the results will at best be patchy (Bohdanowicz and Zientara, 2009). There are some indications that more legislation will be introduced to target essential, possibly environmental, concerns (Van De Merwe and Wöcke, 2007) and it is important that further research is undertaken to help tourism practitioners (many of whom are small businesses) find solutions to industry issues in this regard.

Further reading

Carroll, A. B. (1999) 'Corporate social responsibility: Evolution of a definitional construct', *Business and Society*, vol 38, no 3, September, pp268–295

Carroll, A. B. and Shabana, K. M. (2010) 'The business case for corporate social responsibility: A review of concepts, research and practice', *International Journal of Management Reviews*, vol 12, no 1, March, pp85–105

De Bakker, F. G. A., Groenewegen, P. and Den Hond, F. (2005) 'A bibliometric analysis of 30 years of research and theory on corporate social responsibility and corporate social performance', *Business and Society*, vol 44, no 3, September, pp283–317

Robinson, S. and Kenyon, A. J. (2009) *Ethics in the Alcohol Industry*, Palgrave, London

Caroline Ann Wiscombe

CRISIS MANAGEMENT

A crisis is defined by Devlin (2006) as 'an unstable time for a hospitality organization or for a tourism destination with a distinct possibility for an undesirable outcome which could interfere with the normal operations of the tourism establishment and/or destination which could jeopardize the positive public image or could lead to negative news for the media'. Sikich (2008) suggests that a crisis can be defined as any unplanned event, occurrence or sequence of events that has a specific undesirable consequence. Crisis occurs suddenly, often unexpectedly, and demands a quick response in order to prevent negative impacts. Therefore managing them in an organized way is very important for the successful future outcomes for an organization or destination. Thus, crisis management may be defined as 'actions taken by a company to maintain its credibility and good reputation after a situation has occurred that may affect the company in a negative manner and therefore reduce sales of that company's product or service' (Imber and Toffler, 2008, p149). A crisis can be:

- a natural event, such as an earthquake, a hurricane or a tornado;
- a man-made event, such as a bombing, workplace or domestic violence, war, pollution, flood, explosion, terrorism, theft, a conflict or scandal, stringent regulations, financial manipulation and societal disruption in destinations;
- accidental, such as fires, health-and-safety errors, injuries or fatalities;
- reputational, such as a service failure, bad publicity, issues around equality or poor management of hygiene and safety (Tavmergen and Ozdemir, 2001; Sikich, 2008).

Examples include SARS, the Bali bombings, 9/11 in the US, the Mumbai terrorist attack and the Gulf oil spill. These are all very different crises that had negative impacts upon tourism revenues and international tourism arrival numbers to the affected destinations (Tavmergen and Ozdemir, 2001; Li et al, 2003; Shekkar, 2009).

An important aspect of public relations is crisis management: the management of messages and communication must be delivered swiftly to minimize the impact of negative messages from other sources; the negative impacts of a crisis may also lead to negative publicity and negative images, which may result in loss of revenues. Inevitably, some crises are sudden, which gives further importance to the management of the crisis to minimize the negative impacts.

The application of a crisis management system, staff crisis training, being prepared for all occurrences and risk assessing a range of factors are all valuable components of crisis management. Thus, crisis management, disaster recovery and organizational continuity are critical areas of competence for managers of individual organizations, and multinationals operating in different countries and facing different threats as well as destinations. For large-scale problems, crisis management may be a critical factor that determines the sustainability and success of a destination (Racheria and Hu, 2009).

Planning, documentation, training, conducting drills, testing procedures and providing additional external resources are very important functions to prepare for a crisis. In addition, the following factors are also useful in managing crisis situations effectively (Pirnar, 1994; Tavmergen and Ozdemir, 2001; Walbeek, 2004; Kotler et al, 2006; Fearn-Banks, 2011):

- effective and planned responses;
- the establishment of good communication systems;
- preparation and provision of an adequate emergency response;
- handling media relations;
- crisis information dissemination and a dedicated media spokesperson;
- a crisis plan that comprises a pre-crisis and post-crisis task list;
- crisis blueprints, which enable an organization to set procedures, with clear steps, responsibilities and action plans – each system and process include the following:

  - key personnel;
  - nature and type of crisis;
  - people to be informed/notified with contact numbers, including members of the crisis team;
  - list of actions and tasks to be taken.

Crisis management tools may be summarized as organizations having a written crisis management plan in place, establishing a tourism crisis management task force and selecting and training the initial crisis

Table 2 The UNWTO's crisis guidelines for the tourism industry

Before the crisis: be prepared	Prepare a crisis management plan. Be prepared for promotional activity. Review security systems. Be ready.
During the crisis: minimize damage	Communicate from the frontline. Devise promotional messages. Ensure security of the operation. Conduct tactical research on the situation.
After the crisis: recover tourist confidence	Build communication confidence. Use promotion imaginatively. Evaluate security measures. Use research effectively to build confidence.

responders; rehearsing by conducting 'major incident' exercises; developing a crisis management guidebook; creating awareness among the partners and tourism industry organizations; and partnering with law enforcement officials and crisis management consultants (Sonmez et al, 1999). Further to this guidance is the common practice in the heritage sector of identifying key items to be rescued from a museum, gallery or historic site, as well as specific contingency plans for major events.

Further reading

Cooper, C., Fletcher, J., Fyall, A., Gilbert, D. and Wanhill, S. (2008a) *Tourism: Principles and Practice*, 4th edition, Pearson Education Limited, Essex, UK, p667

Devlin, E. S. (2006) *Crisis Management Planning and Execution*, Auerbach Publications, New York, NY

Fearn-Banks, K. (2011) *Crisis Communications: A Casebook Approach*, fourth edition, Routledge, Oxon, UK

Sonmez, S., Apostolopoulos, Y. and Tarlow, P. (1999) 'Tourism in crisis: Managing the effects of terrorism', *Journal of Travel Research*, August, vol 38, no 1, pp13–18

Tavmergen (Pirnar), I. and Ozdemir, P. M. (2001) 'Turizm sektorunde kriz pazarlamasi ve yonetimi', *Uluslararasi Turizm Arastirmalari Dergisi*, T.C. Maltepe Universitesi, pp111–120

Dr. Ige Pirnar

CRUISE TOURISM

During recent years, the oceans of the world have borne witness to the growth of a major leisure phenomenon, the cruise industry. Cruising, once the holiday of choice for a privileged few, has entered the mass market with an increasing array of products on offer to suit all price ranges. Other sectors of the highly competitive tourism industry might cast covetous glances at the healthy 8 per cent growth that this sector has shown over the last 20 years (UNWTO, 2010a), with its ability to attract new customers while retaining those all-important existing ones (CLIA, 2010). In 2005, world demand for cruises was 14.12 million, of which 9.67 million came from North America, 3.22 million from Europe and the rest of the world accounting for 1.23 million (UNWTO, 2010a). Cruisers from the UK account for the largest group from Europe, followed by Germany and Italy. According to the United Nations World Tourism Organization (UNWTO, 2010a), the average age of the North American cruiser is 49, generally married, university educated and with an annual income of over US$104,000. The demographic trend in the markets is a decline in the average age of cruise passenger. Cartwright and Baird (1999, pxv) define cruising as 'a multi-centre holiday where you take your hotel with you from centre to centre'.

The majority of this growth is due to the development by the major cruise lines of innovative products and the launch of new large ships, resulting in a subsequent increase in passenger capacity. The sector is dominated by three main companies, Carnival Corporation, Royal Caribbean Cruises Ltd and the GHK group, all of which own a variety of brands catering for diverse consumer groups and operating out of different parts of the world:

- Carnival Corporation PLC: the largest cruise company worldwide owns Carnival Cruise Line, Costa Crociere, Cunard Line, Seabourn Cruises, Holland America Line, P and O Cruises, Princess Cruises, Aida Cruise and Iberocruceros.
- Royal Caribbean Cruises Ltd: operates Celebrity Cruises, Azamara Cruises, Royal Caribbean International, Pullmantur Cruceros, and CDF Crosieres de France.
- Genting Hong Kong Ltd (GHK group) (formerly Star Cruises): includes Star Cruises and Norwegian Cruise Line and is the leading cruise line in Asia–Pacific.

The remaining cruise industry is shared among approximately 50 other cruise lines, including, for example, MSC Cruises, operating out of Italy; Orient River Cruises in China; and the Disney Cruise Line, based in Celebration, Florida. It can be difficult to keep track of ship ownership as a feature of the sector is that ships often alter their name once they change hands or are refurbished.

The different brands tend to be linked to one of the five main categories of cruising, each of which target specific customer demographics and needs, while the length of the cruise tends to be closely linked to the free time available to consumers:

1 Budget cruises operate on older, smaller ships with few amenities, focusing on the European market.
2 Contemporary cruises tend to be mass market with resort-style facilities, a heavy emphasis on ship-board activities and entertainment, and are dependent on the continued introduction of new passengers.
3 Premium cruises are targeted at more experienced cruisers with an accent on service and food quality.
4 Luxury cruises focus on a high-quality experience, travelling on small- and medium-sized vessels that tend to sail worldwide and are destination oriented, offering superior service and food.
5 Special cruises include river and exploration cruises that concentrate on niche markets.

The distinction between luxury and premium is increasingly blurred, although luxury tends to infer exclusivity, formal atmospheres and itineraries with uncommon destinations lasting more than ten days.

One of the reasons for the growth in cruising over recent years is the development and introduction of new ships into the fleets, the majority of which have increased passenger capacity. The largest 'mega-ship' in the world is currently the Royal Caribbean *Allure of the Seas*, standing at 16 storeys tall with cabins for 5400 passengers and serviced by 2384 crew members. This particular ship offers 37 categories of accommodation, including balcony cabins overlooking the on-board Central Park. At the luxury end of the market, the Yachts of Seabourn carry only 208 to 450 travellers and boast one member of staff per suite (Yachts of Seabourn, 2010). Some of the new large ships cannot berth in ports due to their size and therefore anchor offshore, using tender boats to ferry passengers to and from the visiting destination port.

As cruise companies target more customers, the products and services on-board have increased. Most ships provide spas and health and fitness facilities, as well as theatres, casinos, shops and a choice of dining amenities. Some newer ships now offer celebrity-endorsed restaurants, ice skating, climbing walls, golf simulators, laser shows and even zip lines. Other vessels also offer culinary demonstrations, guest lectures and wine workshops, as well as a range of shore- and land-based excursions. While the facilities offered are dependent upon the size and age of the ships, the development of the cruise as an all-inclusive resort package at sea, that is highly competitive when compared to similar land-based holidays, has contributed to the expansion of the sector. The cruise ship today is a destination in itself and, like the land-based tourist resort, is one that the tourist need not leave for the duration of their holiday. However, unlike its land-based competitors, the ships and the experiences offered on-board can be repositioned relatively quickly to anywhere in the world.

The main location for cruising is the Caribbean, albeit in a process of long-term decline in its market share, followed by the Mediterranean, Northern Europe and Alaska. There are also a further 20 sub-regions within the global marketplace with a wide range of different itineraries. The cruise industry has now begun to focus on the Asia-Pacific market, with the newly mobile Chinese tourists a certain future target (Koncept Analytics, 2010).

The major cruise companies have the advantage of economies of scale. This allows widespread influence on cruise marketing, operation and deployment trends worldwide. Their domination of the sector has enabled them to erect barriers for potential new market entrants and to increase leverage on cruise destinations in order to maintain low cruise fees (Chin, 2008). Registering ships under the 'Flag of Convenience' for tax purposes (Wood, 2004) enables all of the major cruise companies to recruit their staff on a global basis. Chin (2008) suggests that 74 per cent of cruise lines turn to crewing agents for recruitment, with a general bias towards the higher-ranked positions being filled by those from the Northern Hemisphere and the more manual occupations being serviced by those from the Global South. While tax-free wages are an appeal of working on a cruise ship, six- to nine-month contracts and long working hours are the norm.

Cruising is a fast-evolving sector of tourism, so much so that more research into the overall cruise experience is essential, exploring not only the passengers' perspectives, but those of the crew, from captain to cabin steward, in order to obtain a comprehensive overview of this dynamic industry.

Further reading

Cartwright, R. and Baird, C. (1999) *The Development and Growth of the Cruise Industry*, Butterworth–Heinemann, Oxford, UK

Chin, C. (2008) *Cruising in the Global Economy: Profits, Pleasure and Work at Sea*, Ashgate Publishing Limited, Hampshire, UK

CLIA (Cruise Lines International Association Inc.) (2010) *The Overview: 2010 CLIA Cruise Market Overview*, http://www.cruising.org, accessed 29 October 2011

UNWTO (United Nations World Tourism Organization) (2010a) *Cruise Tourism: Current Situation and Trends*, World Tourism Organization, Madrid

Lisa Power

DARK TOURISM (ALSO THANATOURISM)

Dark tourism may be defined as the act of travel to sites of death, disaster or the seemingly macabre. While the practice of dark tourism has a long history – for example, crowds of people who gathered for Roman gladiatorial games or hordes of spectators at medieval public executions – the contemporary version of the phenomenon has attracted growing academic interest and media attention over the past decade or so. Indeed, dark tourism may include diverse visitor experiences at sites such as the London Dungeon (a purpose-built visitor attraction depicting death and torture), to the Bodyworlds exhibition (an anatomical exhibition using real human corpses), to Ground Zero (the site of the atrocity on 9/11), or to Auschwitz-Birkenau Memorial and Museum (the infamous Holocaust site in Poland).

The term *dark tourism* as a codified research area was brought to mainstream academic consideration in an editorial by Malcolm Foley and John Lennon for the *International Journal of Heritage Studies* in 1996 and, subsequently, popularized in 2000 by their inspiring yet theoretically tentative book *Dark Tourism: The Attraction of Death and Disaster*. Moreover, the increasing weight of coverage with regard to dark tourism over the past few years from the press and broadcast media, as well as the Internet, has been striking. Consequently, Seaton and Lennon (2004, p63) propose dark tourism as a contemporary leisure activity has been aggrandized by the popular press from the status of myth to meta-myth, allowing the media to 'depict it, not just as a genre of travel motivation and attraction, but as a social pathology sufficiently new and threatening to create moral panic'.

Nevertheless, the point to be emphasized here is that, prior to the mid-1990s, dark tourism, as a *generic* term for travel associated with death, atrocity or disaster, had not previously featured in the academic literature as a specific element of consumption in periodic typologies of tourism. Of course, the study of the commodification of death has pedigree in broader sociology, anthropology and museology studies. Most notably, Rojeck (1993) introduced the concept of 'black spot' tourist sites by highlighting relationships between death sites and commercialism, while earlier, Walter (1984) suggested that death at a distance was a kind of voyeuristic pornography for a (Western) society in which there is no easy language for discussing death. However, despite some early works on the study of tourist sites associated with death, an encyclopaedia entry by Seaton (2000) and a subsequent call by Stone (2005) for dark tourism research to be located within social and cultural responses to death and disaster have controversially elaborated upon the range and type of sites that may be included as dark tourism. Additionally, the first-ever dedicated academic research centre – The Institute for Dark Tourism Research (iDTR) – opened in 2011 at the University of Central Lancashire, UK, and acts as 'global hub' for dark tourism scholarship and research.

Although dark tourism has many defining features and consequences, and is both produced and consumed within a plethora of sociocultural and geopolitical environments, attempts have been made to construct dark tourism typologies. Notably, the 'dark tourism spectrum' typology highlights various 'shades' of dark tourism sites, attractions, and exhibitions according to spatial, temporal and interpretative factors (Stone, 2006). Particularly, this 'spectrum of supply' compares, for example, location, site objectives (education, entertainment or 'edutainment'), perceptions of authenticity and so on. In doing so, the model provides a conjectural basis for locating dark tourism sites on a darkest–lightest scale. Although perhaps oversimplifying the complexity of influences on dark tourism supply, the 'dark tourism spectrum' provides a useful conceptual framework for exploring different modes of dark tourism supply and, consequently, a broader base for understanding the phenomenon as a whole. Similarly, Sharpley (2005) offers a 'dark tourism matrix' in which both the supply of and demand for dark tourism are taken into account. In particular, Sharpley proposes a typological model in which dark tourism attractions or experiences are measured by the extent to which a fascination with death is a dominant consumption factor and the supply is purposefully directed towards satisfying this fascination. As a result, it is possible to identify four 'shades' of dark tourism:

1 *Pale tourism* – tourists with a minimal or limited interest in death or the death event visiting sites unintended to be visitor tourist attractions.
2 *Grey tourism demand* – tourists with a fascination with death or the death event visiting unintended dark tourism sites.
3 *Grey tourism supply* – sites intentionally established to exploit death and/or the death event but attracting visitors with some, though not a dominant, interest in death or the death event.

4 *Black tourism* – in effect, 'pure' dark tourism, where a fascination with death and the death event is satisfied by the purposeful supply of experiences intended to satisfy this fascination.

However, while there is no universal typology of dark tourism, or even a universally accepted definition, there has been an increasing trend amongst scholars to use dark tourism as a lens to scrutinize broader sociocultural considerations, managerial and political consequences, or ethical dilemmas. Indeed, a key theme of dark tourism often focuses on the mediating relationship between the cultural condition of contemporary society and broader issues of morality and mortality. In particular, the edited book *The Darker Side of Travel: The Theory and Practice of Dark Tourism* by Richard Sharpley and Philip Stone (2009) attempts to draw together conceptual themes and debates surrounding dark tourism. Consequently, they explore dark tourism within wider disciplinary contexts and establish a more informed relationship between the theory and practice of dark tourism.

Ultimately, dark tourism is a complex, emotive, multidimensional, politically vulnerable, and ethically and morally challenging phenomenon. There are no simple definitions of dark tourism, no simple answers to many of the questions that surround it, and no quick solutions to the many challenges or dilemmas inherent in the development and promotion of dark sites. Nevertheless, as a particular theme in tourism studies, it is not only a fascinating subject in its own right, but it also represents, as with the study of tourism more generally, a powerful vehicle for exploring contemporary social life, practices and institutions. In other words, the principal benefit of studying dark tourism lies in what it reveals, or may reveal, about the relationship between life and death, the living and the dead, and the institutions or processes that mediate between life and death at both the individual and societal level. Indeed, although the term 'dark tourism' implies a focus on death and dying, developing our understanding of the phenomenon may, ironically, tell us more about life and the living.

Further reading

Lennon, J. and Foley, M. (2000) *Dark Tourism: The Attraction of Death and Disaster*, Continuum, London

Seaton, A. (2010) 'Thanatourism and its discontents: An appraisal of a decade's work with some future issues and directions', in T. Jamal and M. Robinson (eds) *The Sage Handbook of Tourism Studies*, Sage Publications, London, pp521–542

Sharpley, R. and Stone, P. R. (eds) (2009) *The Darker Side of Travel: The Theory and Practice of Dark Tourism*, Aspect of Tourism Series, Channel View Publications, Bristol, UK

Stone, P. R. (2006) 'A dark tourism spectrum: Towards a typology of death and macabre related tourist sites, attractions and exhibitions', *Tourism: An Interdisciplinary International Journal*, vol 54, no 2, pp145–160

Stone, P. R. and Sharpley, R. (2008) 'Consuming dark tourism: A thanatological perspective', *Annals of Tourism Research*, vol 35, no 2, pp574–595

The Institute for Dark Tourism Research (iDTR), *http://www.dark-tourism.org.uk*

Dr. Philip R. Stone

DESTINATION IMAGE

The study of destination image has its roots in a number of disciplines, including marketing, sociology, human geography, anthropology, cultural studies and psychology (Baloglu and McCleary, 1999; Gallarza et al, 2002). The study of destination image in tourism literature has been a constant since Gunn's (1972) book *Vacationscape: Designing Tourist Regions*, which was based, in part, on the studies of geography, landscape and architecture from the 1960s. Gunn (1972) introduced the importance and focus of destination image in a functional and critical perspective. The functional perspective is concerned with the formation of the image and its function, especially in marketing and destination selection. The critical cultural perspective is concerned with analysing the way in which destination image creates meaning, and how meaning is manipulated through representation and interpretation (Andsager and Drzewiecka, 2002).

Contrary to the critical perspective, the functional perspective does not relate the image functions to the cultural, political or social context within which they take place. Since 1972, there has been a predominance of studies to assess destination image from a functional perspective (e.g. as a function of marketing) (Gallarza et al, 2002). Nonetheless, there has also been a growing body of literature studying destination image from a critical cultural perspective (e.g. critical evaluation of the representations of people) (Andsager and Drzewiecka, 2002).

Very broadly, in each of these perspectives, destination image is the perception of a place for travel. Destination image is, therefore, defined and discussed in two main ways (Jenkins, 1999):

1 the tourists' perception of a place for travel, and discussed in the source, formation and influence of the image (understood as the interpretation or perception of place);

2 the destination projected image that it represents as its tourism offer, discussed in the destination's selection, management and marketing of images (understood as the representation of place) (see the section on **Semiotics in tourism**).

For the potential tourist, destination image is comprised of three components, which together create a perception of the destination (Gartner, 1993):

1 the cognitive component: what we know about the place;
2 the affective component: what we feel about the place; and
3 the conative component: the active consideration of the place as a potential travel destination.

The conative image component distinguishes the destination image from a general place image, and moves the place image into one of travel action. For example, the image action considerations that surround the selection of a place in which to live (based on a set of rationale factors such as work and family) are often very different, or even opposite, from the considerations in selecting where to take a holiday.

The destination image and the three components are constructed through the development of perception. The cognitive component occurs first: we know the place exists and have some perceived facts about the place. Through further exposure, familiarity and complexity, the affective component is constructed as we form feelings towards the place. If both the cognitive and affective images are positive, the conative image component will be initiated. The initiated conative destination image is distinct from a positive cognitive and affective place image.

Other factors influence the construction of a conative destination image, including a range of individual motivations, and society's messages about the nature and purpose of travel (Baloglu and McCleary, 1999; Andsager and Drzewiecka, 2002) (see **Consumer behaviour in tourism**).

Destination image is clearly constructed through a complex process, dependent upon the potential tourists' characteristics, and the attributes that they consider important. Adding to the complexity, there are three sources or agents of image formation (Gunn, 1972; Gartner, 1993; Jenkins, 1999; Andsager and Drzewiecka, 2002):

1 Organic agents are those from perceived non-tourism sources, including friends and general media, user review sites and other informal sources. These are usually perceived as the most credible

sources and are, therefore, influential in the formation of destination image.

2   Induced agents are those perceived to be from tourism sources, including destination promotions, official websites and tourist brochures. These are perceived as the least credible sources since they represent a sales image that marketers want the potential tourist to purchase.

3   Real agents are the actual experience of the destination, perceived as the most credible, and the most influential in destination image formation.

Of course, most potential tourists' destination image is formed through only organic and induced agents prior to actual travel to the destination (where they are exposed to the real agent). As such, the credible image experienced at the actual destination will be compared within the pre-existing organic and induced constructs (Andsager and Drzewiecka, 2002).

For the destination, image is important to the marketing and alignment of the destination representation with target market tourists' perceptions of an ideal destination (Gartner, 1993). Specifically, it is important to create the most positive and enticing image possible in the mind of the target market. The alignment process is an acknowledgement that potential tourists' complex destination image processes can create a variety of perceptions of place, and some of these may be quite divergent to the actual destination (Gartner, 1993). Indeed, gap analysis studies compare the interpreted (tourists') and represented (destination's) image to the destination reality, and assess how the three image-formation agents create expectations. For a destination, the process to align the interpreted, represented and actual destination images is very difficult and long (Gartner, 1993). The main difficulty is that the image agents able to be used by the destination are less credible and less influential in changing the image, and once potential tourists hold an image it is very difficult to modify it.

Further studies have found that tourists actually search for the destination-represented images, and once found and experienced then represent these back to friends, as a marker of being *There* (Jenkins, 2003). An example would be tourists visiting Paris, taking pictures of the Eiffel Tower as seen in brochures, movies and television programmes, and showing these pictures to friends upon their return home. In this, it is proposed that the initial destination image interpreted by the tourist (via the image formation agents) sets expectations for the experience, and these images need to be experienced for expectations to be met, closing a satisfying hermeneutic circle. Destination image is, therefore, important as a result of its effects on prospective markets' destination selection and its role in consumer satisfaction (Gartner, 1993; Baloglu and McCleary, 1999; Jenkins, 1999).

Destination image, studied from functional and critical perspectives, is the perception of a place for travel. Image is constructed from cognitive, affective and conative components, informed by organic, induced and real agents. In this complexity, destination image is developed and interpreted within personal and societal contexts before actually being experienced. For destinations, the management and marketing of destination image is difficult given the complexity of image-formation processes and the limited access to influential agents. Nonetheless, once an image is interpreted by potential tourists, it is also searched for.

Further reading

Baloglu, S. and McCleary, K. W. (1999) 'A model of destination image formation', *Annals of Tourism Research*, vol 26, no 4, pp868–897
Gartner, W. C. (1993) 'Image formation process', *Journal of Travel and Tourism Marketing*, vol 2, no 2/3, pp191–215
Gunn, C. A. (1972) *Vacationscape: Designing Tourist Regions*, University of Texas, Austin, TX
Jenkins, O. H. (1999) 'Understanding and measuring tourist destination images', *International Journal of Tourism Research*, vol 1, no 1, pp1–15

Dr. Glen Croy

DESTINATION MANAGEMENT

The tourist 'destination' comprises all of those elements that collectively offer day and staying visitors an integrated visit experience and is regarded as the core component of the wider travel and tourism system. Destinations can include countries such as the UK, Thailand or India; a macro-region which brings together several countries, such as the Caribbean, a province or another administrative entity, such as Provence in France or Queensland in Australia; a localized region, city or town, such as New York and Cape Town or the Peak District in England; or a unique locale with great drawing power, such as Yosemite and Zion national parks in the US and the Serengeti in Tanzania.

Conceptually, destinations remain difficult to define due to the nature and diversity of the components that come together to attract visitors, the various stakeholders within and outside of the destination who have an interest in its competitiveness, the myriad of market groups who visit the destination, and the geographical boundaries that more often than not set the parameters for its management. The latter point is particularly significant as most destinations are dissected by geographical, administrative and political barriers which bear no resemblance to the destination as viewed through the lens of the visitor. This does, in fact, highlight the distinction between supply-sided definitions which reflect destinations as a tourist place where activities and products are developed for, and consumed by, visitors and which are delivered in a specific geographical area with a defined planning and management framework, often involving both public- and private-sector operators, and demand-sided definitions which focus more explicitly on the destination as a collection of visit experiences, again in a well-defined geographical area.

The challenges of definition, in part, contribute to why destinations are viewed as such difficult entities to manage. More often than not, however, the principal challenge is the number and degree of complexity in the relationships of the stakeholders who collectively make up the destination in that each stakeholder or stakeholder group often has a particular interest which diverges with the interests and perceptions of others in terms of actual need or priority. This, in turn, makes the harmonization of common destination-wide interests hard to achieve. It is for these reasons that in the study of destinations, systematic and interdisciplinary approaches are advanced as a means by which to grasp the full complexity inherent within destinations. It is important to be aware of the specific interactions among destination stakeholders, and of the need to come to terms with the impacts exerted by the competitive environment on the broader destination. The early work of Leiper (1979, 1990, 1995) was particularly noteworthy in providing a robust platform for the study of destinations, his work set the foundations for more contemporary studies on the relationships among actors and stakeholders within destinations, and the means by which they can collectively manage more effectively the destination 'experience' for visitors.

Although very much still in its infancy when compared to the study of tourism more broadly, research into destinations does, in fact, cover a wide spectrum of activity. While early studies explored the geographical dimensions of destinations (see Gunn, 1972), work by Butler in the early 1980s began to explore the wider conceptualization of tourism and the means by which destinations are planned and managed (Butler, 1980). There then followed a surge of supply-sided studies building on Butler's initial conceptualizations before a number of more specialized areas of investigation appeared in the areas of environmental impacts and the development of destinations in a variety of geographic and political contexts, such as in the case of rural and coastal, and business and convention destinations. In contrast, demand-sided studies focused on destination image and perceptions; destination choice and the modelling of visitor movement; destination marketing and branding; and the more recent trend towards the experiential aspects of destinations.

In an attempt to bring together all of the component parts of the tourist destination, the text by Ritchie and Crouch (2003) provides a valuable overview of the management of destinations in the wider context of sustainability and introduces a suitable conceptual framework upon which to build much future research. Within the broader context of competitiveness, the text introduces the range of policies available to those managing destinations and the means by which destinations can develop and interface more effectively with other sectors across the wider economy. Hence, while the development of policy focuses on macro-level decision-making, the specific management of destinations involves micro-level activity in which the myriad of component parts of the destination 'product' undertake their individual and organizational duties to realize the vision contained in respective policy, planning and development documents. Ultimately, to be competitive, destinations need to attract and satisfy visitors in a manner that is consistent with the overall ambitions of the destination and its multitude of stakeholders, most notably its resident community, more effectively and efficiently than its competitor set of destinations. To achieve such competitiveness, those managing destinations require a mixed skill set of business acumen and environmental awareness to manage the natural and man-made resources available to a destination as effectively as possible and to be fully aware of both demand and supply factors. For example, they need to be cognisant of the timing and scale of demand with regard to managing the destination's resources, while being aware of the products, services, amenities and attractions necessary to satisfy the needs, wants and experiences of visitors.

To conclude, in many parts of the world, at present, those managing destinations are facing a number of considerable challenges. This is set against a backdrop of all destinations operating within a unique environmental and political context to the extent that no ideal blueprint exists anywhere for their generic management. With budget pressures in many public-sector environments, the emergence of the private sector in the management of destinations is growing in many parts of the world, coupled with the trend for destinations to be managed in a more holistic and collaborative sense under the banner of regeneration. Irrespective of the challenges, however, collaboration among all those stakeholders with an interest in the management of destinations is critical, with a significant element of trust necessary across all parties if their collective ambitions are going to deliver a satisfactory destination experience to visitors.

Further reading

Buhalis, D. (2000) 'Marketing the competitive destination of the future', *Tourism Management*, vol 21, no 1, pp97–116

Fyall, A. (2011a) 'Destination management: Challenges and opportunities', in Y. Wang and A. Pizam (eds) *Destination Marketing and Management: Theories and Applications*, CABI, Oxford, UK, pp340–357

Laws, E., Richins, H., Agrusa, J. F. and Scott, N. (2011) *Tourist Destination Governance: Practice, Theory and Issues*, CABI, Oxford, UK

Ritchie, J. R. B. and Crouch, G. I. (2003) *The Competitive Destination: A Sustainable Tourism Perspective*, CABI, Oxford, UK

Wang, Y. and Pizam, A. (eds) (2011) *Destination Marketing and Management: Theories and Applications*, CABI, Oxford, UK

Dr. Alan Fyall

DESTINATION MANAGEMENT ORGANIZATIONS

Destination management organizations (DMOs) are those entities charged with the leadership of destinations, whether on a national, regional or local scale. Although with a strong public-sector bias in many countries, DMOs increasingly represent a partnership between the public and private sectors, with both sectors joining together to enhance the overall competitiveness of the destination through a shared collaborative agenda. The actual scope of DMOs vary considerably, with the specific geographic and political contexts being key determinants in deciding their strategic focus and operational parameters, with no blueprint in existence anywhere for the standardized management of destinations. As such, although all DMOs may seek to achieve long-term competitiveness, the extent to which they share the same organizational characteristics is minimal.

Interestingly, current public-sector budget pressures in many countries around the world are providing a suitable wake-up call for many DMOs in that there is significant pressure to reduce costs and improve efficiency and effectiveness, and in turn to seek new approaches to the progressive marketing and management of destinations. Hence, while a combination of strategy, policy-setting and planning, industry cross-sector representation, product development, marketing, sales and facilitation activity, skills development and training, infrastructure development and the coherent collection of management information and research all remain very valid activities, the extent to which each and more can continue in every DMO around the world is open to question.

With regard to actual composition, while some are membership based, where a membership fee for businesses in the DMO area will often be levied, others represent much looser organizational forms. And while in much of the world DMOs have yet to shake off their public sector bias, in the US DMOs, which are often referred to as convention and visitor bureaux (CVBs), are predominantly private-sector funded and driven and, in part, are funded by local taxation mechanisms such as bed or hotel taxes. Although often regarded as unfair in that a tax is levied on only one of the component sectors of the destination, the cost of alternative measures is either financially prohibitive or politically unacceptable. One often used alternative is that of sponsorship, but this is not issue free as, although frequently successful in the short term (especially for promotional campaigns), there is always a tendency to pander to the sponsor rather than act on behalf of the entire destination in as neutral a way as possible.

Irrespective of current, future or desired 'ideal' activities to be undertaken by a DMO, what is common is the need for a large number of stakeholders in, and often outside, the boundaries of the destination to work collectively and determine an organizational structure that best fits the ambitions of the overall destination. The DMO needs to be recognized and acknowledged as the identifiable lead organization for the destination, enjoy 'buy-in' from across all sectors within the destination, and be able to pull all component parts together in delivering a seamless experience to visitors – all undertaken within a broader policy framework. To achieve this, a sense of independence and degree of neutrality across all sectors is preferable, while the DMO needs to be able to demonstrate an ability to enhance the economic prosperity of the destination and local resident community, and to maximize the positive and minimize the negative impacts of tourism. An increasing priority for many DMOs is the creation and dissemination of a suitable market positioning for the destination and a consequent branding, marketing and distribution strategy to ensure that existing and desired origin markets receive communication in an effective manner. More often than not, this now involves extensive development of destination web pages, often using the prefix 'visit', destination management and reservation systems, and the use of social media and online social networks such as Facebook and Twitter to communicate and build relationships with both consumer and business markets.

Perhaps the most pressing of issues for all DMOs around the world in the current unstable financial climate is the extent to which their success, or otherwise, can be measured, monitored and benchmarked with other destinations. To date, the ability to pinpoint the contribution of DMOs to the development of tourism to a destination has proved elusive, while for many politicians the only metrics that matter are visitor numbers and visitor spend – metrics that in every sense underplay the contribution of DMOs to the wider development, management and marketing of destinations.

Further reading

Fyall, A. (2011b) 'The partnership challenge', in N. Morgan, A. Pritchard and R. Pride (eds) *Destination Brands: Managing Place Reputation*, third edition, Elsevier, Oxford, UK, pp91–103

Fyall, A., Fletcher, J. and Spyriadis, T. (2010) 'Diversity, devolution and disorder: The management of tourism', in M. Kozak, J. Gnoth and L. Andreu (eds) *Advances in Tourism Destination Marketing: Managing Networks*, Routledge: Oxford, UK, pp15–26

Laws, E., Richins, H., Agrusa, J. F. and Scott, N. (2011) *Tourist Destination Governance: Practice, Theory and Issues*, CABI, Oxford, UK

Middleton, V. T. C., Fyall, A., Morgan, M. with Ranchhod, A. (2009) *Marketing in Travel and Tourism*, fourth edition, Butterworth Heinemann, Oxford, UK

Pike, S. (2004) *Destination Marketing Organisations*, Elsevier, Oxford, UK

Wang, Y. (2012) *Tourism Destination Marketing: Collaborative Strategies*, CABI, Oxford, UK

Dr. Alan Fyall

DESTINATION MARKETING

The management and marketing of destinations are closely intertwined, with the terms **destination management** and destination marketing often used interchangeably. This is especially so in the case of those organizational entities established to manage and/or market destinations. In the specific context of destinations, marketing relates to those marketing, promotional, branding and relationship-building activities, often in a collaborative form, undertaken by destinations to:

- raise the profile and awareness of the destination;
- attract new and repeat visitors to the destination;

- build and enhance relationships with those intermediaries and channels of distribution critical for access to markets;
- engage with broader stakeholder groups who benefit from association with a successful tourist destination.

As with the marketing of tourism in a broader sense, destination marketing has passed through a series of life stages in that while its origins lie firmly in product and sales-oriented marketing, more recent trends suggest that many destinations around the world are now focusing on more relational and experiential approaches. Underpinning all marketing activity in the context of destinations is the need to fully understand the motivations, needs and expectations of visitors, their patterns of decision-making and the means by which they search for and use information to make their decisions pertaining to the consumption of destinations. In order to understand such behaviour, extensive market and marketing research is required, most notably to underpin the means by which destinations position and brand themselves in the marketplace and how they then seek to communicate such images to the desired target markets. Destinations that have been particularly successful during recent years in their destination marketing and branding strategies include India, with its Incredible India campaign, and New Zealand, who for a number of years now has focused attention on its 100% Pure campaign, which set the international benchmark for the marketing of destinations by 'places' and 'experiences'.

The future marketing of destinations is presented with a series of challenges and opportunities which reflect the complexity of destinations as an entity to market and the dynamic and sometimes turbulent macro-environment within which many destinations around the world now find themselves. The very complexity of destinations does, in fact, impact directly upon the ability of any one individual or entity to influence the competitiveness of the destination and the consistency of the message being communicated internally and externally to stakeholders. As such, destinations are home to multiple components, suppliers and stakeholders and seek to deliver satisfactory experiences to multiple markets and visitor segments. If not coordinated in a sufficiently coherent manner, strategic efforts to market destinations can be seriously undermined. Set within a backdrop of continuous change, one permanent fixture is the resident community who serve as 'hosts' to visitors to the destination. With their roles as local tax payers and hosts critical to the quality of the public realm and destination experiences, it is ill advised to ignore local residents. Of increasing significance during recent years is the destination's ability to cope with, and counter, crises and disasters, whether they are man-made or natural. Crisis and disaster management and marketing strategies are now essential ingredients for many destinations who can ill afford not being prepared for events that may, in fact, take place outside of the destination, and that cause a shock to their normal pattern of visitation. Perhaps the single biggest crisis facing many destinations is that of economic recession in origin markets, which, in turn, affects the message and packaging or products being communicated to market groups. Although a number of destinations can be viewed as complacent, product driven and lacking in innovation, efforts being made by many to adopt experiential strategies are to be commended, with visitors actively engaged in the co-creation of visit experiences. Such strategies are crucial as a means of avoiding commodification and reflect the increasingly external competitive environment and the need to differentiate oneself distinctively in the marketplace – more often than not through experiential branding exercises and innovative web-based strategies that tap into the growing role and influence of the Internet, social media and online social networks, such as Facebook, Twitter and YouTube.

In order to successfully develop and implement effective destination marketing strategies and plans, it is virtually impossible to avoid collaboration in some shape or form. With such a fragmented group of stakeholders where no single stakeholder can effectively deliver the necessary destination experience to visitors in isolation, the ability to work together to form suitable collaborative networks is critical. Hence, the future success of destination marketing is very much dependent upon the ability of divergent stakeholders to learn, act and deliver together in an environment conducive to trust, where unilateral action by a single stakeholder is to be widely accepted as damaging to the collective development, management and marketing of the destination.

Further reading

Kozak, M., Gnoth, J. and Andreu, L. (2009) *Advances in Tourism Destination Marketing: Managing Networks*, Routledge, Oxford, UK

Li, X. and Petrick, J. F. (2008) 'Tourism marketing in an era of paradigm shift', *Journal of Travel Research*, vol 46, pp235–244

Morgan, M., Elbe, J. and de Esteban Curiel, J. (2009) 'Has the experience economy arrived? The views of destination managers in three visitor-dependent areas', *International Journal of Tourism Research*, vol 11, no 2, pp201–216

Morgan, N., Pritchard, A. and Pride, R. (2011) *Destination Brands: Managing Place Reputation*, third edition, Elsevier, Oxford, UK

Pike, S. (2004) *Destination Marketing Organisations*, Oxford, Elsevier, UK
Wang, Y. (2008) 'Collaborative destination marketing: Understanding the dynamic process', *Journal of Travel Research*, vol 47, no 2, pp151–166
Wang, Y. (2012) *Tourism Destination Marketing: Collaborative Strategies*, CABI, Oxford, UK

Dr. Alan Fyall

DOMESTIC TOURISM

Domestic tourism refers to tourism that occurs within the boundaries of a country. Therefore, according to the United Nations World Tourism Organization (UNWTO) definition, a domestic tourist refers to anyone who is resident in a country and who travels within the same country for not more than one year, other than for the purpose of occupation and remuneration. The domestic tourist refers to those people who stay overnight, while the domestic excursionist refers to those who do not.

Without the need to cross international borders, domestic tourists do not have the concerns about visas, permits and other border controls or restrictions that are required for international travel. This allows greater freedom and flexibility in their travel arrangements. Consequently, domestic tourism accounts for a large proportion of tourism occurring in any country. Since countries range in size and terrain, domestic tourism may require sea and **air transport** to travel from one part of the country to the other. Different regions within a country may vary considerably both geographically, historically and culturally; this provides diverse experiences regarding climate and built and natural environments, which also encourages further domestic tourism.

Although domestic tourism does not bring in foreign currency or spending, which inbound tourism can bring, domestic tourism encourages the redistribution of finances from one location to another within the boundaries of a country. Since domestic and inbound tourists travel within the country, the regional businesses that depend on tourism are likely to benefit from both types. The spending of tourists over a period of time can vary depending on the duration of stay, which emphasizes the reason why destination managers are always keen to focus on increasing the length of time a visitor stays within the destination. With destination planning, domestic tourists can assist in reducing the effects of seasonality in destinations: the peaks and troughs of tourist visitation to any region. Accordingly, domestic tourism creates employment and helps to ensure permanent, rather than temporary, seasonal jobs in these locations. It also encourages the development of new business and, over time, assists in improving the standards and quality to a level at which the tourism product would attract, encourage and support future international tourism.

People travel in order to visit places of interest and/or to acquire new experiences. The need to travel can be physical, emotional, cultural, interpersonal and even for status and prestige. Residents travelling within their country can increase their awareness of their nationality and heritage as they explore its different cultural components (see also **Motivation in tourism**).

With the increasing tendency of international tourists to seek **authenticity** in their experiences, the frequency and presence of domestic tourists, who visit their local attractions and sites, add credibility to these places. It is perceived that the presence of domestic tourists reinforces the notion that the cultural heritage sites are genuine, and not artificial products especially created for international tourists. Consequently, these tourism sites cater for both domestic and international tourists.

Further reading

Archer, B. (1978) 'Domestic tourism as a development factor', *Annals of Tourism Research*, vol 5, no 1, pp126–141

Hughes, G. (1992) 'Changing approaches to domestic tourism', *Tourism Management*, vol 13, no 1, pp85–90

Jafari, J. (1986) 'On domestic tourism', *Annals of Tourism Research*, vol 13, no 3, pp491–496

Dr. Christine Lee

ECONOMICS OF TOURISM

According to the United Nations World Tourism Organization (UNWTO), over the past six decades tourism has experienced continued growth and diversification to become the largest and fastest-growing economic driver in the world. Its high growth and development rates, considerable volumes of foreign currency flows, multiplier effects and infrastructure development are the principal reasons for its impacts upon social and economic development. The export income generated by international tourism ranks fourth after fuels, chemicals and automotive products. For most developing countries, it is one of the main income sources and a major export category, creating much-needed employment and opportunities for development, (Dwyer et al, 2009).

Foreign tourist expenditures are a form of exports for the host country. Tourists spend money on goods and services such as food, transportation, accommodation, tours, entrance fees and souvenirs. For instance, British people travelling to Turkey earn their income in the UK, but spend it in Turkey, therefore injecting money into the economy that was not there before. If the exchange rate is favourable to the foreign tourist because the host country has devalued currency, demand for visitor services will be relatively higher, compared to a pre-devaluation period. By contrast, outbound tourists are considered as a form of import, as people take money out of their home country and spend it in a different host country, purchasing goods and services. Tourist spend can be categorized as:

- direct expenditure;
- indirect expenditure; and
- induced expenditure.

Direct expenditure

This comprises expenditure by tourists on goods and services in hotels, restaurants, shops, other tourist facilities and for tourism-generated exports, or by tourism-related investment in the area. This can be quantified relatively easily through spend per head data and has a direct effect on economic activity in the form of sale revenues; income to businesses for selling goods and services to tourists; salaries and wages to households; employment and taxes; and revenues to government through tourist taxation and fees. The direct economic effects are those that occur at front-line tourism-related establishments.

Indirect expenditure

This results from inter-business transactions which are a result of the direct expenditure. When a tourist spends money in a restaurant, the restaurant will spend some of the money it receives on food and beverage supplies, some of it on transport, heating and lighting, and some on accountancy and other business services. The amount of money circulating becomes smaller at each successive round of activity as money leaks out of the economy in the form of savings and imports, until the amount of money circulating in the economy as a result of the initial tourism spending becomes negligible. All of these subsequent activities are classified as indirect effects, which is much more difficult to measure, but again results in increased employment and economic growth.

Induced expenditure

This is the increased consumer spend that results from the additional personal income generated by direct expenditure – for example, hotel workers using their wages for the purchase of goods and services. Both indirect and induced expenditure are called secondary expenditure. Induced effects which result from induced expenditure include the accrual of wealth amongst residents of the local economy as some of this money is spent locally and some leaks out of the system.

This economic impact of tourism is commonly understood in terms of **multiplier and leakage**, where multipliers are the principal methods available to economists for estimating the economic impacts of tourism upon host societies. The term 'multiplier' is derived from the fact that the value of expenditure is multiplied by some estimated factor in order to determine the total economic impact. As tourists contribute to sales, profits, jobs, tax revenues and income in the host country, tourism multipliers indicate the total increase in output, income and employment. The multiplier is greatly enhanced when money is spent by a tourist and re-spent locally by the community, while money that leaves the tourism economy through multinational hotels represents leakage of money from the economy.

Further reading

Fletcher, J. E. and Archer, B. H. (1991) 'The development and application of multiplier analysis', in J. Fletcher (ed) *Progress in Tourism and Recreational Research*, Frances Pinter, London, pp28–48

Mak, J. (2004) *Tourism and the Economy: Understanding the Economics of Tourism*, University of Hawaii Press, Hawaii

Roya Rahimi

ECOTOURISM

During recent years, ecotourism has attracted significant attention from consumers, conservationists, economic development specialists and others (Lindberg, 1992; Sindiga, 1999; Higham and Lück, 2002). However, ecotourism is entering a period during which it may undergo a more careful scrutiny in order to determine whether it provides the benefits that its proponents suggest. Ecotourism has played, and will continue to play, an important role in terms of providing private-sector development opportunities, creating jobs, and generating financial and political support for the protection and management of natural areas. A frequently cited definition of ecotourism was developed by The International Ecotourism Society (TIES), which states that ecotourism is 'responsible travel to natural areas which conserve the environment and sustains the well-being of local people'. A review of the definitions of ecotourism highlights significant commonalities around conservation, education, local ownership, small-scale development, economic benefits for local communities, the relevance of cultural resources, low-level impacts and sustainability. These points justify a critical evaluation of the plausibility of developing ecotourism operations in accordance with various definitions.

The concept of ecotourism can be considered from different geographical perspectives:

- The North American perspective is based upon the pristine quality of nature, on the pleasure of adventure and on physical activity in wilderness areas.
- The European perspective finds its roots in rural tourism. In many countries, ecotourism is seen as a form of rural tourism, sustainable tourism and in the notion of soft (low-impact) tourism.
- In South-East Asia, it is viewed as a form of responsible tourism with ethical and cross-cultural issues prevailing.
- In Africa and South America, the perspective has changed to a focus of ecosystems historically managed by traditional cultures.

Ecotourism is sometimes considered to provide a sustainable approach to development. Notwithstanding its potentially negative consequences, such as the impacts of building and the generation of wastes, as well as the impact of tourist activities, ecotourism has come to be closely associated, and even sometimes synonymous, with equally

Table 3 Ecotourism stakeholders

Stakeholders	Views
Eco-tourists	Value environmental integrity
Eco-tour operators	Promote nature travel with economic, socio-cultural and environmental focus
Host communities	Require consultation and involvement in planning and management
Host governments	Engage in national policy, planning and development to promote natural areas and cultures
Conservation groups	Ecotourism acts as an incentive to conservation
Academics	Research and debate whether ecotourism is the solution to environmental conservation

Source: Okech (2011)

controversial and much-debated terms such as sustainable tourism and alternative tourism. Weaver (1999) proposed that all tourism forms, in theory, can be differentiated as either sustainable or unsustainable, acknowledging that an understanding of the indicators for measuring and monitoring sustainability is vital, and that tourism which appears to be sustainable in the short term may prove otherwise over a long period of time.

Weaver (2008) highlights some of the types of ecotourism activity, which include:

- aboriginal tourism (linked to cultural tourism);
- celestial ecotourism (comets, northern lights, sky gazing, stargazing);
- flower gazing;
- nature observation (leaf-peeping, bird watching and whale watching – onshore or vessel based);
- nature photography;
- nature activities (hiking, canoeing, camping, fishing, wildlife safaris, wolf calling).

The benefits of ecotourism include:

- an enhanced appreciation of natural environments, both in terms of their intrinsic and economic worth for protection and conservation;
- the educational value of exposing visitors and locals to nature and conservation; and
- the potential of ecotourism to motivate the designation of additional natural areas for conservation and protection.

From an economic standpoint, Lindberg (2001) notes that there are two related, but distinct, economic concepts in ecotourism: economic impact and economic value. A common ecotourism goal is the generation of economic impacts, whether they are profits for companies, jobs for communities, or revenues for parks. Ecotourism plays a particularly important role because it can create jobs in remote regions that historically have benefited less from economic development programmes than have more populous areas. Even a small number of jobs may be significant in communities where populations are low and alternatives are few. The economic impact can increase political and financial support for conservation. Protected areas and nature conservation, generally, provide many benefits to society, including preservation of biodiversity, the maintenance of watersheds and so on. Conversely, pressures originating from inappropriately managed infrastructure and visitor activities can adversely affect the receiving environment. Negative impacts upon terrestrial ecosystems include:

- destruction of plant and wildlife habitats;
- soil and dune erosion;
- soil compaction;
- disruption of soil stability;
- alteration of geological regimes;
- disruption of nutrient cycles; and
- reduction in biodiversity.

While tourism planners recently put local participation in decision-making high on their agendas (see **Community-based tourism**), this has mostly been done to demonstrate consultation, and there is some debate about the true nature of participation in tourism development. Rarely have local people been involved in the planning and implementation of ecotourism ventures such as eco-lodges and eco-tours, nor have they taken part in decisions on whether a project should go ahead or on the distribution of common resources and revenue. Furthermore, Wearing (2001) asserts that the designation of ecotourism sites tends to disentitle the poor by depriving them of their traditional use of land and natural resources. With such an approach, local communities face exploitation and abuse, including the loss of cultural and social identity. This form of development undermines the autonomy of local people by increasing their dependence on outside forces, eroding societies' capacity and potential for self-reliance. Ethnic groups, according to Scheyvens (2000) and Okech (2011), are increasingly being seen as a major asset and 'exotic' backdrop to natural scenery and wildlife. The fact that these people are the target of exploitation and suppression by dominant social groups in state structure has generally been ignored.

Further reading

Honey, M. (2008) *Ecotourism and Sustainable Development: Who Owns Paradise?*, second edition, Island Press, Washington, DC

Lindberg, K. (2001) 'Economic impacts', in D. B. Weaver (ed) *The Encyclopedia of Ecotourism*, CABI, Wallingford, UK, pp363–377

Okech, R. N. (2011) 'Ecotourism development and challenges: A Kenyan experience', *Special Issue: Tourism Analysis: An Interdisciplinary Journal* (forthcoming)

Weaver, D. (2008) *Ecotourism*, second edition, John Wiley, Australia

Dr. Roselyne N. Okech

EDUCATION IN TOURISM

Education has long been a factor in tourist activities – it was the main reason so many young aristocrats travelled around Europe during the seventeenth century, learning about new cultures and visiting sites of historical importance. However, it is only during the last two decades that the importance of education has been recognized in terms of social necessity, marketing and income generation, and most tourist sites now provide some form of educational resource. In addition, there are many other places which are not tourist sites, but which do attract educational visits, and thus become tourist sites for this niche market of 'edu-tourism'.

Ritchie (2003) defines educational tourism as 'tourist activity undertaken by those who are undertaking an overnight vacation and those who are undertaking an excursion for whom education and learning is a primary or secondary part of their trip. This can include general educational tourism and adult study tours, international and domestic university and school students' travel, including language schools, school excursions and exchange programmes. Educational tourism can be independently or formally organised and can be undertaken in a variety of natural or human-made settings.'

The provision of education resources varies, from a school trip to a factory, to a living history activity at a historic site, to an overseas residential field trip or foreign exchange. Invariably, the majority of visits to tourist sites are not generally motivated by a provision for education; but many formal education visits are, and organizations often invest heavily in education provision, which is usually provided free of charge or at a lower cost than standard admission fees and guided tours. While some of this is done for philanthropic reasons, it is also likely either to be seen as a way of encouraging repeat visits outside of the formal education trip, or because the organization is required to provide education as part of its core purpose (charitable organizations and those in the public sector especially).

Ritchie (2003) proposes a continuum for educational tourism which ranges from 'general interest while travelling' to 'purposeful learning and travelling' and suggests that educational tourists can be divided into two sub-groups, linked to their **tourism motivation**:

- tourism first – learning is incidental to the visit (cultural attractions, natural attractions);
- education first – the visit is chosen for educational purposes (a school visit or exchange trip).

Of course, the ultimate purpose for any form of educational tourism is linked to many other niche markets. Examples may include **literary tourism** (visits to find out about famous authors or to see plays performed), **genealogical tourism** (visits to learn about family history) and **heritage tourism** (visits to learn about the cultural past).

Further reading

Ritchie, B W. (2003) *Managing Educational Tourism*, Channel View Publications, Clevedon, UK
Tourism Alliance (2010) *Tourism: The Opportunity for Employment and Economic Growth*, www.tourismalliance.com

Peter Robinson

ENTREPRENEURSHIP

Entrepreneurship is a term which has grown out of economic theory; it is a term without a universal definition but is usually used to describe a person or persons who develop an innovative business idea, taking some level of uninsurable risk to do so. People who are described as 'entrepreneurs' have often started out with no ability to provide evidence to investors that they are capable of developing their innovative idea and therefore have an inability to attract finance; thus, they have to create capital from inherited wealth or by working and saving. Sometimes the risk-taking provides opportunities for speedy development of capital which they reinvest into growing an existing business or for the development of other innovative ideas. However, while entrepreneurship is applied to individuals who commonly start up their own small business based on an idea which services a particular gap in the market or perceived market need, medium- and large-sized companies and organizations can also be termed 'entrepreneurial' if they adopt policies and practices that encourage and strive for innovation. Innovation differs from an extension of existing products (even though this may be quite complex to create) and clearly strives for totally new ideas; companies are innovative when they are 'hungry for new things' (Drucker, 2007, p138) and invest in the resources to produce them.

Entrepreneurship has the power to create new industries and, thus, growth in economies. The tourism economy is no exception; it has been driven by individuals with ideas that satisfied the needs of mass markets and have spawned some of the biggest companies in the world (e.g. Marriott, Hilton, Thomas Cook and Holiday Inn).

Figure 2 Entrepreneurs in the tourism industry

Famous tourism entrepreneurs include John Willard Marriott, Conrad Hilton, Thomas Cook and Kemmons Wilson. Each of these individuals created business empires which grew from small ideas; their companies retain the founder's original values of consumer satisfaction. In addition, the founder's values are often the drivers for **corporate social responsibility** agendas.

John Willard Marriott, who came from a farming background that emphasized hard work through its culture and religion, visited Washington in sweltering heat and saw an opportunity, once he finished university, to start a 'root beer' stand providing refreshments to very hot visitors. The winter months saw the addition of Mexican food products to diversify the product offerings and from this small beginning grew a chain of family restaurants, and then hotels. Today Marriott owns not just hotels and restaurants, but cruise ships and theme parks, employing over 150,000 people worldwide.

Conrad Hilton also had a background that owed a lot to his family culture, having worked in his father's general store. Buying his first hotel, he discovered that a room could be sold more than once per day (a model used today in many city centre and airport hotels). However, his story was not all smooth: risk-taking and the economic climate caused him near bankruptcy before he went on to grow Hilton Hotel Corporation and Hilton Hotels International.

Thomas Cook came to tourism through equally entrepreneurial beginnings, driven by a need to move people from Leicester to Loughborough for a temperance meeting. He commissioned a train from Midland Railways, a risky strategy, and charged travellers for the journey. The success led him to arrange other

---

excursions for pleasure, first within the UK and then into Europe, followed later by trips within the US. Thomas Cook Group PLC now has sales of UK£8.9 billion and 22.5 million customers, operating under six geographic segments in 21 countries; in 2011, it was the number one operator of charter packages.

Kemmons Wilson had four children; after a road trip to Washington, where he found a lack of family-friendly, clean, easily accessible hotels, he realized that there was an opportunity. He opened his first hotel in 1952 and six years later was so successful that there were 50 franchises located across the US. Today the company that he started as Holiday Inns of America is the Holiday Inn brand, part of Intercontinental Hotels, the world's largest hotel chain with over 1300 hotels, selling 100 million guest nights each year.

Nevertheless, 80 per cent of tourism businesses are micro-enterprises (less than 10 employees) and small- (less than 50 employees) or medium-sized companies (SMEs) (less than 250 employees), and their products and services range from an owner-operated 'cycle rickshaw taxi' or a pedicab that carries people around the tourist attractions of London, to massive integrated resorts containing theme parks, hotels, casinos and spas, such as Resorts World in Sentosa, Singapore.

The significance and impact of entrepreneurialism cannot be under-estimated in the development of tourism economies. Tourism's attractiveness to entrepreneurs, its low barriers of entry and the search for innovative ideas with which to both retain and attract even more consumers, and the creation of subsequent wealth have driven gov-ernment strategies in many countries. Goa, for instance, now attracts more visitors than it has population and is responsible for 12 per cent of all total foreign tourist visits, together with 75 per cent of direct charter business to India. It is crucial to the economic success of the region (Dwivedi et al, 2009).

Further reading

Casson, M., Yeung, B., Basu, A. and Wadeson, N. (eds) (2006) *The Oxford Handbook of Entrepreneurship*, Oxford University Press, Oxford, UK

Drucker, P. F. (2007) *Innovation and Entrepreneurship: Practice and Principles*, Butterworth Heinemann, Oxford, UK

Lowe, R. and Marriott, S. (2006) *Enterprise: Entrepreneurship and Innovation: Concepts, Contexts and Commercialization*, Butterworth Heinemann, Oxford, UK

Caroline Ann Wiscombe

ETHNOGRAPHY

Ethnography (from Greek *Εθνος* ethnos = folk/people and *γράφω* grapho = to write) is the flexible, context-specific use of multiple methods to understand a culture and community. It emphasizes people, their knowledge, their ways of interacting, their practices and their discourses, all of which are analysed through the lens of 'participant observation'. Ideally, ethnographies do not only transmit knowledge about a specific place, its people or culture, but also answer broader questions.

The foundation of ethnography is the simultaneous use and later comparison of diverse research results. These can be generated through interviews, group discussions, the analysis of documents and field notes, as well as the use of media, such as image, film and sound. The authority of the ethnographer is granted through the scientific quality of the work and the clear presentation of the research data.

One generally distinguishes two types of ethnographies. There are, on the one hand, the works that discuss particular aspects of, or even whole, cultures in comparative perspective. The interest in cultural comparison goes back to a general search for universalisms – that is to say, cultural markers that are present in all cultures. The existence of belief systems and gender roles, for example, are two of those universalisms. On the other hand, there are monographs that analyse a particular aspect of one culture within its given context.

Different from memories, opinions and descriptions raised by informants, ethnographies are grounded in participation, membership and assistance of the researcher in contemporary cultural phenomena. As such, part of the ethnographic writing is also the description of the ways in which a field has been accessed, what obstacles were faced, how one established trust, and what persons, so called 'gatekeepers', were of particular importance during the research process. Ethnography, therefore, demands the ability to analyse in a self-reflexive manner one's own actions, experiences and perceptions, as well as cultural, social and existential foundations. This is done through reconstructible protocols and diaries about one's own experiences.

Various disciplines have laid claim to ethnographic methods. During the 1960s, its home discipline, anthropology, identified the single-sited authority of the ethnographer and the missing of indigenous voices as a reason for constructive criticism. As a result, ethnographers turned away from realist approaches to their fields of study, as well as the reduction to the one voice of the author. Instead, they adopted the concept of a 'plurality of voices' developed by the linguist Mikhail

Bakhtin (1895 to 1975). Clifford Geertz (1973) enforced this approach in his ethnographic method of 'thick description', a style of writing in which a cultural event is shown from the perspective of all its participants. Those can include author(s), anthropologist(s) and informant(s), but also newspapers, legal texts, etc.

Twenty years later, George E. Marcus, amongst others, added to this approach the emphasis on the interpretation of anthropologists' goals, fears and motivations during and after fieldwork. This led to the production of more experimental 'postmodern' ethnographies. The aim for such ethnographic writing is to formulate new ways through which to combine traditional ethnographic interests in people's actions, cultural symbolisms or everyday practices that take into account a changed spatial perception of the world. Related investigation focuses on subjects within a global system. This is done through the analysis of associations and connections between (field) sites. A so-called 'multi-sited ethnography' generates comparison through research on a particular object of study whose concrete shape and relationships with others are not known beforehand (Marcus, 1998). Consequently, the object of ethnographic study is ultimately mobile and multiply situated. Any ethnography of these objects automatically integrates a comparative dimension in the form of 'juxtapositions of phenomena that conventionally appeared to be (or conceptually have been kept) "worlds apart"' (Marcus, 1998, p86).

The link between ethnography and tourism is as old as the discipline and the phenomenon of organized travel itself. The beginnings of ethnographic study are connected to earliest accounts of travellers, missionaries and explorers. Until today, ethnographic work is part of tourism and vice-versa, mainly through studies of so-called 'developing' countries. Likewise, many social phenomena that ethnographic work has brought to the attention of a wider audience have been incorporated within the tourism industry. Australian companies, for example, provide *kula-tours* with anthropologists as tour guides who introduce tourists to the techniques of exchange among Trobriand islanders (Malinowski, 1922).

Ethnographic efforts to classify types of tourism have been numerous, from international, domestic and business related, to pilgrimage or family visits. Besides those classifications, tourists also form a core ethnographic concern. One central theme has been the notion of 'hosts and guests', along which ethnographies discuss tourist movements and part-time migrations, as well as tourism rituals that create social proximity and reciprocity (Smith, 1978). Tourism is a fast growing and diversifying industry around the world. As such, ethnographers also analyse tourism as a global and globe-making industry (Neveling and Wergin, 2009). Wider questions of marginalization, sub-alteration and other concerns of a postcolonial critique are included in tourism ethnographies.

Many studies have also engaged with the political economy of tourism. They focus on its developmental dimension in peripheral regions of the Northern Hemisphere (Crick, 1989). A timely question is how sustainability as scientific discourse is used in ecotourism projects and in doing so transports and reproduces forms of exotism, (re)writing the history of numerous cultures, people and communities. Other themes include the search for apparently authentic experiences in tourism, as well as the preservation of natural and cultural heritage under UNESCO rules and regulations. Related scientific discourses of the North actively influence the development of new social orders around the globe. As such, ethnographic writing on tourism continues to offer new ways into the socio-political, cultural and scientific complexities of today's world.

Further reading

Crick, M. (1989) 'Representations of international tourism in the social sciences: Sun, sex, sights, savings, and servility', *Annual Review of Anthropology*, vol 18, pp307–344

Geertz, C. (1973) 'Deep play: Notes on the Balinese cockfight', in C. Geertz (ed) *The Interpretation of Cultures*, Fontana Press, New York, NY

Malinowski, B. (1922) *Argonauts of the Western Pacific: An Account of Native Enterprise and Adventure in the Archipelagoes of Melanesian New Guinea*, Routledge, London

Marcus, G. E. (1998) 'Ethnography in/of the World System: The emergence of multi-sited ethnography', in G. E. Marcus (ed) *Ethnography through Thick and Thin*, Princeton University Press, Princeton, NJ

Neveling, P. and Wergin, C. (2009) 'Projects of scale-making: New perspectives for the anthropology of tourism', *Etnografica*, vol 13, no 2, pp315–342

Smith, V. L. (1978) *Hosts and Guests: The Anthropology of Tourism*, University of Pennsylvania Press, Philadelphia, PA

Dr. Carsten Wergin

E-TOURISM

e-Tourism defines a wide range of travel and tourism technologies used within the tourism industry to help manage a range of complex logistical activities to meet customer expectations. Many of these systems are closely linked to aspects of operations management and help to facilitate service delivery, although it is important not to confuse e-tourism with **virtual tourism**, which defines consumer experience rather than business processes, despite the fact that e-tourism can involve virtual tourism.

The most commonly recognized systems are Computer Reservations Systems (CRSs), which manage complex booking requirements and originated in the airline industry and travel agencies, where multiple facilities could be booked at the same time, including air travel, hotel rooms and transfers. Today, CRS systems are adopted throughout the tourism industry for events management, hotel management and travel management. CRS systems are closely linked to Global Distribution Systems (GDSs), which manage the supply chain for the travel industry, linking together the various suppliers of travel and tourism products.

Customer Relationship Management systems (CRM) are an important feature of marketing activities in many businesses, allowing organizations to keep detailed records about their customers, and they can use the data in one of two ways:

1 The offer of special promotions may be based on data collected about a customer's interests during their first visit.
2 The use of CRM is particularly common in hotels to record customers' preferences so that their expectations can be easily met on their subsequent visits – this may include preferred settings for room heating, preferred newspapers or bedding allergies.

Current technologies allow for greater consumer interaction with the travel industry, with consumers able to view destinations online through Google Earth prior to making a travel decision, and being able to use user-generated content on websites such as Tripadvisor to help their decision-making process. Online ticket sales and retail are further developments, and it is important to remember that e-tourism may include buying event tickets, arranging itineraries, and booking travel arrangements, bypassing the traditional tour operator. Other applications considered as e-tourism include the ability to track flights online and the use of biometric passports.

However, perhaps the most notable development in tourism technologies during recent years has been the growth of MP3 music players and Smartphones, allowing travellers to download audio tours, guides, maps and travel information for destinations that they are visiting, offering alternative ways to engage with historic sites and offering new methods of interpretation, giving the tourist a greater awareness and opportunity to interact with the world around them.

English Heritage, the advisory body to the UK government for historic sites in England, provides a variety of functions, including the management of a number of historic sites open to the public. Some of these are found in very rural areas and are unstaffed, with limited interpretation. The ability for individuals to download a podcast tour of the site before their visit brings to life otherwise static sites, and allows interpreters to include living history style commentaries, with actors speaking as previous inhabitants of the site.

Further reading

Buhalis, D. (2003b) *eTourism: Information Technology for Strategic Tourism Management*, Pearson (Financial Times/Prentice Hall), London

Egger, R. and Buhalis, D. (eds) (2008) *eTourism Case Studies: Management and Marketing Issues in eTourism*, Butterworth Heinemann, Oxford, UK

Peter Robinson

EVENTS AND FESTIVALS

The events industry includes meetings, incentives, conferences, exhibitions (MICE), festivals, arts, sports and a range of other activities. Over the last two decades there has been significant growth in the events sector and the industry today makes a significant contribution to business and leisure-related tourism.

The 1960s and 1970s saw the rapid increase of cultural events, including the Notting Hill Carnival in London (established in 1964), the Pilton (now Glastonbury) Festival (1970) and Woodstock (1969). During the 1970s and 1980s there was significant investment in event facilities and infrastructure with the construction of multipurpose venues, including the National Exhibition Centre (NEC) in Birmingham (1976) and the Brighton Centre (1977). The 1980s saw a rapid increase in corporate hospitality and sponsorship at international sporting events, including Formula One, Wimbledon and the Olympics, and many countries are now keen to host these events based upon their potential to draw in tourist numbers. Since the 1990s, events have been recognized as a major driver of tourism and are increasingly used to maximize visitor figures during off-peak periods.

Events are now central to our culture, and increased attendance is linked to an increase in available leisure time and discretionary spending, together with a recognition amongst the tourism industry that events are a useful tool for generating income, and for raising the profile of attractions and destinations. As a result, there is considerable public-sector support for events, especially where access and education can be enhanced as a result. Events are seen as a key element of many strategic development plans, and are an integral part of the tourism offer of many destinations, attracting many thousands of visitors, thereby enhancing economic prosperity, development and regeneration. Indeed, many cities now build their brand on business tourism, conferences and events, including Brighton in the UK, Singapore and Dubai.

Goldblatt (2002) provides a useful definition for events, stating that 'a special event is a unique moment in time celebrated with ceremony and ritual to satisfy specific needs', although within this definition there are four specific event typologies:

1 minor events;
2 special events;
3 hallmark events; and
4 mega-events.

Minor events

These are generally personal events and include parties, celebrations and fundraising and charity events.

Special events

Most events fall into this category – these are activities which are non-routine, and which variously entertain, educate, celebrate or challenge those who are spectating or participating.

Hallmark events

These events are synonymous with the location where they take place and are valuable tourism assets for the host communities. Examples include the Tour de France, Carnival Rio and the Monaco Formula One Race.

Mega-events

These are transient events that move around the globe and attract very high attendances. Countries wishing to host these events often have to bid for them and demonstrate how they will deliver a high-quality event, as well as explaining how the event legacy will impact upon the destination. Examples include the Olympics, the FIFA World Cup and the Commonwealth Games.

When events are applied to a tourism context it has been suggested that there should be six core attributes of the event (Jago and Shaw, 1998), which explain that an event should:

1   attract tourists or tourism development;
2   be of limited duration;
3   be one-off or infrequent occurrence;
4   raise the awareness, image or profile of a region;
5   offer a social experience; and
6   be out of the ordinary.

Event tourism is defined by Getz (1993, pp15–26) as 'the systematic planning, development and marketing of festivals and special events as tourist attractions, catalysts, and image builders'. Examples of the use of events include:

- help to promote a destination and therefore attract tourism;
- raise awareness and develop repeat business;
- create a positive destination image;
- generate income.

Most visitors to city destinations will find an impressive list of sporting and cultural events that compete to capture the attention of tourists. However, there are also negative impacts of events, and these must be considered to ensure that the benefits are not outweighed by the costs:

- legacies that do not bring benefits to a wide area;
- displacement of communities to facilitate the construction of event infrastructure;
- increased house prices and living costs, leading to social dislocation and increased crime;
- increased pollution (litter, traffic and waste);
- damage to heritage sites and use of greenfield sites.

However, these negative impacts may be somewhat mitigated by the construction of replacement housing, improved community facilities, affordable housing schemes and reclamation of brownfield sites, which, together with the event infrastructure, may enhance community participation and community facilities post-event, such as schools and retail facilities. Despite this, though, the negative effects are profound for those directly affected and it is essential that events and event legacy are carefully and thoughtfully planned to bring maximum benefit to communities at minimum cost.

Further reading

Allen, J., O'Toole, W., Harris, R. and McDonnell, I. (2008) *Festival and Special Event Management*, fourth edition, Wiley and Sons, Milton, Australia

Bowdin, G., Allen, J., O'Toole, W., Harris, R. and McDonnell, I. (2006) *Events Management*, second edition, Elsevier, Oxford, UK

Getz, D. (2005) *Event Management and Event Tourism*, Cognizant Communication Corporation, New York, NY

Robinson, P., Wale, D. and Dickson, G. (eds) (2010) *Event Management*, CABI, Wallingford, UK

Peter Robinson

FAMILY TOURISM

There are many permutations of the modern family and what is important in this context is to identify them and consider their impact upon and importance to the tourism industry. According to the Office for National Statistics (ONS, 2009), there are more people living alone, more children raised by single parents and more grownup children still living at home with their parents than ever before. The *Social Trends Report* produced by the ONS (2009) indicates, over a generation, a doubling of adults living alone, a tripling of single-parent households and a significant fall in the percentage of households comprising the nuclear or 'traditional' family (i.e. a couple with children). What is clear from these statistics is that the nature of families and family life has changed considerably over the course of a generation.

For the tourism industry it is important to recognize that these changes will have a far-reaching impact upon the nature of family tourism provision. A knowledge of how family tourism demand influences supply is essential to tourism professionals. The factors affecting and influencing the holiday behaviour of families and the nature of the family holiday experience are instrumental in understanding this diverse market segment.

According to Cooper et al (2008b, p50) the family is 'the fundamental social unit of group formation in society ... [and therefore] the influence of the family on tourism demand is extremely important'. Despite the prevailing economic climate, family tourism is undoubtedly a growth market.

Families are defined as social groups, including at least two family members. The ONS (2011, p3) defines families 'by marriage, civil partnership or cohabitation or, where there are children in the household, child/parent relationships exist'. The family unit consists of one or more parents together with a child or children, and the extended family is likely to consist of grandparents, aunts, uncles and other family members. Family tourism therefore involves the family unit, in all its diversity, and their participation in different forms of tourism activity. The complex and changing nature of the family unit is an important consideration for the tourism industry. Family tourism may therefore be defined as participation by the family unit in travel away from home and incorporating leisure activities pursued in a destination.

Working-class culture incorporated the concept of the family holiday in the mid to late 1800s (Walton, 2000) as resorts such as Blackpool on England's north-west coast, close to the industrial areas of northern England, began to attract those wishing to escape from the urban environment. The advent of the railway initially made such seaside destinations attractive and, for the first time, accessible for day-trippers and holiday-makers.

As transportation developments facilitated travel, the popularity of holidays soared, and by 1936 workers finally gained a week's paid holiday with the advent of the Annual Holiday Bill. Additionally, the holiday camps opened by Butlin and Pontin during the mid-1900s gave families an affordable opportunity for a break from routine. Affordable commercial aviation from the 1960s onwards continued to offer families travel and tourism opportunities that had, for many people, been inconceivable before this time.

Existing research focuses on tourism consumer decision-making within the family unit and gender perspectives within/on the family tourism decision-making process (Decrop and Snelders, 2005; Kang and Hsu, 2005; Kim et al, 2007a; Bronner and de Hoog, 2008; Kozak, 2010). Much of the research considers only the 'traditional' family unit headed by husband and wife, despite recognizing changes in those relationships. Limited additional research focuses on the notion of 'pester power', involving analysis of the influence of young travellers (Nickerson and Jurowski, 2001; Connell, 2005; Connell and Meyer, 2009). The importance of travel for the purpose of visiting friends and relatives (VFR) should not be underestimated, as connections with extended family and friends become increasingly important.

The diverse nature and complexity of the family tourism market means that the tourism industry must constantly adapt its products and services. There are numerous challenges facing both the family tourism market and organizations catering for this segment, not least rising socio-economic inequalities, the proliferation of 'alternative' families (i.e. lesbian, gay, bisexual and transgender families), an ageing population, the aforementioned 'pester power', exponential growth in the use of social media and a corresponding rise in the use of electronic entertainment as a prerequisite for travel and the demand for multigenerational products and services.

Further reading

Bronner, F. and de Hoog, R. (2008) 'Agreement and disagreement in family decision-making', *Tourism Management*, vol 29, pp967–979
Cooper, C., Fletcher, J., Fyall, A., Gilbert, D. and Wanhill, S. (2008a) *Tourism: Principles and Practice*, 4th edition, Pearson Education Limited, Essex, UK
Nichols, C. M. and Snepenger, D. J. (1999) 'Family decision making and tourism behaviors and attitudes', in A. Pizam and Y. Mansfield (eds) (1999) *Consumer Behaviour in Travel and Tourism*, Haworth Hospitality Press, New York, NY
Nickerson, N. and Jurowski, C. (2001) 'The influence of children on vacation travel patterns', *Journal of Vacation Marketing*, vol 7, no 1, pp19–30

Carol Southall

FILM AND TV TOURISM

Film and TV tourism can be defined as tourism to the places where a movie or TV series has been filmed or set. This can include on-location sites such as Monument Valley for many American Westerns, or off-location studio sets. Furthermore, while film tourism can occasionally be a primary motivator for a person to visit a place, it more often plays an adjunct role in the decision-making process. This has been referred to as incidental or even accidental film tourism (Beeton, 2005). The phenomenon has attracted a lot of interest in recent years, and has become variously known as film-induced tourism, movie-induced tourism, cinematic tourism and even set-jetting tourism.

To date, most of the academic work related to film and TV tourism has focused on fictional movies and TV series, with little consideration given to documentaries and reality programmes and their influence on tourism. The popular media gives us the stories of what can be considered 'blockbuster tourism' (such as *The Da Vinci Code*, *The Lord of the Rings* trilogy, the James Bond franchise and the Harry Potter series), leading many to conclude that a popular movie will automatically induce people to visit its sites and settings.

Before the beginning of the twenty-first century, research into the relationship between film, TV and tourism was sporadic and incidental, with the earlier researchers tending to release a few journal articles and then move on to other research areas. This is quite common in a field of research such as tourism, where there is still so much to explore, and our interests often move elsewhere. However, since the publication of *Film-Induced Tourism* (Beeton, 2005), we have seen an increase in the interest and on-going research into this field, especially from younger PhD candidates and academics. While the subject continues to be dominated by studies that do little more than replicate what is already known, a strong push towards developing further knowledge in this field is emerging.

So, what do we know about film and TV tourism, and what are the issues and major research questions we need to address? While fictional movies and TV series can encourage (or induce) people to visit the places in which they were set or filmed, there are many examples where this does not happen, or if it does, it is not due to one movie alone. This is the challenge that currently consumes many researchers and practitioners – how can we predict film and TV tourism success? As understanding of this continues to develop, many of the successful marriages between tourism and film seem to come from what began as a popular book (or series) that was released as a movie or TV series such as *The Da Vinci Code*, *The Lord of the Rings* and the TV series *Heartbeat* or *Wallander* (see Beeton, 2005; Reijnders, 2011), or where a high number of movies/TV have been filmed (e.g. New York). However, cult movies such as *The Blair Witch Project* can also be powerful tourism inducers, particularly if the audience of that film is of the appropriate tourist demographic, as with many of the quirky UK TV series such as *Inspector Morse* (Reijnders, 2011) and the Korean series *Winter Sonata* (Kim et al, 2007b).

A trap that many researchers have fallen in to is that, in their haste to find a 'research or knowledge gap', they claim there is little work in a field, or that it is a recent phenomenon. Both of these factors are evident in much of the work in film and TV tourism; however, the relationship between film and tourism is as old as the moving image itself, with early films of travel featuring heavily in both the fictional and non-fictional realm. The argument of limited literature in this area may have some credence when looking at a specific element; however, over the past ten years a substantial volume of research articles, monographs and related publications on film/movie/TV tourism has been published, along with a growing body of work from Asia, where film and tourism are intrinsically linked. Furthermore, there are studies relating to film and tourism coming out of other disciplines, which is often overlooked in the tourism literature (and vice versa), particularly in the media studies realm. Work by Strain (2003) contributes an anthropological perspective, along with others in the social sciences, including Reijnders (2011).

Further reading

Beeton, S. (2005) *Film-Induced Tourism*, Channel View Publications, Clevedon, UK

Beeton, S. (2012) *Tourism and the Moving Image*, Channel View Publications, Clevedon, UK

Kim, S. S., Argusa, J., Lee, H. and Chon, K. (2007b) 'Effects of Korean television dramas on the flow of Japanese tourists', *Tourism Management*, vol 28, no 5, pp1340–1353

Reijnders, S. (2011) *Places of the Imagination: Media, Tourism, Culture*, Ashgate Publishing, Surrey, UK

Roesch, S. (2009) *The Experiences of Film Location Tourists*, Channel View Publications, Clevedon, UK

Strain, E. (2003) *Public Places, Private Journeys: Ethnography, Entertainment and the Tourist Gaze*, Rutgers University Press, New Brunswick, NJ

Dr. Sue Beeton

GASTRONOMY AND FOOD TOURISM

Historically, the role of food in tourism was much underrated, academically and by the travel industry itself. Yet, since travel began food has been a very important element of the tourist experience. Even going back to Chaucer's *Canterbury Tales*, written at the end of the fourteenth century, food was an essential element of pilgrimage for the characters in the book, and thus an important element of their tourist experience. All tourists have to eat every day, and so destination food is intrinsically important, whether it is a primary or secondary motivation (Quan and Wang, 2004; Okumus et al, 2007). During the last two decades, the study of gastronomy has progressed rapidly, encompassing a range of disciplines, including history, geography, anthropology, ethnography and sociology. Gastro-tourism is now viewed as a distinct sector of the industry (Cohen and Avieli, 2004; Ignatov and Smith, 2006; Kivela and Crotts, 2006; Okumus et al, 2007; Devesa et al, 2009). Gastronomy is a key motivation to travel (van Westering, 1999) and is able to satisfy our neophilic desires to try new foods, which some consider has been fundamental to our ability to succeed as a species, enabling us to derive nutrients from a variety of sources (Veek, 2010). Similarly, the growth in the Slow Food movement, which seeks to provide an alternative and traditional approach to the production of food (as a resistance to the growth of fast food) further emphasizes the changing nature of food in tourism.

This is true whether food is the key focus of the trip or not; many tourists whose primary motivation is not gastronomy are, nevertheless, keen gastronomes and will seek authentic foods, often basing their judgement of the destination upon them (Quan and Wang, 2004; Okumus et al, 2007). For neophilic tourists, eating new foods is a fundamental element of the travel experience, while for others it can be a reinforcement of feelings of 'not belonging' (Veek, 2010). While in resorts and other destinations tourists undertake a range of activities that include aspects of gastronomy (Smith and Costello, 2009), ranging from visiting cafés, bars and restaurants, buying food at shops and markets, tasting experiences, and factory visits to participating in tours of farms and vineyards. By contrast, other tourists exhibit neophobic behaviour, and avoid local foods out of fear of their content, flavour, cost and cleanliness (Cohen and Avieli, 2004). When coerced into eating unfamiliar foods – for example, due to peer pressure or lack of familiar options – some tourists felt that this detracted significantly from their travel experience (Veek, 2010).

For the postmodern tourist, food and gastronomy is increasingly fundamental to their identity formation (Ignatov and Smith, 2006). This is reflective of the central role of food in culture, where food is literally grown out of the 'terroir' – the soil and climate of the region. Tourists consuming locally grown products literally consume the destination and its culture in the flesh (Povey, 2006). Regions where gastro-tourism is buoyant can see the economic benefits to their agricultural economy, as well as having the ability to develop trails, food attractions and market image. Food products can also be used as important elements of other events, which can enhance visitors' satisfaction. In addition, the destination's local pride and self-value are enhanced by visitors' interest in local culture (Quan and Wang, 2004). The economic benefit derived from the increase in purchase of local products for consumption at home is also important to a destination (Sims, 2009). For tourists, this is a tangible way of giving a small part of their holiday to their friends and family at home.

There is also a clear role for gastronomy in the developing discussions and theories of authenticity and its consumption. The very images used in destination marketing, and on postcards, are often of food, and are a vivid symbol of authenticity to the consumer (Markwick, 2001). According to Buckland (2007), tourists who aspire to experience authenticity ascribe high value to the authenticity of their gastronomic experiences. There is a triumvirate relationship affecting the authenticity of any meal, which is an interaction between 'The Self' and the sum of their experiences, 'The Thing' that is actually being experienced and 'The Others', which is the ways in which authenticity is defined by societies (Beer, 2008). Producers in destinations need to ensure that they understand 'The Other' in their visitors' culture is equal to their understanding of their own, and thus become empowered to provide the tourists with an experience that they consider to be authentic. Authenticity, however, is always subjective; it is essentially a personal creation influenced not only by culture but also by the individual's experiences, attitudes and even personality (Reisinger and Steiner, 2006; Morgan et al, 2008).

There is a staged process outlined by Cohen and Avieli (2004) in the development of 'authentic' tourist food, with what are normal local foods being adapted to the visitors' palates. These adaptations, while denigrating the food offering for local people, enhance them for tourists. These stages are:

- The Preparatory Stage: this involves the substitution of less palatable ingredients such as snake or dog – the inclusion of modern preparatory technologies which are applied behind the scenes or can become part of the experience, taking the form of a 'stage show', such as the case of *tepanyaki* cooking. For chefs and production kitchens, this is a balancing act between acceptability to the tourist palate and diminishing authenticity.
- The Presentation Stage: here individuals act as 'culinary brokers', translating the product or experience being offered to the consumer, usually through the menu, which is vital to the visitors' understanding of the food and the way in which it is eaten. The translations need to be cultural as well as linguistic.

For tourists unfamiliar with new cuisines, it is very challenging to put together different elements of a meal in an unfamiliar gastronomic setting, which has led to the emergence of the popular 'set meal' option (Cohen and Avieli, 2004). Other participants in the tourist experience also act as intermediaries and enhance the translation of foods, including travel representatives, tour guides, waiters and local friends. The structure and style of the service is of secondary importance, and will only have significance if they are very different from the visitors' expectations or perceptions. A good example is where Thai restaurants dig out spaces in the floor to enable Western tourists, unused to sitting on the floor, to experience the traditional *kantok* low table, while still being comfortable (Cohen and Avieli, 2004). As resorts develop they tend to offer an increasingly internationalized range of foods, often to the point that the more adventurous experiential tourists move on to less developed areas.

Another key aspect of gastronomy's relationship with tourism is in the area of heritage food. Heritage attractions now often feature kitchens, and focus more on the lives of servants and ordinary people than on the leisured classes and aristocracy. Consumption of heritage food is linked to the consumption of place and the value of old British pubs, many of which are heritage attractions in themselves, and the food served therein (Howe, 1996), as well as the significance of historically valuable restaurants or 'historant'. Josiam et al (2004) explored this relationship, where actual consumption of heritage could take place. Restaurants and other eating places that are heritage sites do have the advantage of attracting visitors on the basis of their listing as an historical site, avoiding the intrinsic disadvantages around planning and development, particularly regarding health and safety legislation and the changes to kitchens and service areas that this necessitates.

This section has briefly discussed several aspects of the relationship between tourism and gastronomy, as well as the rapidly establishing sector of gastronomic tourism. From the discussions in the areas of motivation, tourist experience, authenticity and heritage, it is possible to conclude that gastronomy always has, and always will have, an important role in the wider tourism industry, and it has proved itself to be a very important tool for those who are developing and marketing destinations (see also slow food within the **Slow tourism** entry).

Further reading

Beer, S. (2008) 'Authenticity and food experience – commercial and academic perspectives', *Journal of Foodservice*, vol 19, no 3, pp153–163

Povey, G. (2006) 'Factors influencing the identity of regional food products; a grounded theory approach', *Cyprus Journal of Sciences*, vol 4, pp145–157

Reisinger, Y. and Steiner, C. J. (2006) 'Reconceptualising object authenticity', *Annals of Tourism Research*, vol 33, no 1, pp65–86

Sims, R. (2009) 'Food, place and authenticity: Local food and the sustainable tourism experience', *Journal of Sustainable Tourism*, vol 17, no 3, pp321–336

Smith, S. and Costello, C. (2009) 'Segmenting visitors to a culinary event: Motivations, travel behavior, and expenditures', *Journal of Hospitality Marketing and Management*, vol 18, pp44–67

Veek, A. (2010) 'Encounters with extreme foods: Neophilic/neophobic tendencies and novel foods', *Journal of Food Products Marketing*, vol 16, pp246–260

Ghislaine Povey

GENEALOGICAL (OR ANCESTRAL) TOURISM

Genealogical tourism represents a niche segment of the market and has potentially been historically undervalued, but is now becoming recognized as a valuable tool for destination promotion. In 2009, VisitScotland hosted a Homecoming Festival to appeal to genealogical tourists who wanted to travel to the country of their ancestors' origins and to learn more about their family history.

Engagement in genealogical tourism may be a result of an interest in family history, or may be part of a desire to understand the contextual and cultural heritage of the family. In addition to the places and sites where people used to live and work, visits to graveyards and churches to see memorials and burial sites, as well as to inspect historic records are becoming increasingly popular.

Although a worldwide phenomenon, genealogical tourism is most common amongst diasporas (communities removed from their homelands) or where there has at some time been mass emigration (e.g. from England to Australia, and from Ireland to England and the US). Relatively little data is available specific to this segment, although evidence suggests that it is a growing sub-sector of tourism.

Santos and Yan (2010) explain this growth, at least partially, as a result of 'the increasing sociological awareness of the post-industrial society that we currently live in' and suggest that 'not only does it help to mitigate the desires and anxieties about our age, genealogical tourism also encourages us to take a more humanistic approach toward issues of belonging, home, heritage and identity'.

Further reading

Santos, C. A. and Yan, G. (2010) 'Genealogical tourism: A phenomenological examination', *Journal of Travel Research*, vol 49, no 1, pp56–57

Peter Robinson

GEOGRAPHIES OF TOURISM

The concept of geographies of tourism denotes the scope of new developments and extensive multidisciplinary interest that has broadened the geographical approaches towards exploring the complex notion of tourism. According to Williams (1998, p16) 'Tourism (with its focus upon travelling and the transfer of goods and services through time and space) is essentially a geographical phenomenon.' This is, in part, an important definition of the relationship between tourism and geography in that it reminds us of basic considerations; but it also alludes to many other important themes that exist within the framework of time, space and mobility issues linked to tourism. Tourism and geography are mutually linked by their shared interests in resources and people. The geographies of tourism contribute to our understanding of tourism's inter-relationship with the human and physical characteristics of the world.

As a result, tourism's significance is now being recognized as an integral part of social, political and economic life, having wider obligations than just commercial concerns, and seen less as an ephemeral activity and marginal field of study, but one that offers and commands far more academic scrutiny (Franklin and Crang, 2001; Hall and Page, 2006).

Developing this further, Hall and Page (2006) recognize the substantial contribution of geographers to the field of tourism studies, acknowledging, amongst others, the works of Butler (1980); Pearce (1981, 1987); Mathieson and Wall (1982); Shaw and Williams (1994, 2002, 2004); and Pigram and Jenkins (1999). However, they also highlight the scope of new developments and research foci that has led to the notion of tourism geographies, stating 'that there is more than one paradigmatic approach towards the geography of tourism and tourism management' (Hall and Page, 2006, p4). Moreover, they claim that the geographical focus of tourism has benefited and expanded with the input of other social sciences – namely, sociology and cultural studies, anthropology, landscape architecture, urban and regional planning, and environmental science and management.

A key, but relatively neglected, theme within tourism studies is the exploration of international political power within the geographical setting. It is suggested here that political, economic and environmental instability are probably the most challenging issues facing humanity today. During recent years, the geopolitical map of the world has become highly unstable and volatile, wrought with dramatic and continual change. For example, wars, revolutions, political and economic crises, environmental disasters, earthquakes, tsunamis, volcanic eruptions, health warnings and terrorism have heightened safety and security, challenging the certainties within modernist scientific ideology and crucially impacting upon tourism activity. In this age of uncertainty, global mobility and, in turn, tourism are increasingly becoming affected by the frequency of crises. Geopolitics (the relationship and interaction between geographical, political and economic factors) is a significant concept for understanding the influence of ideological and economic forces that affect world order. S. B. Cohen (2003) provides a comprehensive background to geopolitics and international relations, including a short section on the geopolitics of tourism in the Caribbean. The historical, political and cultural geography of regions contributes to a broader understanding of critical issues – for instance, the geopolitics of the eastern Mediterranean region, especially the political/geographical divide that continues to affect communities, such as the on-going impasse in Cyprus and the protracted conflict between Israel and Palestine. Indeed, appreciating the political history and geography of a country/region is fundamental to understanding the complexities of political instability and their relationship with tourism.

Other significant geopolitical themes that have a vital relationship with tourism are the notions of sustainability, globalization and development. Geopolitical approaches to tourism critically explore the global production and consumption spaces of travel and trends of global tourism organizations – in particular, assessing the dominance of the cruise, hotel and airline industry in this process, critically evaluating the contradictions and problems related to tourism sustainability notions.

An integral theme of the geographies of tourism is the concept of mobility, explaining and examining why, when, how and where people move to engage with tourism (Hall and Page, 2006). Despite the increasing levels of crisis, it is now recognized that we are witnessing the travel and movement of people all over the world on an unprecedented scale. A vital consideration is how political, technological and economic factors have enabled mobility and time barriers to be reduced, contributing to the phenomenal global flow of tourists. Interdisciplinary approaches are now examining these global movements, focusing on a world made up of flows. The new mobilities paradigm explores inconstant travelling identities, attempting to map this perpetual movement of people, commodities, capital and information, rather than compartmentalize flows. Developing this from a travel perspective, Hannam and Ateljevic (2007) state that leisure, tourism, travel business and migration activity cannot easily be observed as separate elements; rather, they have become blurred and need to be analysed together in their fluid interdependence.

This increased level of mobility creates particular conflicts and contradictions (e.g. regarding transport policy, long-haul travel and sustainability), raising questions over taxation and travel industry regulations (Duffy, 2002; Hannam and Ateljevic, 2007). Clearly linked to this is the major challenge facing future development: the impact of climate change upon tourism (see also **Sustainable tourism**). All aspects of tourism are affected by climate change, but equally tourism has to be assessed with regard to its direct and indirect effects on climate change. Increased mobility has to be considered against the ways in which tourism development shapes places, creating opportunities, but also altering conditions for local people who can be displaced by new infrastructure and superstructures linked with leisure and tourism development. Enclave developments for cruise ships, such as the segregated area at Labadee in Haiti, are a stark reminder of spatial inequalities – tourism luxury existing alongside poverty and destruction. Thus, tourism planning creates and offers a variety of spatial challenges in a variety of geographical settings. Again, this problem of how to achieve more sustainable forms of tourism development, with far more community participation and stakeholder interaction, while increasingly seen as central to achieving desired outcomes, remains generally elusive. Alternative development paradigms need to be considered alongside the omnipotent model of development: neoliberalism. Other related planning themes that rely on geographical interpretation are the post-industrial regeneration and gentrification initiatives that have been part of the continuing ideological and material transformation of urban and rural landscapes during the last 30 years. Tourism-led urban regeneration has specifically been criticized as 'servicing the pleasures of the well-to-do' and neglecting peripheral run-down areas in cities (Hall, 2005, p194). Nevertheless, we are witnessing a re-imaging of cities through iconic architecture and leisure and tourism event-led regeneration that have redefined the role of the city (see **Urban tourism**) (Smith, M. K., 2009).

It is also important to consider the cartographic dimension – the production of maps – the geographer's tool to measure space and create boundaries. The historian MacKenzie (2007, pp20–21) in his study 'Empires of travel', which examines the cultural phenomenon of imperialism, shows the significant effect that the ideology of Modern Empire had on societies: how the development of the traveller's handbook was a vital part in this process of 'marking and miniaturisation', unveiling a 'complete mindset', reducing and compressing the globe into a few books and atlases. This cartographic representation of the world can be viewed as socially constructed forms of knowledge, meaning and power relationships. Influential cultural theorists, such as the post-colonial theorist Edward Said, have examined the imaginative geographies. In his study *Orientalism*, Said (1978) argued that orientalist scholarship in the form of travel writings created the illusion of colonial subjects and places as inferior, while portraying the West as rational and powerful, which, he argues, assisted in the legitimization of colonial rule. Therefore, Said's work and the concept of imaginative geography continues to constitute a significant narrative for today's debates on tourism's links with **neo-colonialism**, dependency paradigms and alternative development models such as sustainability.

The cartography of nations and territories is also an important consideration in past and present land-use conflicts and heritage dissonance issues connected with tourism activity and promotion. Indeed, the politics of culture and heritage remains an important theme, especially with tensions that exist in nations that trade on their past. Maps were also fundamental when designating protected areas. The geography of nature and wildlife conservation impulses during the 19th century created wildlife parks in Africa and the Far East which are now popular attractions for tourists. However, these parks are contested areas, with many conflicts and perspectives on conservation ethics and social and cultural constructions of nature to consider – for example, challenges to the imposition of Western protected area legislation, conservation ideas and values (Neumann, 1996; Jepson and Whittaker, 2002; Adams and Hutton, 2007). Furthermore, territorial promotion and the visual language of regions (how tourism authorities use visual culture, maps, guidebooks and symbols) also represent part of a geopolitical narrative (Crouch and Lubbren, 2003; Burns et al, 2010). Finally, new mapping technologies in the form of geographic information systems (GIS) are contributing to spatial analysis in tourism, measuring space and assisting in tourism development and planning. They can be used to explore the effects of changing land use, map new transport networks and examine impacts upon environmentally sensitive areas. However, Hall (2010) also considers the possible problems with future commodification and privacy concerns. No doubt these are concerns that are again linked with the power and politics of control and ownership, which is a constant theme in the geographies of tourism (Behaire and Elliot White, 1999; Hall, 2005).

Further reading

Hall, C. M. (2008) *Tourism Planning: Policies, Processes and Relationships*, Pearson Education, Harlow

Hall, C. M. (2010) 'Spatial analysis: A critical tool for tourism geographies', in J. Wilson (ed) *Space, Place and Tourism: New Perspectives in Tourism Geographies*, Routledge, London

Hall, C. M. and Page, S. J. (2006) *The Geography of Tourism and Recreation, Environment, Place and Space*, Routledge, London

Hall, C. M. and Page, S. J. (2008) 'Progress in tourism management: From the geography of tourism to the geographies of tourism – a review', *Journal of Tourism Management*, xxx, pp1–14

Harry Cameron

GEOTOURISM

Geotourism is used interchangeably to discuss sites of geological interest, such as the European Geoparks project, and to describe the geographical character of a place, leading to some potential confusion.

The concept of geotourism as geography was officially recognized in a 2002 report from the then Travel Industry Association of America (now the US Travel Association) and *National Geographic Magazine*, which had used the term as early as 1997. Unlike **ecotourism**, geotourism in this context considers the physical structures, land use and development of a tourist destination from an ethically responsible perspective. It is defined by the National Geographic Society as 'tourism that sustains or enhances the geographical character of a place – its environment, culture, aesthetics, heritage, and the well-being of its residents'.

By contrast, the term is used by Dowling and Newsome (2006) to discuss sites of geological significance, which may include caves, rock formations, mountains, cliffs and other natural resources, all of which require careful management. There are, as illustrated by these two authors, many debates around the management of these sites, given their appeal to adventure tourists.

The European Geoparks project identifies sites which 'include a particular geological heritage and a sustainable territorial development strategy supported by a European program to promote development. It must have clearly defined boundaries and sufficient surface area for true territorial economic development' (Europeangeoparks.org). The economic development aspect is often linked to tourism development, hence 'geotourism', and the areas are designated as geoparks based on their scientific quality, rarity, aesthetic appeal or educational value. They may also include sites of archaeological, ecological, historical or cultural significance which are linked to the geological heritage of the geopark.

Further reading

Dowling, R. K. and Newsome, D. (2006) *Geotourism*, Elsevier–Butterworth-Heinemann, Oxford, UK

European Geoparks (2011), http://www.europeangeoparks.org/isite/page/2,1,0.asp?mu=1andcmu=7andthID=0

Peter Robinson

GLOBALIZATION

Globalization is the term used to encapsulate the processes by which all people, societies and cultures interconnect through communication, transport and trade. The term is closely linked to the development of a world economy (i.e. the integration of national economies in an international market through trade, foreign investment and global flows of capital, as well as migration, the spread of technologies and military presence). Globalization is, as a result, driven by a combination of economic, technological, sociocultural, political and biological factors, and also refers to the transnational circulation of ideas, languages, arts and popular culture. The on-going importance of national, international and multinational businesses, of borders, economies, taxes and legislation, however, turns the above into an idealist definition of the concept (see **Mobility**).

In realist approaches to the phenomenon of globalization, focus has been on changing population numbers and social networks that indicate an increased complexity within globally informed communities. Hierarchical notions have also been prominent in works on the effects of globalization since colonialism, one of the central forces behind the globalization process of today's capitalist world system. These include the famous 'global versus local' distinction, but have also analysed more complex re-workings of centre–periphery relations. These are highlighted, for example, in debates on mega-cities as centres of financial accumulation, scientific training and artistic production, as well as political decision-making (Sassen, 2000).

Tourism is one of the largest industrial sectors of the world economy and as such a central figure in globalization debates. It generates the circulation of great quantities of money, labour, ideas and imaginations. For several decades, images created and sold on the tourism market have been an integral part of the imagined hierarchical ordering of the world as described above. Notions of 'developed' and 'underdeveloped' regions, for example, remain prominent both on the global scale of tourist routes between developed and developing world destinations, and in the rural versus urban dichotomy played out in the tourism industry of the Northern Hemisphere.

Tourism as a global industry generally allows for tourists from the North to imagine themselves in a privileged position compared to those people who live in the places they visit in the South. On the other hand, the inhabitants of such holiday destinations are well aware of the financial possibilities offered by global tourism as a leisure-time activity. In addition, global flows of foreign investment no longer only move unidirectional from so-called 'developed' to 'underdeveloped' regions. In the global tourism economy, the numbers of Chinese, Indian or Russian customers, for example, have greatly increased over the years. However, the majority of tourists still emanate from Northern countries, and most of the income generated from tourism also remains in these countries.

As a significant part of the globalization process, tourism is not only affected by, but has an effect on, the spatial and socio-economic forms that globalization takes on. Landscapes and cultures are greatly influenced by globalization when it comes to developing, staging and consuming tourism. Furthermore, the industry provides for specific conceptions of values and morals, as well as a spatial positioning of cultures, peoples and places within the world economy (Terkenli, 2002). This calls for a fundamental critique of the globalization discourse and strategy. Such reconsideration of globalization is, for example, concerned with 'local' tradition and landscapes, while simultaneously informed by the analysis of standardized strategies linked to capitalist notions of development, marketing and control (Tsing, 2000). Indeed, movements such as Cittaslow and slow tourism are reactions to the homogenized, globalized brands that operate within the tourism and hospitality sectors.

Such 'globalist' understanding of tourism development projects reveals conflicts and alliances among local populations, national politics, tourists, international companies and organizations in the making of a tourist destination. Globalization in this model becomes a matrix of the past, present and future production of tourist sites, and of the different actors involved.

Further reading

Meethan, K. (2001) *Tourism in Global Society: Place, Culture, Consumption*, Palgrave, Basingstoke, UK

Mowforth, M. and Munt, I. (2009) *Tourism and Sustainability. Development, Globalisation and New Tourism in the Third World*, third edition, Routledge, Abingdon, Oxon, UK

Sassen, S. (2000) *Cities in a World Economy*, second edition, Pine Forge Press, Thousand Oaks, CA

Terkenli, T. S. (2002) 'Landscapes of tourism: Towards a global cultural economy of space?', *Tourism Geographies*, vol 4, no 3, pp227–254

Tsing, A. (2000) 'The global situation', *Cultural Anthropology*, vol 15, pp327–360

Dr. Carsten Wergin

HEALTH AND WELLNESS TOURISM

Tourism which focuses on health and wellness has been identified as a rapidly growing sector within contemporary tourism (Smith and

Puzko, 2009). The global movement towards fitness and health has created a long-term demand for both health and wellness services and products (Cooper and Malcolm, 2009). However, the history of health and wellness tourism dates back to the use of natural mineral and thermal baths for therapeutic purposes in ancient times. For example, the earliest spa reference is circa 1700 BC, with the Greeks, Romans and Ottomans leaving a legacy of Baths across Europe. The ancient civilizations of the Middle East and Asia also contributed to the development of an ethos for health and wellness in terms of yoga, meditation, massage and herbal medicines.

It has been noted that definitions of health and wellness tourism are almost endless, with health, wellness, medical and spa sometimes being used interchangeably (Smith and Puzko, 2009). Concepts of health and wellness have different connotations in dissimilar cultures, and meanings are also affected by the globalization of wellness products, further complicating the standardization of definitions. Health and wellness tourism can be divided into two broad and sometimes overlapping categories – in Europe, for example, tourism involving the use of mineral and thermal waters at spa towns for leisure and also for prescribed treatments falls into both categories.

Health tourism, specifically in terms of healthcare, was defined as 'the attempt on the part of a tourist facility (e.g. hotel) or destination (e.g. Baden in Switzerland) to attract tourists by deliberately promoting its healthcare services and facilities, in addition to its regular tourist amenities' (Goodrich and Goodrich, 1991). Medical tourism, where people travel to another country specifically for a medical treatment, has become a distinct niche of health tourism (Connell, 2006). While a number of Asian countries (e.g. Thailand and India) have dominated this market, most countries have tried to enter the field, as evidenced by numerous studies, such as a report on Canada's health and wellness tourism industry (Supapol and Barrows, 2007) and a study of Macao's potential for receiving health tourists from the People's Republic of China (Lam et al, 2011). For some countries, medical tourism is seen as a tool for economic development and/or diversification of the tourism product. For example, in the Caribbean, Cuba has a long-standing and well-developed health tourism product and now a number of others are entering the broader health and wellness market, each with a different focus on products and services: Jamaica (wellness), Puerto Rico (medical) and Barbados (infertility) (Arellano, 2011). An on-going issue at these locations and others about instigating health and medical tourism is that locals must first have adequate access and that this should not be compromised by any health tourism initiatives.

Whereas health tourism can include a medical or treatment component, wellness tourism is generally considered to have a more holistic focus on the physical, emotional and spiritual well-being of the individual and does not include medical treatment. Wellness tourism includes the growing area of spa tourism, and many countries seek to brand themselves as spa destinations (Joppe, 2010). Health club and spa facilities, once limited to resorts located around natural mineral springs, are now an accepted part of new hotel and resort developments. Options for incorporating the health/spa concept range from providing a swimming pool and a sauna to fully outfitted gymnasiums with trained staff, to spa resorts providing exclusive health, fitness and beauty services (Gee, 1996).

In conclusion, key issues in the development of tourism related to health and wellness are market segmentation, product standards and development, as well as destination branding (Smith et al, 2010b). Markets can be segmented by interests, purpose and products, as well as by cost. In the case of medical tourism, markets can be segmented by purpose, complexity of treatment, type of care and cost. Each subset of both health and wellness tourism has its own particular developmental issues. For example, specific issues related to the area of medical tourism include the privatization of healthcare, uneven access to healthcare and the accelerated globalization of healthcare services (Connell, 2006). In the case of spa tourism, development issues include marketing, treatments and competitiveness.

Further reading

Cooper, P. E. and Malcolm, C. (2009) *Health and Wellness Tourism: Spas and Hot Springs*, Channel View Publications, Bristol, UK
Smith, M. and Puzko, L. (2009) *Health and Wellness Tourism*, Butterworth-Heinemann, Oxford, UK

Dr. Lee Jolliffe and Dr. Jenny Cave

HERITAGE TOURISM

Heritage tourism describes visits to sites of interest because of their heritage value. The United Nations Educational, Scientific and Cultural Organization (UNESCO, 2010) defines heritage as 'our legacy from the past, what we live with today, and what we pass on to future generations'. This explains effectively the philosophy behind the conservation movement that protects the sites which tourists then visit. The fact that these sites are often very popular with visitors relates to their ability to define and explain the cultural heritage of a group or groups of people and this therefore supports the importance of access to heritage sites.

Heritage is defined by Tilden (1996, cited in Goulding, 1999) as 'an activity which aims to reveal meanings and relationships as an art, and revelations based upon information whose aim is not instruction but provocation'. It is important to note that many definitions of heritage make reference to the concept of culture and cultural tourism, and such an example is provided by Dallen and Boyd (2003, p5) who suggest that cultural or heritage tourism 'goes beyond the visitation of sites and monuments, to include consuming the way of life of places visited'.

It has also been suggested that in tourism terms, heritage becomes a commodity that embodies notions of romanticism, local pride, nationalism, mythology and nostalgia, and by being commoditized heritage becomes used for contemporary purposes and, consequently, is defined as a type of tourism, bringing economic benefits to the region where the heritage site or sites are located. Heritage is a relatively broad concept and encompasses a number of different types of attractions, some more **authentic** than others. Heritage attractions may include:

- mythical sites and characters;
- reconstructions of real places;
- new sites where there was nothing before;
- locations where significant features no longer exist;
- museum collections;
- medieval 'fayres';
- vernacular building styles;
- ways of life of people in the past/culture;
- industrial archaeology;
- stately homes;
- art galleries;
- battlefields;
- castles;
- historic waterways;
- cathedrals;
- ancient and prehistoric sites.

Most heritage sites and attractions fall under public- and voluntary-sector ownership, and ownership is often a contested issue when it comes to heritage sites. In most countries the public sector plays a significant part in the management of historic sites, some of which are within public-sector ownership, and some in private- or voluntary-sector ownership. Regardless of who owns the site, there is a general recognition that effective stakeholder management is essential to ensure the survival of heritage sites and attractions.

Especially important sites are designated as World Heritage sites, which means they are formally recognized through UNESCO. Examples of sites in this category include the Sydney Opera House, the Ironbridge Gorge, the Tower of London, the Great Wall of China, the Acropolis and Lake Malawi National Park. At a national level, organizations such as The National Trust (of which there are many globally) also work to preserve cultural heritage and to provide access; but there is a continual challenge to manage the delicate balance between access and conservation/preservation. Indeed, this is just one example of the many topics for debate around heritage tourism, as follows.

Access

Access may be determined, in part, by the popularity of the site, which may elevate a site to national or international profile, such as Stonehenge, but will at the same time increase the conservation costs and level of protection required by the site. Ironically, the designation of World Heritage status may further increase demand from tourists.

Interpretation

The presentation of heritage also requires some careful consideration because to narrate the story of the site and to explain its significance requires sensitivity. While there are a myriad of tools available to the interpretation specialist, these have to be applied carefully and appropriately to the site. Examples of the methods adopted for interpretation include guided tours, audio-guides, brochures, guidebooks, signage, an interpretation centre or visitor centre, historical re-enactments, living history (where actors dress up and act out the role of a historic character) and interactive exhibitions.

Ownership

The question of whose heritage is commonly asked, and the altruistic view is that heritage is a shared resource that belongs to the widest community who can benefit from it. This raises issues around the notion of admission charges, opening hours and other restrictions placed upon sites by their owners. Indeed, there is good reason for limited opening hours as some historic artefacts can be damaged by excessive exposure to light and humidity, and these costs increase as visitor numbers rise.

Admission charges

An admission charge is not just an income-generation tool, but a visitor-management tool. The fragile nature of many historic buildings makes it impossible to allow unlimited admission, and a charge goes some way to limiting visitor numbers. In instances where even this is not enough of a deterrent, timed and/or pre-booked ticket systems may also be used.

Authenticity

Managers of heritage sites have a continual challenge to consider the interpretation and promotion of a site to meet the needs of consumers and to provide the facilities required of a visitor attraction, while seeking not to compromise the historical integrity of the site and, therefore, its authenticity and value as an educational resource.

Events

Events are increasingly popular at heritage sites and are used to increase visitor numbers and broaden the educational appeal of the site, narrating its history and engaging a wider and younger audience. Most events are related to the cultural heritage of the site, although there are examples of historic venues hosting music concerts and fireworks performances to maximize the revenue generated by the site without impacting upon the sensitive features of the place.

The on-going management of many heritage sites relies heavily on volunteers, many of whom choose to participate because they have an interest in the site and its long-term preservation. This **serious leisure** often extends beyond the interpretive to 'closed-season' activities, such as working in conservation, restoring contents, cleaning the property and helping with management tasks, and is also manifest in outdoor conservation and working holidays.

During recent years, many heritage sites have also become the location for films and documentaries. Sites include Chatsworth House (*Pride and Prejudice*), Phi Phi Islands (*The Beach*), Lacock Abbey (*Harry Potter*) and Angkor Wat in Cambodia (*Tomb Raider*). This growth in media interest has manifested itself in **film and TV tourism** and further develops the appeal and breadth of heritage as a tourism commodity.

Further reading

Dallen, J. T. and Boyd, S. W. (2003) *Heritage Tourism*, Pearson Education Limited, Harlow, UK

Southall, C. and Robinson, P. (2011) 'Heritage tourism', in P. Robinson, S. Heitmann and P. Dieke (2011) *Research Themes for Tourism*, CABI, Wallingford, UK

Timothy, D. J. and Boyd, S. W. (2006) 'Heritage tourism in the 21st century: Valued traditions and new perspectives', *Journal of Heritage Tourism*, vol 1, no 1, pp1–16

UNESCO (2010) *World Heritage List*, http://whc.unesco.org/en/list

Peter Robinson

HOSPITALITY

Hospitality is defined as 'the reception and entertainment of guests, visitors or strangers with liberality and goodwill' (Harrison and Enz, 2005) and 'the provision of products and services provided to those away from home' (Nykiel, 2005). However, in the context of tourism (if defined as the temporary short-term movement of people outside the places where they normally live or work, together with the activities they undertake), then hospitality can be promoted as the provision of food, beverage and accommodation which accompanies these visits. Nevertheless, hospitality is also used to describe leisure, meetings and conventions, and is included in the use of travel and attractions (Ottenbacher et al, 2009). In addition, two further precepts must be considered. The first is that food and beverage can be consumed by those not moving far from the place where they live or work, such as staff canteens or hospitals, and these are also defined as hospitality. The second is that hospitality is not just a product (a meal, a drink, a bedroom), but is also a service which is underpinned by culture and has a social dimension. Thus, there is a difference between hospitality as a product or experience and hospitableness which is derived from the giving of authentic kindness and perhaps by generosity (Pizam and Shani, 2009).

Hospitality as a service grew from consumer demand. Moving away from home encouraged the provision of lodging houses for both business and leisure needs, eating out as part of daily life also became more commonplace. Restaurants and other associated facilities have diversified as consumer tastes have become more sophisticated and the attraction of particular tourism markets to those services has become more challenging. Thus, in the twenty-first century, tourist resorts will include a plethora of food and beverage concepts and a wide range of accommodation.

The creation of genuine cultures of hospitality can change over time as tourism becomes vital to the infrastructure of communities, this has occurred in Lyme Regis in the west of England, where once tourists were branded 'grockles' and treated as interlopers, tolerated from May through to September each year during the main holiday season. This culture has changed to one of a 'year-round' welcome as the service sector has grown through the notion of shorter breaks both during holiday periods but also 'out of season'; the town has also become more economically stable.

Those working for larger organizations may work towards a 'branded' notion of hospitality service that, if not well managed, could appear less than sincere; the creation of hospitable settings is important to tourism as there may be some uncertainty and fear associated with the new setting. In addition, hospitality may involve helping guests to have a good time by engaging them in activities and conversation (Crick, 2000; Guerrier and Adib, 2000; Tracey, 2000; Constanti and Gibbs, 2005; O'Connor, 2006). Examples of this in practical settings include the hotel reception enquiring after the guests' journey as they check in; the guest experience would be enhanced if the reaction to negative incidents resulted in a courteous response, whether this was expressed sympathy, cups of tea or additional assistance with baggage. It also describes the role of the 'travel rep' whose responsibility it is to enhance guest experience by the engagement in, and selling of, a range of activities in which they too may engage.

In its 2009 summary of the global industry, Data Monitor described hospitality as divided into three key areas: hotels (hotels, resorts and cruise lines), leisure (including food and beverage outlets, but also theme parks and golf courses) and resorts (integral complexes). This clearly answers earlier difficulties which found the description of an international hospitality industry a struggle and, it could be argued, is a clear indication of how much the business has both grown and been globalized. Brotherton (2003) had only been able to truly segregate the international industry into sectors of hotels, restaurants and contract foodservice; but The Institute of Hospitality, an international organization with representation in 100 countries around the globe, defines their remit as covering all sectors of the industry, including hotels, contract catering companies, restaurants, pubs and clubs, as well as leisure outlets, theme parks and sports venues.

Nevertheless, hospitality subdivisions are largely defined within national contexts rather than across international boundaries as not all sectors exist in every country, although this is also changing rapidly. One such example might be pubs, bars and clubs, which are a key sector in the UK hospitality industry but which tend not to be owned in large numbers across international boundaries despite the globalization of brewing and drinks manufacturing. Finding a national body that can separate out hospitality facilities from tourism provision is also difficult; People1st, the UK sector skills council which represents hospitality and tourism to government, lists 14 clear categories for the industry (see Table 4). This list certainly supports the view that it is easier to include travel, lodging, food service, gaming clubs, attractions, entertainment and recreation in any national definition (Nykiel, 2005).

Some subdivisions of the hospitality industry are discussed in less than clear terms due to the notion that they all provide the same product; accommodation is one such sub-section. Accommodation, or lodging, can include hotels, cruise ships, self-catering facilities, spas, hostels or holiday camps and then within these divisions are further subsets.

Hotels can be allocated into segments using price or type of visit, with each divided into sectors, as shown in Table 5. Nevertheless, each category of hotel may then appear in more than one sector, such as boutique hotels appearing both by price and in the luxury travel category.

Other ways of identifying differences in accommodation is through the use of 'rating systems'. The rating system for catered and self-catered accommodation varies extensively throughout Europe. In France, room size is a major factor in whether it will receive a high rating. To gain four stars, the room must measure at least 15 square feet, or for smaller establishments, 10 square feet. To gain four stars or more in Austria, all floors of a hotel must be soundproofed. In China, hotels are generally classified into star-rated hotels, boutique hotels (generally individual hotels), serviced apartments, Comfort Inn (the chain of budget hotels),

Table 4 The 14 industries in travel, tourism and hospitality

1 Contract food service providers	8 Membership clubs
2 Events	9 Pubs, bars and nightclubs
3 Gambling	10 Restaurants
4 Holiday parks	11 Self-catering accommodation
5 Hospitality services	12 Tourist services
6 Hostels	13 Travel services
7 Hotels	14 Visitor attractions

Source: People 1st (2011)

Table 5 Hotel segmentation

By price	Leisure travel	Family travel	Business travel	Luxury travel
Budget hotels	Resorts	Extended stay hotels	Meeting/ planning hotels	Resorts
Mid-priced hotels	Spa hotels and resorts		Corporate hotels	Luxury hotels
Boutique hotels	Suite hotels with casinos	Suite hotels	Airport hotels	Casinos
Luxury hotels	Pet-friendly hotels	Pet-friendly hotels	Extended stay hotels	Boutique hotels

Source: Hotel Rooms (2011)

Chinese courtyard (unique concepts often in historic buildings) and hostels (which can be dormitory style or house group-based rooms).

In the UK the tourist board rating includes all types of accommodation (see also **Operations management in tourism**), hotels (rated using a star system from 1 through 5 and a red star to indicate one of the top 200 hotels in the country), guest houses (rated using diamonds), self-catering accommodation (star system), camping and caravanning sites. This latter category is rated via 1 to 5 stars, but can also be awarded Gold and Silver awards from the tourist board or a Sparkling Diamond award via the Royal Automobile Club (RAC) for especially high standards of cleanliness. The UK tourist boards also define accommodation to include other types of facility (bed-and-breakfast, inns, restaurant with rooms and campus accommodation) for which they also rate using star-based categorization; some are also able to achieve Gold and Silver awards.

Rating hospitality quality is not limited to hotels. Restaurants have their own codes, the most famous of which is the Michelin Star System published each year with stars awarded for cuisine in addition to separate ratings for service and ambience. In the US, *Mobil Travel Guides* and the American Automobile Association award stars and diamonds, respectively, via guidebooks. It is through these publications and rating systems that we are continually reminded of the links between hospitality, travel and tourism.

Hospitality is a huge employer; in the US, since 2010, travel jobs grew 1.7 times faster than any other sector, while India's travel and tourism industry (which includes all hospitality sectors) is the world's third largest employer and is vital to its economic progress. The cruise sector alone employs 400,000 people at sea, and with 5 per cent growth per annum will need a further 250,000 by 2020 (*Cruise Industry*

News, 2008). It is surprising, therefore, that the global industry still has a reputation as offering primarily low-skill employment, although for entrepreneurs it has provided lucrative opportunities. Employees in hospitality are often asked to provide memorable customer experiences and certainly to make guests feel welcome, special and even important; but often the roles they occupy are servile (such as waiting staff) or linked to dirty work (room attendants or kitchen porters) (Shamir, 1980; Patullo, 1996; Guerrier, 1999). While pay, training and other benefits have undoubtedly improved through consideration of **corporate social responsibility** and increased legislation, high employee turnover continues to be a problem in many parts of the world (Moncarz et al, 2009; Chalkiti and Sigala, 2010).

The significance of hospitality, with all its connotations, to the tourism experience is vital. The stay within a location or venue will be affected by the products and service they receive in restaurants, cafés and bars, as well as the hospitality shown by the wider service sector, such as taxi drivers and retail shops. The wider community is also a part of the hospitality culture; an invitation to take tea inside the home of Moroccan Berbers while on a walking holiday in the Lower Atlas Mountains may not be on the tourist itinerary, but the hospitality of the people makes a serious impact upon the tourism experience.

Further reading

Brotherton, B. (2006) 'Some thoughts on a general theory of hospitality', *Tourism Today*, issue 6, autumn, pp8–19
Institute of Hospitality, http://www.instituteofhospitality.org
Wood, R. and Brotherton, B. (eds) (2008) *The Sage Handbook of Hospitality Management*, Sage Publications Ltd, London

Caroline Ann Wiscombe

HUMAN RESOURCES MANAGEMENT

Human resources, or personnel, describes the department responsible for managing the people within an organization. Tracey (2004) defines human resources (HR) as: 'The people that staff and operate an organization; as contrasted with the financial and material resources of an organization. HR is also the organizational function that deals with the people and issues related to people such as compensation, hiring, performance management, and training.' HR is also claimed to be the single 'biggest cost' for tourism enterprises and needs to be seen instead as an investment. The service society is characterized by three kinds of service jobs:

1 large numbers of low-skilled, low-pay jobs;
2 a smaller number of high-skilled, high-income jobs;
3 a few jobs in the middle of these two extremes.

Many businesses in the tourism sector operate globally and employ people in several different countries. This brings with it a number of issues related to cultural and legal differences, regional taxation rules and market entry strategies. In order to address these challenges, different approaches are required towards recruitment, training, motivation and compliance with international laws. It further requires managers and HR departments to be increasingly aware of diversity and cultural differences.

Staff within a business play an essential role in the customer experience, emphasizing the importance of investment in human resources and explaining why staff are also considered as 'human capital' in some segments (Brocaglia, 2011). Human resource management (HRM) focuses on the role and needs of individuals within an organization, including:

- *Human resource planning (HRP)*. An assessment of present and future needs of the organization in comparison with present resources and future predicted resources. The aim is to bring demand and supply into balance. The existing workforce profile (numbers, ages, experience, forecast capabilities, etc.) is determined and adjusted for a specified period of time regarding turnover rate, planned staff movements and retirements.
- *Job evaluation*. An analysis of the job (i.e. study of the tasks, responsibilities, necessary qualifications, reporting policies, equipment used, etc.) to design job descriptions and job specifications. It enables the employer to know what characteristics, qualities and attitudes applicants should possess.
- *Recruitment*. The process of attracting, screening, and selecting qualified people for a job. The process can be carried out by the HR department or by a recruitment agency or executive search firm (for senior positions).
- *Training and development*. This aims to develop the skills and improve the performance of employees. For effective training and development, careful planning (sometimes thorough training needs analysis) is essential.

- *Performance management.* HR staff will be trained to manage grievance, disciplinary and dismissal issues with staff.
- *Appraisal.* A tool that is used to assess, manage and motivate staff, to support staff development (and their future career development) and to discuss progress. Appraisal is usually carried out by line managers, using a process designed by the HR department. It often includes a process of setting targets for the next year.
- *Labour and employee relations.* 'Labour relations' is a concept that refers to any dealings between management and employees concerning the terms and conditions of employment. It includes employees', employers' and unions' legally protected activities; unfair labour and management practices; union-organizing activities; union recognition and representation elections; collective bargaining; and union contract administration.

Further reading

Baum, T. (2006) *Human Resource Management for Tourism, Hospitality and Leisure: An International Perspective*, Thomson Learning, London

Haslinda, A. (2009). 'Evolving terms of human resource management and development', *The Journal of International Social Research*, vol 2, no 9, pp180–186

People 1st, http://www.people1st.co.uk/research/sector-skills-assessments

Dr. Ebru Günlü and Roya Rahimi

HYPER-REALITY

As a phenomenon of the 'postmodern' world and its philosophy, hyper-reality characterizes the ways in which the human consciousness communicates with the surrounding world (Alrouf, 2010). It is increasingly common in 'postmodern' daily life. Visits to shopping centres or supermarkets put the individual into a situation where true reality is left behind and a different 'hyper' reality prevails. The individual ceases to be able to distinguish between reality and the state of hyper-reality. Lighting levels put visitors into the mood to make purchases. The background sounds, whether music or other sounds, are pitched at a perfect volume so that it's not intrusive but prevents the individual from feeling that the area is too silent. Even the smells that pervade the senses are manufactured and designed to put the visitor in the mood to buy.

Similarly, when a tourist enters an airport they are on the verge of leaving their reality behind and of entering what is largely a fantasy world, the experience of which is largely formed by their expectations and imagination of the destination's reality. Often tourists purchasing an all-inclusive package have little contact with the real culture of the country they visit, seeing only the inside of their 'resort hotel' with food which caters to their cultural preferences, and even shopping within the perimeter of their enclave. Ventures into the surrounding towns and sites are carefully managed by mediators, filtered to ensure that the experiences are positive, not too shocking or intense, still having their bubble of hyper-reality maintained around them. The essence of hyper-reality is that there is an enhancement of what is 'real' that is undetectable to the individual observing this, and tourism resort planners are keen to ensure that the hyper-reality they create is perceived to be authentic (Alrouf, 2010).

Baudrillard (1993) proposes that we live in a world which is no longer real but is a fabrication of a reality that never actually existed, while Eco (1986) suggests that we are becoming accustomed to the 'authentic fake'. For Eco (1990), historical sites with enhancements – rebuilding damaged areas alongside original historical remains – are examples of entering hyper-reality. Alrouf (2010, p52) purports that hyper-reality implies a 'reality by proxy'. Examples from the tourism industry are frequently used by key theorists in this area, particularly those of resorts such as Las Vegas, which are created at sites with no previous history or relevance. Disneyland is another such resort which was made from a site with no previous relevance. On entering Disneyland, all sight of the rest of the world is lost and the visitor is engulfed in Disney culture and Disney reality. It has even proved to be exportable to countries with strong cultures of their own, such as France and Japan. According to Debord (1995), this creation of a spectacle that can only be viewed but is never part of the reality of modern life is easily extrapolated to include the rapid growth in events and festival tourism.

The hyper-reality bubble is fundamentally important to those involved in **literary tourism** and **film and TV tourism**, as these tourists are engaged in visiting not the destination, but a fantasy of that destination. For example, while tourists who are on *Lord of the Rings* tours are physically in New Zealand, they are, in their hyper-reality, visiting Middle Earth, a setting in the book written by J. R. Tolkien upon which the film is based (Carl et al, 2007).

It can be concluded that while the underpinning theories of hyper-reality are still developing, this is an important phenomenon for those working in tourism, particularly those involved in the development of resorts, festivals and events, as well as tours and sites relating to literature and film. It is an area where more research is needed.

Further reading

Alrouf, A. A. (2010) 'Regenerating urban traditions in Bahrain. Learning from Bab-Al-Bahrain: The authentic fake', *Journal of Tourism and Cultural Change*, vol 8, no 1–2, pp50–68

Baudrillard, J. (1993) *The Transparency of Evil*, Verso, London

Carl, D., Kindon, S. and Smith, K. (2007) 'Tourists' experiences of film locations: New Zealand as "Middle-Earth"', *Tourism Geographies*, vol 9, no 1, pp49–63

Debord, G. (1995) *Society of the Spectacle*, Zone Books, New York, NY

Eco, U. (1986) *Faith in Fakes*, Vintage, New York, NY

Eco, U. (1990) *Travels in Hyperreality*, Harvest Book, New York, NY

Ghislaine Povey

INDEPENDENT TRAVEL

Independent travel refers to travel that has been directly arranged by the traveller. This may be for one individual or for a small group who are travelling together. These travellers can be domestic or international tourists and are also referred to as free independent travellers (FIDs). Independent travel contrasts with **mass tourism**. Mass tourists purchase their travel, transport and accommodation as a prearranged package through a travel agent. However, independent tourists may book individual elements of their holiday (flights, accommodation, activities) either online or through a specialist travel agent.

The concept of independent travel is not new. The Grand Tours of the seventeenth and eighteenth centuries in Europe, which formed a part of the upper classes' cultural education, is an example of independent travel. In modern times, backpackers comprise a significant proportion of independent travellers, with their travel experience being largely self-planned or arranged. Backpacking is a relatively new term, evolving from the travellers referred to as 'drifters'. With **globalization** and an increasing demand, the development and status of backpacking improved over time, as did the concept of the Grand Tour, which historically experienced a similar evolution.

For the increasing number of travellers who are seeking an authentic tourist experience, independent travel may be perceived to offer the only way to participate in this experience. Independent travel also encompasses tourists who participate in **special interest tourism**, such as **dark tourism**, ethical tourism, **religious tourism** and other **niche tourism**. However, according to levels of supply and demand, today many agencies and tourism organizations will promote and assist tourists who travel independently by providing them with advice, published information, travel guides, lists of hotels and other useful information. Independent tourists comprise domestic, inbound and outbound tourists. With increasingly affordable international travel, the economic contribution of independent travellers is often believed to be higher than the spend per head figures for organized mass tourism because individuals spend a longer period of time within specific regions or communities, although certain mass tourism markets (e.g. US travel to the UK) are still recognized as very lucrative, as are certain mass tourism products, such as **cruise tourism**. During recent years, with modern technology, **e-tourism**, the Internet, social networks and various technologies have encouraged and enabled many more tourists to become independent travellers.

Further reading

O'Reilly, C. C. (2006) 'From drifter to gap year tourist: Mainstreaming backpacker travel', *Annals of Tourism Research*, vol 33, no 4, pp998–1017

Sørensen, A. (2003) 'Backpacker ethnography', *Annals of Tourism Research*, vol 30, pp847–867

Towner, J. (1985) 'The Grand Tour: A key phase in the history of tourism', *Annals of Tourism Research*, vol 12, pp297–326

Tsaur, S. H., Yen, C. and Chen, C. L. (2010) 'Independent tourist knowledge and skills', *Annals of Tourism Research*, vol 37, no 4, pp1035–1054

Dr. Christine Lee

INFORMATION TECHNOLOGY

The term information technology, or IT, refers to all technologies with a user interface, which includes mobile devices, networking, computer hardware and software, the Internet, cloud computing and Web 2.0. In the current information age, considerable information and communication takes place using technology and for this reason the acronym ICT – information communication technology – was coined. ICT covers any product that will store, retrieve, manipulate, transmit or receive information electronically in a digital form. Its adoption within tourism organizations is essential, as it underpins global distribution systems, marketing activity, customer relationship management and a range of consumer and academic research resources. Its importance for the sector should not be underestimated as it forms the lynchpin of user-generated content and social media, and **virtual**

tourism is arguably at the heart of the development of software such as Google Earth.

During the past two decades, the adoption of ICT has been a key success factor in enhancing hotel performance (Siguaw et al, 2000; Sigala et al, 2001; Sirirak et al, 2011), improving operational productivity, lowering distribution costs, generating economies of scale through the supply chain and reducing travel costs across multinational chains. It can also play a part in enhancing customer satisfaction, reducing operating costs, increasing market share, and improving employee performance and service (David et al, 1996; Buhalis and Main, 1998; Jones, 1999; Huang, 2008; Tae et al, 2008; Karadag et al, 2009; Zelenka, 2009). In short, ICT has revolutionized the entire tourism industry (Buhalis and Law, 2008). Different forms of ICT have been widely adopted by, among others, travel agencies, hotel chains, airlines, tourism management organizations, car rental agencies and food and beverage outlets. ICT has also been used in supporting dis-intermediated marketing and the distribution of tourism products (Huang, 2008).

It is also generally accepted that the emergence of ICT has resulted in the rapid growth of the electronic marketplace associated with tourism (Norzaidi et al, 2007). Globalization and liberalization of ICT, parti-cularly via the Internet, is regarded as the most cost-efficient tool for any business to gain bigger markets and the chance to compete with other rival organizations in attracting customers to their products, services and information (Tan et al, 2009). The favourable characteristics inherent in the Internet such as speed, user friendliness, low cost and wide accessibility have allowed electronic commerce (e-commerce) to be increasingly diffused globally, bringing countries together into a globally networked economy (Chandran et al, 2001; Gibbs and Kraemer, 2004), and also in terms of pursuing efficiency and quality (Mougayar, 1998).

Research related to the adoption of technology has generally been underpinned by communication theory (Scott Morton, 1991; Thorp, 1998; Luengo-Jones, 2001) to support studies on the identification of barriers and drivers of this adoption (Kauffman and Kumar, 2005). Different levels of technology usage can be identified in tourism busi-nesses (Battisti and Stoneman, 2003) – namely, intra-firm and inter-firm adoption. Intra-firm is normally when one technology is fully adopted by an organization from its purchase to the full integration as part of the business strategy. On the contrary, inter-firm approach technology adoption takes place among tourism businesses regardless of the level of integration.

Table 6 Innovation theory

Elements of the theory	Processes involved in each element
Social system	The social system would relate to a group of individuals who are engaged in achieving a specific goal. These individuals will be innovators, early adopters, early majority, late majority and laggards.
Communication channel	The communication channel relates to the means by which a message is communicated, which can include heterophilic (different) or homophilic (similar) individuals. Communication will be better between homophilic individuals; however, a certain degree of difference in relation to their knowledge about the innovation will be needed.
Time factor	A time factor will be involved in the innovation–decision process, innovativeness, and innovation's rate of adoption.
Characteristics of the innovation	The characteristics of the innovation also have an effect on its likely adoption, which is defined according to its relative advantage, compatibility, complexity, triability and observability of the potential results emerging that it yields.

Source: Rogers (1969)

The adoption of technology in the tourism sector generally uses the innovation theory that was modelled by Rogers (1969), which outlines the process by which innovation, including ICT, is embraced by users. The four main elements of the process are outlined in Table 6.

As outlined by Otto and Ritchie (1996), tourism is a service industry in which creating and sustaining a competitive global advantage is critical. There is a strong emphasis in the service sector on the consumer, and this consumer-centric position requires the service innovation to continue to meet and satisfy individual customers as consumers become increasingly sophisticated in their expectations. Hence, the role of ICT in supporting this service innovation has become critical.

In conclusion, ICT has played a phenomenal role in transforming the tourism industry globally. New innovations are transcending the efficiency and capacity of the industry, and the new systems are so powerful in their capabilities that they may change traditional under-standing and experience. For corporate and business managers in the tourism sector, the continual innovation within ICT poses a challenge to managers who must decide which are beneficial and worthy of investment, but who must also first understand the potential benefits of the innovation in order to make this decision. Some ICT is critical to competitive success, especially user-generated content which is beyond the control of businesses. Consequently, ICT has, and will continue, to fundamentally revolutionize the tourism industry.

Further reading

Buhalis, D. (2003a) *eTourism – Information Management*, Prentice Hall, Harlow, UK

Inkpen, G. (1998) *Information Technology for Travel and Tourism*, Addison Wesley Longman, Essex, UK

Poon, A. (1993) *Tourism, Technology and Competitive Strategies*, CAB International, Wallingford, UK

Sheldon, P. (1997) *Tourism Information Technology*, CAB International, Wallingford, UK, and New York, US

Werthner, H. and Klein, S. (1999) *Information Technology and Tourism: A Challenging Relationship*, Springer, Wien and New York

Dr. Vikneswaran Nair

LEISURE

The Latin translation of leisure literally means 'to be free' (Cooper et al, 2008b). According to Sharma (2005, p138) and Cooper et al, (2008b, p16), leisure is the time available to an individual after work, sleep and other basic needs have been met. Williams and Buswell (2003, p5) stated that leisure can be viewed in terms of residual time, activity, function, state of mind or an experience. Stockdale (1985) identified three main ways in which the concept of leisure is used:

1 as a period of time, activity or state of mind in which choice is the dominant feature; in this sense leisure is a form of 'free time' for an individual;
2 an objective view in which leisure is perceived as the opposite of work and is defined as non-work or residual time;
3 a subjective view which emphasizes leisure as a qualitative concept in which leisure activities take on a meaning only within the context of individual perceptions and belief systems and can therefore occur at any time in any setting (Hall and Page, 2006, p3).

Youell (1995) emphasizes that a comprehensive definition of the term leisure would necessarily include all of the following elements:

• time outside of a formal employment situation;
• time over and above that which is devoted to necessary household chores;

- time outside sleeping, eating and personal hygiene functions;
- time at the disposal of the individual;
- time when an individual has the freedom to choose what to do.

Historical development in leisure and **recreation** goes back to ancient times when there was little opportunity for true leisure and recreational pursuits and the distinction between work and leisure was often blurred. The leisure opportunities which did present themselves were usually associated with festivals and celebrations of a religious or spiritual nature. There is, however, evidence of some travel for purely recreational purposes, with the first Olympic Games taking place in 776 BC. The Greeks, and particularly the Ancient Greek philosophers, were the first to begin to distinguish clearly between work and leisure. They commended the sensible use of free time and promoted a balance between work and play as the route to a healthy individual and a healthy society. Sport was encouraged and many of the words we associate with sport and recreation derive from Ancient Greek (e.g. stadium, decathlon and gymnasium). The rise of Christianity during the Dark Ages (AD 400–1000) relegated leisure activities to those associated with worship and religious festivities. Later, during the Middle Ages (up to approximately AD 1500), leisure became the privilege of those in power who enjoyed hunting, jousting, music and dance. Leisure, in general, towards the end of the Middle Ages was beginning to take on an unpleasant character with activities such as gambling, drinking and blood sports becoming the pastimes of the increasingly corrupt nobility.

During the Renaissance – a cultural movement that spanned roughly the fourteenth to the seventeenth century – the reformation movement was also developing in Europe, leading to the 'Protestant work ethic', which attacked the excesses and corruption of the pleasure-seeking nobility and led to a sharp decrease in the availability and respectability of leisure and recreation. During the early seventeenth century, the healing powers of spa waters became widely accepted among the aristocracy, leading to the development of spa resorts both in Britain and in continental Europe. The Industrial Revolution of the eighteenth and nineteenth centuries brought about profound changes to the way of life, not least in relation to leisure and recreation (Youell, 1995, pp44–47). World War I (1914–1918) brought a temporary halt to the more active forms of leisure, with much time being spent on activities such as needlework, knitting, board games and reading. The inter-war years (1918 to 1939) saw a return to many of the leisure pursuits that had become popular in Victorian times. 'Taking fresh air and exercise' was regarded as a very healthy activity either in the countryside around towns and cities or at seaside resorts. New forms of communication, such as posters, guidebooks and radio, stimulated the public to travel further afield in search of different leisure experiences. The 1950s boom after the end of World War II (1939 to 1945) created more employment and meant that people had greater disposable income with which to purchase the many new consumer and leisure products which were coming onto the market (Veal, 2002, p11). Fashion, music and youth culture were to have important influences on the pattern of leisure during the 1960s, 1970s and 1980s. During the1980s, tourism and leisure development became a recognized element of the inner city and regeneration agenda, and evaluative research pointed to its effectiveness (Maitland, 2007, p26).

A Charter for Leisure, drawn up by the international organization World Leisure in 1970, was revised and approved by the World Leisure Board of Directors in July 2000 (World Leisure Organization, 2011). It declares leisure to be a right, extols the virtues of leisure and exhorts governments to make provision for leisure as a social service; but it stops short of declaring access to leisure facilities and services as a right (Veal, 2002).

Today, leisure can be perceived in many contexts: individual, community, national and international. Its delivery is both local and global. Moreover, global conditions affect each country far more now than in the past; the world economic climate, for example, has an impact upon every nation. The terrorist tragedy inflicted on the US on 11 September 2001 had, and will continue to have, profound effects, not only in the military, political and economic arenas, but also in our ways of life, including leisure. The international tourist market declined, and visitor attractions and activities were affected in many major cities throughout the world. In spite of international and national tensions, however, leisure and recreation continue to flourish and spending on leisure is projected to grow (Torkildsen, 2005, p3).

Increased leisure time and longer periods of vacation, together with rising real incomes in the wake of sustained economic growth, is one of several factors that are responsible for the continued growth of international tourism in the modern world (Cooper et al, 2008b, p192). On the other hand, tourism, recreation and leisure are generally seen as a set of interrelated and overlapping concepts (Hall and Page, 2006, p3). If leisure is a measure of time, and recreation embraces the activities undertaken during that time (Cooper et al, 2008b), then tourism could be considered to be simply one of those leisure activities. Conversely, a central part of the tourism experience usually focuses on leisure and recreational activities (Newsome et al, 2007, p6).

It is clear that leisure and recreational activities differ greatly in the degree of physical effort required from the individual; passive activities, such as watching television or listening to the radio, involve little in the way of exertion, whereas active recreational pursuits – for example, jogging, gardening and DIY (do-it-yourself) – demand much greater effort (Youell, 1995, p5). Leisure pursuits take place in cities and towns, small villages, the countryside and mega-urban centres. Leisure experiences occur inside buildings or outside and sometimes in either location. Recreation can be and is found everywhere – all the places and spaces in which people gather to play, enjoy and relax. The physical characteristics of different seasons provide opportunities for year-round activity. Mountainous venues, for instance, may offer activities in both winter (e.g. skiing) and summer period (e.g. biking, paragliding, etc.). Recreation is pursued 24 hours a day as well. Ski areas open at first light to give would-be lift ticket purchasers the chance to check out snow conditions. Some health clubs open at 4.30 a.m., enabling early risers to work out before heading to work. Recreation and leisure is 'all the time' in an additional way. Play is essential for children. The same holds true at the other end of the life cycle, as recreation provides stress reduction for overworked adults and social support for older people living on their own (O'Sullivan, 2006, pp4–6).

Driver (1999) identified the benefits of leisure as improved conditions, prevention of a worse condition, and realization of a psychological experience (O'Sullivan, 2006, p8). Various factors influence participation in leisure and the types of activities that are preferred by different groups in society. Some of the more important factors include:

- availability of leisure time;
- income level;
- personal mobility;
- culture and demography (age, gender, cultural background, etc.);
- provision of leisure and recreation facilities;
- long-term changes in society (Youell, 1995, p5).

According to Burkart and Medlik (1981, p223), much of this increased leisure time is spent in and about the home, mainly in the immediate environs of the towns and districts in which people live and work. Cinemas, theatres, dance halls and concert halls provide many of the outlets for the increased leisure time of the community devoted to indoor pursuits outside the home, when leisure time is counted in hours, half-days and evenings. Parks, sports fields and other facilities fulfil the same roles as providers of local outdoor recreation. The daily and, still to a great extent, weekly leisure time gives rise to the demand for essentially local leisure facilities.

Recreation and leisure are increasingly tied to the fields of tourism and sport. Understanding these relationships is important for the success of leisure service managers (Mclean et al, 2008). According to Weiermair and Mathies (2004, p171), tomorrow's consumers have high expectations of travel and leisure products: free time needs to provide both relaxation and thrill; people no longer want to buy products or services, but experiences; work, leisure and education seem to merge into one purchasable bundle; adventure and relaxation, as well as fun and health consciousness, are no longer contrasts. Service quality is such a key strategic and operational issue because of the potential for variation and variability of service in the different contexts and the growing importance of leisure and tourism to the individual and to society. Leisure and tourism managers need to know more than operational management; they need to know how to manage quality. Knowledge and understanding of the consumer and of the concepts of leisure and tourism, including the way in which they are consumed and experienced, are becoming increasingly important and even represent the difference between success and failure (Williams and Buswell, 2003, p3).

Developments in leisure (and recreation) will be influenced by social, political and economic, cultural and environmental, and technological factors. Future discussions on leisure time are likely to be very broadly based and to reflect some of the changes in the relationship between work and leisure. Leisure industries should focus particularly on how to ensure that economic growth, as well as rising incomes, also enables people to achieve a sensible balance between work and leisure (Clark, 2001, p81).

Further reading

Hurd, A. R., Barcelona, R. J. and Meldrum, J. T. (2008) *Leisure Services Management*, Human Kinetics, Champaign

Inkpen, G. (1998) *Information Technology for Travel and Tourism*, second edition, Longman, London

Leitner, M. J. and Leitner, S. F. (1996) *Leisure in Later Life*, Haworth Press, New York, NY

Robinson, L. (2004) *Managing Public Support and Leisure Services*, Routledge, Oxford

Rojek, C. (2010) *The Labour of Leisure*, Sage Publications, London

Sharpley, R. and Telfer, D. J. (2002) *Tourism and Development: Concepts and Issues. Aspects of Tourism*, Channel View Publications, Clevedon, UK

Timothy, D. J. (2005) *Shopping Tourism, Retailing, and Leisure: Aspects of Tourism*, Cromwell Press, London

Tribe, J., Font, X., Griffiths, N., Vickery, R. and Yale, K. (2000) *Environmental Management for Rural Tourism and Recreation*, Cassell, London

Dr. Gul Gunes

LGBT TOURISM

LGBT (lesbian, gay, bisexual and transgender) tourism is a term used to replace the more familiar 'gay' tourism focus, so endemic within both academic and commercial literature and the tourism industry itself. While 'gay' is generally perceived as referring to gay men and lesbians, gay tourism has historically been 'used in a wider, more generic sense as a surrogate for LGBT tourism which may reflect that "gay tourism" is a more recognisable or user friendly term' (Southall and Fallon, 2011, p218). According to Hughes (2006), there is a lack of literature relating to bisexual and transgendered travel. Indeed, much existing literature focuses on the tourism predications of gay men and lesbians.

The use of the term LGBT tourism reflects the fact that, increasingly, organizations such as InterPride (the international association of Pride festival organizers) and IGLTA (the International Gay and Lesbian Travel Association) 'explicitly acknowledge this more inclusive concept in describing their activities' (Southall and Fallon, 2011, p218).

Estimates of the economic significance of the LGBT tourism market vary considerably worldwide; however, what is clear is that an increasing number of tourism organizations and destinations are targeting LGBT travellers.

LGBT tourism is defined as 'any tourism activity, either specifically designed to attract the LGBT (lesbian, gay, bisexual and transgendered) market, or one that, by nature and/or design, appeals to and is ultimately pursued by the LGBT market' (Southall and Fallon, 2011, pp220–221). An integral component of the concept of LGBT tourism is the interaction and relationship between producers and consumers. It is also important to note the use of other terms referring to LGBT tourism, such as queer tourism and 'pink tourism' (Hughes, 2006), which reflects the demarcation of gay men in Nazi Germany concentration camps by the use of pink triangles and the symbol of community for which it now stands.

As homosexuality has become more accepted worldwide, it has provided the travel industry with another market segment on which to focus; however, gay tourism itself is considered to date back to the 'Grand Tour' of the Victorian era. The Grand Tour afforded homosexual noblemen both cultural education and the opportunity to express their sexuality more freely (Clift et al, 2002), a form of tourism referred to as 'homosexual tourism' (Graham, 2002). Littlewood (2001, p24) indicated that 'the erotic opportunities of the Grand Tour were homosexual as well as heterosexual'.

The Stonewall Riots of 1969 marked the start of the gay rights movement both in the US and worldwide. The Stonewall Inn in Greenwich Village, New York, was the focal point of the LGBT community's fight against persecution (New York Area Bisexual Network, 2010). The first Gay Pride marches in 1970 in Los Angeles, Chicago and New York, commemorating the anniversary of the riots, were the start of what has now become a series of such events worldwide, bringing together the gay and straight communities in a celebration and remembrance of the original struggle for acceptance.

The emergence of gay neighbourhoods, or 'gayborhoods' (Clift et al, 2002), following de-industrialization during the late twentieth century, led to the increasing popularity of urban environments as gay enclaves and subsequent 'gay-safe' destinations for the gay travel market, examples of which include Greenwich Village in New York and Canal Street in Manchester. It was in the 1990s when gay and lesbian travellers, perhaps emboldened with increasing worldwide recognition and acceptance of gay and lesbian rights, began to break away from the confines of all-gay environments. The concept of gay tourism was steadily becoming incorporated within mainstream tourism provision.

The recognition and subsequent growth of the 'gay travel market' was economically driven and initially based upon the perception of gay men, in particular, as high earners, keen travellers and high travel spenders (Hughes, 2002, 2004). This is also noted by Pitts (1999, p32) who describes the 'viable, potentially lucrative, chic and high brand loyal [lesbian and gay] market'. While this may be the case, it is also true to say that the numbers of LGBT families with children are increasing, thus suggesting a more restricted disposable income. Significantly, the market has further developed due to increasing recognition, transforming attitudes and legislatory changes, such as the UK's Civil Partnership Act, 2004, and the Equality Act (Sexual Orientation) Regulations, 2007.

While there are some operators specializing in the LGBT market, offering tourism products and services to 'gay-friendly' destinations, such operators are comparatively few. A trend away from 'all-gay' travel has been identified in recent research, with surveys finding that fewer gay men and lesbians are looking for an 'all-gay' environment (Community Marketing Inc., 2011). The anonymity of the online society in which we live has enabled the LGBT community to access information and make independent travel arrangements without fear of 'outing' themselves (Kaur Puar, 2002). It is important to note that the holiday activities of LGBT travellers are not dissimilar to those of the 'straight' or heterosexual community, in respect of sightseeing, eating and drinking out and sunbathing (Pritchard et al, 2000).

With estimates of the LGBT population worldwide continuing to rise, the importance of defining LGBT tourism and measuring participation should not be underestimated. It is estimated that between 1 and 20 per cent of the UK's adult population is gay; however, it is difficult to ascertain the true value of the LGBT market due to discrepancies in research, from definitions to methodology (Southall and Fallon, 2011). The growing events industry is supported by the LGBT market, not only through attendance and participation in 'Pride' events and conferences, but also through increasing participation in sports tourism through events such as the Gay Games (Pitts, 1999). As recognition and acceptance of the LGBT community grows, as civil partnerships and marriage become accepted cultural practice, and as mainstream tourism providers recognize the economic benefits of this potentially lucrative market, LGBT tourism provision will become increasingly important.

Further reading

Clift, S., Luongo, M. and Callister, C. (eds) (2002) *Gay Tourism: Culture, Identity and Sex*, Continuum, London

Hughes, H. L. (2004) 'A gay tourism market: Reality or illusion, benefit or burden?', *Journal of Quality Assurance in Hospitality and Tourism*, vol 5, no 2/3/4, pp57–74

Hughes, H. (2006) *Pink Tourism: Holidays of Gay Men and Lesbians*, CABI, Wallingford, UK

Pritchard, A., Morgan, N., Sedgley, D., Khan, E. and Jenkins, A. (2000) 'Sexuality and holiday choices: Conversations with gay and lesbian tourists', *Leisure Studies*, vol 19, pp267–282

Southall, C. and Fallon, P. (2011) 'LGBT tourism', in P. Robinson, S. Heitmann and P. U. C. Dieke (eds) (2011) *Research Themes for Tourism*, CABI, Wallingford, UK, pp218–232

Carol Southall

LITERARY TOURISM

Literary tourism is travel induced by, or associated with, works of literature, authors and the places featured within literature. Early fiction is regarded as the first tourism-inspiring medium. This literature presented images of new places, with unique and wondrous stories, motivating people to visit and experience a place for themselves. With increased access to literature and travel, literary tourism activity remains an area of growth.

There are five themes within literary tourism:

1 travel to places written about or written in; places associated with the story or the author;
2 travel to places with significant book collections; generally experiencing unique or historical libraries and personal book collections;
3 travel to literary destinations; destinations whose bookshops attract tourists;
4 literary festivals and events celebrating and promoting authors and books;
5 retrospective exposure to literature works and authors presented in film, which is closely linked to the first theme.

Predominantly, the study of literary tourism has focused on travel to places featured within books. Literary tourism destinations include Monterey Peninsula and Salinas Valley, US (John Steinbeck's *Cannery Row*), Prince Edward Island, Canada (Lucy Maud Montgomery's *Anne of Green Gables*) and Transylvania, Romania (Bram Stoker's *Dracula*) (e.g. see Squire, 1996, and Muresan and Smith, 1998). Literary tourism destinations associated with authors include the Lake District, England (Beatrix Potter), Stratford upon Avon, England (William Shakespeare), Laugharne, Wales (Dylan Thomas) and Chawton, England (Jane Austen) (e.g. see Herbert, 2001). The effect of literary works and their authors can make a significant impact on a destination. For example, over 100,000 tourists a year are motivated by *Anne of Green Gables* to visit Prince Edward Island, Canada (Fawcett and Cormack, 2001).

Some of these literary icons may be more associated now with film, rather than the books where the tales originate. For example, *Anne of Green Gables* has been made into movies and television series, and *Dracula* has also been adapted for film on numerous occasions (see **Film and TV tourism**), as well as featuring heavily in a number of television shows (Squire, 1996; Muresan and Smith, 1998). Other recent examples include *Eat Pray Love* and the *Harry Potter* series of films. This filmic representation may create demand to literary sites, and dislocated tourist demand to sites associated with the film rather than the literary works. For example, *The Lord of the Rings* is now associated with the film's location of New Zealand, and the 1990s adaptation of *Pride and Prejudice* attracted tourists to Lyme Park in Cheshire, chosen to represent 'Pemberley', but with no connection to the novel.

In cases of literary tourism to book collections, especially to significant historical or personal collections, the authors and the stories are almost insignificant. For this literary tourism it is individual books, the collector or collection of books that attract the tourists. Examples include Pepys's Library in Cambridge, England; the Lilly Library in Indiana, US; the Bodleian Library in Oxford, England; the Library of Congress in Washington, DC, US; and the National and University Library in Strasbourg, France.

Travel to literary towns is more specifically for places with a cluster of bookshops, usually selling used and antiquarian books (Seaton, 1999). Examples of book towns include Hay-on-Wye, Wales; Redu, Belgium; Bredevoort, The Netherlands; and Becherel, France. Other book precincts or permanent markets in urban areas share this literary tourism theme.

Travel to book fairs and events range from large-scale book fairs, writers' festivals and symposia, through to literary events, including book signings and book launches. Two examples of book fairs are the Turin International Book Fair in Italy and the Frankfurt Book Fair in Germany; each attracts about 300,000 tourists a year. Examples of writer and reader festivals include the Australian Festival of the Book, Australia; the International Literature Festival, Berlin, Germany; the Vancouver International Writers Festival, Canada; and the Hong Kong International Literary Festival, China. Tourists may also experience book signings and book launches at bookshops and the like.

The actual effect of literary works on tourists is not well documented. It is difficult to separate out literature from other reasons an individual may have for visiting a destination, and the literary theme may be a part of a wider set of tourism motivations. The historical relationship between a place, literature and associated writers make it difficult to identify a specific impact of the book or author upon tourist numbers, or changes in visitation (as is often noted for film tourism). Furthermore, the location of the literary site, in some cases, also precludes the identification of literary tourist numbers due to many other prominent attractions, or the location is too remote to allow any effective recording of visitor numbers.

However, many destinations have developed marketing strategies (see **Destination marketing**) to further emphasize the link to their literary past and to attract tourists, using the iconic events described in books or lived by the authors. What is evident is that literary tourism does exist and is being used by regions to market themselves to tourists. Although the effectiveness of many of these strategies is not evident, the anecdotal evidence and the continuing survival of these destinations do indicate that literary tourism is an effective motivator for tourists, or at least creates awareness of the destination.

While a large number of tourists visit literary sites, only a few purposefully chose a location because of its literary association. As a result, literary tourists are very much a niche market. True literary tourists are knowledgeable enthusiasts or even pilgrims of a book or author (Herbert, 2001; Smith, 2003). For the majority of tourists, however, literary tourism is incidental to their travel, with the literary theme forming a small part of their itinerary. In noting this incidental nature of visitation to literary sites, it is still likely that the literary association influences tourists' perceptions and motivations to visit the destination.

Further reading

Herbert, D. (2001) 'Literary places, tourism and the heritage experience', *Annals of Tourism Research*, vol 28, no 2, pp312–333

Seaton, A. V. (1999) 'Book towns as tourism developments in peripheral areas', *International Journal of Tourism Research*, vol 1, no 4, pp389–399

Smith, K. A. (2003) 'Literary enthusiasts as visitors and volunteers', *International Journal of Tourism*, vol 5, no 2, pp83–95

Squire, S. J. (1996) 'Literary tourism and sustainable tourism: Promoting *Anne of Green Gables* in Prince Edward Island', *Journal of Sustainable Tourism*, vol 4, no 3, pp119–134

Dr. Glen Croy

MARKETING FOR TOURISM

Although there are literally dozens of definitions for marketing, most of them vary slightly within a broad consensus – that is, the marketing concept refers to a process that organizations undergo with the end goal of satisfying individual customers and organizational objectives. This process covers activities such as planning and executing the formation, pricing, promotions and distribution of ideas and goods (Bennett, 1995). This definition, generally accepted by many marketing managers and academics, essentially posits marketing as a process that focuses on finding, satisfying and retaining customers while the business makes profit.

The beginnings of the marketing concept, in general, and marketing theory, in particular, can be traced back to the early 1900s in the US. This is the period when scholars in the field of economics realized that demand could be influenced by factors other than the sheer existence of supply. They started to comprehend that demand represented desire and power to purchase. They also theorized that new experiences with advertising and communication were establishing a desire to purchase a product amongst consumers. Early contributions to the body of knowledge in marketing thought were focused on the opportunities for growth in sales and distribution, given the rapid advancements in rail and road transport. As such, many theories were borrowed from economics relating to distribution and commodity markets. It was during these years between 1900 and 1910 when the concept of marketing was first identified and a name given to the discipline. As a consequence of the dominance of economics applications, most, if not all, the marketing theories that emerged for the next 50 years were focused on the promotion and selling of physical goods. It was not until the 1960s and 1970s when large-scale commercial service operations were established that scholars began to shift their attention towards the marketing of services. Although there has been recognition that the marketing of goods also implies the obligation to supply associated after-sales services, the first marketing conference devoted to service industries by the American Marketing Association only took place in 1981.

Tourism marketing is often explained as a type of service marketing because of its intangible, inseparable, non-perishable and heterogeneous nature. In any case, Gilbert (1992) provides a relatively early definition of tourism marketing as an application of the process defined in general marketing terms to the particular characteristics relevant to the tourism industry. Therefore, tourism marketing refers to the process of exchange between tourists and tourism-related establishments for certain benefits. This means that tourism marketing is concerned with the processes by which tourism establishments make managerial decisions, and understanding how these decisions, in turn, affect tourist choices. It is not surprising, then, that this definition of tourism marketing does not differ very much from the definition of general marketing. This is because the principles of marketing, in general, can be applied across all business segments. What is different, however, as some have argued, is that some marketing management tools employed in other business sectors cannot be applied in tourism. For example, service development is much more complex for a destination as opposed to other service divisions such as banks. This is because a wide range of suppliers are involved and a combination of services is offered whenever a destination is marketed. In addition, the destination can only provide a rather rigid supply of facilities which can only be gradually adjusted, in contrast to patterns of tourist demand, which may change constantly, if not rapidly.

Perhaps these are the reasons why the recognition of marketing theories and research in tourism studies has been slow. This was observed by March (1994), who found it ironic that the discipline of marketing has been underutilized by tourism practitioners and policy-makers, both in the private and public sectors. He cautioned that this slowness of the tourism industry in adopting marketing practices is detrimental because it hinders the growth potential of the industry at large and the commercial capability of individual tourism players. Whether or not coincidental, the years after Gilbert's (1992) definition and March's (1994) observation saw an increase in the number of new tourism academic journals, academic articles and conference tracks on tourism marketing. From these, new streams of tourism marketing research have started to emerge, with branches such as destination marketing, vacation marketing and hospitality marketing. Then, there are divisions of tourism research which do not specifically carry the term marketing, but are essentially focused on the process of segmentation and marketing to specific profiles of the tourist market. Some of these examples are **sports tourism**, **adventure tourism**, **dark tourism**, **sex tourism**, **LGBT tourism**, space tourism and purple tourism.

Topics that are addressed in the process of marketing include segmentation, communication mix, marketing mix, distribution, pricing, promotion, competition and marketing strategy. The key concepts are defined briefly in Table 7, and it should also be noted that

Table 7 Principal tourism marketing concepts

Segmentation	The identification of different groups of people within the market place who share similar characteristics and can be identified as potential consumers
Communication mix	The mix of methods used to communicate to consumers, which may include email, websites, direct mail and advertising
Marketing mix	Often described as the 7Ps, the marketing mix helps to outline the marketing of a service or product in terms of product; price; place (distribution); physical evidence; process; people; promotion and position

marketing is closely aligned to **tourism strategy, destination management, destination marketing** and **destination image**.

In the interest of brevity, published studies on tourism marketing will be presented briefly, with the aim of providing an overview rather than specifying in detail what each of these studies entails. Within academia, studies have looked into the various aspects of distributing destinations and tourism products. This includes investigations into different distribution channels for the varied tourism experiences; the gatekeepers and challenges for using any of these channels; and the roles of travel intermediaries and information technology in the distribution chain. Tourism scholars have also looked into the applications of marketing mix in the context of travel and tourism. They have also researched topics related to the process of establishing costs and pricing strategies for any tourism products and services, whether accommodation, transportation, tour packages or experiences. Research on tourism marketing has attempted to understand the tourist segments and their travel behaviour, as well as how best to appeal to these segments (see also **Consumer behaviour in tourism**).

There have also been many studies conducted on branding and packaging a destination; developing an image for destinations; and, more importantly, how to develop and market new tourism destinations. Then there are studies that concentrate on tourism advertising, which in itself consists of an enormous body of work ranging from public relations, word-of-mouth advertising, online advertising and international advertising. It also covers the best strategies for employing media use, and each form of media (from television, radio and magazines to billboards, exhibitions and media) has been researched from multiple perspectives and multiple contexts. Tourism marketing research has also covered post-consumption – that is, scholars have attempted to understand the antecedents of tourist (dis)satisfaction after they have experienced a product or service (see also **Operations management in tourism**). From this, studies have branched out into understanding tourist complaints and complimenting behaviours, and how best to recreate the desired outcomes for both the customers and tourism practitioners. In terms of products, investigations have been carried out on meals and restaurants, flights and any other form of transportation, hotel rooms, hotel staff, travel packages, heritage sites, shopping malls, events, cultural and religious places, and specific tourism activities such as hiking, skiing, bungee-jumping and white-water rafting. In addition, many studies within tourism marketing have been replicated for different contexts, and contexts here can refer to different settings, locations and destinations or different cultures, religions or values.

The importance of marketing for tourism becomes evident when the main sectors of the tourism industry (from tourism policy-makers to travel organizers, destination organizers, **accommodation providers**, **transport** providers and other related product suppliers) come together to manage tourists' needs and demands through a wide range of marketing applications. Tourism marketing is also becoming more important as technology enables societies to become more global. When **globalization** takes place, destinations, people and places become ever more interdependent. The globalization of tourism in this sense has many implications in terms of **culture**, politics and economics, and should be given fitting considerations by tourism marketers. After all, it is only a practical management response to the volatile industry conditions and market demand that are usually found in international tourism.

Further reading

Chaudhary, M. (2008) *Tourism Marketing*, Oxford University Press, Oxford, UK
Gilbert, D. C. (1998) 'Tourism marketing – its emergence and establishment', in C. P. Cooper (ed) *Progress in Tourism, Recreation and Hospitality Management*, CBS Publishers, New Delhi, pp77–90
Holloway, J. T. and Plant, R. V. (1992) *Marketing for Tourism*, Pitman, London
Hudson, A. (2008) *Tourism and Hospitality Marketing: A Global Perspective*, Sage Publications Ltd, London
Kotler, P., Bowen, J. T. and Makens, J. (2006) *Marketing for Hospitality and Tourism*, fourth edition, Prentice Hall, New York, NY

Dr. Catheryn Khoo-Lattimore

MASS TOURISM

Although there is a common view that mass tourism has been, is and will be the dominant form of travelling in the future, its definition, advantages and disadvantages are contested. Mass tourism is therefore 'one of the most important concepts in the academic field of tourism management' (Lomine and Edmunds, 2007, p123). In very general terms, mass tourism relates to the scale of tourism and tourism parti-cipation rates (Swarbrooke, 2007). It can be defined as the mass movement of people to a specific destination where tourism develop-ment 'exists as a means by which to concentrate people in very high densities' (Fennell, 2008). As an economic activity, it is supposedly based on short-term free-market principles of profit maximization (Orams, 2001) following Fordist production principles.

Often, the development of mass tourism is strongly associated with the creation of the package holiday. Accordingly, it could be defined as the relatively recent phenomenon of simultaneous mass (large) movement of tourists who purchased a package of tourism experiences and services (industrially organized tourism) to a particular destination (see, for example, Altobelli and Kirstges, 2008; Cooper and Hall, 2008; Hannam and Knox, 2010). At the same time, it has an elitist connotation 'as it often implies travel by poorer, less well-educated people to destinations that the wealthier and "more discerning" do not travel to, or have ceased to travel to' (Cooper and Hall, 2008, p62). However, the global participation in mass tourism is still a privilege for residents of the wealthier countries of the developed world.

Some authors believe the 'birth of mass tourism' happened on 5 July 1841 when Thomas Cook organized a railway trip for 570 people from Leicester to Loughborough and back (e.g. Hall, 2007b; Cook et al, 2010). The fare of 1 shilling covered third-class return standing tickets, a cup of tea and a ham sandwich. Historically, it was the first package tour (Cook et al, 2010). Before then, travelling was mainly reserved for a privileged minority of the upper class (Sharpley, 2006); but the packaging of different tourism products (e.g. travel to/from destination, accommodation and food) as part of the process of reducing the costs of a holiday opened travelling to the 'masses'. Cook therefore started a new phase in the history of travel – namely, domestic mass tourism or the mobility era (Cook et al, 2010). It provided the basis for the later expansion into international mass tourism.

Other authors argue that mass tourism refers to the historical phenomenon of outbound international tourism that started to develop in Europe during the late 1950s (e.g. Sharpley, 2006; Lomine and Edmunds, 2007). It was driven by the growth of air travel following World War II, the introduction of modern jet airliners, cheaper air travel prices and the introduction of the packaged tour (Altobelli and Kirstges, 2008). Statistics published by the United Nations World Tourism Organization (UNWTO) confirm this growth. It estimates that tourism numbers grew from approximately 25 million in 1950 (UNWTO, 2011b) to 935 million in 2010 (UNWTO, 2011a). However, this development of tourism was not only driven by the expansion of air travel, but by a number of overlapping changes that are closely connected to industrialization and national identity.

Industrialization, which began at the end of the eighteenth century in England, describes the shift from a society based mainly on agriculture to one based on industrial mass production of goods in large-scale urban factories using mechanical methods (Cook et al, 2010). Over time, industrialization and industrial capitalism produced the basic conditions for tourism demand and mass tourism: increased personal wealth and disposable time in the form of paid annual leave for the great majority of people in industrialized countries. These economic and social changes facilitated the move from a static to a mobile society (Holden, 2005). The desire to spend leisure time away from home and the creation of (mass) tourism infrastructure is therefore very closely connected to industrial capitalism (Mowforth and Munt, 2009).

Another important element in the evolution of mass tourism is the formation of modern nation states and national identity during the nineteenth century (Franklin, 2003a). It was in the interest of the new nation states to see their residents travelling through their own country to experience selected symbols of national identity (e.g. Shaffer, 2001) as common heritage and later to discover foreign countries to explore where and why they were 'different'. Even today in times of globalization, national identity and national image is recreated through national tourism branding to mass markets.

Additionally, industrialization and the establishment of modern nation states facilitated a variety of other changes in tourism, making it possible for the working class to travel in great numbers. These changes included:

- new technological developments – in particular, transport technology and transport infrastructure (e.g. railways and cars for domestic tourism during the nineteenth and early twentieth centuries and jet planes for international tourism during the second half of the twentieth century) and later information technology (e.g. computer technology and the internet since the late twentieth century);
- socioeconomic and political transformations – namely, the democratization of tourism (Urry, 1990) that extended tourism to all sectors of (Western) society (Hannam and Knox, 2010);
- the surfacing of an industrialized tourism industry that transferred the principles of Fordist accumulation to tourism, especially through the large-scale reproduction of a standardized tourism product to reduce the cost and the promotion of these cheap package tours for mass consumption (Hannam and Knox, 2010).

International mass tourism experienced rapid growth during the mid-1960s with, first, criticism of its environmental and sociocultural impacts appearing during the early 1970s, mainly in the context of the European Alps as a mass tourism destination (e.g. Young, 1973), before developing into an established feature of tourism critique in the 1980s (e.g. Krippendorf, 1987). Poon (1993, p4), for example, characterized mass tourism as tourism that is 'consumed en masse in a similar, robot like and routine manner, with a lack of consideration for the norms, culture and environment of the host country visited'. Consequently, alternative tourism as a 'different' model of tourism than mass tourism emerged. It is often described as the good option in comparison to 'bad' mass tourism (Weaver, 2001). However, it is highly questionable if 'good' small-scale alternative tourism will be able to make the tourism industry sustainable or can replace mass tourism (Cohen, 1987) as tourism numbers have to remain small for it not to defeat its purpose, yet there are nearly 1 billion international tourists worldwide. Some believe, therefore, that mass tourism is in a far better position than small-scale tourism to make tourism activities more sustainable (Clarke, 1997; Weaver, 2006) as 'there is no inherent reason why a large scale [tourism] product cannot be sustainable' (Weaver, 2001, p77). In this sense, mass tourism needs to be accepted as a reality that has to minimize its negative impacts and maximize its positive contributions to become more sustainable.

Further reading

Cook, R. A., Yale, L. J. and Marqua, J. J. (2010) *Tourism: The Business of Travel*, fourth edition, Prentice Hall, Upper Saddle River, NJ
Franklin, A. (2003) *Tourism: An Introduction*, Sage Publications Ltd, London
Hannam, K. and Knox, D. (2010) *Understanding Tourism: A Critical Introduction*, Sage Publication Ltd, London
Mowforth, M. and Munt, I. (2009) *Tourism and Sustainability: Development, Globalisation and New Tourism in the Third World*, third edition, Routledge, Abingdon, Oxon, UK

Dr. Dirk Reiser

MEDICAL TOURISM

Medical tourism is categorized as a segment or sub-sector of health tourism defined by Erfurt-Cooper and Cooper's textbook (2009, p6) as 'any kind of travel to make yourself or a member of your family healthier' and as briefly travelling abroad for healthcare services for reasons such as lower-priced or higher-quality treatments.

The definitions and classifications of health and wellness tourism vary, as they do for health, medical and wellness tourism. Several scholars do not differentiate between wellness tourism and medical tourism and place wellness-related categories under the general term of medical tourism. For instance, one typology (Voigt et al, 2010, p30) suggests the four medical tourism categories of:

1 Illness: medical check-ups, medical surgery, dental treatment.
2 Wellness: beauty care, spa treatment, yoga, herbal healing.
3 Enhancement: cosmetic surgery.
4 Reproduction: fertility treatment and birth tourism.

Thus, the general definition of the health and wellness tourism industries is generalized as 'products and services made accessible to people travelling from their place of residence for health reasons', whereas medical tourism specifically focuses on conventional healthcare (medical) services by including operations and services (including cosmetic surgery) such as rhinoplasty and weight reduction surgery, medical surgery (from highly invasive operations such as organ transplantation and cardiac and orthopaedic surgery to dental, eye and reproductive/IVF operations, as well as health screenings) (Pirnar, 2007). Regarding this perspective, medical travel may be defined as the travel portion of the medical tourism trip where the tourist makes use of healthcare services, either purchased as the main purpose of the trip or surplus of the travel package (Epstein and Meyers, 2009).

Medical tourism is not a new concept since its roots can be traced back to Greek pilgrims who travelled overseas for medical care. 'This was limited to the upper classes, moving from developing countries to developed ones, when health care was inadequate or unavailable at home. Now, however, the direction of medical travel is changing towards developing countries' (Pocock and Phua, 2011; see also Williams and Williams, 2011). The medical tourism industry has recently evolved to focus more on surgical procedures in countries where the cost is significantly cheaper than in the patient's home nation. According to different patterns of medical tourist flows, medical tourism may be divided into two categories, according to the characteristics of the target market (Phua and Chew, 2002; Phua, 2011):

1 quality-sensitive medical tourism targeting quality-sensitive medical tourists who are usually affluent people looking for professional or sophisticated health services such as organ transplantation or open heart surgery;

2 price-sensitive medical tourists who are generally from the middle classes, and are reasonably well informed and educated about foreign destinations and the healthcare services and prices that they offer.

Due to the positive economic and social impacts of medical tourism, more and more countries are becoming medical tourism destinations. The global top ten in 2010 include Brazil, Costa Rica, India, Korea, Malaysia, Mexico, Singapore, Taiwan, Thailand and Turkey. China, Puerto Rico, the United Arab Emirates and the US are becoming more popular destinations amongst medical tourists.

The prices of health tourism products vary substantially from region to region and from one country to another; thus, health procedures across the world show a 200 to 800 per cent cost difference, which creates various demand patterns for global medical tourism.

In order to attain customer satisfaction in medical tourism, it is important that the supplier meets the individual expectations and perceptions of the medical tourists (Edelheit, 2009; Epstein and Meyers, 2009; Pirnar and İçöz, 2010), which include:

- a real or perceived lack of medical services at home;
- availability of care or treatment that is unavailable or illegal in the home country;
- avoidance of prolonged waiting periods in the home country;
- lower costs of medical care abroad: the customer looks for less costly treatments and procedures than those in his or her own country;
- personal reasons, including convenience and privacy: an individual may, for example, be embarrassed to get surgery at home and want to keep it secret;
- the opportunity to access experimental or controversial treatments, procedures or care;
- the perception of serious governmental and private-sector investment in healthcare infrastructure;
- a high international patient flow to the destination, indicating low risks involved with the surgery;
- improved service by health personnel and the opportunity to combine medical treatment with a visit to an exotic destination;
- political transparency and stability within the destination;
- ease of access to tourism infrastructure;
- a sustained reputation for expertise in the area of medical treatment that is required;
- a history of healthcare innovation and achievement;

- the successful adoption of best practices, case studies and cutting-edge medical technology within the destination;
- the availability of internationally trained, experienced medical staff: individuals may seek high standards and levels of quality which are unaffordable or unavailable at home.

Criteria for deciding on destinations for medical tourism encompass many variables, such as (Mueller and Kaufmann, 2001, p5; Phua and Chew, 2002; Yildirim, 2005; Kaur et al, 2007, p421; Pirnar, 2007, pp35–38; Pirnar and İçöz, 2010; Turkeli et al, 2011):

- a hygienic environment;
- standardization and uniformity of healthcare services;
- a high level of quality (an increasingly decisive competitive factor);
- fewer limitations imposed by regulatory agencies, specialists and/or procedures;
- a broad commitment to international accreditation, quality assurance and transparency of success results;
- an expanded range of services;
- highly qualified staff (trained technically as well as in personal skills);
- the value proposition: good low cost–high quality ratio;
- recognized expertise;
- accreditation by the medical tourist's own home country;
- owned by the medical tourist's own home country's healthcare corporations;
- staffed by doctors with credentials from the medical tourist's own country;
- successful marketing and promotion;
- services that are covered by medical insurance;
- availability of different/unique touristic attractions or opportunity for unique cultural/heritage experiences; availability of pre- or post-operation travel packages;
- availability of alternative tourism products within the destination;
- destinations where foreign visitors feel welcome and safe;
- destinations that are politically stable with a relatively high standard of living;
- availability of internationally accepted standards or quality certifications for health services offered;
- destinations that offer extraordinary and unique surgery or treatment methods;
- technological creativeness;
- better logistics services;

- destinations that are ranked high in terms of perceived medical care quality image;
- destinations where major languages, such as English, Spanish and French, are widely spoken.

Competitive advantage in the medical tourism market is achieved through low-cost leadership and/or differentiation through the offer of high-quality services (by improving the service and logistics) and applying marketing strategies such as branding, consumer relationship management and innovative marketing techniques (Turkeli et al, 2011). In terms of differentiation, ethical conduct and hygiene control are important quality differentials since some countries have a reputation for unethical applications, such as the illegal purchase of organs and tissues needed for transplant, and many medical tourists face the risk of acquiring infectious diseases or may have problems on return flights after surgery (York, 2008) – all of which must never occur if competitive advantage is sought by medical destinations.

Further reading

Connell, J. (2006) 'Medical tourism: sea, sun, sand ... surgery', *Tourism Management*, vol 27, pp1093–1100

Erfurt-Cooper, P. and Cooper, M. (2009) *Health and Wellness Tourism: Spas and Hot Springs*, Channel View Publications, Clevedon, UK

Pocock, N. S. and Phua, K. H. (2011) 'Medical tourism and policy implications for health systems: A conceptual framework from a comparative study of Thailand, Singapore and Malaysia', *Globalization and Health*, vol 7, p12

Dr. Ige Pirnar

MICRO- AND MACRO-ENVIRONMENTS

It is important for organizations in the tourism sector to be able to evaluate their external operating environment and any internal factors affecting organizational performance. There are three essential tools that enable this type of analysis, which can be used within **marketing for tourism, tourism strategy** and **operations management**.

SWOT Analysis

The SWOT Analysis (strengths, weaknesses, opportunities and threats) provides a good overview of the internal workings of an organization and is useful for planning the future direction of the business and assessing its internal workings. The analysis is designed to measure the strengths and weaknesses of the organization (internal factors) and the opportunities and threats that exist in the wider operating environment:

- Strengths are the activities that the business does well.
- Weaknesses are the areas of activity that could be improved upon.
- Opportunities may include new market opportunities or closure of competitors.
- Threats may include new competitors.

PEST Analysis

The PEST Analysis provides an evaluation of the external operating environment assessing political, economic, sociocultural and technological factors. It is most useful in its extended PESTEL form, which also encompasses environmental and legal factors, or as STEEPLE (which adds ethics); but context must be given here to the notion that legislative issues are often related to political factors and so duplication may occur. PEST, like SWOT, is useful for marketing processes, but can be further adapted for marketing as a DEPICTS Analysis. DEPICTS assesses demographic, economic, political, infrastructural, competitor, technological and sociocultural factors.

Porter's Five Forces

Ostensibly used as a competitor analysis, Porter's five forces assess the marketplace and the factors that influence and shape the activities of a business. The model considers:

1 Threat of new entrants: some markets are difficult to enter; it is, for example, difficult to build a new theme park, so there are a number of barriers to entry. It is relatively easy, however, to start a bed-and-breakfast, so there is a greater threat of new entrants who could become competitors.
2 Power of suppliers: the more important and larger the supplier, the greater their ability to squeeze the profits of the businesses that they supply, especially if there are no substitute products.
3 Power of buyers: if businesses rely on a small number of buyers for most of their income, the buyer is able to negotiate price, affecting business profit margins. Competitive marketplaces also tend to lead to more flexible competitive pricing.

4 Threat of substitute products: this factor measures the ease with which consumers can switch to a competing product or service, and the lower the cost of switching, the easier it becomes to lose customers.

5 Competitive rivalry: this final factor assesses the degree of competition between businesses, and usually the higher the competitive rivalry the lower the return on investment.

Further reading

Porter, M. (1980) *Competitive Strategy: Techniques for Analyzing Industries and Competitors*, Free Press, New York, NY

Robinson, P. (ed) (2009) *Operations Management in the Travel Industry*, CABI, Wallingford, UK

Peter Robinson

MOBILITY

Mobility means the state of someone or something being in motion. Different forms of mobility include academic mobility, economic mobility, social mobility, migration and cosmopolitanism, as well as travel and tourism for recreation and leisure purposes.

Mobility has always played a central role in the development of people, cultures and communities. People inscribe places and spaces with meaning as they move. Nomadic ways of life and mass migrations remain a significant counterpoint to tendencies of nation- and frontier-building that have shaped world history. Political, social and environmental barriers have had important effects on human development, while mobile ways of life have disrupted attempts to impose particular kinds of social and political order.

While travellers were first concerned with the acquisition of knowledge about landscapes, cultures and markets, this interest quickly changed to exploitation and conquest. The creation of the modern Atlantic World during the slave trade and colonization, for example, created large movements of populations in diverse regions affected by the development of European empires. Movement from the South to the North became more important after decolonization, a result of the uneven development of the world economy (see **Globalization**).

Related scholarly literature is dominated by concepts and metaphors through which authors describe intensified spatial and temporal realities. Popular terms include de-territorialization, re-territorialization, scape, time–space compression, network society and flow. The time–space compression, for example, has been identified as a central element of post-modern movement. It is seen to produce particular non-places, such as airport lounges that facilitate but also demand mobility. Related scientific analysis puts emphasis on the influence of transnational ties, sociocultural outlooks and technologies of transport, knowledge and information. Lifestyle mobilities further affect such thinking as they blur traditional boundaries between work and leisure or home and away.

During the early twenty-first century, not only more people but also information, images and goods moved differently than before. The mobility of people has become more dynamic and complex, but also controllable due to technological, social and cultural development in transportation, border control, media and communication surveillance. Another timely issue in the mobility paradigm concerns social media, such as the mobile phone, that are important tools used to shape communication and social environments – for example, enabling hosts and guests to offer or book tickets, and to compare hotels and prices. At the same time, social media and digital arts allow for new communication possibilities. They create alternative public spaces such as web forums or blogs where travellers broadcast, discuss and criticize their diverse experiences of places, tourist sites, travel agencies and others.

While this has led to an almost common-sense perception of a world in constant motion, not all movements are valued equally. The very techniques and processes that produce mobility also result in immobility and exclusion. Some countries, for example, continue, raise or even introduce new legal and physical barriers to prevent movement, whether human, animal or viral. Other barriers to mobility include the imposition of visa and immigration restrictions, as well as the efforts of some countries to control their citizens' relations with the outside world – for example, through censorship of transnational media channels such as the Internet.

People who wish to continue mobile ways of life often conflict with other interests. This is exemplified by many indigenous groups with a demand for recognition of their land rights. There are further implications of immobility, bearing in mind the wide variety of reasons why people cannot or do not wish to move. Related analytical questions towards contemporary forms of mobility, immobility and tourism aim to understand the global impact of the mobility of people, capital and images. This is highlighted, for example, in more recent anthropological studies of tourism (see **Ethnography**). It is argued that tourism, in particular, is visibly affected by how places and technologies enhance the mobility of some people and heighten the immobility of others (Hannam, 2006).

Mobility in tourism is closely linked to the three modes of transport: ground, marine and air transport. The growing expansion of international tourism continues to have a large impact upon the development of local and global infrastructures, logistics and technology. These might enhance but also hinder mobility – for example, if one contrasts the new generation of double-deck aircrafts such as the Airbus A380 with the invention of electronic passports that are meant to better control people's movements.

Further themes and issues address destination management, the accessibility of certain regions compared to others, as well as problems of noise pollution caused through tourism and transport, especially in highly concentrated areas such as islands or cities. While ordinary pedestrians, for example, might lose their prominent position in some places to other traffic participants, tourists like to walk through city space. In some places this has triggered a renaissance of inner-city pedestrian areas. Other topics of the tourism–mobility relationship include the regional economic conditions that benefit from, or hinder, tourism and mobility development. They also address post-colonial (re)appropriations of space and related power mechanisms that continue within and through the interconnections between tourism and transport and more general interdependencies beyond human/non-human or subject/object dialectics.

Further reading

Duval, D. T. (2007) *Tourism and Transport: Modes, Networks and Flows*, Channel View Publications, Clevedon, UK

Franklin, A. (2003b) 'The tourist syndrome: An interview with Zigmunt Bauman', *Tourist Studies*, vol 3, no 2, pp205–217

Hannam, K. (2006) 'Heritage tourism and development III: Performances, performativities and mobilities', *Progress in Development Studies*, vol 6, no 3, pp243–249

Hannerz, U. (1998) *Transnational Connections: Culture, People, Places*, Routledge, London

Lash, S. and Urry, J. (1994) 'Mobility, modernity and place', in S. Lash and J. Urry (eds) *Economies of Signs and Space*, Sage Publications, London, pp252–278

Dr. Carsten Wergin

MOTIVATION

Heitmann (2011) comments that 'motivation is a state of need or a condition that causes the tourist to take action … to take a holiday which is likely to bring satisfaction by addressing the ... need' and suggests that 'studying tourist motivation seeks to answer why people want to travel and if they travel why they travel to certain destinations and why they engage in certain activities while on holiday'.

Explaining motivation, therefore, essentially means explaining how individuals and groups make decisions about purchasing products and services, and choosing where to visit. As a starting point, Kotler et al (2010) suggest that this decision process is comprised of five stages, although it should be noted that at every stage of the process the individual may be affected by cultural, social, personal and psychological characteristics:

1   A recognition that the individual needs a change from their current state (e.g. busy at work) to a desired state (e.g. a state of relaxation).
2   In order to achieve this desired state the individual seeks information about places where this desire can be realized, which may include recommendations, tourist information, media coverage and advertising.
3   The individual then needs to evaluate alternative options – of all the potential destinations selected in stage 2, which of these is going to meet the desired needs of the individual; different levels of importance will be placed on different attributes.
4   The fourth stage sees the individual choosing specific products and services, although this may be tempered by family arrangements and unexpected situations such as increased prices or loss of income.
5   The final stage of the process is post-purchase behaviour – having purchased the product the individual may feel satisfied or dissatisfied, which then relates to the individual's expectations and whether or not these have been met.

Page and Connell (2009) suggest that factors influencing purchase decisions include the situation where the decision is made, the point of purchase information, previous experience, personal preferences, the specialist or routine nature of the purchase, the influence of the salesperson and individual personality.

The individual as a decision-maker is influenced by the society (the interrelationships that connect them, such as place of living, religious beliefs, etc.) to which they belong; this, in turn, creates their cultural backgrounds, which are the determinants of basic behaviours. It is important to recognize that society and culture defines the beliefs and values that are important to an individual. It also dictates food, clothing and art and, therefore, how people choose to travel.

Demographic factors also play a part in determining travel decision-making. Age, gender and social class all influence consumer behaviour, and people in the same age group or social class tend to exhibit similar behaviour, tastes and preferences. In addition, some personal factors also play a part in the decision-making process – these include lifecycle, occupation, level of income, lifestyle and personality. It is important to refer to the **Marketing for tourism** entry to see how this data is used by marketers to identify and design products and services that cater for certain consumer segments.

Various theories and concepts have been developed to explain motivation, giving consideration to societal and individual influences. The key theories are explained as follows.

Anomie enhancement

In this model, Dann (1977) argues that both social and psychological factors influence motivation, suggesting that the individual is in a state of anomie within his society and daily environment, and it is the act of travelling that allows the individual to achieve a state of ego-enhancement. Dann's model assumes that escape is socially determined.

Escape-seeking

This theory, proposed by Iso-Ahola (1982), explains motivation as a combination of escaping (the norm) and seeking (a desired need), which act simultaneously. The theory also suggests that decision-making is comprised of a personal (psychological) component and a social (inter-personal) component, and as a result proposes four dimensions for motivation: personal seeking; personal escape; interpersonal seeking; interpersonal escape. This theory suggests that the need for escape is driven by psychological factors.

Seven psychological motives

Crompton (1979) suggests that there are seven psychological (or push) motives, which include: escape from a perceived mundane environment; exploration and evaluation of self; relaxation; prestige; regression; enhancement of kinship relationships; facilitation of social interaction. There are also two cultural (pull) motives: novelty and education.

Push–pull factors

This model is a central idea of tourist motivation and is heavily underpinned by the work of Dann (1977) and Iso-Ahola (1982). The pull factors are those which are specific to the destination and that allow the destination to attract or 'pull' someone to visit. The push factors are those which drive the internal motivations to seek change and new experiences because of a need to get away from everyday routine.

Although this theory is easily applicable, there are some problems in identifying which factor has more influence on the decision or which factor comes into play first. Generally, it is the push factors that lead to the decision; but the pull factors can play an equally important role in influencing the final decision.

Maslow's Hierarchy of Needs

The hierarchy of needs is probably the most recognized framework for explaining motivation, but it must be understood in the correct context, as it was developed for employee motivation rather than tourist behaviour. Maslow (1943) identifies five different needs, starting with basic needs, which must be fulfilled before the subsequent levels are achieved:

1 physiological (thirst, hunger, sleep and sex);
2 safety (security, stability, protection);
3 social (love, affection, belongingness, interpersonal relationships);
4 esteem (self-esteem, self-respect, prestige, status);
5 self-actualization (growth, advancement, creativity).

When it is applied to tourism the model may explain some specific motivations – for example, individuals may travel to meet new friends, others may travel because of the prestige of a destination, others to enhance and develop their skills. However, these motivations are not necessarily ranked in the order suggested by Maslow and may be individual factors, thus limiting the applicability of Maslow to tourist behaviour.

Travel Career Ladder

This model from Pearce (1988) is based upon Maslow, but takes the model and explains it as a ladder, where the traveller climbs each of the different rungs, starting at the bottom (rung 1) and progressing to the top (rung 5):

1 relaxation needs;
2 stimulation needs;
3 relationship needs;
4 self-esteem/development;
5 fulfilment.

Tourists are not considered to have only one level of need; instead, one set of needs in the ladder acts as the most dominant one, and it may be self-directed (such as relaxation) or directed at others (such as opportunities to meet new people and make new friends). The ladder also explains usefully how individuals may stay at one level, or may progress up the ladder, motivated by changes in lifestyle or life stage. This may be exemplified by a person taking their first overseas holiday and seeking a safe environment, but recognizing that once they are confident travellers they may start to explore and seek different requirements on the ladder. Criticisms of this model tend to focus on the fact that the model is a continuum that does not prioritize different factors, recognize how a traveller may change while they are on holiday or consider that different holidays may be taken for different purposes by the same individual (to amuse children on one holiday and to take part in adventure tourism for another holiday).

Motivation by purpose

Travel motivators can also be explained in relation to the purpose of the holiday taken. McIntosh et al (1990) proposed five categories of motivations which reflect the ideas of Maslow's hierarchy (see Table 8).

Table 8 Travel motivation

Travel motivator	Explanation
Physical	Physical motivators indicate the need for physical activities. This can be either the need for rest, relaxation and simple things such as getting a suntan or for active participation in exercise and health-related activities – any activity motivated by the desire for reducing tension or refreshing the body while on holiday.
Emotional	Emotional motivators indicate the influence of emotions on travel behaviour, and could include travelling activities related to romance, adventure, spirituality, escapism or nostalgia.

Table 8 (continued)

Travel motivator	Explanation
Cultural	Cultural motivators indicate the need or desire to explore and learn about the destination, its culture, its heritage, or to generally expand one's horizon and knowledge through travelling to new places.
Interpersonal	Interpersonal motivators indicate the need for maintaining existing relationships or developing new relationships. This includes visits to family, friends and relatives, or the holiday is taken in order to meet new people.
Status and prestige	Travelling is motivated by the desire to enhance one's status, receiving attention and appreciation from others, but can also include travelling for the purpose of personal development (e.g. increasing knowledge or learning new skills).

Source: McIntosh et al (1990)

The notion of motivation is important in all aspects of tourism studies, but it is crucial that it is understood in the context of different types of tourism and alongside **consumer behaviour.**

Further reading

Hall, C. (2005) *Tourism: Rethinking the Social Science of Mobility*, Pearson Education, Harlow

Heitmann, S. (2011) 'Authenticity in tourism', in P. Robinson, S. Heitmann and P. Dieke (eds) *Research Themes for Tourism*, CABI, Wallingford, UK

Kotler, P., Bowen, J. and Makens, J. (2010) *Marketing for Tourism and Hospitality*, fifth edition, Prentice Hall, New York, NY

Page, S. and Connell, J. (2009) *Tourism: A Modern Synthesis*, Cengage Learning, Hampshire

Ryan, C. (2002) *The Tourist Experience*, Continuum, London

Peter Robinson

MULTIPLIER AND LEAKAGE

Tourism can have significant economic impacts upon a destination, including the generation of incomes and creation of jobs. An injection of spending by tourists into a destination will bring about various indirect and induced impacts, the total equating to some multiple of the original injection of spending. This multiple is known as the 'tourism multiplier' for that destination.

A tourism multiplier can be calculated for an entire economy or for a specific destination. It is defined as the ratio of direct to indirect (and sometimes induced) economic impacts of an increase of tourist spending. Direct impacts result from the expenditure of money by tourists on food and drink, accommodation, souvenirs, recreation equipment, car parking, admission fees and other purchases. This represents direct revenue for the organizations involved in the transactions. A proportion of this direct revenue will, of course, be needed to pay for supplies. Once these have been paid for, any revenue that remains will be direct income for the organization, which will be distributed as wages, salaries and profits. Direct employment relates to the number of jobs directly supported by this direct expenditure.

The overall impact of additional expenditure in the destination economy is not, however, limited to these direct impacts. Some of the supplies will be purchased from other businesses within the local area, keeping the money within the local economy. These are known as indirect impacts and take the form of indirect incomes and indirect employment. Spending on supplies from outside the destination economy, meanwhile, is known as leakage. The third type of impact, known as induced impacts, arises from the re-spending of wages, salaries and profits earned directly or indirectly as a result of the initial increase in expenditure. As residents of the specified destination economy earn income from their involvement in tourism, they will also spend a proportion of this additional money in the local area. The incomes created in this way are known as induced incomes and the jobs associated with such spending are known as induced employment.

The total impact of an increase in spending is thus the sum of the direct, indirect and induced impacts, while the overall increase in employment is the sum of the direct, indirect and induced employment impacts. Additional expenditure by persons engaged in leisure and tourism therefore has a 'ripple' effect in the local economy, with the final impact being a multiple of the initial injection of expenditure. This is caused by the recirculation of money around the destination economy and is known as the multiplier effect. The size of the multiplier effect is determined to a significant extent by the propensity of money to be retained in the destination. Thus, the size of the multiplier is closely associated with rate of leakage from the local economy; each one is determined by the other.

Multiplier analysis identifies a single multiplier coefficient which specifies how large the overall impact of income or employment will be in comparison to the initial injection of expenditure. Extreme care is, however, needed in interpreting multiplier coefficients, as there are a number of different versions in common use. First, there are three major varieties of multiplier: income, output and employment. The output multiplier measures the effect of additional expenditure in the local economy upon the level of output of that economy. The income multiplier is the most commonly quoted of all multipliers and is usually regarded as the most important indicator of the impact of spending in a destination. It measures the relationship between an initial injection of expenditure and the increase in incomes in the local economy that are associated with this, including wages, salaries and profits. The employment multiplier, meanwhile, measures the increase in employment associated with a specified increase in initial expenditure, usually in terms of the number of full-time equivalent jobs associated with a specified amount of initial expenditure.

Second, there are two different formulations of each of these three major varieties of multiplier coefficient: ratio (conventional) multipliers and Keynesian (proportional) multipliers. Ratio multipliers relate the final impact of an increase in expenditure to the direct income that it creates. Consequently, ratio multipliers are always greater than one. They tend, however, to be of limited use to planners and policy-makers because the level of investment required to achieve a desired increase in final income is not readily discernible. Keynesian multipliers, on the other hand, relate the final impact directly to the amount of direct expenditure in question. This makes them easier to apply and to interpret. It is also a simple matter to compute the equivalent ratio multiplier from the Keynesian multiplier, while the reverse is not true. Keynesian multipliers may be less than, greater than or even equal to one.

Third, there are two types of each variety and formulation of multiplier, known as type I and type II multipliers. The former include only the direct and indirect impacts of the initial increase in spending, while the latter include not only the direct and indirect impacts but also the induced impacts.

The different formulations of the multiplier coefficient are summarized in Figure 3, along with a highly simplified worked example of each in the case of an income multiplier.

Thus, using either the Keynesian or ratio multiplier, an initial increase in expenditure of UK£100 on the part of tourists would be expected to result in an increase in direct incomes in the local economy of UK£40. This would then go on to be multiplied up so that an additional UK£60 of final income is added to the local economy using the type I multiplier, or UK£70 using the type II multiplier. The second of these totals is larger simply because it includes induced as well as direct and indirect incomes.

E = initial injection of expenditure (e.g. UK£100)
D = direct income (e.g. UK£40)
I = indirect income (e.g. UK£20)
N = induced income (e.g. UK£10)

Keynesian, type I	$\dfrac{D + I}{E}$	$\dfrac{40 + 20}{100}$	0.6
Keynesian, type I	$\dfrac{D + I + N}{E}$	$\dfrac{40 + 20 + 10}{100}$	0.7
Keynesian, type I	$\dfrac{D + I}{D}$	$\dfrac{40 + 20}{40}$	1.5
Keynesian, type I	$\dfrac{D + I + N}{D}$	$\dfrac{40 + 20 + 10}{40}$	1.75

Figure 3 Versions of the multiplier coefficient .

A further difficulty in interpreting multiplier coefficients is that their size depends ultimately upon the extent to which injections of expenditure are retained and re-spent in the destination economy concerned. Consequently, the more narrowly the economy is defined, the lower the multiplier will tend to be. This is because there is a greater propensity for expenditures to leak out of a more narrowly defined economic space. It also tends to be the case that more remote and more rural locations tend to have a higher multiplier effect, even after allowing for the above effect. This is because poor communications tend to reduce expenditure leakages from the specified economy. Islands, in particular, tend to have higher multiplier coefficients relative to mainland economies. On the other hand, the nature of modern mass tourism means that for many small island developing states (SIDS), the rate of leakage of income from the economy is relatively high. Many SIDS are forced to import consumer items from abroad, such as global brands of food and drink products, in order to satisfy more institutionalized tourists' tastes. This may be reinforced by tourists' expectations of luxury and having all of the home comforts while staying in a holiday destination. This has a depressing effect on the tourism multiplier, so that many SIDS economies support relatively low multiplier effects.

Multiplier analysis is widely used in assessing the economic impacts of tourism. Essentially, there are two approaches to developing estimates of multiplier coefficients. The first is through the collection of the primary data needed to establish the relevant coefficients of expenditure leakage from the economy in question. This approach tends, however, to be technically complex and data intensive. An alternative approach, which has been developed in the UK by the New Economics Foundation, is known as LM3 (Sacks, 2002). This is a much less data-intensive approach that uses surveys of local businesses and households to estimate the share of leakages from the economy during only the first three multiplier rounds. This limits the amount of data required to generate functional multiplier coefficients. Furthermore, it is argued that in most cases the majority of relevant spending and re-spending tends to takes place during first three multiplier rounds (Sacks, 2002). The second approach is to borrow coefficients from previous studies of similar economic activities. This tends to introduce a degree of subjectivity in the analysis, since the researcher must decide how applicable the coefficients derived from other studies are likely to be to the specific context at hand. Sometimes researchers choose to adapt these borrowed multiplier coefficients in order to make them more applicable to the activity and/or economy in question, which adds additional subjectivity to the process. As such, multiplier studies must always be interpreted with care.

Further reading

Archer, B. H. (1995) 'Importance of tourism for the economy of Bermuda', *Annals of Tourism Research*, vol 22, no 4, pp918–930

Archer, B. H. and Fletcher, J. (1996) 'The economic impact of tourism in the Seychelles', *Annals of Tourism Research*, vol 23, no 1, pp32–47

Fletcher, J. and Archer, B. H. (1991) 'The development and application of multiplier analysis', in C. P. Cooper and A. Lockwood (eds) *Progress in Tourism, Recreation and Hospitality Management: Volume 3*, Belhaven Press, London, pp28–47

Sacks, J. (2002) *The Money Trail: Measuring Your Impact on the Local Economy Using LM3*, New Economics Foundation and the Countryside Agency, London

Witt, S. F. (1987) 'Economic impact of tourism on Wales', *Tourism Management*, vol 8, no 4, pp306–316

Dr. Brian Garrod

NATURE TOURISM

In its broadest sense, nature in tourism involves experiencing natural places, typically through outdoor activities that are sustainable in terms of their impact upon the environment. These can range from active to passive and include everything from bushwalking and adventure tourism experiences to sightseeing, scenic driving, beach experiences and wildlife viewing.

The concept of nature-based tourism is broad and encompassing. It is therefore unsurprising that establishing an exact definition has proved to be both difficult and is a source of on-going debate among researchers (Tangeland and Aas, 2011). Despite this, particular elements are common among many of the definitions – namely, that learning, recreation and adventure take place in natural surroundings. Nature-based tourism is frequently used synonymously with other terms such as **sustainable tourism, green, rural, alternative, adventure** and **responsible tourism**. Lindberg (1991) argued that it is possible to define nature-based tourism in a number of ways, with the distinction between nature-based tourism and mass tourism being particularly important.

Those participating in nature-based tourism choose activities such as bird-watching, kayaking, and hiking, with the intent of getting in touch with nature, escaping the stresses of daily life, and seeing landscapes and wildlife. Other categories of nature-based tourism include 3S (sun, sand and sea) tourism, **adventure tourism, wildlife tourism**, extractive tourism (hunting and fishing) and some types of **health tourism** (Weaver, 2008). According to Vespestad and Lindberg (2010) nature-based experiences are debated within research around tourism motivation and consumer behaviour, referring to, for instance, the recreation experience preference (REP) scale, which is a psychometric scale measuring dimensions of people's recreation experience. Moreover, research on nature-based tourism often attends to wilderness, wildlife or ecotourism.

Nature-based tourism is distinguished from other tourism forms by its natural area setting which may allow for a variety of modes of engagement with the natural environment, including commercial outdoor recreational-based activities such as trekking, hiking, canoeing and climbing.

Properly planned and managed, nature tourism can have minimal impacts upon the environment, and can be a useful method to protect and enhance social and cultural values, as well as to contribute to the economic well-being of residents. Effective planning and development are essential for a community to benefit from nature-based tourism (see also **Community-based tourism**).

Reliable data on nature tourism is difficult to identify, partly because of the lack of consensus around definitions, and the myriad activities which could be included, although the few reliable estimates suggest that the scale of the economic impact of (and risks associated with) greater numbers of nature tourism is impressive. Nature tourism activities, even with proper management and government initiatives, can and do damage natural resources. The management objectives of nature tourism should focus on minimizing damage (see **Corporate social responsibility** and **Sustainable tourism**). Popular sites are often overused and degraded and, as a result, they can lose many ecological functions and amenities, including wildlife and their habitats, which are the very resources that created the destinations in the first place. Improper location and design of tourism developments have destroyed beaches and dunes, ruined scenic views and eroded fragile resources. Assessing and monitoring the impacts of nature tourism upon natural resources is an important responsibility for all stakeholders. Developing an attractive tourism economy that is part of a community's economic base requires careful planning and coordination among those who design, build, manage and market nature-based tourist attractions.

Further reading

Buckley, R., Pickering, C. and Weaver, D. B. (eds) (2003) *Nature-Based Tourism, Environment and Land Management*, CABI, Wallingford, UK

Hall, C. M. and Boyd, S. (eds) (2005) *Nature Based Tourism in Peripheral Areas: Development or Disaster?*, Channel View Publications, Clevedon, UK

Tangeland, T. and Aas, O. (2011) 'Household composition and the importance of experience attributes of nature based tourism activity products: A Norwegian case study of outdoor recreationists', *Tourism Management*, vol 32, pp822–832

Vespestad, M. K. and Lindberg, F. (2010) 'Understanding nature-based tourist experiences: An ontological analysis', *Current Issues in Tourism*, 10 September

Dr. Roselyne N. Okech

NEO-COLONIALISM

The term 'neo-colonialism' can only be ascribed to countries that were previously a part of an empire: British, Portuguese, Dutch or one of the several other conquering powers of the eighteenth and nineteenth centuries. Some of these countries were and remain developing countries in South Asia, Africa or South America; but it should be remembered that the US, Canada and Australia, too, were all once colonies!

According to Nkrumah (1969, pix), 'Neo-colonialism of today represents imperialism in its final and perhaps its most dangerous stage.' Writing over 40 years ago at a time when Great Britain had already led the Commonwealth for more than two decades, he saw that, in essence, nothing had really changed and that although many countries, previously the subject of international sovereignty, appeared independent, the reality was they were as dependent as ever. His concerns were that although countries became independent by name, they remained dependent by nature either to their former governing power or the capitalist economy with which they 'traded'. The economy of Senegal, for instance, is based upon the sale of phosphate mining, fertilizer production, groundnut oil and commercial fishing, all of which are exported.

Rhodesia was different than most other colonies and remains both an interesting and, yet, sad anomaly within Southern Africa. Now named Zimbabwe, in 1965 the local government in Rhodesia declared a 'unilateral declaration of independence' and broke away (without consent) from the British Commonwealth. It remains one of the most troubled and poorest, yet potentially rich, countries in Africa.

Central to the concept of neo-colonialism is that of leakage. Much of the post-colonial investment around the world has been made by private organizations and multinational countries that have their headquarters in their home country. While profits generated provide for local employment, the hard fact remains that much of the money never reaches the country at all.

Today, neo-colonialism in tourism describes the dependence that developing countries place upon leisure visitors from the developed world. They may, but not exclusively, be from the country that once ruled them from a distance. For instance, Tanzania, once a colony of Germany (until 1919), historically receives more arrivals from other generating areas than from the ex-mother nation. Moreover, it is likely that the motivation for visiting is more complex and varied. The country may attract those seeking a shared heritage experience, perhaps architectural style or historical links, while other visitors will be attracted by the heat, wildlife or both!

The precursor of neo-colonialism, however, is the unhealthy overreliance upon developed nations for their livelihood, where the country does not have a balanced economy. Originally Kenya was claimed over 500 years ago by Vasco da Gama of Portugal for its location as a naval base for the trade routes to the East. Subsequently, settlers arrived and built up a demand for ivory and big game hunting. Happily, today visitors shoot film rather than guns. But although, on the face of it, Kenya continues to generate much wealth, it can correctly be described as operating as a neo-colonial state: without tourism, the economy would collapse – as it did following the bombing of the Paradise Hotel in 2002.

Further reading

Hall, C. M. and Tucker, H. (2004) *Tourism and Post-Colonialism*, Routledge, Abingdon, Oxon, UK

Lozanski, K. (2007) *Violence in Independent Travel to India: Unpacking Patriarchy and Neo-Colonialism, Tourist Studies*, Sage, London

Manyara, G. and Jones, E. (2007) 'Community-based tourism enterprises development in Kenya: An exploration of their potential as avenues of poverty reduction', *Journal of Sustainable Tourism*, vol 15, no 6, pp628–644

Zavala, I. (2000) 'The retroaction of the postcolonial: The answer of the real and the Caribbean as thing: An essay on critical fiction', *Interventions*, vol 2, no 3, pp364–378

Geoff Shirt

NICHE TOURISM

Niche tourism is, to all intents and purposes, a typological framework in which a relatively small market segment can be identified. Defined as 'special interests, culture and/or activity based tourism involving small number of tourists in authentic settings' (Novelli, 2005, p9), the principal aim of niche tourism is to subdivide broader tourism markets into manageable and targetable areas. In turn, niche tourism offers a pragmatic framework in which destinations, sites and attractions can be marketed, promoted and, ultimately, consumed as a tourist experience. Arguably, the concept of 'niche tourism' has emerged in recent years as a counterpoint to traditional 'mass tourism' and the often negative connotations that mass tourism can bring to environmental and sociocultural degradation. In an age of globalization and its resultant homogeneity within tourism destinations and tourist experiences, niche tourism represents, potentially, a certain amount of diversity and differentiation. Subsequently, niche tourism implies a more sophisticated set of practices and values that distinguish niche tourists from their mass tourist counterparts. Often used interchangeably with the term **special interest tourism** (which focuses upon tourist demand and tourist activities), niche tourism focuses on the supply of tourism markets. However, given the diverse nature of niche tourism products, different general approaches may be utilized to identify markets:

- *A geographical and demographical approach:* the location and people involved in both the production and consumption of tourism, whether in urban, rural, coastal or alpine environments, and the specific activities that tourists are engaged in.

- *A product-related approach:* the emphasis on facilities, including the presence of tourist activities, hospitality provision, attractions and other amenities, which are influenced by tourists' needs, wants and desires.
- *A customer-related approach:* the emphasis on tourist requirements and expectations that focus upon value and quality, and which are delivered through a marketing orientation.

Niche tourism is largely borrowed from the term 'niche marketing', where, first, there is a place in the market for a specific product and, second, there is a specific market for a product. In other words, the clear premise of niche tourism is that the market is not viewed as a simple homogenous collective mass with general needs but, rather, as specific sets of individuals with certain needs relating to the qualities and features of a particular product. Consequently, niche tourism may be further divided and segmented into 'macro-' and 'micro-' niches. At the one end of the niche tourism spectrum, relatively large market sectors or *macro-niches* (e.g. urban tourism, rural tourism, environmental tourism, etc.) are capable of additional segmentation into *micro-niches* (e.g. business tourism, farm tourism, adventure tourism, etc.). At the other end of the niche tourism spectrum, tourism is focused on very precise activities and small markets that, in turn, make it difficult to segment further. Table 9 illustrates niche tourism components, although these are neither exclusive nor exhaustive.

Table 9 Examples of niche tourism components

Macro-niches	Micro-niches (examples)
Culture and heritage	Religious/pilgrimages Educational/research Genealogy Industrial heritage/sites of historical 'significance' Art/literary/movies/'celebrity'-inspired sites Dark tourism/dark heritage (e.g. slavery heritage sites/ memorial museums and exhibitions/sites or shrines of death, disaster, murder or atrocity/prisons/battlefields/ cemeteries and sites of internment)
Environmental	Nature and wildlife Ecotourism/slow travel/transport tourism Adventure Alpine Geotourism Space tourism Coastal tourism

Table 9 (continued)

Macro-niches	*Micro-niches (examples)*
Rural	Farm tourism Camping/caravanning Gastronomy tourism/food festivals Agricultural shows Music events Sport Arts and crafts Photography/painting
Urban	Business tourism/MICE tourism (meetings, incentives, conferences and exhibitions) Music Sport Volunteering Medical tourism Art/galleries/special events/museums

Further reading

Lew, A. A. (2008) 'Long tail tourism: New geographies for marketing niche tourism products', *Journal of Travel and Tourism Marketing*, vol 25, no 3–4, pp409–419

Macleod, D. V. L. (2003) 'Culture and the construction of a niche market destination', in D. V. L. Macleod (ed) *Niche Tourism in Question*, University of Glasgow Chrichton Publications, Dumfries, Scotland, pp30–44

Novelli, M. (ed) (2005) *Niche Tourism: Contemporary Issues, Trends and Cases*, Elsevier, Oxford, UK

Sharpley, R. and Telfer, D. J. (2002) *Tourism and Development: Concepts and Issues*, Channel View Publications, Clevedon, UK

Dr. Philip R. Stone

OPERATIONS MANAGEMENT

Operations management in a tourism context has emerged from the principles of operations management within manufacturing and provides a model which explains the processes in an organization and the way in which they interrelate and impact upon each other. The use of the model enables managers to understand how changes to one aspect of a business, such as increasing capacity, may have a positive or negative impact upon other aspects, such as revenue management and quality management. It also provides systems for monitoring and measuring operational activities, and identifying and solving problems within an organization.

Operations management, in its simplest explanation, describes the way in which inputs into the business (people, money, information and assets) are transformed (through capacity management, quality management, revenue management, etc.) into a single output, which, for the service sector, has to be satisfied customers. This is illustrated in Figure 4; but it is useful, first, to provide some further definitions of operations management.

Needle (2000, p296) suggests that operations management can be explained as 'concerned with the transformation of a variety of inputs such as information, people, material, finance and methods into a variety of outputs such as goods, services, profit, customer and employee satisfaction ... the centrality of the function means that operations has a significant influence on costs and revenue as well as organizational structure' (cited in Clark and Johnston, 2000). Swarbrooke (2002, p239) explains that 'it is about marshalling the attractions resources, notably the staff and physical equipment such as machinery, to provide a satisfactory service for the customer, and an acceptable rate of

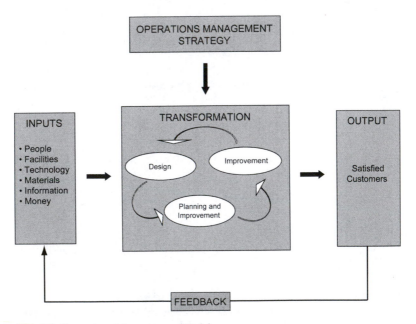

Figure 4 Operations Management Model

return on the use of these resources ... the goal ... is the smooth and efficient operation of the site.

Operational activities are governed by operational strategies, which provide an evaluation of the external operating environment, through PEST (political, economic, sociocultural and technological factors) and SWOT (strengths, weaknesses, opportunities, threats) analyses, and tend to focus on particular short-term goals such as enhancing customer service, improving quality or developing new products.

There are a number of specific tasks and concepts associated with operations management. These are defined as follows.

Capacity Management

Capacity describes the maximum number of people whom the organization can process at any one time. It may be defined by safety limits (inside building), licensing requirements (outdoor events) or carrying capacity (the ideal maximum in a rural environment). Tourism provides an interesting study in capacity management because there are some very predictable aspects of capacity planning (seasonality, holiday periods) and some extremely unpredictable considerations (poor weather, public mourning), which can variously increase or decrease visitor numbers, or entirely change the types of visitors and therefore determines the type of activities that may be required on any particular day.

Crisis Management

This is the point when a risk becomes a reality. A crisis could be financial, environmental, internal or external to a business, and requires very careful management. A crisis is the point when stability and order becomes chaos, and it is often the aftermath of the crisis rather than the relatively short period of a crisis that must be managed effectively as they are longer term. The management of a crisis depends upon the initial response, the clarity of leadership, the effectiveness of communication and the speed with which information is disseminated. It also relies upon an effective planning process in preparation for a crisis – usually referred to as a contingency plan; this document sets out the procedures for a host of potential crisis scenarios.

Demand Management

Demand defines the quantity of a product or service that consumers want and the level they are willing to pay for it. It does not always translate into real visitor numbers and not everyone will want to pay the price.

Design

Design is an essential element of operations management, defining the way in which processes, systems, facilities, products and jobs operate in order to achieve organizational objectives around customer satisfaction and experience.

Facilities Management

Facilities management describes the control of the physical assets of an organization, both those on public view and those behind the scenes. In a tourism context, such management can range from relatively simple groups of tasks to very complex management requirements.

Forecasting

Forecasting provides managers with techniques for long-term planning based upon qualitative and quantitative methods, which can vary from consultation with experts (the Delphi Technique) to extrapolation of previous years' visitor figures.

Productivity

Productivity describes the ratio of inputs to outputs. The lower the input and the higher the output, the greater the productivity, although there is a balance required to ensure sensitivity to the management of quality, queues and customer service. This makes productivity a very good measure of the health of an organization because profitability offers no measure of the effectiveness of the processes that led to the profit or, indeed, if the profit hides a wasteful transformation process.

Project Management

Project management defines the coordination of a variety of tasks, which may run concurrently or may be sequential, and which need managing from the start to the completion of a project, while managing financial and human resources alongside the project. Projects are often managed using Gantt charts and Critical Path Analysis.

Queue Management

Related to capacity management is the management of queues, and what has become known as 'queuing theory', which states that people may choose to leave a queue or to not join it if it seems too long. There are management solutions to this problem, including queue time signage, activities and entertainment as a distraction or fast-track ticketing.

Revenue Management

This term explains the management of income generation within an organization, and focuses on the development of revenue based upon factors such as demand and capacity management.

Service quality

The management of quality is important in tourism – as consumers are purchasing an experience, the measure of their enjoyment is based on their own previous experiences and the expectations that are created through marketing activities.

Yield Management

This is a revenue maximization technique which offers more sophisticated assessments of income-generation opportunities by increasing net yield based upon available capacity, offering discounts, developing secondary spend and identifying opportunities to increase capacity.

Further reading

Burke, R. (2006) *Project Management: Planning and Control Techniques*, Wiley and Sons, Chichester, UK

Greasley, A. (2006) *Operations Management*, Wiley and Sons, Chichester, UK

Heizer, J. and Render, B. (2006) *Principles of Operations Management*, sixth edition, Prentice Hall, New Jersey

Hill, T. (2005) *Operations Management*, second edition, Palgrave Macmillan, Basingstoke, UK

Pender, L. and Sharpley, R. (eds) (2005) *The Management of Tourism*, Sage Publications, London

Slack, N., Chamber, S. and Johnston, R. (2007) *Operations Management*, fifth edition, Prentice Hall, Harlow

Peter Robinson

PLANNING FOR TOURISM

Prior to mass tourism development in the mid-twentieth century, planning for tourism tended to be site specific. Individual hotels/resorts were built, access to the area was improved, and a tourism promotional campaign was conducted (Inskeep, 1991). In the post-World War II period, researchers point out that the rapid growth of the global tourism industry has increased the complexity of tourism planning, resulting in the need for concerted multiple actions, participants, fields of knowledge, levels of decision and implementation (Branch, 1985; Gunn, 1994; Hall, 2000).

Tourism planning is a socio-political process of deciding where decisions are prepared for action in the future (Chadwick, 1971, p24; Dror, 1973, p330; Veal, 1992). This process can occur at a number of scales (e.g. international, national, regional, community or site levels). Through the planning process, goals are set and policies are elaborated for implementation, with the participation of key interest groups and individuals from the public and/or private sectors (Dror, 1973, p330; Hall, 2000). The process traditionally follows a systematic, phased approach, incorporating problem identification, goals and objectives, an inventory of primary and secondary information, analysis, plan creation, recommendations, implementation, monitoring and evaluation (Cooper et al, 2005).

The aims of tourism planning are to anticipate and regulate change in the **tourism system** to promote orderly development in order to increase the social, economic and environmental benefits (Murphy, 1985, p156). Planning for tourism also provides opportunities for tourists to have enjoyable, satisfying experiences and to improve the way of life for residents and destinations. In addition, the process shapes and controls physical patterns of development, conserves resources, provides a framework for promoting destinations, and provides a process for integrating tourism with other sectors (Mathieson and Wall, 1982; Gunn, 1994; Williams, 1998; Mason, 2008).

Researchers (Getz, 1987; Hall, 2000; Dredge and Jenkins, 2011) identify a number of tourism planning traditions that have developed with the advent of mass tourism (see Table 10). These traditions are not mutually exclusive or necessarily sequential, which demonstrates how any approach to tourism planning necessarily requires a mix of traditions in terms of their practical application (Getz, 1987; Hall, 2000; Dredge and Jenkins, 2011). As Dredge and Jenkins (2011, p14) state, each tradition offers something useful in the mix of knowledge, method, approaches and analytical tools.

Table 10 Tourism planning traditions

Tradition	Summary
Boosterism	Tourism development is inherently good. Focus on economic benefits to host community. Little attention is given to negative impacts.
Economic/industry oriented	Industry is used by governments to achieve economic growth and regional development. Public support occurs through incentives, research and marketing assistance.
Land use/physical/ spatial	A rational, scientific approach based on capacity of sites/ destinations to withstand tourism development. Tendency for destinations to evolve or decline in relation to the market demand and the quality of resources.
Community based	A bottom-up, systems approach emphasizes development *in* the community rather than development *of* the community. Tourism is based on local participation and capacities to satisfy the users, reward the owners and protect environmental resources.
Sustainable development	Provides secure livelihoods that minimize resource depletion/degradation, cultural disruption and social instability. Managing impacts takes precedence over market economics. Local control of resources and long-term commitment to sustainability.
Normative/ prescriptive	Provides guidance on the content of policy for developing and managing tourism.
Predictive	Makes predictions about possible causes of various policy actions on tourism.
Procedural	Provides advice on how to plan and manage tourism.
Descriptive/ explanatory	Seeks to understand and develop knowledge about how policy is made and outcomes occur.
Evaluative	Evaluates the dimensions of policy, including content, delivery, process, outcomes and impacts.

This complexity in terms of the practical application of planning traditions also indicates the way in which planning for tourism is affected by multiple stakeholders' interests. These interests can reflect personal and group values, ideology or perceived benefits (Gunn, 1994; Hall, 2000; Dredge and Jenkins, 2007). Tourism planning's origins and drivers are influenced by the thoughts, ideas, actions and collaborations of a diverse set of actors, agencies and institutions representing government, business and community (Veal, 1992; Coccossis, 1996; Dredge and Jenkins, 2011). Current research trends in planning for tourism (Dredge and Jenkins, 2011, p2) reflect the:

- increasing interest in a critical, social constructionist approach to address why tourism planning happens (Dredge and Jenkins, 2007; Stevenson et al, 2008);
- integration of concepts from other disciplines (e.g. geography and sociology) to explain planning processes and the complexity of planning systems (Tribe, 2004); and
- increasing knowledge from reflective practice and attention to ethics and values that is stimulating critical, interpretive theoretical development (Tribe, 2002; Jamal, 2004).

Planning requires not only an understanding of the demands and needs of various stakeholders and interests, but also understanding the changing values and needs of community and society, and the broader socio-economic–environmental context within which planning occurs. Recent success points to the adoption of networks, innovation and new models of governance.

Further reading

Dredge, D. and Jenkins, J. (eds) (2011) *Stories of Practice: Tourism Policy and Planning*, Ashgate, Surrey, UK

Getz, D. (1987) 'Tourism planning and research: Traditions, models and futures', Paper presented at the Australian Travel Research Workshop, Bunbury, Western Australia, 5–6 November 1987

Gunn, C. (1994) *Tourism Planning*, third edition, Taylor and Francis, New York, NY

Hall, C. M. (2000) *Tourism Planning, Policies, Processes and Relationships*, Prentice Hall, Harlow

Inskeep, E. (1991) *Tourism Planning: An Integrated and Sustainable Development Approach*, John Wiley and Sons, New York, NY

Dr. John S. Hull

PRO-POOR TOURISM

Pro-poor tourism, or PPT, describes an approach to tourism development and management, primarily in developing countries. Ashley et al (2001) explain that 'PPT strategies aim to unlock opportunities – for economic gain, other livelihood benefits, or engagement in decision-making – for the poor'. They also note that 'Certain characteristics of tourism enhance its pro-poor potential. It can be: labour intensive; inclusive of women and the informal sector; based on natural and cultural assets of the poor; and suitable for poor areas. Harnessing tourism for pro-poor growth means capitalising on these features, while reducing negative impacts on the poor. Potential for *change* stems from the continued "master planning" role of governments, and strong commercial and international interest in sustainable tourism.'

As a result of this philosophy, PPT lends itself to being a useful development strategy, and both Ashley et al (2001) and Hall (2007b) provide a series of examples that prove the benefits of PPT. It enables poorer communities to participate in the development of tourism products, and the benefits include:

- increased opportunities for local employment;
- increased opportunities for local entrepreneurship;
- development of shared community income;
- development of new products;
- opportunities for training;
- enhanced capacity for tourism;
- management of (sometimes fragile) resources;
- net socio-cultural benefits;
- improved infrastructure and services, and better community access to these;
- supportive policy development;
- improved communication between the private sector and local communities;
- development of mechanisms for consultation;
- full stakeholder involvement in tourism management;
- addressing supply and demand issues;
- non-financial benefits such as better health and crime reduction.

The Pro-Poor Tourism Partnership is a collaborative research initiative between the International Centre for Responsible Tourism (ICRT), the International Institute for Environment and Development (IIED) and the Overseas Development Institute (ODI). It seeks to support PPT through research, strategy development and raising awareness of PPT and its various benefits. The Pro-Poor Tourism Partnership notes that 'any type of company can be involved in Pro-Poor Tourism – a small lodge, an urban hotel, a tour operator, an infrastructure developer. The critical factor is not the type of company or the type of tourism, but that an increase in the net benefits that go to poor people can be demonstrated.'

Further reading

Hall, C. M. (2007b) *Pro-Poor Tourism: Who Benefits? Perspectives on Tourism and Poverty Reduction*, Channel View Publications, Bristol, UK
Pro-Poor Tourism Partnership (2011) *www.propoortourism.org.uk*

Peter Robinson

PUBLIC SECTOR

The public sector, whether operating at national, regional or local level, can be defined as that part of the economy in which production is undertaken on behalf of the government, usually by state-owned agencies and organizations, for the benefit of its citizens. It thereby contrasts with the private sector, which is that part of the economy where the means of production are normally owned by commercial organizations, and the voluntary (or 'third') sector of the economy, in which production activities are undertaken solely by non-governmental and not-for-profit organizations. The boundaries between these three sectors of the economy are, however, becoming more blurred in contemporary society, especially in the context of tourism, where collaboration between organizations working in all three sectors is increasingly common. Tourism destination marketing strategies, for example, are increasingly being delivered by public–private partnerships (PPPs), which tend to comprise organizations from all three sectors of the economy.

The size and scope of the public sector varies according to the economic system adopted by the citizens of the country in question. This, in turn, tends to determine the remit that the public sector has in regulating, organizing and directly producing those goods and services that are relevant to the tourism industry. States that operate under broadly socialist economic systems, such as the People's Republic of China, tend to favour large public sectors, comprising state organizations with extensive scope and powers to shape the economy. They also tend to favour state ownership of the means of production. Such states often intervene heavily in tourism – for example, by implementing strategic plans for the development of tourism. Many operate state airlines, tourism resorts, accommodation, leisure centres, tour operation companies and even state travel agencies. Some socialist countries undertake to provide holidays either for the disadvantaged in their society, who cannot easily afford a holiday or are otherwise prevented from taking them due to their family circumstances – a phenomenon sometimes known as social tourism – or for those whom the state wishes to reward.

States with broadly libertarian economic systems, such as the US, tend to favour a relatively small public sector with limited scope and power to influence the way in which the economy operates. This view is based on the belief that free markets are the most efficient allocators of resources among competing economic uses, so the role of the state should be restricted to those circumstances in which the price mechanism is deemed to fail. The role of the public sector in tourism in such countries tends therefore to be greatly circumscribed, with government intervention being limited to ensuring that the necessary conditions exist for tourism to thrive under the direction of market forces.

Many states do, of course, operate between these two economic systems, taking a middle path that adopts characteristics of both. States with broadly liberal or social-democratic economic systems therefore tend to intervene more heavily in some areas and aspects of the economy than others. The remit of the public sector in tourism also tends to depend on the perceived economic or political importance of tourism in that country. Where tourism is a major component of the national economy, or where it has been identified as a major vehicle of economic development, governments will tend to intervene more widely and more intensively. Many countries, for example, have established separate tourism ministries within their governments. Most have also established a National Tourism Organization (NTO), often with a network of regional tourism organizations operating beneath it.

Many NTOs will, however, be technically independent from the state, having their own constitution and a board of directors appointed from outside government. Their usual purpose is, nevertheless, to implement government policy on tourism matters and to allocate public money for specific purposes among organizations operating in its tourism industry. Most NTOs have both a marketing function and a development function. Their marketing function is first to develop the government's tourism marketing strategy and then to implement it. The latter may take the form of:

- maintaining a website, often with a web portal through which to channel potential tourists to appropriate tourism destinations, tour . operators, accommodation providers and other tourism businesses;

- developing and maintaining a destination brand image for the country;
- running promotional activities for the country as a tourism destination, such as television advertising campaigns;
- licensing and grading hotels and other establishments, thereby helping tourists to make informed choices when coming to visit the country;
- maintaining a network of tourism offices in key tourist-origin markets;
- promoting national festivals and events;
- providing certain tourism facilities, such as tourist information centres (TICs); although these are often the responsibility of organizations operating at the regional or local level, the NTO may manage TICs at major transport hubs and destination gateways.

Many governments do not actively promote domestic tourism, so the NTO will sometimes not cover this market sector. In contrast, NTOs often have a specialist division to market to the business tourism sector. Increasingly, NTOs worldwide are carrying out their marketing function in collaboration with tourism organizations operating in the private and voluntary sectors of the economy.

The development function of NTOs, meanwhile, encompasses at the very least a role in coordinating the development of the tourism industry. This often equates to a strategic planning function, the purpose being to ensure that tourism activities are developed in appropriate combinations in the locations where they are needed. The NTO may also be charged with aligning the spatial and sectoral development of tourism with the regeneration strategy of the country as a whole. Given the complex and fragmented nature of the tourism industry, it is normally the role of the NTO to promote and coordinate activities from which the sector as a whole would stand to benefit. The NTO may thus be involved in providing training schemes and activities intended to help develop the tourism workforce. These kinds of activity may well be undertaken in collaboration with the private and voluntary sectors.

Visit Wales is a good example of an NTO. Formerly known as the Wales Tourist Board (WTB), Visit Wales is now part of the National Assembly for Wales (the devolved regional government) and sits in the Department of Heritage. Visit Wales's primary role is to develop national tourism policy, encourage investment in the tourism industry of Wales and market Wales as a tourism destination both domestically and overseas. The latter marks a change from the remit of the WTB, which was primarily to market Wales to the rest of the UK, the responsibility falling to Visit Britain to market Wales, along with the other constituent countries of the UK (England, Scotland and Northern Ireland), to overseas markets. The mission of Visit Wales is to 'maximise tourism's contribution to the economic, social and cultural prosperity of Wales' (Welsh Assembly Government, 2011, p1).

Beneath the level of the NTO, there are usually regional or destination-area tourist boards. In the case of Wales, there are four Regional Tourism Partnerships (RTPs): Tourism Partnership Mid Wales, Tourism Partnership North Wales, South West Wales Tourism Partnership and Capital Region Tourism. Visit Wales devolves part of its funds to the RTPs to fund their work, which is to implement regional tourism strategies consistent with those developed at the national level by Visit Wales. The RTPs in Wales seek to add a regional dimension to the way in which strategy is implemented, helping to enhance the competitiveness of tourism in the regions, thereby enabling them to make a greater contribution to the well-being of the people of Wales as a whole. To do this, they work in partnership with Visit Wales, local authorities and local tourism organizations to undertake marketing and business-support activities.

There are a number of reasons why a government – whether at the national, regional or local level – might deem it desirable to intervene in the tourism industry, including:

- *Contributing to wider government objectives.* For example, the government may wish to use tourism as a 'growth-pole' strategy in an attempt to assist an area of the country that is deemed to be in need of further development or regeneration.
- *Coordinating the development of tourism.* Because of the complex and fragmented nature of tourism, it can be argued that only governments have the authority and position to coordinate tourism development.
- *Correcting market failures.* This could involve introducing policies to protect the natural environment from the negative impacts of tourism or the regulation of health and safety standards in the construction of hotels and holiday resorts.
- *Directly producing 'public goods'.* These would not be produced by the free market. Examples include highways and street lighting, which are infrastructural prerequisites to the development of tourism resorts.
- *Producing or subsidizing merit goods.* These will be under-produced by the free market. As such, it is often considered necessary for the government to intervene in order to enhance provision. Examples

include leisure centres and museums, both of which can serve as important tourist attractions.

- *Resolving conflict.* Because of the many stakeholders involved in tourism there is a strong potential for conflicting interests to arise. For example, conflicts between residents and tourism interests can easily arise in a city destination. When these prove difficult to resolve, it may be deemed appropriate for the government to step in to mediate a solution.

States are also involved at the supranational level through their membership of various intergovernmental organizations and multinational agencies. Prominent among these is the United Nations World Tourism Organization (UNWTO), which came into being as the World Tourism Organization in 1974 (the UN prefix was added in 2005). As a specialized agency of the United Nations, the remit of the UNWTO is to serve as the lead international organization in the field of tourism. As such, it aims to serve the world community 'as a global forum for tourism policy issues and a practical source of tourism know-how' (UNWTO, 2011a, p1). As of 2011, membership of the UNWTO comprised 154 countries, 7 territories and more than 400 affiliate members, the latter representing the interests of the private sector, educational institutions, tourism associations and local tourism authorities. The inclusion of these affiliate members sets UNWTO apart from the other UN specialized agencies.

Other tourism organizations at the supranational level include the International Air Transport Association (IATA) and the International Civil Aviation Organization (ICAO). There are also a number of important regional bodies with a tourism remit, such as the Pacific Asia Travel Association (PATA) and the European Travel Commission (ETC).

Further reading

Cooper, C., Fletcher, J., Fyall, A., Gilbert, D. and Wanhill, S. (2008b) *Tourism: Principles and Practice*, 4th edition, Pearson Education Limited, Essex, UK

Page, S. J. (2007) *Tourism Management: Managing for Change*, second edition, Butterworth-Heinemann, Oxford and Burlington

Dr. Brian Garrod

RECREATION

Recreation is considered to be the activities that individuals carry out in their **leisure** time. It is, however, too simplistic to say that a definition of recreation is concerned only with activities. The term 'recreation' comes from the Latin word *recreatio*, meaning that which refreshes or restores (Youell, 1995, p4). According to McIntosh and Goeldner (1990, p10), recreation describes the action and activities of people engaging in constructive and personally pleasurable use of leisure time. Recreation may include passive or active participation in individual or group sports, cultural functions, the appreciation of natural and human history, non-formal education, travel for pleasure, sightseeing and entertainment.

Recreation opportunities and activities can be, and are, found in all the places and spaces in which people gather to play, enjoy and relax (O'Sullivan, 2006, p4). For example, local authority sport and leisure services provide many recreational opportunities, including (Robinson, 2004, p4):

- sport and physical recreation (playing fields, golf courses, etc.);
- informal recreation (open spaces, urban parks and gardens, etc.);
- countryside recreation (country parks, national parks, picnic sites, etc.);
- cultural services (concert halls, theatres, art galleries, etc.);
- tourism, conservation and heritage (information services, historic sites, nature reserves, etc.);
- education-related services (adult education, youth clubs);
- library services (branch and mobile libraries);
- entertainment, catering and conferences (public halls, pavilions, restaurants, bars, etc.);
- housing, community and social services (play centres, city farms, community centres, etc.).

Public-sector provision for leisure and recreation is primarily concerned with encouraging participation and maximizing the use of facilities, therefore providing a beneficial service to local and regional communities. Groups including the unemployed, disabled people, rural dwellers, ethnic minorities and women have been the focus of local, regional and national campaigns in an attempt to increase participation in leisure and recreation (Youell, 1995, p11). Mclean et al (2008) explain the social functions of community recreation as:

- enriching the quality of life;
- contributing to personal development;
- making the community a more attractive place in which to live and visit;
- preventing anti-social uses of free time;

- improving intergroup and intergenerational relations;
- strengthening neighbourhood and community ties;
- meeting the needs of special populations;
- maintaining economic health and community stability;
- enriching community cultural life;
- promoting personal health and safety.

Leitner et al (2004), Bell (2008) and Mclean et al (2008) evaluate recreation in modern society and emphasize that:

- Important factors that have promoted the growth of recreation and the park movement range from increasing discretionary time and growing affluence to increased interest in health and fitness and concerns about the natural environment.
- Increasing pollution of outdoor recreation resources caused by industrialization created a need for an organized movement to work for the conservation of these resources. The recreation movement was instrumental in the creation of national, state and municipal parks.
- The changing nature of the political, economic and social environment has forced park and recreation agencies to re-evaluate traditional approaches to delivering public parks and recreation. Many communities are utilizing the human services approach by serving all sectors of the population. Many of these communities and others are also building major recreation centres with membership fees and programmes catering to upscale populations.
- Outdoor recreation is the big growth area in leisure activities today. As the populations of more countries develop and become more urbanized, and as most people's work becomes less and less connected with soil, many more people are seeking to regain some kind of connection with nature and with wild landscapes, even if it is only for short periods at infrequent intervals. There are many reasons for visiting and exploring the outdoors: physical exercise, release from the stress of city life, fresh air, getting closer to nature, enjoyment of the scenery, hunting and fishing, walking the dog, an occasion to meet family and friends ... the list goes on.
- Children give gradually less of their time to playing outdoors, despite the positive effects of being exposed to the natural environment.
- Larger numbers of people are visiting rural areas. While recreational activities undertaken in rural areas are increasing and diversifying, raising issues of competing traditional/new, passive/active pursuits and the need for adequate planning and management to cope with contrasting demands from mass and niche requirements. Until

perhaps 30 years ago, most leisure activities in rural areas were related closely to the intrinsic environmental setting, and could be characterized as relaxing, relatively passive, perhaps nostalgia related, with forms of activity such as walking, picnicking, fishing and landscape photography. Many of these activities represented an escape from urban life into an environment of contrasting pace and setting where the physical and human elements were thought to blend in harmony. While such 'traditional' recreational practices are still widely pursued in rural areas, other activities have grown in appeal. These are generally more active, competitive, prestige or fashion related, perhaps technological, modern, individual and fast, such as survival games, off-road motor vehicle driving and hang-gliding.

- The baby boomers are beginning to retire and have a major impact upon parks and recreation facilities. They have more discretionary income than ever before and are willing to spend it on experiences, through participation in programmes, health and fitness, and adventure recreation.

- Sport is increasing its influence and importance in the local, national and international arena. Youth sports are taking on the forms and actions of professional sports, frequently to the detriment of participants.

- Wellness will continue to be a major issue in leisure and recreation field, but obesity is the most immediate issue facing public parks and recreation agencies. Major efforts are being made to provide health and wellness opportunities, control obesity and preserve cardiovascular health through parks and recreation.

Recreation planning is about assessing the demand, both actual and potential; about assessing the capacity of the land base to meet that demand in a sustainable way; and about using available resources wisely to optimize the potential (Bell, 2008, p23). McCool and Patterson (2000) suggested, instead, focusing on understanding what conditions are desired, what impacts are acceptable and unacceptable, and what actions will lead to accepted goals (Newsome et al, 2005, p155).

Outdoor recreational activities such as camping, biking, backpacking, boating, hunting, fishing, skiing and mountain climbing depend heavily on parks, forests and water areas (Mclean et al, 2008, p14). Recreational trampling can have an effect on many types of woodland soil and vegetation. Compaction is the most noted effect on forest soils resulting from recreational trampling (Tribe et al, 2000, p20). Enjoyment of outdoors causes relatively little environmental damage, compared with major land-use impacts, but all the principles such as wise use of non-renewable resources, carrying capacity, environmental quality, and acting in a precautionary manner have relevance to access planning and design (Bell, 2005, p24).

As far as possible, any recreation provision should be planned and designed with sustainability in mind (Bell, 2008, p23). If essential environmental resources cannot be adequately sustained, they, in turn, cannot sustain economic and other human activity. The imperative has emerged, therefore, to adopt patterns of development that can fulfil socio-economic objectives without reducing the ability of natural resources to sustain us in the long term: this goal is referred to as sustainable development (Tribe et al, 2000, p23).

Further reading

Hall, C. (2005) *Tourism: Rethinking the Social Science of Mobility*, Pearson Education, Harlow

Kelly, I. and Nankervis, T. (2001) *Visitor Destinations*, John Wiley and Sons, Milton, UK

Keyser, H. (2002) *Tourism Development*, Oxford University Press, Cape Town, South Africa

McMahon, U. and Yeoman, I. (2004) *Sport and Leisure Operations Management*, Thomson, London

Pigram, J. J. and Jenkins, J. M. (1999) *Outdoor Recreation Management*, Routledge, London

Torkildsen, G. (2005) *Leisure and Recreation Management*, fifth edition, Routledge, Oxford

Verbole, P. (2005) 'The role of education in the management of rural tourism and leisure', in D. Hall, L. Roberts and M. Mitchell (eds) *New Directions in Rural Tourism*, Ashgate Publishing Limited, Hampshire, UK, pp183–189

Dr. Gul Gunes

REGENERATION

Regeneration is a recurring theme within tourism, as tourism is often seen as a catalyst for economic growth and is used both as a rationale for regeneration and to spark further regeneration. Some areas are regenerated with the aim of appealing to tourists, and once visitors start arriving the economy grows, new businesses are developed and further inward investment follows. Often this process is supported by public-sector funding together with private-sector investment. However, regeneration should not be taken to refer only to urban environments, but also to the renewal and improvement of rural areas, exemplified by the creation of the National Forest in the centre of the UK, an area that was covered with mines and opencast sites, but which is now being returned to nature, providing access, recreation opportunities and new leisure-related businesses.

Although tourism can be the catalyst for regeneration, the benefits are shared by both visitors to the area and also by the host community, who benefits from an improved quality of life, better standards of living, new facilities and employment opportunities. However, regeneration alone is not enough and it is important for **destination management organizations** to provide marketing and business support to underpin an emerging tourism economy.

During recent years, events have been used as the catalyst to bring in tourists to a destination, which is why the public sector increasingly places an emphasis on bidding for major events, which justify public-sector investment and leave a lasting legacy. In addition, the media coverage given to major events further enhances global awareness of the host destination. These longer-term impacts are, in the context of events, referred to as event legacy and are often considered to be the essential justification for hosting many large-scale tourism-related events.

One of the most significant examples of urban regeneration has been the redevelopment of London's St. Pancras Station. This imposing Victorian station, fronted by a large Victorian Gothic Hotel, had suffered many years of neglect with only basic maintenance provided to keep the building in a usable state. Its famous glass arched ceiling had been largely covered up with cheaper metal alternatives and the station concourse was dark and dingy and covered in grime from steam and diesel locomotives. The decision to run Eurostar Services to Europe from St. Pancras facilitated a UK£5.8 billion project which included the restoration of the station, the creation of a shopping mall in the station's old cellars, the reopening of the old hotel as a luxury 5-star hotel, together with the creation of apartments and a link to King's Cross Underground Station. The station houses coffee shops, restaurants and artwork and has been designed to be a destination in its own right. However, this regeneration project has acted as a catalyst for the regeneration of the King's Cross area of London, with new public spaces, cultural venues, retail offers and accommodation, demonstrating the role of tourism in the regeneration of urban areas and the link between regeneration and the development of new destinations.

Further reading

Smith, M. (2006) *Tourism, Culture and Regeneration*, CABI, Wallingford, UK

Peter Robinson

RELIGIOUS TOURISM

Religious tourism is perhaps the oldest formally recognized tourism product, as people travelled on pilgrimages to visit sites of religious importance. Once at the destination they would often pay for prayers to be said, a business that was so lucrative that Durham Cathedral in England had nine altars built to cope with the demand from pilgrims visiting the tomb of St. Cuthbert.

The Church Tourism Association (2007) defines religious tourism as 'promoting best practice in welcoming visitors to places of worship and developing the tourism potential and visitor experience of a unique part of our historical and contemporary sacred heritage' and Woodward (2004) explains that 'tourist activity at religious sites represents an important source of income for many faith institutions and organizations, generating funds for maintenance and repair'.

In contemporary tourism, religious sites are considered to be valuable tourism resources and important sociocultural centres. Some of the most notable religious tourism sites include Mecca, Vatican City and Rome, Istanbul, Santiago de Compostela, Jerusalem, Bethlehem, Rio de Janeiro and Lourdes. In many cases, the religious site forms the core purpose of a visit or the central feature of the destination.

There are many contested issues around religious sites and their use for tourism, often defined by the beliefs and values of the community who use the site, together with the views of others who live in the communities served by the religious site. Three user groups can be easily defined – worshippers, tourists and the community; but the community and tourists may or may not be worshippers. This raises issues for one of the most common debates around religious sites: the challenge of levying an admission fee to generate tourism income. Often the fee is waived for local people on the basis of their use of the building as their local centre of worship; but many visitors may also be there for the same purposes and not as sightseeing tourists.

Additional management issues revolve around other forms of income generation, including the positioning of retail and catering facilities within religious buildings. Of course, income generation is essential to manage the impact of high visitor numbers and to pay for on-going repairs and maintenance; but that is not to say that many people disagree with this commercialization of religious sites. The same contested issues are less prevalent at many older sites where worship no longer takes place, and admission charges to these sites seem to generally meet with less resistance.

Interpretation is an important feature of the religious site in a tourism context, both narration of the architecture and history of the site, and also the religion itself. Many involved with sites of worship believe that tourism is acceptable within sacred spaces if it is tempered with religious messages.

Managing access to religious sites is a further contested issue. During recent years many sites have been kept locked because of vandalism and theft, although modern security systems have helped to address some of these problems. Damage is, of course, caused by a minority and the use of volunteer wardens to supervise and interpret the site has proved successful in many instances.

However, the scope of religious tourism extends beyond the doors of the physical building, and there is an increased interest in visiting graveyards for genealogical research and, in the case of older grave-yards where maintenance may be infrequent, to find unusual and rare wildlife and flowers, or to admire different grave architecture – especially those with old mausoleums and tombs. It is also important to define spirituality and spiritual tourism within the context of religious tourism, and these may both include visits to military graveyards and sites such as the National Memorial Arboretum in the UK, where visitors can participate in services, wander in the countryside, visit specific memorials and experience other ways of finding peace.

Current destination management encourages many of these sites to work together to form networks that build capacity for tourism visits. This helps to broaden the narration of the cultural heritage of a destination; given the centrality of religion to the location of the site, it is important to consider the role of the community within the management of the site and the issues that exist around cultural authenticity. The major problem facing many sites, though, is that they are not recognized as important sacred sites and are thus commoditized for tourism, such as at Uluru, Ayres Rock, in Australia.

There are also growing numbers of examples of communities finding new uses for religious sites for events, festivals and meetings, some of which bring in tourists and help to raise further income. Where sites are no longer used for worship they may still be an important tourist destination, and groups such as the UK-based Friends of Friendless Churches continue to maintain and, in some cases, develop these sites for tourism and events.

Further reading

Shackley, M. (2001) *Managing Sacred Sites: Service Provision and Visitor Experience*, Continuum, London

Shaw, G. and Williams, A. (2004) *Tourism and Tourism Spaces*, Sage Publications, London

Timothy, D. J. and Olsen, D. H. (2006) *Tourism, Religion and Spiritual Journeys*, Routledge, London

Woodward, S. (2004) 'Faith and tourism: Planning tourism in relation to places of worship', *Tourism and Hospitality Planning and Development*, vol 1, no 2, pp173–186

Peter Robinson

RESPONSIBLE TOURISM

Responsible tourism seeks to maximize the benefits of tourism, whilst minimizing its negative impacts. It was defined at the World Summit on Sustainable Development in Cape Town in 2002 as 'tourism that creates better places for people to live in, and better places to visit'. The concept is supported by the Responsible Tourism Partnership, which helps businesses and communities to develop responsible tourism, and it is emphasized each year by the annual World Responsible Tourism Day, held to coincide with the World Travel Market exhibition. The aims of responsible tourism are to:

- minimize negative economic, environmental and social impacts;
- generate greater economic benefits for local people and enhance the well-being of host communities, improving working conditions and access to the industry;
- involve local people in decisions that affect their lives;
- make positive contributions to the conservation of natural and cultural heritage, and to the maintenance of the world's diversity;
- provide more enjoyable experiences for tourists through more meaningful connections with local people, and a greater understanding of local cultural, social and environmental issues;
- provide access for physically challenged people;
- be culturally sensitive, engendering respect between tourists and hosts, and building local pride and confidence (see www.responsibletourismpartnership.org).

The ideology of responsible tourism is underpinned by the notion of sustainable development, so many of the principles of **sustainable tourism** are equally applicable to responsible tourism; but the idea of responsibility places an emphasis on individual consumers, business leaders and other stakeholders, and describes ownership of responsible tourism behaviours, rather than an overall emphasis on sustainable working. This focus on responsibility should, it is argued, be driven by a concern around global warming, environmental destruction, cultural erosion and global poverty (see also **Tourism in developing countries**).

Responsible tourism should not be considered to be a form of niche tourism in the way that ecotourism and other green products may be discussed – rather, it is concerned with the impacts of tourism for local people, environments and economies and can, therefore, be applied to any type of tourism destination, including urban destinations and cities, as well as rural areas, and may be equally relevant to both the developing and the developed world. It is suggested that the net result of responsible tourism is the development of better quality, ethically sound holidays.

Further reading

Spenceley, A. (2008) *Responsible Tourism: Critical Issues for Conservation and Development*, Earthscan, London
The Responsible Tourism Partnership, www.responsibletourismpartnership.org

Peter Robinson

RURAL TOURISM

Rural tourism generally refers to visits to places outside major metropolitan areas. The concept has developed over the years to become a complex, multifaceted activity where it is no longer viewed as just tourism that takes place in the countryside. Rather, the notion of rural tourism has become much more specific, with definitions now encompassing the agricultural aspect associated with its development. For example, Killon (2001, p167) defined rural tourism as:

> … a multi-faceted activity that takes place in an environment outside heavily urbanised areas. It is an industry sector characterised by small-scale tourism businesses, set in areas where land is dominated by agricultural pursuits … It should be seen as offering a different range of experiences … [where] the emphasis … is on the tourist's experience of the products and activities of rural areas.

In particular, **rural tourism** includes farm- and station-based holidays, special-interest holidays, nature-based and **ecotourism** holidays, walking, cycling, climbing and riding holidays, **adventure**, **sport** and **health tourism**, hunting and angling, **educational travel**, **arts**, **heritage** and historic recreation, **festivals** and **events**, **food** and **wine** tourism, cultural and social experiences, and, in some areas, ethnic tourism (see, for example, Lane, 1994; Cox Innal Communications, 1996; Butler et al, 1998; Hall et al, 2005a; George et al, 2009). While this illustrates the broad nature of rural tourism, there is some debate over the extent to which certain areas and activities actually qualify as being traditionally rural in character. For example, Lane (1994) and, more recently, George et al (2009) argued that although tourism may take place in rural areas, some tourism developments, such as theme parks and villages/resorts, are much more 'urban' in form, with the only difference being their outer-metropolitan location. In response to such questions, Lane (1994, p14) concluded that the concept of rural tourism in its purest form should be:

- located in rural areas;
- functionally rural, built upon the rural world's special features of small-scale enterprise, open space, contact with nature and the natural world, heritage, 'traditional' societies and 'traditional' practices;
- rural in scale – both in terms of buildings and settlements – and, therefore, usually small scale;
- traditional in character, growing slowly and organically, and connected with local families; it will often be controlled locally and developed for the long-term good of the area; and
- of many different kinds, representing the complex pattern of rural environment, economy, history and location.

This categorization of 'rural tourism' has since been adopted by the Organization for Economic Co-operation and Development (OECD) in their reports and documents to assist rural regions which are contemplating tourism because it represents areas for differentiation and competitive advantage (George et al, 2009).

The development of rural tourism is frequently undertaken due to the potential it has to contribute to the regeneration of rural areas, both socially and economically. Indeed, rural tourism is now seen to be a 'solution' to many of the problems that rural communities around the world face. This is particularly evident in locations where the traditional 'agriculture' industry faces issues of globalization, resulting in increased economic pressure and, in some instances, decline. In this respect, tourism is viewed by rural locations to be a central means by which they can adjust themselves economically, socially and politically, especially when it comes to new sources of income, employment and the repopulation of rural communities (Sharpley and Sharpley, 1997;

Hall, 2007). Diversification and regeneration through rural tourism has been shown to create the following benefits:

- stimulation of local business;
- employment opportunities;
- further regional development;
- development of regional infrastructure, facilities and services, including recreational facilities that can be used by rural residents and tourists;
- diversification of income; and
- enhanced quality of life.

Although the development of rural tourism has apparent benefits for communities, it also provides challenges when it comes to the destruction of the local environment. Thus, there is an increased emphasis on rural locations adopting sustainable practices in relation to enhancing and promoting their resource base. Indeed, there are many examples around the world where rural tourism is adopting sustainability practices while, at the same time, benefiting rural communities through tourist visitation and expenditure (see, for example, George et al, 2009).

Further reading

Beeton, S. (2006) 'Rural tourism communities', in *Community Development through Tourism*, Landlinks Press, Collingwood, UK

Journal of Sustainable Tourism (1994) *Special Issue: Rural Tourism and Sustainable Tourism Development*, vol 2, pp1–2

Page, S. and Getz, D. (1997) *The Business of Rural Tourism: International Perspectives*, International Thomson Business Press, Oxford, UK

Roberts, L. and Hall, D. (2001) *Rural Tourism and Recreation: Principles to Practice*, CABI Publishing, Wallingford, UK

Dr. Lisa Melsen

SELF AND OTHER

The terms Self and Other within tourism discourse refer to potential transformational outcomes and consequences between tourist and native encounters. Furthermore, the Self and the Other often refer to alleged differentiation and disparities between tourism-generating cultures (i.e. the Self within 'developed' countries), and tourism host cultures (i.e. the Other within 'developing' countries). However, this rather simple notion of transformation or differentiation between one culture and another camouflages complex sociocultural and geopolitical interrelationships between the tourist Self and the so-called native Other. Moreover, the concepts of the Self and the Other, borrowed largely from sociological and anthropological discourse, can be traced back throughout history from the contact made by early European travellers with foreigners from *other lands*. As Seaton (2009, p76) notes, 'these travellers returned from remote places with tales of societies where they had witnessed bizarre physical differences, extraordinary customs, strange judicial and religious practices – in short, with all manners of *differences*'.

With the evolution of tourism from the Grand Tour to the twentieth century, and the fact that European cultures dominated printing as a popular medium from the fifteenth century onward, these early perceptions of 'other' cultures were perpetuated and promoted in books, journalism and graphics across the world. Indeed, tourist guidebooks from the late eighteenth and much of the nineteenth century were not entitled 'tourist' guidebooks but, rather, 'strangers' guides' (Seaton, 2009). Thus, the Other became a term to distinguish and categorize observed differences by (European) travellers, and later adopted by (dominant Western) anthropologists who compared their own cultures and societies with those they were studying. In short, the Other has been typically used to denote 'people not like us' (i.e. the Self). As Hawthorn (1994, p141) suggests, 'to characterise a person, group or individual as "other" is to place them outside the system of normality or convention to which one belongs oneself'.

The anthropological conception of the Self and Other was most notably promulgated by Said (1978) in his seminal work on *Orientalism* – that is, a composite and adverse view of Eastern cultures

Table 11 (Early) conceptual differences between the Self and the Other

Own societies of the Self	Societies of the Other
Modern, evolving	Timeless, traditional
Civilized	Primitive
Superior	Inferior
Rational-scientific	Superstitious, ignorant
Humane	Savage, cruel, cannibalistic
Christian	Heathen
Worldly	Naïve, innocent
Disenchanted	Enchanted, mysterious

Source: adapted from Seaton (2009)

constructed by imperialists who perpetuated the East as the Other of the West (i.e. its opposite). Of course, Said's work has been both augmented and criticized by post-colonial analysts such as Kennedy (2000) and Warraq (2007) for its overtly political biases.

In particular, much of this post-colonial discourse has been focused on the conceptualizing of the Other as hegemony, by which imperial cultures dominate, through representations and discourses inscribed, and transmitted through, a range of institutions such as the media, education, academia and governments. Moreover, this post-colonial paradigm of the Self and the Other has been prominent in the (re)presentation of both place and people and, subsequently, allowed the imaginary construction of the Other by the powerful over the powerless.

In the context of the Self and Other, this power/powerless dichotomy has largely driven tourism scholarship, whereby the focus has often been on relations between tourists and indigenous populations. Indeed, tourism has often been viewed as the (Romantic) pursuit by the Western Self of the Other. Consequently, and notwithstanding its critics, tourism is often allied to motivations for temporal and spatial encounters with other cultures. In turn, the tourist is stimulated, consciously or unconsciously, by attributing extremes of imagined difference from their own culture(s) (Seaton, 2009). As Hollinshead (cited in Jafari, 2000, p420) suggests, tourism theory has largely adopted post-colonial perspectives of the Other and Othering:

Other[ing] is the imaginary construction of different/alien people by external individuals who remain marginal (yet powerful) in that encounter with their exotic 'others'. The Othering of foreigners tend to deny these others of genuine identifications as they are conspiratorially (but often unconsciously) appropriated. The management/development practices, and the narratives of tourism, regularly further the capture/destruction of others.

However, the conceptualization between the Self and Other within tourism is not just a malign mechanism to imagine and (re)present other cultures. Indeed, the almost infinite way in which place and people are identified with images creates possibilities of difference. This difference can generate compulsions of positive and negative desire to visit such places and people, as well as instil potential transformations in the tourist or host, either during or post-visitation. Yet, the Other is part of the social imaginary of the Self, whereby individuals draw upon diverse experiences, opinions and perceptions. In so doing, the Self creates a sense of the Other, which, ultimately, allows for both escape, regression and potential transformation of an individual's life-world.

Further reading

Kennedy, V. (2000) *Edward Said: A Critical Introduction*, Polity Press, Cambridge
MacCannell, D. (2011) *The Ethics of Sightseeing*, University of California Press, Berkeley and Los Angeles
Seaton, T. (2009) 'Purposeful Otherness: Approaches to the management of thanatourism', in R. Sharpley and P. R. Stone (eds) *The Darker Side of Tourism: The Theory and Practice of Dark Tourism*, Channel View Publications, Bristol, UK, pp75–108
Urry, J. and Larsen, J. (2011) *The Tourist Gaze 3.0*, Sage Publications, London

Dr. Philip R. Stone

SEMIOTICS

Although semiotics is well established within tourism studies, the phraseology of semiotics is used as a convenient label for the analysis of the signs and images produced and utilized by the tourism industry. Semiotics may be simply defined as the study of signs and images, upon which the tourism industry is heavily reliant, as these signs add meaning to destinations and sites.

In order to achieve this, the tourism industry and marketers adopt and develop a semiotic language of tourism that is used when promoting and marketing destinations that employs conventions that signpost experiences and perceptions. Urry (2002, p139) explains that 'one learns that a thatched cottage with roses around the door represents "ye olde England", or the waves crashing on to rocks signifies "wild, untamed nature"; or especially, that a person with a camera draped around his/her neck is clearly a tourist'. Or similarly, as Culler (1981, p158) comments, 'All over the world the unsung armies of semioticians, the tourists, are fanning out in search of the signs of Frenchness, typical Italian behaviour, exemplary Oriental scenes.' These signs, though, do not have to be in picture form. They can just as easily be represented in words and colours. Examples of this include:

- Semiotics in image: images of empty beaches − signifying peace and quiet, space and relaxation.
- Semiotics in text: use of words such as 'fun' and 'escape' − these define expectations of the experience offered by the destination.

- Semiotics of colour: red suggests 'stop' or danger, green suggests safety or 'go'.

However, the interpretation suggested here is not necessarily the same – indeed, for somebody living next to a quiet and deserted beach there is nothing exotic or different, and so they may seek somewhere with less than perfect weather that is, perhaps, urban or busy, in contrast to daily life. The meaning of images then, such as **motivation** and **consumer behaviour**, are defined by the cultural and societal background of the individual. Furthermore, gender is also involved in understanding semiotics, so images of people relaxing on a beach may influence men and women differently depending upon the gender, composition and pose of those relaxing.

Semiotics also refers to the method of research which analyses brochures, flyers, travel guides and postcards, and explains a research method where common images, scenes and styles are coded and understood in quantitative terms.

Further reading

Barthes, R. (1982) *Empire of Signs* (translated by R. Howard), Jonathan Cape, London

Botterill, D. (2001) 'The epistemology of a set of tourism studies', *Leisure Studies*, vol 20, no 3, pp199–214

Culler, J. (1981) 'Semiotics of tourism', *American Journal of Semiotics*, vol 1, pp127–158

MacCannell, D. (1999) *The Tourist: A New Theory of the Leisure Class*, University of California Press, Los Angeles, CA

Rose, G. (2001) *Visual Methodologies*, Sage Publications, London

Tresidder, R. (2011) 'The semiotics of tourism', in P. Robinson, S. Heitmann and P. Dieke (eds) (2011) *Research Themes for Tourism*, CABI, Wallingford, UK

Urry, J. (2001) *The Tourist Gaze: Leisure and Travel in Contemporary Society*, TCS, London

Peter Robinson

SERIOUS LEISURE

The concept of serious leisure is most readily associated with the work of Stebbins (1982, 1992), who distinguishes between two types of leisure pursuit: serious leisure and casual leisure. Stebbins's central argument is that the post-industrial society will offer fewer jobs, jobs with shorter working hours and, hence, more leisure time, and jobs that are less likely to require the progressive acquisition and application of specialist skills and knowledge. He goes on to argue that leisure will generally play an increasing role in people's lives and, more specifically, that serious leisure will represent an increasingly important avenue through which personal fulfilment will be achieved. Serious leisure can thus be defined as:

> ... the systematic pursuit of an amateur, hobbyist, or volunteer activity that participants find so substantial and interesting that, in the typical case, they launch themselves on a career centred on acquiring and expressing its special skills, knowledge and experience.
>
> (Stebbins, 1992, p3)

Stebbins (1982) further argues that serious leisure is defined by six qualities, which together distinguish it from casual leisure. These are:

1   *The occasional need to persevere.* If the participant wishes to maintain the same level of satisfaction over time, he or she will need to overcome various challenges and obstacles that arise in following the pursuit. Indeed, the greatest satisfaction from serious leisure often comes at the end of the activity rather than during it, as the participant looks back and recognizes the adversities they have faced and how they overcame them.

2   *The ability to follow a 'career path' in the pursuit.* Serious leisure pursuits have a career path that the participant follows. This career path is often unique to the individual participant and is shaped by his or her particular motivations, experiences and choices. The career path may not always take an upward trajectory. For example, as the participant becomes older, he or she may become less proficient at certain activities (e.g. many sporting activities or certain artistic pursuits).

3   *The individual gains specially acquired skills and knowledge.* In order to progress in their chosen leisure 'career', the participant may require special skills and knowledge, which they may learn from others, acquire for themselves or learn from experience.

4   *The individual seeks durable benefits.* While the participant in casual leisure seeks thrills or fun, these rewards are often ephemeral. The serious leisure participant, in contrast, seeks to build their character through greater self-esteem, self-knowledge, pleasure of achievement, enhancement of self-image, social networking, a feeling of belonging or even the creation of a tangible product (e.g. works of art).

5 *A different social world.* Serious leisure enthusiasts are part of a distinct community, the ethos of which is derived from the shared interest in the leisure pursuit of its members. Each group has its own routines, practices, hierarchy and language. Such groups are usually held together by semi-formal mediated communication, such as newsletters, electronic bulletin boards and so on.

6 *Strong identification with the leisure pursuit.* Springing from the previous five, the final characteristic of serious leisure is that participants tend to be avid enthusiasts of their chosen pursuit. Casual leisure pursuits are generally 'too fleeting, mundane and commonplace to generate distinctive identities' (Stebbins and Graham, 2004, p6).

For Stebbins, then, the term 'serious' is not intended to convey such qualities as gravity, solemnity, distress or anxiety; rather, it is intended to convey earnestness, sincerity, importance and care. Even if the former are often associated with 'serious' leisure pursuits, they are not what define it. Instead, it is about commitment to an endeavour, even if there is no social or personal obligation to do so. Someone involved in serious leisure is not simply a 'dabbler' in the pursuit but an enthusiast who is looking for the durable benefits associated with it.

As noted in the above definition, Stebbins (1982) argues that there are essentially three types of serious leisure participant – amateurs, volunteers and hobbyists:

1 *Amateurs:* those who pursue a leisure activity that would normally be associated with a paid profession, such as amateur archaeologists, sportsmen and women, entertainers and so forth. They participate, however, not in order to earn a living but as a satisfying way of passing their leisure time.

2 *Hobbyists:* those whose endeavour has no direct professional equivalent. Stebbins identifies four types of activity that can be pursued by hobbyists, any of which may be practised as casual or serious leisure. The first is 'collectors', who typically gather items such as fine art, rare books or vintage cars. Serious collectors develop a deep technical knowledge of the production, provenance and commercial value of such items. Collectors of more everyday items such as beer mats or matchboxes are considered by Stebbins to be unlikely to be serious leisure participants in that it is difficult to acquire a technical appreciation of such items. The second type of hobbyist, termed 'makers and tinkerers' by Stebbins, includes those who follow leisure pursuits such as toy-making, needlecrafts and boat restoration. Participants acquire technical skills, as well as

specialist knowledge, and the benefits include the production of a tangible artefact, such as a garment. Stebbins also includes those who breed and display animals among this group. Third are 'activity participants', who engage in non-competitive leisure activities such as angling, bird-watching, hang-gliding, hunting, body-building, surfing, skiing and video-gaming. The fourth category, 'players', are those participating in competitive sports such as ball sports, racquet sports, fencing and athletics.

3 *Volunteers:* those who engage in work for no financial reward. Two features distinguish serious volunteers from serious amateurs and serious hobbyists. The first is that serious volunteers undertake their pursuit primarily for reasons of altruism, although it is recognized that there is often an element of self-interest in volunteering. Examples of this include unemployed people volunteering to undertake a role in order to obtain work experience, or volunteers at sports events, such as race marshals, in order to gain free tickets or to enjoy some greater involvement with the sport. The second is that volunteer work is directed by others. This turns volunteers into 'outsiders' in the organization they are working for. Stebbins and Graham (2004) argue that volunteering (see **Voluntary (third) sector in tourism**) has become an increasingly important form of serious leisure.

There has been some debate regarding how far the concept of serious leisure might be directly applicable to the context of tourism. Stebbins (1992) makes a case to argue that some cultural tourists may be considered serious leisure participants. When the cultural tour is an extension of the participant's 'serious' hobby, then the individual may be considered to be practising serious leisure. However, when cultural tourism is performed in the context of recreational tourism (e.g. in the form of an excursion as part of a mass tourism product), the participant is more likely to be engaging in casual leisure. Stebbins goes on to suggest that any type of special interest tourism (Weiler and Hall, 1992) may have a serious leisure basis to it.

Kane and Zink (2004), meanwhile, explore the extent to which even 'packaged' adventure tourism may be considered a market of serious leisure. They argue that while adventure tourism fits comfortably within serious leisure, the guided or packaged tour has been described as 'insulated adventure', where the participant exchanges freedom and independence of decision-making for the safety and structure of an organized tour. This might suggest that packaged adventure tourists tend to identify with casual rather than serious leisure. The results of

Kane and Zink's research, however, suggested that participants in a packaged kayaking tour in New Zealand tended to exhibit many of the qualities and behaviours associated with serious leisure participants. Going on the tour enabled participants to authorize their qualifications as serious leisure enthusiasts, including perseverance, skills acquisition, identity, ethos and commitment to a leisure career. This suggests that associating recreational tourists with casual leisure and special interest tourists with serious leisure is not entirely tenable.

Further reading

Jones, I. (2000) 'A model of serious leisure identification: The case of football fandom', *Leisure Studies*, vol 19, no 4, pp283–298

Kane, M. J. and Zink, R. (2004) 'Package adventure tours: Markets in serious leisure careers', *Leisure Studies*, vol 23, no 4, pp329–345

Stebbins, R. A. (1982) 'Serious leisure: A conceptual statement', *Pacific Sociological Review*, vol 25, no 2, pp251–272

Stebbins, R. A. (1992) *Amateurs, Professionals, and Serious Leisure*, McGill–Queens University Press, Montreal, Quebec

Stebbins, R. A. and Graham, M. (2004) *Volunteering as Leisure: Leisure as Volunteering – An International Assessment*, CABI, Wallingford and Cambridge

Dr. Brian Garrod

SERVICE QUALITY

Service quality as a concept has gained a wide interest in tourism literature during the past few decades and has been assigned a number of definitions. In the tourism sector, service quality has been viewed as 'quality of opportunity' (Lee et al, 2007), which comprises the service attributes and organizational resources that are supplied and managed by the service provider. However, the management of quality in a service context can be very daunting because:

- Quality is intangible and instantaneous.
- Quality must be assured beforehand.
- Quality relies on people, their skills, behaviour and knowledge.

For these reasons and many more, a considerable amount of effort has been expended to understand the notion of quality in the service context. There are two perspectives to the conceptualization of service quality:

1 the Nordic perspective, which delineates service quality in a universal term as possessing two dimensions: functional and technical quality;

2 the American perspective that operationalizes service quality in terms of five service characteristics: empathy, tangibility, assurance, responsiveness and reliability.

Both of these perspectives are based on the disconfirmation paradigm, which assumes that consumers judge a product or service, and, more appropriately in tourism, an experience, by comparing *expectations* prior to consumption with the *performance* of the product's attributes post-consumption. So far, research conducted into service quality has been based on this expectancy–(dis)confirmation notion, which assumes that consumers evaluate a product (or, in a tourism context, the service experience) by comparing their expectations with the actual service experience. This method was used in the development of the SERVQUAL model (Parasuraman et al, 1985), which has been widely used in services management research, in general, and tourism and leisure related studies, in particular.

The use of SERVQUAL has, however, received extensive theoretical and operational criticism despite its popularity in literature. Other approaches such as importance-performance and performance-only models have been found to have performed better in terms of validity and reliability.

Despite external factors, the importance of service quality is a very high priority for most travellers. Academic discussion in this area is likely to continue to inform planners' and managers' actions and possibly shape their implementation and evaluation of service quality strategies in the industry. A number of quality assurance systems exist in tourism and hospitality. Examples include the Visitor Attraction Quality Assurance Scheme (VAQAS) in the UK and the Q Mark in Spain. VAQAS is an accreditation and assessment system for visitor attractions that want to improve the quality of customer experience. It is managed by VisitEngland and assesses a four-stage process of pre-arrival, visit, debrief and reporting. Q Mark for tourism quality in Spain is based on the need to develop a management model that facilitates service delivery to meet visitors' expectations and, hence, gain a competitive edge. The system's certification and monitoring duties span the breadth of the Spanish tourism industry and includes Spanish facilities in other countries.

In addition, tourism organizations often carry out in-house investigation of the effectiveness of their service delivery mechanism and evaluation of visitors' perception of their service. This can be done in a number of ways, such as focus group, comment card, online survey and through reviewing websites such as TripAdvisor.

Further reading

Kandampully, J., Mok, C. and Sparks, B. (eds) (2001) *Service Quality Management in Hospitality, Tourism and Leisure*, Haworth Hospitality Press, Binghamton, NY

Williams, C. and Buswell, J. (2003) *Service Quality in Leisure and Tourism*, CABI, Oxford, UK

Ade Oriade

SEX TOURISM

The World Tourism Organization (UNWTO) defines sex tourism as trips organized from within the tourism sector, or from outside this sector but using its structures and networks, with the primary purpose of effecting a commercial sexual relationship by the tourist with residents at the destinations. Sex tourism in a general tourism context is special interest tourism where the travel motive is driven by specific expressed interests of individuals and groups. It is destination specific and based upon unique supply and demand elements (such as underage sex in Thailand and male prostitution in the Caribbean). Much has been written and said about the linkage between tourism and the sex trade (Ryan and Hall, 2001; Kibicho, 2004, 2005; Okech, 2007). Relatively few studies on the subject of tourism and the sex trade have been carried out because of the ethical challenges of conducting research with participants or with the sometimes illegal supply side of the industry. Representations of sex and sexuality are integral to contemporary tourism (see **Semiotics in tourism**) and sexual references are often made to the most innocuous of sites – examples include descriptions of beaches as 'her' in ascribing adjectives to explain the beach experience in East Asian travel brochures.

It is important to consider the construction of gender identities within tourism, and aligned to this the notion that frontline workers in the tourism industry should be female, well presented and 'sexy' (Filby, 1992; Tyler and Abbott, 1998), demonstrating the centrality of sexual identity to a broad range of tourism contexts. Attitudes and behaviours of tourists, employers and colleagues, as well as marketing practices, need to change in order to create greater equality. Issues of tourism-related rape, trafficking and sexual assault are increasing, while there are also on-going debates and campaigns against sex tourism and child sex tourism, in particular. The main reasons for entering the trade identified by commercial sex workers include unemployment, family problems, pleasure, part-time work, adventure, lucrative earnings and perceived prestige. Most women are willing to quit the trade if they can find a better alternative.

It must be noted that evidence shows that sex tourism violates legislation and human rights in many countries, although there are other complex and interrelated human rights issues around race and sexual orientation, and in many countries sex tourism flourishes as a result of the continued dominance of the male gender, in contrast to the Westernized identity construct where traditional male and female roles have been 'largely emptied of meaning ... with greater fluidity of gender ... [which] has produced female consumption of male prostitution, Gay or Pink Dollar Tourism [see **LGBT tourism**], and re-mapping of the geography of tourism according to "safeness" of manifestation of difference' (Smith et al, 2010a).

Indigenous peoples are particularly vulnerable to market-driven sex tourism, losing their customary and religious freedom and, ultimately, their cultures and capacity for self-sufficiency. Women and children are at very high risk where tourism economies are built upon exploitative labour practices, and where sex tourism occurs. Another factor to be considered is the health risks associated with sex tourism. When people travel, not only do they carry their genetic makeup, disease pathogens and vectors, and accumulated immunologic experience, but they also transport their capacity to introduce diseases into new regions. As is the case in most littoral areas, risky behavioural patterns involving substance misuse and casual/unprotected sexual encounters constitute a prevalent hazard particularly due to the pervasiveness of the sun, sea, sand tourists, many of whom, amongst younger travellers, may also be seeking casual sexual experiences, although this may not define them as a sex tourist in the traditional sense. Furthermore, risky encounters occur between beach boys and white foreign women, between locals and exotic visitors, and between paedophiles and victims of child sex tourism. Sex tourism linked to poverty has been blamed, in part, for the AIDS increase in some Asian and African countries.

The linkage of sex tourism with the alarmingly fast spread of HIV/ AIDS needs to be recognized, and an appropriate education campaign delivered through all tourism stakeholders in a destination is needed. Existing literature has shown that the marriage between tourism and the sex trade is a reality of international tourism, accounting for a sizeable portion of all tourism activities. However, it would be inaccurate to suggest that the sex trade is created by tourism alone. It existed in society long before current levels of tourism. If, however, we are to control and reduce its impacts, it will be necessary to understand the trade from all sides, and to develop positive and sustainable ways forward, emphasizing the need for further research. A number of recent studies have added insights into the phenomenon, but there are still areas that require more attention. Unfortunately, the current subject is highly charged with emotions, social prejudices, sociocultural issues and political bias. Many international tourism organizations have passed resolutions and have declared their willingness to cooperate with the authorities in countering sex abuse at all levels. The delivery of an effective solution in many destinations will be difficult to achieve, however, because local issues, including a lack of enforcement and continued demand from tourists, are difficult challenges to address.

Further reading

Kibicho, W. (2005) 'Tourism and the sex trade in Kenya's coastal region', *Journal of Sustainable Tourism*, vol 13, no 3, pp256–280

Okech, R. N (2007) 'Sex tourism and its effect on women: Case study of the coastal region in Kenya', *International Journal for Women and Gender Research*, vol 1, no 1, pp75–83

Robinson, P., Lueck. M. and Smith, S. (2012) *Tourism*, CABI, Wallingford, UK

Ryan, C. and Hall, C. M. (2001) *Sex Tourism: Marginal People and Liminalities*, Routledge, Oxon, UK

Smith, M., Macleod, N. and Robinson, M. H. (2010) *Key Concepts in Tourist Studies*, Sage Publications, Oxford, UK

Dr. Roselyne N. Okech

SHOPPING AND TOURISM

Shopping is a significant and pervasive tourist activity (Timothy, 2005). As such, it is an important but secondary component (Timothy and Boyd, 2003) of the **tourism system** that can affect the success of a tourist destination (Gunn and Var, 2002). Tourist shopping can make a significant contribution to local economies, particularly in destinations known for shopping. It is thus important to understand the motivations for shopping activity, as in some cases tourists may travel for this purpose or are influenced in their destination choice by opportunities for shopping. Essential aspects of tourist shopping are the authenticity of the products in relation to the local area and the quality of the shopping experience.

When shopping, many tourists are interested in purchasing items that are indigenous to the local area or region. They also look to purchase items that will act as a souvenir or memory of their visit or that they can give to others on their return home as a marker of their visit (Gordon, 1986). In their search for authentic souvenirs, tourists are often attracted to local or native marketplaces, noted to be rich in ethnicity. Studies of souvenirs collaborate that tourists have various motivations for purchase, and identify the fact that differing types of tourists will be attracted to different types of souvenirs. Littrell et al (1994) identified four types of souvenir shoppers in terms of motivation:

1 ethnic, art and people;
2 history and parks;
3 urban entertainment;
4 active outdoor.

There have been studies of tourist shopping precincts and villages; for example, Getz (1993) examines planning and development strategies for tourist shopping villages, while Frost (2006) links **heritage tourism** with such shopping villages in Australia. In addition, tourist-oriented malls, such as the West Edmonton Mall in Canada and the Mall of America in Bloomington, US, that aim to create a shopping experience for visitors have been studied (LeHew and Wesley, 2007). Cross-border activity as a characteristic of international tourism shopping has also received some attention in the literature (e.g. Timothy and Butler, 1995).

The shopping experience itself is also important, as tourists can be encouraged to spend more when shopping if the displays are attractive. Gift shops are often located in tourist facilities, such as hotels and attractions, providing an added amenity for visitors needing to purchase necessities or souvenirs, and creating an additional revenue stream for these properties. Shopping as an activity also forms a major part of cruise tourism, either occurring at 'on-board' shops or during shore visits.

In all types of tourist shopping situations, from tourist shopping districts to shopping malls to shops in resorts and on cruise ships, it is important for retailers to understand why tourists buy and how satisfied they are with their experience. It is therefore necessary for these operating shops to continually strive to maintain and improve the visitor shopping experience, while at the same time ensuring the availability of authentic souvenirs of place.

Further reading

Gordon, B. (1986) 'The souvenir: messenger of the extraordinary', *Journal of Popular Culture*, vol 20, pp135–146

Littrell, M. S. et al (1994) 'Souvenirs and tourism styles', *Journal of Travel Research*, vol 33, no 1, pp3–11

Timothy, D. J. (2005) *Shopping Tourism, Retailing and Leisure*, Channel View Publications, Clevedon, UK

Dr. Lee Jolliffe and Dr. Jenny Cave

SLOW TOURISM

Slow tourism has emerged from the Slow Food and *Cittàslow* (Slow Cities) movements, and there is, therefore, little in the way of research and definition for the concept. Its evolution can be traced through these two cultural movements.

Slow food

During an anti-McDonald's protest in Rome 1986 the term 'slow food' was coined as a rallying call for those who wanted to halt the invasion of standardized Americanized 'fast food' (and culture) into the heart of Rome. A second influence on the formation of the movement was the death of 19 Italians who drank cheap wine that had been mixed with methanol. In reaction to these events, Carlos Petrini formed the embryonic Slow Food Movement, which was officially launched in December 1989 in Paris. Since then the movement has gone from strength to strength and has attracted 100,000 members from over 150 countries worldwide (Slow Food, 2011).

Cittàslow

Slow City, *Cittàslow* or *Città Lenta* (hereafter Slow City) is both an urban social movement and a model for local governance. The concept seeks to extend slow food's philosophy to all aspects of urban living, providing an agenda of local distinctiveness and urban development. While having a political anti-globalization message, it distinguishes itself from other protest groups as globality is used for positive purposes, exploiting global communicative potentials for the promotion of food and cultural differences and fostering networks and transnational cooperation.

Central to the meaning and concept of slow tourism is the shift in focus from achieving a quantity and volume of experiences (while on holiday) towards a focus on the quality of (generally fewer) experiences. It is a form of tourism that respects local cultures, history and environment, and values social responsibility while celebrating diversity and connecting people (tourists with other tourists and with host communities) and is characterized by the enjoyment of discovery, learning and sharing. This 'slowing' of the pace of a holiday provides opportunities to interact and connect with local people and places on a deeper level. This facilitates a more detailed exploration of the cultural environment in which the holiday is taking place and results in a more rewarding and memorable experience for the participants.

The slow tourist focuses much more on immersion with local life and an understanding of places they visit beyond their initial tourist offer. Slow tourism activities while on holiday do not differ much from other types of tourism; but again the key characteristics of engagement, immersion and slowness are central to the experiential philosophy of 'slow' that requires more integration, research and lingering within the environment to acquire more knowledge and form stronger memories. While slow tourists are likely to engage with any type of attraction, the smaller 'hidden gems' are likely to be the most rewarding. Hence, authenticity becomes a focal point for the slow tourist and much of the experience is driven by the search for **authenticity**.

Slow travel is an even more recent emergence from the slow movement, but the principles remain the same. The opportunity to stay in self-catering facilities allows the traveller to become more integrated within the community, to partake of community services, to visit local hostelries and to purchase local produce. It moves away from the idea of the 'resort' or the 'holiday park' (which are, conversely, noisy and exciting, with fast food provision and instant entertainment) and seeks to offer a more traditional lifestyle, which may bring with it many benefits to the local community that are prevented by the inclusive nature of resort-type facilities, thereby stymieing the potential economic benefits for local communities.

One key observation here is the move away from airline travel and the use of slow transport or forms of transportation that fit the slow philosophy. Air transport is considered to be an epitome of globalization and, hence, an antidote to slowness. Instead, slow tourism requires the use of slower and more environmentally friendly forms of transport. Furthermore, within destinations, public or local transport should be used much more in order to encourage the closer connection with locals and local culture. As slow tourism is also characterized by more active pursuits, hiking and cycling are tourism activities that fit the concept well, being forms of transportation that encourage the tourist to engage more with the destination, landscape and local environment.

Slow travel is clearly exemplified by narrow-boats or heritage railways, where these are part of the tourism infrastructure that can be used for travelling; but they do represent a mode of travel which is relatively polluting for the environment. By contrast, travel that follows the true nature of the slow concept – traditional and low impact (e.g. horse-drawn carts) – still exists in some parts of the world not just for the benefit of tourists but as a necessity for the community. The Island of Sark in the UK Channel Islands is one example and represents a deliberate decision by the islanders to focus on traditional forms of transport (horses, donkeys and bicycles), and is the opposite of the situation in some countries, such as rural Romania, where these same methods of transport are chosen because they are affordable. The majority of travellers see this as part of the quaint and authentic nature of the destination, regardless of the socio-economic and sociocultural issues that create these scenarios. This idea, of course, derives from its polar opposite of fast-moving commuter trains and busy stations and instead looks back to a reflective and quieter past.

Further reading

Dickinson, J. and Lumsden, L. (2010) *Slow Travel and Tourism*, Earthscan, London

Hall, M. C. (2006) 'Introduction: Culinary tourism and regional development – from slow food to slow tourism?', *Tourism Review International*, vol 9, no 4, pp303–305

Heitmann, S. and Robinson, P. (2009) 'Slow cities – the Emperor's new clothes or (another) solution for sustainable tourism management?', Paper presented at the BAM Conference, Brighton, UK, 15–17 September 2009

Heitmann, S., Robinson, P. and Povey, G. (2011) 'Slow tourism', in P. Robinson, S. Heitmann and P. Dieke (2011) *Research Themes for Tourism*, CABI, Wallingford, UK

Knox, P. (2005) 'Creating ordinary places: Slow cities in a fast world', *Journal of Urban Design*, vol 10, no 1, pp1–11

Mayer, H. and Knox, P. (2006) 'Slow cities – sustainable places in a fast world', *Journal of Urban Affairs*, vol 28, no 4, pp321–334

Peter Robinson

SOCIETY AND CULTURE

The concepts of 'society' and 'culture' are a key element of tourism. Early travellers were actively seeking out new cultures and new communities, and much of today's developed world is heavily influenced by the art, architecture and food of these early tourists. As indicated by Sharpley (2008) in *Tourism, Tourists and Society*, the relationship between tourism, society and culture can be viewed from two perspectives: the influence of society and culture on tourism, and the influence of tourism on society and culture.

Looking at the context of tourism, 'society' encapsulates an aggregation of people related to each other through persistent relations in the development of tourism (Mayhew, 1968). The understanding of local culture within a society is imperative for the planning and development of tourism, which itself is often based upon the distinctive culture of the destination. When society is discussed within tourism, it is a multifaceted term that encapsulates travellers and host communities and describes their individual and integrated activities. Many tourism theories rely heavily on the notion of society, as it defines the environment within which our sociocultural practices, behaviours, morals, ethics and norms are developed within the communities in which we live.

It is important to fully understand the cultural impact that tourism creates in a society, especially the direct and indirect interaction of host communities with tourists. In many studies into the relationship between different societies and cultures, it is suggested that the host communities are regarded as the weaker party, often the result of a neo-colonial view of the host as servant (especially in developing countries). This is especially evident in research related to the concepts of **pro-poor tourism** and **community-based tourism**. The impact that tourism brings about is termed acculturation, which describes the way in which the value systems and behaviours of a society and culture are influenced by visitors to that culture, thereby threatening its indigenous identity.

The ideas of 'society' and 'culture' are often used interchangeably to mean sociocultural in multidisciplinary studies including in tourism. Franklin and Crang (2001) used the term 'touristic culture' to describe travel in order to experience culture as more than the physical travel itself. It is the preparation of people to see other places as objects of tourism, and similarly the preparation of places (and their peoples) to be seen. By contrast, Galdini (2007) and Gezici and Kerimoglu (2010) suggest that cultural tourism is not just the visual consumption of cultural artefacts (such as architecture, art and artefacts) and the places that house them, such as galleries, theatres and museums, but also the way in which visitors are given the opportunity to absorb and experience some sense of place.

Hence, 'society' and 'culture' may be considered to be a part of sociology – the scientific study of society, social institutions and social relationships. Tourists visiting a community or place create relationships that typically differ from the indigenous population. Thus, the influence of society and culture in tourism needs to be well understood, especially in consideration of the impact upon the individual, their family and society at large (Goeldner and Ritchie, 2006).

The extent of the cultural distance that the visitor wishes to maintain may result in decisions on how unfamiliar the traveller wants his or her environment to be. Interaction and assimilation to the society and culture may not, therefore, be the same for different groups of travellers.

Tourism has significant effects on society. The very presence of visitors in a country, city or home (i.e. homestay) affects the living patterns of local people. The way in which visitors conduct themselves and their relationships with the citizens of the host country often have a profound effect on the way of life and attitudes of local people. This results in security and crime issues and resentment between locals and host communities. The negative social and cultural effects on a host society can be identified as follows, and often emerge from neo-colonial views of people in different, and often developing, countries:

- undesirable activities that are introduced to the host, such as gambling, prostitution, drunkenness and other excesses;
- demonstration effect of local people wanting the same lifestyle and luxuries as those indulged in by tourists;
- racial tension where there are differences between the tourists and their hosts;
- servile attitude developed on the part of tourist business employees which pay frontline 'serving staff' a very low salary;
- 'trinketization' or 'commodification' of culture, crafts and arts to produce volumes of souvenirs for the tourist trade;
- standardization of employee roles in every country;
- the erosion of cultural pride if visitors view people and communities as entertainment, to be gazed at;
- rapid changes in local ways of life if tourist numbers exceed the carrying capacity of the destination;
- disproportionate numbers of workers in low-paid, menial jobs.

The right balance of society and culture for tourism is not always a solution and neither is it a way to attract more tourists and, consequently, more money (Moulin, 1995). Instead, it is important to get the host community to better understand the benefits of tourism and to educate tourists about the communities whom they are visiting In this light, it is critical to understand the change of local identity and values when studying local societies and culture. Conventional and traditional forms of tourism practices can result in the change or loss of local identity and values as a result of:

- *Commercialization of local culture:* this is evident when local religious cultures, customs, traditions and festivals are reduced to conform to tourists' expectations, resulting in what has been called 'reconstructed ethnicity' or 'commodification'.
- *Standardization of tourism experience:* diversity in society and culture is what makes tourism experiential. Hence, destinations that try to accommodate and satisfy tourist desires risk standardization as they seek to deliver the same products and services as other successful destinations.
- *Adaptation to tourist demands:* in many destinations, tourists seek souvenirs, arts, crafts and other cultural manifestations. In response, craftsmen have made changes in the design of their traditional local products to fit in with tourists' tastes. Hence, cultural erosion may occur in the process of commercializing and sustaining cultural goods.

Four basic elements that need to be adopted in promoting good-quality cultural tourism that emphasize the local society include:

1 an environment with aesthetic value and which influences tourism buying behaviour;
2 facilities which facilitate the stay and enjoyment of tourists;
3 events which bring life to the community and create a year-round destination;
4 well-trained staff who can deliver high-quality tourist experiences.

The following factors determine the development of any society and culture: time and common residence; shared activities and the degree of involvement in them; the characteristics of members; and the kinds of leadership present. These factors were further categorized by Pearce et al (1996) into four theoretical approaches to society and community, with particular relevance to tourism impacts. They include:

1 The social systems approach: emphasis is placed on the role of social relations and the dominance of group membership.
2 The human ecological approach: emphasis is placed on living together and adapting to a setting which develops distinctive characteristics.

3 The interactional approach: this is seen as the sum of regular social interactions of individuals.
4 The critical approach: attention is given to the power of key groups in the decision-making process.

In conclusion, understanding the interrelations of society and culture within the context of tourism is an important part of the responsible tourism concept. The social responsibility of every stake-holder in the tourism industry is critical for the sustainability of tourist sites that are rich in culture and community engagement. Experiential learning from community engagement will deliver a more experiential tourism offer, and will leave a lasting impression on visitors.

Further reading

Goeldner, C. R. and Ritchie, J. R. B. (2006) *Tourism: Principles, Practices and Philosophies*, tenth edition, John Wiley and Sons Inc, New Jersey
Howitt, B. and Julian, R. (2002) *Heinemann Society and Culture*, Heinemann, Port Melbourne, Australia
Lovat, T. (ed) (2000) *New Society and Culture,* second edition, Social Sciences Press, Katoomba
Sharpley, R. (2008) *Tourism, Tourists and Society*, fourth edition, Elm Publications, Huntingdon

Dr. Vikneswaran Nair

SOCIOLOGY

Many aspects of tourism emerge from the principles of sociology, the study of society. The sociologist Boorstin, in his 1962 study, claimed that tourists were cultural idlers, generated from modern institutions, especially mass media. Such negative criticism influenced other research, and since the mid-1970s the studies around sociology and tourism have often become seminal articles which underpin a considerable volume of many aspects of current tourism research. One such study was MacCannell's (1973, 1976); in his view, tourism was considered a symbol of 'modern society', where it is seen as a modern pilgrimage in pursuit of **authenticity**.

Cohen (1984, p373) defined the sociology of tourism as 'an emergent specialty concerned with the study of touristic motivations, roles, relationships and institutions and of their impact on tourists and on the societies who receive them'. However, further studies have resulted in significant challenges to this definition, in both theory and methodology (Dann and Cohen, 1991, p156). Yasumura (1994, p4) proposes a sphere of sociology of tourism. In this framework the phenomenon of tourism is described in levels of a sociological space, as actors, social interaction, social systems and the modern world system. According to the levels of this sociological space, pioneering works of sociology in tourism are classified into four subjects: tourist types; hosts and guest relations; sociocultural impacts; and international mass tourism.

Two important studies focusing on the guest–host interaction are by Doxey (1976) and Butler (1975). Doxey (1976, pp26–27) proposed the 'irridex' model, which suggests that tourism development causes stresses in the local community since it is perceived to be destroying value systems and causing communities to lose their identities. In contrast to the irridex model, Butler's (1975) model focused on the complexity of the interactional process on two determinant factors: social attributes of visitors (the length of stay; their racial and economic backgrounds) and the carrying capacity of the local community (the level of economic development and the spatial distributions of economic and other activities).

Sociology is closely aligned to studies of motivation and consumer behaviour, as decision-making is heavily influenced by a range of societal influences, either directly or indirectly through personal decisions made as a result of the individual's societal background.

The typology that gained some of the greatest recognition was the twofold distinction made by Gray (1970) between 'sunlust' and 'wanderlust' tourists. The sunlust tourist seeks relaxation in warm climates, while the wanderlust traveller has a desire to explore and to learn about different cultures (Corcoran et al, 1996, p106).

Plog's model (1973) describes tourists' personality types along a continuum that approximates a normally distributed curve. The continuum is divided into the following segments:

- *Psychocentrics:* home-loving travellers who seek familiarity and safety in their choice of destination.
- *Allocentrics:* the confident, outgoing travellers who are keen to see new places and try new things.
- *Mid-centrics:* this position describes the mid-point between psychocentrics and allocentrics, although it has since been recognized that this can be explained as a continuum, so there are those who are near-psychocentric and near-allocentric travellers. Those with near-allocentric tendencies are among the first major wave of adopters, after a destination has been found by the allocentrics,

while the near psychocentrics are most likely to try a destination once it has been well travelled.

One of the main themes of the sociology of tourism is the 'guest and host interaction'. Although most early research emphasized the effects of tourists on local people, recent research has generated the idea that this effect is mutual. Therefore, in the sociology of tourism the interaction between the 'host' and the 'guest' should be addressed reciprocally.

Cohen (1972, 1979) classified tourists into four types according to the degree to which they seek familiarity and novelty:

1 *The organized mass tourist* prefers to travel with a group, with a fixed itinerary and a tour guide. Familiarity is at the highest level and novelty at the lowest.
2 *The individual mass tourist* is not necessarily a member of a group but prefers a planned itinerary. Familiarity is more important than for the explorer and novelty is lower.
3 *The explorer* travels alone but seeks the comfort of his or her home in terms of accommodation and transportation. Security is still important. Familiarity is lower than for the individual mass tourist and novelty is higher.
4 *The drifter* is an adventurous tourist who integrates with the local community. Familiarity is at the lowest level and novelty is at the highest.

Smith (1989, pp11–14) proposed a further typology of tourists which also considers environmental factors (the number of tourists, their goals and 'their adaptation to local norms) in order to describe seven types:

1 explorers;
2 elite tourists;
3 off-beat tourists;
4 unusual tourists;
5 incipient mass tourism;
6 mass tourism;
7 charter tourists.

In his study, Krippendorf (1987) categorized local people into four clusters, which enabled the conceptualization of certain characteristics, themes and experiences:

- *In direct contact with tourists:* locals who depend upon tourism and would be unemployed without it. They welcome visitors.

- *Partial contact:* locals who have frequent contact with tourists but derive only part of their income from tourism. They feel more critical about the disadvantages of tourism.
- *In unrelated business:* locals who are the owners of businesses which do not have a regular contact with tourists. Tourism is a purely commercial matter.
- *No contact:* locals who have no contact with tourists (although they may resent the negative impacts of tourism, such as overcrowding).

Local perceptions of tourists is worthy of analysis. However, research shows that an unbalanced relationship between locals and tourists might involve many complex social-cultural phenomena. Such social-cultural phenomena should thus be examined in terms of interactional processes (Yasumura, 1994, p6). In general, a distinction between intrinsic factors and extrinsic factors influencing the residents' perceptions of tourism is made (Wassler, 2010, p10):

- *Intrinsic factors:* age, gender, dependency upon tourism, education and community attachment.
- *Extrinsic factors:* seasonality, overcrowding, increased traffic, cultural differences between host and guest, types of tourists and the stage of development of the tourist destination.

All of these factors are still relevant to current tourism research, which continues to evaluate and re-evaluate the nature of tourism and tourist behaviour within a sociological context.

Further reading

MacCannell, D. (1976) *The Tourist: A New Theory of the Leisure Class*, Schocken Books, New York, NY
Urry, J. (2002) *The Tourist Gaze*, second edition, Sage Publications, London
Urry, J. (2003b) 'The sociology of tourism', in C. Cooper (ed) *Classic Reviews in Tourism*, Channel View Publications, Clevedon, UK

Dr. Ebru Günlü and Roya Rahimi

SPA TOURISM

Spa tourism is increasingly recognized as a growing sector of the tourism industry (Messerli and Oyama, 2004; Bushell and Sheldon, 2009; Smith and Puczko, 2009; SRI International, 2010). Although definitions vary greatly, the sector can be defined from a tourism perspective as 'travelling away from home, overnight for the purpose of engaging with products and services that maintain or improve health and wellbeing' (Hall, 2003; Mintel, 2007). Spa tourism is not a new phenomenon. Indeed, the concept of travelling for curative-related benefits is an ancient one. From prehistoric times through to the modern age, different cultures and societies across the world have engaged with and recognized the beneficial effect of herbal remedies, hot and cold compresses, massages, steam and mud baths, and waters (Crebbin-Bailey et al, 2005).

However, today, spa tourism has evolved into a multi-million-dollar international industry, which numbers a wide range of integrated spa, tourism and hospitality providers and a multitude of products and services that may or may not involve the use of natural resources, such as, for example, mineral waters (Mintel, 2007; Cohen and Bodeker, 2008; D'Angelo, 2010). Working along a continuum, contemporary spa tourism experiences span from the more traditional medical-oriented treatments geared to rehabilitate or to heal and recuperate, to wellness, well-being, beauty and pampering experiences. Within this reasoning, treatments such as galvanic baths, underwater tractions, and CO_2 injections offered by traditional and integrated medical suppliers sit along the same continuum as Swedish and Thai massages, aroma and crystal treatments, Hamman practices, chocolate baths and meditation programmes. It can be argued that the wide spectrum of experiences observable today not only reflects the vast cultural heritage traditions of spa tourism destinations and regions worldwide, it also evidences the increased globalization and commercialization of the concept (Smith and Puczko, 2009).

However, on close analysis, the growth in supply of products and services geared at curing, improving and/or holistically maintaining the 'body, the spirit and the mind' is also representative of broader societal and individual concerns towards health, wellness, well-being and overall quality of life (Bushell and Sheldon, 2009). Concerns in relation to an aging population and an awareness of 'global' diseases, combined with increased national health systems and health insurance costs, global financial market instability, and environmental issues such as climate change and global warming are just some of the drivers behind the fragmentation of the offer observable today. It is within this context that spa tourism can be also understood as a versatile yet key product within the recently acknowledged medical and wellness tourism industries (Bushell and Sheldon, 2009; Global Spa Summit, 2011). Furthermore, it is one that does not simply sit alongside, but rather enhances the provision of products such as dental treatments, surgery safaris, meditation retreats, wellness cruises and courses on how to eat and sleep well. Indeed, as Mintel (2009) points out, while in recent years '14.6 million adults worldwide have experienced some sort of health and wellness activity while on holiday, it is the use of spas and spa facilities which makes up most of this figure.'

Spa tourism consumer behaviours and perceptions mirror the influences of industry supply, with culture, globalization and economics being among the most prominent drivers behind the emergence of new, once-untapped markets both in traditional and emerging destinations (Manacap-Johnson, 2011). Urry's (2007) notion of mobilities, and specifically the twenty-first-century growth in circulation of ideas, money, technologies and people, combined with the growing de-differentiation of tourism from other spheres of cultural activities (Rojek and Urry, 1997), clearly illustrate spa consumer behaviour and preferences towards spa tourism destinations and treatments. Indeed, it can be argued that increased exposure to global spa tourism norms and practices, combined with an enhanced presentation of the products, has led to international travellers seeking ever-more unique and multifaceted cultural experiences both abroad and at home. This is evidenced each year within the spa industry trends predictions and, specifically, those trends that signal the increased consumption of traditional 'authentic' cultural traditions in spa tourism experiences. The continuous redrafting by global economic movements of the spa tourism consumer landscape and markets' characteristics has also enabled the emergence of new consumer markets such as the 'Emerging Seven': Brazil, China, India, Indonesia, Mexico, Russia and Turkey. These markets are in addition to the more mature ones of Europe and North America (in particular, the US) (Tabacchi, 2008).

Spa tourism has developed quickly since the inception of mass travel, and in parallel with the growth in consumer spending ability and the search for tailor-made individual tourism experiences (Mintel, 2007). Yet, as the first decade of the twenty-first century ends with the onset of a global economic recession, it is important to raise the question as to what extent the supply and demand for spa tourism products, services and experiences will continue to follow similar growth and modalities. However, throughout history, spa tourism has demonstrated that it is a resilient industry, and one capable of reinventing itself on more than one occasion. Furthermore, as the search for health preservation, holistic maintenance and an altogether better quality of life becomes an essential part of consumers' lifestyles (Euromonitor International, 2011b), it is not implausible to suggest that the future of spa tourism looks encouraging.

Further reading

Connell, J. (2006) 'Medical tourism: sea, sun, sand … surgery', *Tourism Management*, vol 27, pp1093–1100

Erfurt-Cooper, P. and Cooper, M. (2009) *Health and Wellness Tourism: Spas and Hot Springs*, Channel View Publications, Clevedon, UK

Jansen-Verbecke, M. and Diekmann, A. (2008) *The Future of Historic Spa Towns: Spa Symposium Workbook*, Castermans, Belgium

McNeil, K. R. and Ragins, R. J. (2005) 'Staying in the spa marketing game: Trends, challenges, strategies and techniques', *Journal of Vacation Marketing*, vol 11, no 1, pp31–39

Puczko, L. and Bacharov, M. (2006) 'Spa, bath, thermae: What's behind the labels?', *Journal of Tourism Recreation Research*, vol 31, no 1, pp83–91

Sharpley, R. (2008) *Tourism, Tourists and Society*, fourth edition, Elm Publications, Huntingdon

Dr. Iride Azara and Isobel Stockdale

SPECIAL INTEREST TOURISM

The term 'special interest tourism' (SIT), defined here as the identification of specific groups of tourists according to their defined interests, activities or participation, is often utilized in conjunction with **niche tourism** marketing. While niche tourism focuses upon typologies of tourism supply, SIT is concerned with tourist demand features and characteristics. In other words, SIT attempts to categorize visitor types according to specific motivations and, ultimately, to classify groups of individuals who consume particular experiences or certain types of tourism product. However, while SIT may offer a useful framework to target potential tourists, the term, as well as the methodology used to determine categories of special interest tourists, can be misleading. Moreover, the extent of how 'special' is special interest tourism should be driven by valid, rigorous and measurable parameters, which not only allows potential markets to be targeted, but also markets that are significant in terms of both volume and accessibility. For example, nature-based tourism is often labelled as special interest tourism, yet this micro-niche is broad enough to include diverse but potentially interrelated special interest activities such as bird-watching, flora and fauna painting, landscape photography, fishing, rambling and safaris.

Consequently, it would seem that a key issue with SIT is the emergence of an academic cottage industry which creates and recreates taxonomic categories of apparent special interest tourism, without paying due attention to the extent of the market size and the practicalities of accessing that market. Arguably, therefore, in terms of ramification and without an authoritative and definitive list of special interest tourist activities, *all* tourism might be considered 'special interest', as the mass tourism market becomes ever more fragmented and specialized. Nevertheless, despite typological and methodological concerns, SIT potentially allows industry practitioners such as travel agents and tour operators to create, group and promote tourism products and services that are directly allied to individual interests, as shown in Table 12. Consequently, SIT allows for the triangulation of tourism supply, demand and marketing, and in so doing, further divides a homogenous tourism market into a multiplication of heterogeneous market segments.

However, if SIT is to stand up to academic scrutiny, rather than being a superficial label with which to tag fashionable tourist activities, then any conceptual application needs to distinguish between both situational and enduring involvement in tourism. In other words, *situational involvement* is specific to the actual stimuli of the tourist experience and its context and, subsequently, is related to feelings of excitement, anticipation, anxiety, tensions, pleasure, thrills and so forth. Meanwhile, *enduring involvement* in tourism suggests that SIT incorporates broader notions of lifestyles that may be considered important to individual tourists, thereby creating a kind of 'life narrative' for those individuals who consume, and are seen to consume, particular tourist experiences.

Table 12 An example of special interest tourism and its relationship with niche tourism

Niche tourism		Special interest tourism
Macro–niche	*Micro–niche*	*Tourist activity*
Environmental	Coastal tourism	Beachcombing
		Canoeing/kayaking
		Fishing
		Gastronomy/picnics
		Kiting
		Music events/art shows
		Outdoor pursuits and games (e.g. paragliding/ beach frisbee/cricket/volleyball/etc.)
		Photography/painting
		Rambling/hiking
		Retail/souvenir shopping
		Sailing/boating
		Scuba diving/snorkelling
		Sunbathing/naturalism
		Surfing
		Wildlife/bird watching

Therefore, SIT has the potential to project high symbolic value to individuals (e.g. eco-tourists and their views on environmentalism), which, in turn, extends beyond the initial consumption of the holiday and into the overall 'life narrative' of an individual. Consequently, rather than simply utilizing SIT as a marketing endeavour, SIT can draw attention from the purely behavioural and motivational aspects of the actual tourist activity. Ultimately, the idea of categorizing individuals according to particular interests, values and beliefs allows for a more sensitive approach to cognitive components of how tourism, in general, and special interest tourism, in particular, can be used to reaffirm lifestyle choices and values in a world that appears ever-more fragmented.

Further reading

Douglas, N., Douglas, N. and Derrett, R. (eds) (2002) *Special Interest Tourism*, John Wiley and Sons, Chichester, UK

McKercher, B. and Chan, A. (2005) 'How special is "special interest tourism"?', *Journal of Travel Research*, vol 44, no 1, pp21–31

Sharpley, R. and Stone, P. R. (eds) (2011) *Tourist Experience: Contemporary Perspectives*, Routledge, Abingdon, Oxford, UK

Traucer, B. (2006) 'Conceptualising special interest tourism: Frameworks for analysis', *Tourism Management*, vol 27, no 2, pp183–200

Dr. Philip R. Stone

SPORT TOURISM

Academic interest in sport tourism has grown in recent years, but it is important to note that it is not a recent arrival in the 'tourism marketplace' (Weed, 2006, p305). Indeed, the earliest documentation of sports tourism was the ancient Olympics in 776 BC (Neirotti, 2003; Weed, 2006). Developments in transportation during the Industrial Revolution enabled the growth of sports participation and passive spectatorship by improving access both nationally and internationally. The rise in popularity of adventure sports such as skiing and mountaineering in Europe during the late 1800s facilitated the development of the active tourism market, with commercial operators quickly realizing the potential of the natural environment. Thus, there is a clear correlation between the development of sport tourism and the history of adventure tourism.

As disciplines, sport and tourism have historically been treated separately, although with retrospective analysis it is clear to see their interrelationship. However, increasingly, they have become linked through key influences and trends, including their mutual contribution to economic regeneration; increased media focus on national and international sporting events such as the Olympic Games and the football World Cup; and society's increasing awareness of the benefits of sporting activity for health and well-being (Hudson, S., 2003). Economic regeneration is the key driver for London's 2012 Olympics.

While there are numerous definitions of sport tourism (Roberts, cited in Roberts, 2011), most revolve around the key principles of travel away from home, active and passive involvement, and the element of competition, whether through direct involvement or as a spectator. It is accepted that some sports are an integral part of the adventure tourism offering, such as skiing and, more recently, mountain biking; however, definitions are generally divided into sport tourism and adventure tourism.

Sport or sports tourism refers to involvement in travel away from home to participate in sporting activity, watch sport or visit a sport attraction either competitively or non-competitively (Hudson, S., 2003). The supply side of sport tourism (Neirotti, 2003) includes natural (national parks) and human-made (stadiums, museums) attractions that provide the tourist with things to see and do related to sport; resorts (complexes with sports as their main focus and marketing strategy – for example, ski and golf resorts); and events (sporting activities that attract participants and spectators – for example, mega-events such as the Olympic Games). Increasingly, there are a significant number of mixed-use resort destination developments in key tourist areas worldwide. Such developments combine hotels, entertainment, leisure and sporting activities, retail outlets and attractions. As short breaks replace or supplement longer holidays, multigenerational family holidays become more popular and adventure sports become more mainstream, such mixed-use resorts offer, for many people, an appealing combination of sport and adventure activity within a specific and demarcated setting.

Increased media exposure of key sporting events during recent years has significantly raised the profile of sports and sporting events. This factor combined with those sporting 'icons' awarded celebrity status through high-media profile serves to attract an increasing audience, as well as participants. Competing for a share of non-traditional markets, such as the family market, has also led to sports events enhancing their offering by adding additional events to their main focus. An example of this is a racecourse offering a family fun day, where provision is made for the needs of families, with attractions such as children's rides and entertainment, alongside the key race meeting focus.

As with leisure tourism, the impact of budget airlines on sports tourism should not be underestimated, with increased demand for national and international sporting events due to ease, convenience and affordability of access. What is clear is that an ageing population, increased leisure time, a growing awareness of the health benefits of physical activity and growth in the domestic tourism market offer a significant opportunity to sport tourism entrepreneurs.

Further reading

DCMS (2007) *Winning: A tourism Strategy for 2012 and Beyond*, http://www.vis itbritain.org/Images/DCMS-Tourism2012Strategy_fullreport_tcm29-14543. pdf, accessed 23 August 2011

Euromonitor International (2011a) *City Travel Briefing: London and the Olympic Games Global Briefing*, London

Hudson, S. (ed) (2003) *Sport and Adventure Tourism*, Haworth Hospitality Press, London

Neirotti, L. D. (2003) 'An introduction to sport and adventure tourism', in S. Hudson (ed) *Sport and Adventure Tourism*, Haworth Hospitality Press, London

Roberts, C. (2011) 'Sport and adventure tourism', in P. Robinson, S. Heitmann and P. U. C. Dieke (eds) *Research Themes for Tourism*, CABI, London, pp146–159

Weed, M. (2006) 'Sports tourism', in J. Beech. and S. Chadwick (eds) (2006) *The Business of Tourism Management*, Pearson Education Limited, Harlow

Carol Southall and Linda Phillips

STAKEHOLDERS

The effective management of stakeholders in tourism is essential and can comprise a very complex range of individuals and organizations, frequently defined as those with an interest in the activities of an organization, and who can influence its strategic direction. Stakeholders may include:

- local communities;
- neighbours;
- local authorities;
- banks and financiers;
- other businesses;
- landowners;
- developers;

- members and friends of an organization;
- conservation groups;
- lobby and pressure groups.

The stakeholder analysis model makes it possible to map out the varying levels of interest and conflict amongst these different groups, which enables specific issues to be highlighted. Examples could include customers who may resist increases in admission prices; local communities who may be concerned about environmental impact; staff who want an increase in salary; and shareholders who are keen to see a return on their investment. These competing needs require careful balancing, which presents a manager with some complex difficulties.

The model is based upon an assessment of the varying power and interest of each stakeholder. Power is defined as the stakeholders' ability to actually influence decisions made by the organization, while interest is defined by the stakeholders' desire to influence organizational decisions. Based upon these two factors, stakeholders can be categorized as those who should be kept informed, those who are key players and must be actively involved, those who need to be kept satisfied, and those who have so little interest that only a minimal effort is required. Regardless of where they appear in the model, communication and consultation is essential to manage stakeholders successfully.

Of particular importance is the recognition that stakeholders can change categories, so a separate analysis must be carried out for all major decisions. In many large organizations it is possible for stakeholders to create an opposition to the business and to force the organization to take decisions that they may be unwilling to adopt (see Figure 5).

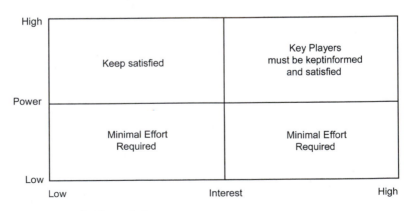

Figure 5 Stakeholder analysis

Further reading

Hall, C. M. (2008) *Tourism Planning: Policies, Processes and Relationships*, Pearson Education, Harlow
Page, S. and Swarbrooke, J. (2001) *The Development and Management of Visitor Attractions*, Butterworth-Heinemann, Oxford, UK

Peter Robinson

SUSTAINABLE TOURISM

The publication of *Our Common Future* (WCED,1987) signalled the beginning of a global focus on the sustainability of all types of development. 'The Earth is one but the world is not' acknowledges that we all depend upon one biosphere for sustaining our lives. Sustainability is predicated on the notion of tourism development that meets the needs of the present without compromising the ability of future generations to meet their own needs (WCED, 1987). The sustainable management of tourism is based upon recommending ways in which shared concern for the environment is based on greater cooperation among developing countries and between countries at different stages of economic and social development. Such management should lead to the achievement of common and mutually supportive objectives which take account of the interrelationships between people, resources, environment and development, linking sustainability through global concerns. This was the intention of the Rio Earth Summit in June 1992, which resulted in Local Agenda 21.

The creation of national parks in the US during the nineteenth century marks the origins of systematically managing sites of special social, cultural and environmental significance. Originally, such interventions were based upon the need to protect species and maintain the biota of specially identified zones. Such sites were selected and then interventions planned to segregate commercial activities from the places designated as of special cultural and natural heritage. Visitor management practices, first developed in the mid-twentieth century, are adjusting to the pressure of visitor numbers using carrying capacity concepts such as:

- Limits of Acceptable Change (LAC) – balancing resource protection with recreational use;
- Visitor Area Management Plans (VAMPs) – identifying and managing visitors' use of special cultural and ecological sites using designated zones; and

- Tourism Optimization Management Modelling (TOMM) – managing beneficial impacts from visitors and minimizing negative sociocultural, environmental and economic impacts.

Sustainable tourism needs to identify who could benefit and what, why and how these beneficiaries need external support and funding. This approach, using stakeholder theory, has usually identified the players who can benefit from practices which manage tourism's capacity to expand and diversify. Policies supporting sustainable tourism have been included in destination development strategies to identify within stakeholders the need for, and the method of, public-sector interventions. In general, destinations' public-sector accountabilities have identified initial interventions which support private-sector entrepreneurs through strategy documents.

In the private sector, for example, the tour operator TUI in Europe has rewritten vision and mission statements to incorporate Agenda 21 and the greening of packaged holidays. In the UK, Tourism Concern represents the interests of hosts at destinations of less developed nations and is largely led by volunteers with concerns over exploitative practices.

What remains to be undertaken is a review of outcomes identifying and ranking the quality and indicators of sustainability that have emerged. Indicators that may be used in assessing positive impacts and barriers to sustainable tourism development can include the employment in direct and indirect supply of goods and services; percentages of total employment in tourism and related services (direct/indirect); gender of employees; depreciation/appreciation of the currency; change in the number of mega-events; change in type and intensity of public-sector support; expectations of public-sector support; ingenuity of contemporary suppliers; the relative attractiveness of suppliers (quality of welcome and coherence in value/supply chain); ageing of host community; seasonality in supply and demand of goods and services; strength in the supply chain (vertical/horizontal/diagonal); strength of ties with manufacturing, mining and agriculture (primary industries); strength of new business creation and longevity (compared to a basket of enterprises); competitiveness of the tourism offer versus a range of comparable destinations' products and services; existence and acknowledgement of push-and-pull factors on demand, including safety, security, political stability, health, privacy, space to play and space to rejuvenate; strength of the domestic (tourism) industry; strength of networks/partnerships; existence of a neo-liberal approach (by regulation) to entrepreneurship – fiscal policy and taxes, the unique identity of products and services (branding) and identity of destination; and the extent to which sustainability indices can be used by the destination in marketing and promotion.

Increasingly, tourism development is discussed as sustainable tourism development. In the face of social, economic and environmental stresses, development must consider the positive aspects of tourism, balanced with an appraisal of the negative impacts, resulting in a managed approach incorporating systems thinking. Hall and Lew

Table 13 Issues in sustainable development

Direct or indirect employment	The net increase in employment as a result of tourism or related industries (indirect) or decreasing employment in tourism or related industries.
Gender of employees	Short-termism in employment offers, gender imbalance, poor career opportunities for recruits.
Depreciation/ appreciation of the currency	External factors affecting demand and the strength of suppliers to pay for expensive imports required for tourism development.
Change in the number of mega-events	Connection between holiday and business travel established and the capacity for infrastructure to support meeting, incentives, conferences and events demand (MICE markets).
Expectations and intensity of public-sector support	Capacity of local and central governments to fund skills development and provide incentives to small business entrepreneurs as well as multinational corporations.
Ingenuity of contemporary suppliers	Existence of enterprise culture and entrepreneurs taking risks with new business in response to new target markets.
Quality of experience (suppliers, welcome)	Existence and extent of mechanisms to measure the quality of provision and guests' experiences.
Ageing of visitors	Acknowledging the ageing and adjusting the supply of appropriate products for key target markets.
Seasonality	Improving yield management and better forecasting of demand to maximize return on investment and smooth the peaks and troughs of demand to match perishable products.
Supply chain	Exploring and monitoring horizontal as well as vertical supply chains with tourism-related supply businesses, thereby minimizing import leakages and maximizing the multiplier effect with indirect and induced expenditure by visitors.
Durability of businesses	Ensuring robust supply with ongoing investment. Typical tourism operations are small and micro-businesses (with fewer than five employees) and few survive the first five years of operations.

Table 13 (continued)

Competitiveness	Ensuring the offer to visitors is complementary to wider development agendas but that services offered are differentiated sufficiently to ensure continuing demand.
Safety, security, health	Minimizing negative impacts of perceived and actual perils for visitors. The existence of terrorism is a contemporary concern.
Strength of domestic tourism	In many destinations domestic demand equals demand from international visitors.
Networks and partnerships	Contemporary success stories typically feature well-integrated networks and partnerships between suppliers and public-sector and private enterprise. Risks and rewards can be shared.
Fiscal policy and taxes	Incentives by governments in lower goods and service taxes for tourism operators.
Branding and identity	Ensuring the contemporary offer reflects shared vision and goals of host communities as well as tourism operators.

(1998) identify that 'holistic planning, preservation of essential ecological processes, protection of human heritage and biodiversity, sustaining productivity for the long-term and achieving a better balance between fairness and opportunity between nations' (citing WCED, 1987).

In contemporary good practices the focus is on demand and supply in tourism, especially where profits are sustained through the allocation of scarce resources. Simultaneously, market-led destinations identify a tide of rising individualism and the dismissal of low-yield and high-cost mass tourism. We should therefore acknowledge divergent patterns of consumption by visitors to a destination. Consumerism and the power in meeting contemporary demand requires a focus by tour operators on two parallel issues: informed and net-savvy customers aware of their consumer rights and an increased range of products available in the market. Not only does sustainable tourism demand that operators minimize negative social and environmental impacts at destinations, it also requires an understanding of the role of fashion and trends in consumption patterns. Without acknowledging the power of consumers' demand we cannot address the continuing supply of sustainable products.

Future areas for exploration include ways in which consumers and suppliers can identify good practices in sharing experiences that have been trialled and tested in other places so that stakeholders can place value on the explicit (outward-facing) and tacit (processes used by developers) knowledge. This can be seen where development has positively benefitted the host community in creating a resource base that all can share by those identified as intellectually and practically able to champion sustainable tourism development management practices (Hollinshead and Jamal, 2007, p85).

The achievement of sustainable tourism evolves from a mix of public- and private-sector incentives for tour operations and accommodation providers helping to monitor, manage and review negative social, environmental and economic impacts of tourism. The capacity to develop tourism will still depend upon practices limiting visitors, zoning recreation and increasing yield from visitors to help reduce these impacts. Long-term sustainable tourism also requires visitors and operators to consider learning ways in which tourism can provide opportunities for hosts to improve quality of life and a clearly beneficial experience for guests and hosts. In taking a positive view of development through sustainability, stakeholders can install systems that will enable participating in networks extending into vertical, horizontal and diagonal supply chains in retail, transport and services such as publishing, health, information technology and communication. At the same time, stakeholders can identify the skills required to engage the learning community. Recently, useful work has been published using North American and Australian best practice case studies (see, for example, Dredge, 2006; Higgins-Desbiolles et al, 2010; Toomaney, 2010). Sustainable tourism is concerned with education and skills enhancements that reflect the interdependent nature of tourism as an enterprise, and the support that tourism can bring through sharing skills and learning between less-developed destinations and not-for-profit organizations. In the UK, Tourism Concern is just one of many such enablers.

Further reading

Cerina, F., Markandya, A. and McAleer, M. (2010) *Economics of Sustainable Tourism*, Routledge, Oxon, UK

Chon, K. and Edgell, D. L. (2006) *Managing Sustainable Tourism: A Legacy for the Future*, Routledge, Oxon, UK

Liburd, J. and Edwards, D. (2010) *Understanding the Sustainable Development of Tourism*, Goodfellow, Oxford, UK

Peter Wiltshier

TOUR OPERATIONS

On 5 July 1841, a special train trip from Leicester to Loughborough and back marked the historical beginning of tour operations. Thomas

Cook had organized this tour, targeting members of the South Midland Temperance Society. It also encompassed entertainment; a band played music for the travellers at the train station (Swinglehurst, 1974). Today this concept covers the commercial creation and distribution of holiday package or inclusive tours, and represents a significant market volume in terms of revenues and participants generated. According to Holloway (2009), three factors contributed to the growth of package holiday tour production and sales in Europe during the second half of the twentieth century: the expansion of leisure time, greater discretionary income, and low package holiday costs.

There is the notion of the tour as a product, which is designed and assembled; however, unlike in the case of manufactured physical goods such as a washing machine, the components of a tour (e.g. hotel accommodation or air transportation) are useful services in their own right. Providers of travel and tourism services are referred to as *principals*. Figure 6 shows the structure of distribution channels, highlighting how the principals' offers find their way to the consumer.

Principals can sell their services directly to tourists via websites or own sales outlets. As an alternative, they can sell indirectly via tour operators and/or travel agencies. Both of these belong to the business category of *intermediaries*. In an economic context, these have the role of creating markets by bringing sellers and buyers together (Cooper et al, 2008a). The use of intermediaries provides benefits to the supply side as well as to the demand side: principals are able to sell in bulk and transfer, at least partly, the risk of unsold capacities to the tour

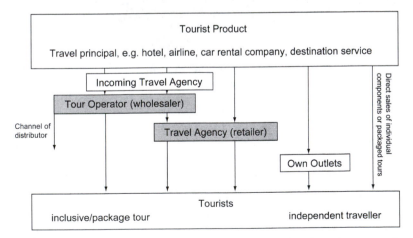

Figure 6 Structure of distribution channels (Source: adapted from Cooper et al, 2008b)

operator, and they can reduce promotion and distribution costs through the multiplying effect of the intermediaries' outreach. Consumers can reduce transaction costs in searching for suitable travel offers. They also gain from specialist knowledge and participate in bulk discounts passed on by tour operators (Gee et al, 1997; Cooper et al, 2008a; Holloway, 2009).

As shown in Figure 6, tour operators can be understood as wholesalers in the tourism market; buying the services of principals in large quantities and selling them in individual units to consumers via travel agents who, following the same logic, are classified as retailers. In this sense, a tour operator's work is functionally similar to wholesale companies in other industries. A major difference, however, is that the tour operator does not buy products. It secures future space or capacities in hotels, airlines, etc., usually by reserving more or less large blocks or allotments (Gee et al, 1997) to form a package tour. In this sense, tour operators differ from wholesalers of other industries, as they change the nature of the purchased services. Therefore, it can be argued that tour operators are also principals, creating new products (Holloway, 2009).

The package tour is also described as a bundle of services, goods and experiences (Shaw and Williams, 2004) or a 'series of integrated travel services' (Holloway, 2009, p559). Thus, it can be considered as a complex composite good, with the following three major components:

1 *transport* between a place of residence and a tourist destination;
2 *tourist attractor*, representing the main reason for travelling there, such as sights, scenery, climate, theme parks, golf courses, etc. – the attractor is typically the core component;
3 *tourism infrastructure*, including hotels, airports, roads, marinas, services, food, etc.

(Letzner, 2010)

It has to be taken into consideration that tour operators have differing levels of control over package tour components. Whereas airline, shuttle bus or hotel services can be negotiated and selected from contract partners, the tour operator does not have any direct influence on the climate or landscape. Hence, despite the importance of some of the natural tourist attractors, the sourcing of package tour components is limited to principals' services. Figure 7 presents the value chain of a package tour based on these services.

Depicting the package tour's path from the individual principals' service components through to the customer reached via retail agents

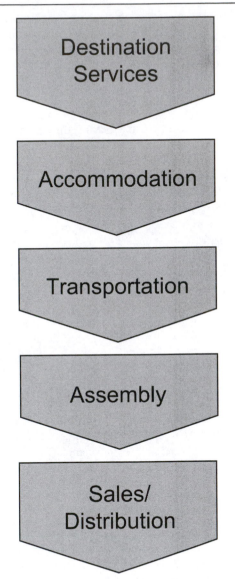

Figure 7 The package tour value chain (Source: adapted from Freyer, 2006, p218)

at the sales/distribution level, this value chain places the tour operator at the *assembly* stage. It thus emphasizes the role of refining components and finishing the product. Tour operators share major operational challenges with protagonists of other industries in today's competitive business environment: on-going improvement in customer service

(Fitzsimmons and Fitzsimmons, 2008) and, at the same time, cost reductions along the entire value chain (Chase et al, 2007).

Tour operators frequently engage in vertical or horizontal integration. The former occurs when a firm gains control over elements at a preceding or subsequent value chain level. The latter occurs when a firm attains increased consolidation or control within their own value chain level. Both integration approaches can be pursued through mergers, alliances or takeovers (Weaver and Lawton, 2010). During recent years, major tour operators have built integrated corporations in order to benefit from all value chain levels. With such a move they acknowledge that **operations management** is more significant than in other industries, as fixed capacities are defined before offer and calculation is finished, and fixed costs account for up to 80 per cent of total cost. In addition, seasonality leads to higher dispatch and flexibility needs (Born, 2004). Furthermore, value-added services provided along the entire value chain yield the benefits of differentiating the firm from its competition and of building relationships that bind customers to the organization (Chase et al, 2007).

Recent trends add more challenges to tour operations: There is an on-going phenomenon of disintermediation, characterized by the rise of Internet platforms replacing or bypassing traditional tour operation intermediaries (Weaver and Lawton, 2010). Another development opens opportunities of re-intermediation; operators once again can add value through a concept referred to as *dynamic packaging*. With real-time access to hotel, airline and rental car capacity databases, which may be owned by various principals or wholesalers, 'virtual' tour operators provide a wide variety of flexible choices to travellers. This concept reflects the trend towards mass customization also known from other industries such as car manufacturing. Dynamic packaging adds complexity as well as intensified competition to the field of tour operations (e.g. through online-savvy market entrants). There is also increasing complexity in international supply chains. Schwartz et al (2008) point out that tour operators have to manage a process, ensuring that products and services along the entire tour value chain are procured in ways that meet the buyer's specifications and address the critical need of improving sustainability performance. Hence, it seems appropriate to conclude that 'the tour operating industry is changing faster than any other sector in tourism' (Schwartz et al, 2008, p298).

Further reading

Cook, R. A., Yale, L. J. and Marqua, J. J. (2009) *Tourism: The Business of Travel*, fourth edition, Prentice Hall, Upper Saddle River, NJ

Font, X. and Cochrane, J. (2005) *Integrating Sustainability into Business: A Management Guide for Responsible Tour Operations*, United Nations Publications, Blue Ridge Summit, PA

Page, S. and Connell, J. (2009) *Tourism: A Modern Synthesis*, third edition, Cengage Learning, Hampshire

Volker Rundshagen

TOURISM AND THE ENVIRONMENT

Tourism is vitally important for many economies: it provides Egypt, for example, with its main source of foreign currency, with 9.8 million visitors per annum; similar numbers visit Singapore (around 10.2 million). Tourism is vital to Kenya's growth strategy and currently accounts for 10 per cent of gross domestic product (GDP), while in India it is seen as a major provider of economic growth. For the 26 coral atolls in the Indian Ocean that form the Republic of the Maldives, tourism accounts for 17 per cent of GDP, and there are more visitors to the islands there each year than there are indigenous population. But the impact of visitors upon the environment has been enormous; in 1983, after ten years of international tourism development, the sea was polluted with garbage and piles of waste were to be found in most resorts. More importantly, perhaps, the coral reef was irreparably damaged through its use as decorative material on buildings and due to the increase in sewage disposal (Saeed, 1998). It is for these reasons that tourism is seen as having a high impact upon the environment within which it operates and why the importance of responsible tourism was highlighted at the Earth Summit at Rio de Janeiro in 1992 (WTTC, 2002).

Tourism depends upon a total environment, both the physical and social construct in which it takes place, to attract visitors; examples include the beach in Goa, India, the heritage experienced through visiting the Pyramids in Egypt, the music encapsulated in the Bayreuth Festival, and the religious experiences promoted by the ten-yearly performance of the Oberammergau passion play in its tiny Austrian village and original amphitheatre. People and place come together in this way to provide a totality of 'the tourist gaze' (Urry, 2002). The cohesion of people and place, whether created by natural phenomena, such as the 'hot springs' in Iceland or a man-made development of integrated resorts or large-scale sporting events in the 638 square kilometre island of Singapore, create an impression which can enhance or detract from the destination, affecting both visitors and communities.

If the core environment, that which visitors were attracted to experience, is not protected, then tourism (through increased visitor numbers which may cause congestion, waste, litter, corrosion to natural paths, damage to flora and fauna, or noise pollution) has the potential to destroy (Pigram, 1995). The maintenance of the setting, therefore, is crucial to tourism's success and the economic multipliers which it creates; as a result, there have been increasing discussions on how environments can be protected.

The environment can be defined as our surroundings: the external conditions affecting development or growth (Chambers Dictionary, 2008). However, this can be made up of both natural and fabricated settings, some of which are existent to the host communities, with others created to support tourism. Environmental management is often regarded as protecting both natural resources and/or the natural environment, which may include beaches, mountains, lakes, waterfalls, forest or desert (Beerli and Martin, 2004); but is also important in conserving scarce resources, such as groundwater or energy. Environmental management is also involved in culture and heritage preservation for ancient monuments or landmarks, famous buildings or experiences, such as shopping in the *souks* of Marrakech, or the buildings and lifestyle to be observed and experienced in Luang Prabang (Peterson and McCarthy, 2000). The natural environment is affected by man-made attractions such as Disneyland, Paris or Sentosa Resort, Singapore; but once built they become part of a tourism environment that is itself an ecosystem, affected by and affecting external surroundings or creating a new geography (Henderson, 2010). Finally, the internal framework, such as airports, roads, restaurants, hotels, access to essential healthcare, emergency services and policing infrastructure, leisure or recreational facilities, public toilets and waste disposal facilities are all elements of the environment (Sawkar et al, 1998; Jayawardena et al, 2008; Dwivedi et al, 2009; Ball and Taleb, 2011).

Both host communities and tourists have a responsibility to the environment, whether that is maintenance, preservation or enhancement. Mensah (2007) argues that **sustainable tourism**, the regulated use of tourism resources, is important to protect these assets for the future. In addition to pollution and depletion of natural resources, the way in which the tourist product is consumed will make an increasing impact upon future tourism markets (Sawkar et al, 1998). Examples of such consumption include the overdevelopment and 'bucket and spade' image of Los Christianos and Playa das Americas on the Island of Tenerife, which, without the hindsight of planning and environmental management, was pushed as an early destination for international visitors, particularly German and British tourists. This has resulted in the loss of the original fishing villages and much of the heritage and culture of the Canarias, making it difficult to attract more diverse and sophisticated tourist markets. However, environmental protection is only one part of the sustainable tourism agenda (UNEP, 2005).

The fact that tourism depends upon environmental quality is a central precept of its development. Often, arguments on the environment concentrate on rural areas; but in city areas the protection of urban wildscapes and the provision of green spaces are seen as climate change response options providing practical solutions that attract both domestic and international visitors, while reclaimed land provides a lucrative and useful development (Henderson, 2010; Kitha and Lyth, 2011). Environmental damage is not seen as being as controversial in urban development; but even so, problems encountered during construction need to be addressed. These may include noise pollution, waste disposal, rising levels of energy and water consumption, as well as soil erosion and sediment runoff (Henderson, 2010).

To be sustainable, or to successfully continue, changes to the environment in which tourism takes place must be seen by the host community and by visitors as positive compensations. For example:

- Economic or financial benefits are seen through increased personal income, continuity of employment, development of export markets for local produce, foodstuffs or handicrafts, as well as support and diversification in local cottage industries, such as agriculture and fisheries. As a result, the local environment is richer, more stable and has a diversified economy.
- Social or cultural benefits may increase services – for instance, health and social care, community facilities (such as restaurants, shops or leisure activities) and an increased education through exposure to alternative lifestyles, as well as through the knowledge of local history and cultures. In addition, social mobility can be encouraged through employment and exposure to tourism, as well as the provision of better transport (e.g. airports in Hong Kong, Singapore and the Maldives were all improved for tourist visits but have greatly enhanced the mobility of local populations). Bus services in rural areas such as the Lake District in Cumbria and Lyme Regis, Dorset, in the UK were both extended to accommodate visitor need as locals were not sufficient in number to make the service viable, but benefit from this tourism provision. Political benefits could include a more cohesive 'local' or regional society who maintain their unique political boundaries, such as has been developed in

both Goa and the Maldives, and promotion of tourism within legal or constrained frameworks has proved very successful for Niagara, Ontario, in Canada through the Niagara Gateway Project (Jayawardena et al, 2008). Other political benefits include environmentally active civil societies – for instance, the Lyme Society, which fights to maintain the unique historical infrastructure of the town of Lyme Regis in the UK, and more tourism-orientated regional councils, as has proved beneficial in Alcúdia, Mallorca, where a Special Plan for the Protection of the Historic Centre was developed (Peterson and McCarthy, 2000).

- Environmental or conservation improvements may incorporate regulatory and enforcement frameworks seeking to provide amenity enhancement, such as beach cleaning, parks management, waste removal and the protection of unique resources (e.g. the Coral Reefs in the Maldives), or the provision of environmental education. Tourism examples include the partnership of the Forestry Commission, Natural England, United Utilities (the water authority) and The National Trust, with other stakeholders working in Ennerdale, Cumbria, under the umbrella title Wild Ennerdale (www.wildennerdale.co.uk).

The positive outcomes from tourism must include a serious review of the negative consequences of current visitor activity, and analysis of what actions are currently being taken to overcome these, before developing coherent and strategic plans for environmental management, or what is more commonly termed responsible tourism development. Some of the negative impacts upon the tourism environment are illustrated in Table 14.

Societies' values are constantly in a state of change, and certainly Western tourists have become more eco-centric; thus, there is an increase in complaints from tourists that include quantity of litter on beaches, proper maintenance of beaches, overcrowding of resorts, encroachment by other than like-minded people (e.g. the hippie scene, which was prevalent in Goa for a time) and noise (Sawkar et al, 1998; Jayawardena et al, 2008; Dwivedi et al, 2009; Ball and Taleb, 2011).

More importantly, perhaps, is the development of tourism which seeks to build on current market trends where infrastructure and permits have not kept up with demand, and then cause communities to fracture in their support of such growth. One example of this are cruise ships visiting the Northern Territories, Australia, whose captains land them at deserted beaches. Visitors then walk over the historical burial grounds of native Australians, where groundwork to support tourism

Table 14 A sample of environmental negatives for the tourism industry

Over-construction	Overcrowding	Sewage increase and disposal
Energy or power cuts	Higher prices for basic services such as taxis	Aggression from traders (the British are termed 'fish and chips' in the souks of Marrakech)
Increase in crime (both petty theft and more serious assaults)	Congestion	Waste
Litter and littering Groundwater depletion Damage of natural resources through exploitation (e.g. coral reefs in the Maldives)	Corrosion Water scarcity Damage of natural resources through usage (e.g. footpath erosion on popular walkways or from use by 'off-road vehicles')	Beach degradation Coastal erosion Disruption and dispersion of cultures
Labour influx which takes jobs from local people	Conflict over use of scarce resources (e.g. locals' use of transport is limited at the height of the season)	Increased cost of living for basic commodities and house prices for local populations
Increased number of undesirable social problems	Seasonality of income and employment	Reduction in available living space as homes are bought as 'second homes' in popular destinations
Subject to economic market forces and therefore tourism may be unstable	Costs of training guides and managers	Lack of contribution from private providers (some countries are now charging a bed tax to hoteliers)

such as signage and toilets is lacking and permissions to land have not been granted; volatile local conditions result. Visionary tourism ventures that seek to open natural environments to more visitors by educating people on wildlife and habitats within the area are to be commended; but with no toilets, no waste bins, limited overnight accommodation and a ban on camping that is not enforced (resulting in human faecal matter left behind walls on private land, and beside pathways where other visitors and children walk), sustainability and responsibility come into question. Developers of tourism need to take a very holistic and long-term view of the impact of their project. Research into a variety of sites in China that were granted World Heritage status show the risks connected to tourism exploitation (Wang and Pizam,

2011), while environmental degradation remains a real danger (Ko and Stewart, 2002).

Expanding tourism provides a dichotomy for communities. **Heritage tourism** depends upon **authentic** experiences for its existence, but the addition of ever more visitors must by its very nature detract from this (Peterson and McCarthy, 2000). In addition, even the most stunning of natural resources, such as Niagara Falls in Ontario, Canada, are not enough to support tourist stays of longer than one or two days in length. This does not provide enough sustainable income to maintain an industry capable of competing on the world stage; thus, great care is needed to plan and manage infrastructure and products to strengthen and sustain tourism development. This is seen to work well when including the community and other local, regional and national stakeholders (Peterson and McCarthy, 2000; Jayawardena et al, 2008).

Tourism brings much needed economic benefits and, in some cases, an enhanced social structure for local communities; however, this has also been shown to negatively affect the environment. Hotels, for instance, have the highest negative impact upon the environment of all commercial buildings except hospitals (Bohdanowicz and Martinac, 2007), and although some large corporations have acted to improve this situation, it sometimes appears as if these are driven more by cost savings, improved company image or legal compliance (WWF-UK and IBLF, 2005). Neither is it just the role of government (local, regional or national) to legislate for protection of the tourist environment; individual tourism operations (some of which are very small businesses) need to clearly understand their impact and act through increased **corporate social responsibility** initiatives, introducing more sustainable practices to protect and enrich the environment in which they trade. Factors to be considered may include using natural resources in a sustainable manner; reducing environmental impacts when developing tourism; maintaining biodiversity; promoting only low-impact tourism; incorporating green technologies; reducing, reusing and recycling (and making this easy for tourists to do); being less wasteful and practising water and energy conservation; reducing environmental pollution; and, finally, educating visitors (through signage, brochures and multimedia communication technology) on what is being achieved and why (Van de Merwe and Wöcke, 2007; Sheldon and Park, 2011).

Further reading

UNEP (United Nations Environment Programme) (2003) *Tourism and the Local Agenda 21: The Role of Local Authorities in Sustainable Tourism*, UNEP, Paris

UNWTO (United Nations World Tourism Organization) (2005) *Making Tourism More Sustainable: A Guide for Policy Makers*, UNWTO, Madrid
WTTC and WTO (1996) *Agenda 21 for the Travel and Tourism Industry towards Environmentally Sustainable Development*, WTTO, London

Caroline Ann Wiscombe

TOURISM EDUCATION

The first tourism qualifications emerged during the early 1970s, and the origins of tourism research, which underpins tourism curricula, are variously embedded in geography, sociology and business studies, amongst others. It is the development of theory that helps to define tourism as a subject area in its own right. Since the 1990s, the increase in tourism-related courses has been encouraged by the growth of the industry and the increased recognition by employers of the benefits of related qualifications. Furthermore, increased tourism research has helped to further the development of teaching and research in tourism and its related disciplines. As a result, it is often taught alongside the subjects of travel, hospitality, events, entertainments, leisure and sport as equally distinct but synchronous areas of study. Tourism itself has diversified into specific specialist areas with courses that include **ecotourism, adventure tourism, rural tourism** and **destination management**, and students often study tourism alongside business studies and languages. In all of these cases the subject may be taught from two perspectives: tourism management and tourism studies. Students of the former are likely to have skills which extend beyond their subject area and equip them to work in most areas of the service industries. Students of the latter frequently engage in greater subject-specific research and help to grow the knowledge around specific tourism themes, such as **dark tourism** and **wildlife tourism**.

In addition, the growth of academic and practitioner membership of professional bodies such as the Tourism Society and the Tourism Management Institute (TMI) has brought the two together more closely in discussion forums, while the accreditation of programmes by trade bodies gives credibility to university courses. Furthermore, continuing professional development (CPD) through professional associations (such as the Institute of Travel and Tourism) also adds value to the benefits of having an industry qualification.

As evidenced in this section, tourism has come a long way as a subject of study and research since the first courses were developed almost 40 years ago. The number of courses, the variety of tourism subjects and the continued interest in the subject from students all point to a successful and increasingly professional subject area. In order to maintain the continued growth of the subject and to ensure that qualifications continue to appy, it is important to look to the future. It will remain crucial for educators to work closely with their local employers to design and develop courses that appeal to students and create industry-ready staff when they graduate. Tourism relies heavily on customer-facing frontline staff and supervisors and all tourism students therefore require both qualifications and experience as they enter the industry.

The increased focus on employability skills throughout tourism courses and the growing relationship between industry and education will continue to draw the two together to ensure that the next generation of students are fit for purpose in a dynamic and changing business environment, and that tourism education keeps up with the changes and needs of the tourism industry in the future, while yielding benefits for educators and employers and the students themselves.

Further reading

Airey, D. and Tribe, J. (2005) *An International Handbook of Tourism Education (Advances in Tourism Research)*, Elsevier Science, Oxford, UK

Peter Robinson

TOURISM ETHICS

Ethical tourism, as a movement, is considered to be a continuance, if not a branch, of a larger phenomenon called ethical consumption. According to Cooper-Martin and Holbrook (1993), ethical consumption occurs when consumers are affected by ethical concerns during their decision-making, purchasing and consuming experiences. Consistent with this definition, Cowe and Williams (2011) characterized ethical consumers as people who are influenced by environmental or ethical considerations when choosing products and services. The rise of ethical consumption in the 1990s was driven by issues such as child labour and the controversy over genetically modified organisms. Ethical consumerism is intentionally buying things that are made in a morally correct way. By doing so, a minimal harm to or exploitation of humans, animals and/or the natural environment can be achieved (Barnett et al, 2005). Favouring ethical products, while boycotting unethical ones by demonstrating a negative purchasing behaviour, is the essence of ethical consumerism.

The ethical consumption movement, which became the new buzz-word in tangible products, then began to receive more and more attention in intangible services. Barnett et al (2005) and, more recently, Cowe and Williams (2011) argued that although ethical consumption is a subject of increasing interest and research, the ethical market is not well understood and comparatively little research has been carried out to assess the prospects for promoting social and environmental issues through the market. Moreover, England (2010) noted the business opportunities that ethical consumption represents and warned of the threat posed to businesses which ignore this important trend. The significant increase in the number of people who are concerned about ethics has led to a move towards ethic-based decisions and ethical consumption in a wide range of products and/or services, including tourism services (Weeden, 2001; Goodwin and Francis, 2003).

Tourism is one of the world's largest industries, generating an esti-mated 17 per cent of global gross domestic product (GDP), employing 300 million people and transporting nearly 920 million international travellers per year – these figures are expected to double by 2020 (UNWTO, 2011a). While these figures and expected tremendous growth ratio can be perceived as being beneficial to the people of the countries visited by tourists (by providing employment and increasing national earnings), there are some ways in which tourism could be detrimental to local communities (Jones, 2011). Weeden (2001) noted that the increase in tourism figures has placed enormous stress on the natural environment in destinations, as well as in the social fabric of the local communities. Environmental concerns (such as global warming and pollution) have generated a mainstream interest in natural settings, preservation and sustainability. As a result, concepts such as **eco-tourism** (environmentally friendly tourism) and **sustainable tourism** (low-impact tourism) have not only emerged but also grown in popu-larity. These concepts gave birth to sub-concepts such as **responsible tourism** (tourism that creates better places for people to visit and live in), **volunteer tourism** (tourism that involves volunteering for a charitable cause) and ethical tourism (tourism based on ethical behaviour).

Ethics, in a broad sense, is concerned with what is right or wrong, good or bad, fair or unfair, responsible or irresponsible, where it aims to achieve and maintain morally correct conducts (Barnett et al, 2005). The term ethics stands for a systematic attempt to make a cohesive, rational whole out of one's individual and social moral experiences (Bird and Hughes, 1997). In the same vein, ethical tourism is composed of activities where the participants purposely choose to visit/consume/ use destinations, companies and services that are following an ethical code of conduct which aims to minimize the negative consequences of tourism on the environment, local people and local economy (Hultsman, 1995). Moreover, ethical tourism attempts to create a positive impact upon the local environment, culture and people, while restoring the balance that might be disturbed by 'greedy mass tourism' (England, 2010).

According to Weeden (2001), ethical tourism is an established term and is closely related to ecotourism and sustainable tourism concepts by sharing common grounds, such as the well-being of the local community and environment. However, by considering the needs of tourism stakeholders, ethical tourism goes beyond just minimizing the possible negative effects of tourism development (Goodwin and Francis, 2003). Although the idea of involving stakeholders in tourism development is being discussed along the lines of responsible tourism, according to ethical tourism, both tourists and providers of tourism services must take responsibility for their behaviour and attitudes (Upchurch, 1998). One of the outcomes of the General Assembly of the United Nations World Tourism Organization (UNWTO, 1999) was the development of a 'global code of ethics for tourism' in order to serve as a frame of reference for the stakeholders in world tourism at the dawn of the next century and millennium. Many of the ten articles which were proposed at this assembly are highly related to ethical tourism – for example, mutual understanding and respect between tourists and the host community; sustainable development by ethical conduct; and fair benefits to host countries and communities. Similarly, the World Trade Organization (WTO, 2000) posited that for a tourism activity to be considered ethical, three fundamental criteria must be followed:

1 Make optimal use of environmental resources.
2 Respect the sociocultural authenticity of host communities.
3 Ensure viable long-term economic operations by providing socio-economic benefits to all stakeholders that are fairly distributed.

Ethical tourism promotes the idea that local people should own or be involved in the development of tourism and not simply provide a cheap labour force. Only by doing so can local communities benefit from the tourism activities taking place in their own country.

In considering the importance of ethical tourism, a great responsibility also falls on the tourists themselves. According to Wheat (1999), the conscious uproar of the 1990s was a reaction to the uncaring tourism consumption of the 1980s. During the last two decades, many tourists from affluent countries began to worry about the impact that tourism generates upon local communities (Fennell and Malloy, 2007). At the start of the twenty-first century, this movement acquired momentum and demanded that more be done to both protect the environment and benefit local people. Academic attention given to this movement showed a parallel increase, particularly in the number of researchers who have proposed guidelines and/or lists of things to do to for both tourists and tour operators who are aiming to be ethically correct (Hultsman, 1995; Upchurch, 1998; Weeden, 2001). Table 15 provides a few related points.

As Wheat (1999) noted, ethical tourism worldwide is not something that can just happen overnight, considering how fast tourism is growing. On the other hand, Jones (2011) stressed that fundamental changes can happen should changes be made to the way in which tour operators operate tourism, and the way in which local people are involved in and benefit from it. This is possible given how governments worldwide are becoming more concerned about resources and involving citizens in tourism development studies. Finally, an increasing number of tourists are becoming aware of issues within ethical tourism. As a consequence, they are also choosing to participate in moral tourism

Table 15 Ethical behaviours

Ethical tourists should...	*Ethical tourist operators should...*
Minimize air travel when/if possible – the biggest cause of global warming.	Establish a clear policy for ethical tourism both in home and host countries.
Spend locally; use services offered by local people.	Commit funds to become a more ethical operator.
Bargain fairly: it may be part of their culture.	Write down best industry practices and learn from them.
Respect and read up on local traditions and way of life.	Produce and disseminate codes for your customers to follow.
Do not litter: waste disposal can be problematic.	Take time to research destinations and local companies that you do business with.
Use water sparingly: excessive usage may cause water shortage.	Set clear annual targets for improvements towards more ethical business.
Check the ethical stance of your tour operator.	Use annual reports to publicize what you have been doing to promote ethical business.
Boycott countries with politically repressive regimes.	

activities (Goodwin and Francis, 2003). Even those who have not yet done so reported that they are interested in contributing to ethical tourism in some way (England, 2010). This is important as ethical tourism can only be effective when all these parties work together in creating, maintaining and improving the morality of tourism activities.

Further reading

Barnett, C., Cafaro, P. and Newholm, T. (2005) 'Philosophy and ethical consumption', in R. Harrison, T. Newholm and D. Shaw (eds) *The Ethical Consumer*, Sage Publications, London, pp11–24

Cooper-Martin, E. and Holbrook, M. B. (1993) 'Ethical consumption experiences and ethical space', *Advances in Consumer Research*, vol 20, pp113–118

Fennell, D. A. and Malloy, D. C. (2007) 'Codes of ethics in tourism: Practice, theory, synthesis', in *Codes of Ethics in Tourism: Practice, Theory, Synthesis*, Channel View Publications, Clevedon, UK

Hultsman, J. (1995) 'Just tourism', *Annals of Tourism Research*, vol 22, no 3, pp553–567

Weeden, C. (2001) 'Ethical tourism: An opportunity for competitive advantage?', *Journal of Vacation Marketing*, vol 8, no 2, pp141–153

Dr. Catheryn Khoo-Lattimore

TOURISM HISTORIES

Although the concept of tourism histories would seem to have become increasingly documented in an ever-growing body of interdisciplinary contributions to this field, Walton (1997) suggests that this process has been problematic as historians have been reluctant to take tourism seriously, with tourism studies and the social sciences failing perhaps to fully embrace the contribution that history can make to understanding tourism. This, in part, can be explained by tourism business management's objectivist and positivistic approaches (Franklin and Crang, 2001; Tribe, 2004; Ateljevic et al, 2005), and therefore the reluctance to acknowledge the qualitative value of the humanities (Walton, 2009). Another contributory factor could be Tribe's observation that 'the canon of Tourism studies is fragmented, the subject remains a somewhat Cinderella area in the academy and its academics range from management scientists and economists, through cultural geographers and anthropologists to sociologists' (Tribe, 2010a, p7). But there is no mention of historians here and their role or lack of it in this disconnected area. Walker (2010) suggests that tourism history can no longer be said to be the 'neglected *enfant*', acknowledging the number of books and articles that have been published over the last decade, as well as the founding of the International Commission for the History of Travel and Tourism in 2001 at the University of Lancashire in the UK.

The *Journal of Tourism History* was launched in 2009, with the editor of the journal (Walton, 2009) stating that the primary objective is to try to bridge the gap between the largely ahistorical field of 'tourism studies' and the history of tourism as practised by historians. The key development is that by also embracing an interdisciplinary approach, drawing from cultural geography, sociology and cultural studies, a wider and complementary picture can emerge of tourism's history.

The historical dimension to the study of tourism provides opportunities to investigate, explore and crucially link the past with the present. Historical investigations offer a more serious examination and scrutiny of earlier narratives, revisiting and unpacking cultural myths, and exploring identities, relationships and representations. Walton (2005, p3) reinforces this argument by commenting that historical interpretation is 'ultimately fluid contested and always open to challenge'. New studies are always changing the picture by adding new dimensions and perspectives. Interesting themes, such as the commodification of history by the tourism industry and its manifestation in heritage management representation, are critical battle grounds over historical validity and commercial constructions of the past. Dark tourism and World Heritage site representation are all contested areas which require balance between commodification, history shaped by present-day needs and historians as interpreters of the past (Walton, 2005; Smith, 2009).

By asking 'What has been tourism's history?', the geographer Towner (1996) challenged earlier assumptions, questioning simplistic notions of tourism's evolution as geographical diffusion from one or two core areas, dominated by Western cultural experiences and arguing that more attention should be paid to tourism's past in non-Western societies and cultures. As part of the process of broadening and challenging such notions, the *Journal of Tourism Histories* includes articles and reviews covering every aspect of the history of tourism engaging with other disciplines and theoretical approaches and embracing an international perspective to historical study. Tourism histories can contribute to a far more expansive understanding of tourism's past, offering a range of themes and possibilities. Importantly, tourism's history has also at its disposal a wealth of untapped archive sources, literary sources, travel guide books, diaries, maps, posters, newspapers, local government planning documents, oral histories (exploring past holiday experiences) and other related journals. The range of material in the book *Histories of Tourism: Representation, Identity and Conflict* (Walton, 2005) is a good example of the quality and diversity of international subject matter that exists in this field.

A final topic to consider which illustrates very well the wealth of material that can exist on particular themes is the history of the British seaside. Over the last 30 years there has been a growing body of material from geographers, sociologists and historians on the growth and development of seaside tourism; significantly, many of these authors have also dealt with the later notions of decline at the British seaside. This abundance of research on the British seaside has produced challenging new perspectives on this phenomenon, especially for the nineteenth and early twentieth centuries. This has contributed to the growing realization that the British seaside conceals far more complex and important themes than perhaps had been generally understood. The scale of the seaside economy and the related demographic factors also make an overwhelming case for the importance of the seaside as a continuing field of study.

The disciplines of cultural geography and political science are offering new perspectives on the seaside; however, not much is known about the detailed interplay at a local level between the various stakeholders, interest groups in resorts, private business groups and local authorities during this period. Walton's extensive research and particularly his work on Blackpool highlight the importance of understanding the political dimension, and the power and politics of early resort development. An important theme here is the growth in municipal enterprise, the local state and its involvement in seaside tourism, acknowledging the concomitant growth in municipal enterprise that was necessary for the financing of essential undertakings, such as coastal zone protection, promenades, piers, bathing pools, advertising and entertainment provision. By focusing on the detail, tourism histories can unpack the crucial links that offer a more informed picture of events, moving away from simplistic accounts (e.g. the extent and scale of decline at the British seaside).

The notion of decline has now received far more attention from geographers and historians. The critical and questioning work of Walton and the study of Gale (2005) in his paper on the North Wales resort of Rhyl raise important questions of accuracy and of detail when examining this notion of decline. Gale's work questions the tendency to present resort decline as an evolutionary process, with an overemphasis on competition and resource depletion, factors that are synonymous with the consolidation, stagnation and post-stagnation phases of the tourist area lifecycle. He argues for more analysis of economic restructuring, political and cultural change, and less emphasis placed on competition and resource depletion as reasons for decline, the factors usually cited as being the main contributors to resort stagnation. Or, as Walton suggests, do we need to question the widespread assumption that the British seaside fell into terminal decline at some point during the 1960s? This material has also been influential when considering and justifying methodological approaches to the study of the British seaside. It also highlights in some of the current material the limitations of the research and where there is a need for more scrutiny and depth of analysis. Gale and Botterill (2005) develop this angle further with a pertinent title to their article: 'A realist agenda for tourist studies or why destination areas really rise and fall in popularity'. This work offers a further dimension to tourism studies and, importantly, how we examine and study seaside resorts. Gale and Botterill (2005) build in this article a critique of what they term 'orthodox' methods and ideas, represented by the tourism area lifecycle, and suggest why a realist philosophy of social science may offer a more satisfactory understanding of destination development and the notion of decline − qualitative analysis that illuminates the debate.

In summary, the concept of tourism histories offers a detailed examination and scrutiny of tourism's past, revisiting and unpacking cultural myths, exploring identities, relationships and representations. However, the most important and continuing development will be the wealth of material yet to emerge from the growing interdisciplinary approach, which is drawing more material from cultural geography, sociology and cultural studies, thus allowing a wider and complementary picture to emerge of tourism's history.

Further reading

Towner, J. (1991) 'Approaches to tourism history', *Annals of Tourism Research*, vol 15, issue 1, pp47–62
Towner, J. (1995) 'What is tourism's history?', *Tourism Management*, vol 16, issue 5, pp339–343
Towner, J. and Wall, G. (1991) 'History and tourism', *Annals of Tourism Research*, vol 18, no 1, pp71–84
Walton, J. K. (1997) 'Taking the history of tourism seriously', *European History Quarterly*, vol 27, no 4, pp563–571
Walton, J. K. (ed) (2005) *Histories of Tourism: Representation, Identity and Conflict* (Tourism and Cultural Change), Channel View Publications, Clevedon, UK
Walton, J. K. (2009) 'Tourism histories', in T. Jamal and M. Robinson (eds) *Sage Handbook of Tourism Studies*, Sage Publications, London, pp115–129

Harry Cameron

TOURISM IN DEVELOPING COUNTRIES

According to Oppermann and Chon (1997, p4), the term *developing countries* is a misleading phrase, the extremely wide parameters used in any meaningful definition being too great. Nevertheless, it remains in contemporary parlance (Telfer and Sharpley, 2008), but is becoming superseded by others such as *developing world* (Timothy and Nyaupane, 2009) and *less* and *least developed countries* (Shaw and Williams, 2004). This is because governments strive for greater differentiation and seek a fairer comparison of each in the global marketplace. Each phrase is used as both a generic standalone term and one linked to activities such as tourism and manufacturing, to name but two.

The terms of reference for the developing countries are where it can fulfil two of the following three criteria:

1   a per capita income of less than US$355;
2   a share of industrial production less than 10 per cent;
3   a literacy rate lower than 20 per cent among the population aged 15 years and above (Oppermann and Chon, 1997, p4).

Where tourism is found within these countries, it is invariably associated with low numbers but high impact in terms of the behaviour demonstrated by the host community. Tourism is often blamed for all 'ills' of such societies – crime, prostitution and low wages amongst this list; but this is not always valid as such comments and statements ignore the availability and impact of satellite television, global media and phone technology.

For some, the term 'developing countries' may be unfamiliar. Some of these are locations that may still be seen within the parameters of a much more well-known term: 'third world'. As will be seen, the latter term has become both obsolete and, historically, invariably derogatory.

The word 'third', by definition, assumes the existence of both a second and, indeed, *first* world. So, historically, who would be included within this description? These would be developed countries within a free market economy (e.g. the UK, North America, Japan and South Korea) – countries that may be perceived to have been successful in terms of gross national product (GNP), a balanced economy and having the capacity to provide healthcare and, perhaps, a stable birth rate. But if there is a first, there must be a second to be a third. Prior to 1989, this term was (albeit silently) used to refer to the Soviet Union: countries that were subservient to the centralized government based in Moscow (Oppermann and Chon, 1997). In 1989, the Berlin

Wall was breached and by 1991, the Soviet Union had begun to break up into self-autonomous nations, including Poland, Belarus and Lithuania. Without a second, it should be obvious why no one should refer to countries as being 'third world'!

There is another reason why the term should no longer be used. Often, the designation 'first' was taken as being *first class*, these national economies having made it somehow (implying the term elite). Invariably, 'third world' countries, until 1989, were in this position because they had not had similar resources or opportunities made available to them, as had the other two groupings. They were thus often regarded as *third class*, inferior, even being associated with having a primitive lifestyle. It is undoubtedly true that most countries either designated as being a developing one or being least developed are in the Southern Hemisphere and in either South America or Africa.

For a period, the countries previously known as 'second world' may be referred to in the literature as being fSU, meaning former Soviet Union (Shmyrov, 2001). But this term is now infrequently used, given the rapid commercialization of certain tourism destinations such as Prague, Krakow and Budapest as they embrace the West's values (and charge Western prices!).

There are several established models used to explain tourism development in such countries, almost irrespective of their categorization. The first two are suggested by Oppermann and Chon (1997), followed by a later model by Telfer and Sharpley (2008).

The Diffusionist Paradigm suggests that all tourism development has implications for four main areas: the destination, the transport infrastructure, the tourist and the receiving host. Each element develops along a shared journey, informing and often limiting development along thresholds. Put simply, over a period of time the destination upgrades its transport system and each wave of leaving tourist informs the host as to what the incoming ones will require. The host will ask or demand action to be taken by the government in order that this cycle moves to the next level. This approach may encourage what are known as 'enclaves' or 'hotspots' to be created. Although these terms do not have the same meaning, either or both may be the result.

An enclave is where a high level of development is found in a small area (e.g. a fully enclosed hotel complex in Jamaica). The location is attractive to Western tourists as the location has sun, sea and sand. The wider area may also have serious crime levels. Accordingly, a hotel may make it a priority to collect the visitor from the airport and provide everything he or she needs onsite until the end of the holiday. The tourist and local community do not mix at all. A 'hotspot' is quite different. This is an area where, for whatever reason, the potential and capability exists to attract high numbers of tourists. Capital cities and premier rural locations may lure vast crowds at certain times of the year, which has been a deliberate policy decision made by the planners, learning from visitor questionnaires. New Orleans is a city built on jazz. The municipal authority arranges for several large outdoor festivals during the peak season with small niche gatherings 'off-season'; but whatever time of the year one makes a visit, there is always a jazz-related string of events taking place. This allows accommodation and other service providers to employ regular full-time staff.

The Sector Paradigm suggests that there are two very different types of tourist (Oppermann and Chon, 1997): the institutionalized and non-institutionalized – those who want a structured and prearranged experience, and those who want the opposite. The latter grouping seeks an authentic local experience, whereas the former wants a 'home from home'. Governments invariably prefer the former, bringing inward investment from hotel chains and visitors with high levels of disposable income. The problem with this approach is often that of 'leakage'. The multinational hotel chains are invariably based elsewhere and the majority of the money never comes near the resort. In a non–enclave setting, some peripheral spend may be witnessed and local employment created; but the majority of wealth created remains in the generating area rather than the destination.

The Four Platform Approach has been identified by Telfer and Sharpley (2008) and focuses upon what was not really an issue for Oppermann and Chon in 1997 – that of sustainable development:

- advocacy – positive vehicle (1960s);
- cautionary – awareness of the negative (1960 to 1970s);
- adaptancy – alternative development (1980s);
- knowledge and shared experience.

Initially, advocacy (by third parties) was welcomed, bringing the needs of an area to the attention of those with money to invest and to the media. However, by 1970 there were several examples of tourism development being seen in a less favourable light. Often this was caused by 'templates' simply being lifted from one area to another; this model did not always 'fit', but needed to take account of cultural differences in a physically different environment. Today all successful development needs to take account of a balanced judgement, considering a wide variety of factors.

As is confirmed elsewhere in this book, sustainability is concerned with providing communities (or countries) with the opportunities to sever the strings of reliance placed upon them by other countries and/ or benefactors. This concept used to be about the demand side of the industry dictating what it would purchase or wish to have made available. Today it is moving to a position where a community is no longer allowing someone else's voice to create the supply, instead appreciating what is demanded and providing it. For instance, governments of least developed countries no longer simply take advice from one potential high-profile developer, but instead adopt a much more cautious approach by inviting a wider consultation process.

It is unlikely that the global community will ever become a universal marketplace, with every team playing on a level playing field. Indeed, national cultural differences and individual specialisms are the very factors that attract the tourism industry and, ultimately, the tourist to the destination.

Further reading

Reisinger, Y. (2009) *International Tourism: Cultures and Behaviours*, Butterworth Heinemann, Oxford, UK
Shmyrov, V. (2001) 'The Gulag Museum', *Museum International*, vol 53, no 1
Telfer, J. and Sharpley, R. (2008) *Tourism and Development in the Developing World*, Routledge, Oxford, UK
Timothy, D. and Nyaupane, G. (2009) *Cultural Heritage and Tourism in the Developing World*, Routledge, Oxford, UK

Geoff Shirt

TOURISM LIFECYCLE (AND DESTINATION LIFECYCLE)

The origination of the concept of the tourism lifecycle, sometimes known as the destination lifecycle, is usually credited to Butler, whose influential article on the subject was published in 1980. Butler built on the ideas of Plog (1973), Cohen (1972) and Doxey (1975), combining their ideas with the marketing concept of the product lifecycle to explain how the nature of tourism areas (otherwise known as destinations or resorts) changes over time. Butler refers to this as his 'tourism area lifecycle' (TALC) model and argues that tourism areas typically progress through a series of distinct stages as they develop over time, beginning with a stage of 'exploration', then 'involvement', moving

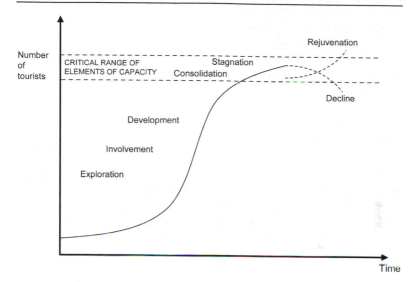

Figure 8 Butler's Tourism Area Lifecycle Model

on to 'development', fourthly 'consolidation' and next 'stagnation'. After this, the tourism area may either 'decline' or it may undergo 'rejuvenation'. This is illustrated in Figure 8.

The stages of the TALC are explained by Mason (2003) as follows:

- *Exploration:* at the earliest stages, the area is 'discovered' by the tourism industry. Initially, there are few 'pioneer' tourists, who tend to be more adventurous in disposition (Plog's 'allocentrics' and Cohen's 'drifters'). Tourists come in small numbers, are specialist in their interests and are drawn mainly by the indigenous attractions of the area. Interaction between locals and tourists remains informal and cordial, corresponding to Doxey's first stage of 'euphoria'.
- *Involvement:* at this stage, interaction between locals and tourists begins to become more commercial, basic services being provided to the latter by the former. The beginnings of a tourist industry become evident in the area. Increased advertising brings more tourists to the area, who tend to come from a limited range of origin markets.
- *Development:* this stage is when the area begins to experience commercial tourism development. Tourist facilities such as accommodation and attractions are built. Tourism 'high' and 'low' seasons emerge. There is greater involvement in tourism by individuals and organizations based outside the local area, with inward

investment taking place. Local people begin to take tourism for granted or have little interest in it (Doxey's 'apathy' stage). Yet, tourism numbers grow very quickly and may even outweigh the resident population during the high season.

- *Consolidation:* by this stage, tourism has become a major part of the local economy, located in a well-delineated tourism business district – the tourism resort. Some of the initial facilities are, however, already in need of repair. Tourist numbers grow less quickly and the tourism sector will often try to extend the tourism season. Frictions frequently arise between tourists and locals, corresponding to Doxey's 'annoyance' stage.
- *Stagnation:* in this stage, tourist numbers stop growing. A peak has been reached as the area reaches maximum capacity. The resort has a well-established image but it is no longer considered fashionable. Tourist facilities are often in great need of renewal and reinvestment. Tourists are institutionalised (Plog's 'psychocentrics' or Cohen's 'organized mass tourists') and relations between local people and tourists are often highly strained (Doxey's 'open antagonism' stage).

At this point the tourism area will *decline* if it is left to its own devices, or intervention will be undertaken so that the area undergoes *rejuvenation:*

- *Decline:* if the tourism area is left to decline it will not be able to compete with tourist areas that are at earlier stages in their life-cycles. It will appeal less and less to holiday-makers and more and more to those looking for weekend stays and day trips, if it is still accessible to large numbers of people. Property turnover will be high and tourist facilities will be gradually replaced by non-tourism ones as the area moves out of tourism.
- *Rejuvenation:* this stage, in contrast, will require intervention in order for it to happen. There are two ways to accomplish this: one is to add human-made attractions such as casinos (as in the case of Atlantic City, US) or theme parks; the other is to take advantage of previously untapped natural resources (such as winter sports in Aviemore, Scotland). Combined public- and private-sector responses are often necessary in order to overcome the constraints the area is likely to be facing, such as an inability to raise investment capital. The new markets for these attractions may be akin to Plog's allocentric tourist but are much more likely to be special interest tourists.

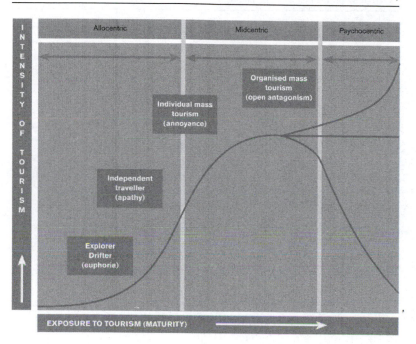

Figure 9 Composive Tourism Lifecycle Model (Source: Cooper et al, 2008b)

Cooper et al (2008b) provide a composite model in which the tourist typologies of Plog and Cohen, and Doxey's 'irridex' of tourist–resident antagonism, are superimposed on Butler's TALC curve (see Figure 9).

It would not be an exaggeration to say that the TALC model has been the subject of considerable academic interest, perhaps more so than any other concept in the study of tourism. Mason (2003, p26) argues that the TALC is 'Probably the single most important theory in tourism contributing to planning and management.' Whether the TALC model actually constitutes a 'theory' *per se* will be discussed shortly. Nevertheless, it is hard to disagree with Mason's statement about the importance of the TALC as a model. Indeed, the model has proven very popular as a research focus. A number of scholars have, for example, attempted to apply the TALC model to actual tourism destinations. Agarwal (1997), for example, applies the TALC model to the seaside resort area of Torbay in south-west England. Her study found that while the model generally fitted the case of Torbay, there were a number of important differences:

- The stages of development were not discrete but tended to overlap with each other.
- Unlike the TALC model, local residents were involved from the outset in providing tourist infrastructure.
- In at least one part of the tourism area (Paignton), the tourist type did not change as the resort developed.
- The decline phase of the cycle is not necessarily irreversible; decline need not be terminal.

Other applications of the TALC include Getz's (1992) study of Niagara Falls in Ontario, Canada. The study is interesting in that there is a city servicing tourism on either side of the falls, which straddle the Canada–US border. Getz's study finds many points of divergence from the TALC model, including a relatively poor fit with the later stages. Indeed, the term 'maturity', rather than 'stagnation', might better describe the stage at which the tourism area reaches its maximum capacity. At the time Getz was writing, the Niagara Falls tourism area showed no sign of going into decline. Meanwhile, elements of consolidation, stagnation, decline and rejuvenation were all considered to coexist in the tourism area. Getz (1992, p767) therefore argues that the stages of the TALC tend to be 'collinear and perpetual'.

Getz (1992) goes on to argue that the two cities servicing tourism at the falls have clearly gone through distinctly different life cycles. For example, Ontario's Niagara Falls had only recently begun to see the need to plan for tourism, while New York's Niagara Falls had invested heavily in tourism since the 1970s in an attempt to arrest its wider economic decline. The study also found that capacity constraints can bite at any stage in the lifecycle. Many of these are political rather than environmental in nature and can be overcome through policy and planning. Getz concludes that tourism planners should, as a result, be less concerned with identifying the stage of development that their tourism area is in and more interested in monitoring a wider range of indicators that will assist successful tourism planning.

The TALC has also been applied to places as far afield as the Bahamas, Grand Cayman, Atlantic City, the Smokey Mountain region of North Carolina, Cyprus, the Isle of Man, Minorca, Lancaster County in Pennsylvania, the Algarve, Malta, Sri Lanka and the Scottish Highlands (Lagiewski, 2006).

The TALC model has received a wide range of criticisms, including the following:

- As a universal model, the TALC fails to take account of the uniqueness of place – for example, the desire or ability of locals to resist the external influences that drive the development stage.
- There is an implicit assumption that all tourism areas are bound to go through these stages, that there is no overlap between the stages, and that tourism areas must go through them in the prescribed order, with no temporary reversals possible.
- The stages of the cycle are very difficult to determine, except with the benefit of hindsight. As such, the model does not present us with a 'theory' that can be tested (so it is not, technically, a theory at all).
- The model does not adequately separate causes from consequences. For example, is the 'decline' of a tourism area caused by changing patterns of production or consumption, or are these a consequence of the tourism area being in decline?

The model may therefore better be thought of as a conceptual framework than a theory. Nevertheless, it is considered useful for a number of reasons (Mason, 2003):

- The model emphasizes dynamism, which is a distinctive feature of most tourism areas.
- There are limits to growth, or capacity constraints, beyond which the tourism area cannot progress unless action is taken to relax them.
- There are triggers in the development of the tourist area, which can bring about significant changes in its nature and the way in which it functions.
- The model emphasizes the importance of **destination management organization** in shaping the way in which a specific tourism area passes through the lifecycle.
- The model adopts a long-term perspective, which is vital in understanding how tourism areas work and how they can best be managed.

As a conceptual framework, the TALC model has undoubtedly had a major influence on tourism studies and is likely to continue to do so in the foreseeable future.

Further reading

Agarwal, S. (1997) 'The resort life cycle and seaside tourism', *Tourism Management*, vol 18, no 2, pp65–73

Butler, R. W. (1980) 'The concept of the tourism area cycle of evolution', *Canadian Geographer*, vol 24, no 1, pp5–12

Butler, R. W. (2006) *The Tourism Area Life Cycle*, two volumes, Channel View Publications, Clevedon, UK

Getz, D. (1992) 'Tourism planning and destination life cycle', *Annals of Tourism Research*, vol 19, no 4, pp752–770

Mason, P. (2003) *Tourism Impacts, Planning and Management*, Elsevier Butterworth-Heinemann, Oxford and Burlington

Dr. Brian Garrod

TOURISM POLICY

Tourism policy can be defined as the sum of the deliberate actions undertaken by a government to influence tourism. Often the government's intention is to favour the tourism sector in some way. The assumption is that enabling the tourism sector to expand or to become more efficient will bring positive impacts to the economy, society and/or environment in which tourism takes place. At the same time, governments often recognize that some tourism impacts may be negative, in which case tourism policy may be needed to restrict the growth or influence of tourism, thereby serving to protect the economy, society and/or environment in which it is taking place.

Hall (1994) argues, however, that this definition may be over-simplistic insofar as it fails to capture the full complexity of tourism policy-making. First, many government policies that are not primarily intended either to promote or to restrain tourism nevertheless have significant implications for tourism as an activity. A topical example is the recent imposition of stricter security measures within airports, such as the use of luggage restrictions and full-body scanners. While they are intended neither to encourage nor to restrict tourism, such measures have undoubtedly had major implications for the sector. Secondly, Hall (1994) argues that non-governmental interests can have an important influence on tourism policy-making. The tourism policy community tends to be large and very diverse, comprising a wide array of pressure groups, such as industry organizations and community groups, as well as a variety of media organizations and influential individuals, including academics. The highly complex and fragmented organization of tourism as an economic activity implies that such interests tend to be multiple, diverse and often in diametric opposition to one other. These basic features of tourism serve to complicate the process of tourism policy-making and can have a significant bearing on its outcomes. As such, the format and substance of tourism policy can be highly sensitive to the specific political and economic context in which it is made and implemented.

The scope of tourism policy therefore tends to be broader than is the case with most other economic sectors. It is nevertheless possible to identify some common concerns of tourism policy at the national level. These might be said to include:

- maximizing the potential of tourism as a source of incomes, jobs and foreign exchange earnings;
- ensuring that the education sector provides the knowledge, skills and training required for the tourism sector to meet its true economic potential;
- spreading the benefits of tourism fairly among stakeholders, including people living in tourism destinations who may or may not be involved directly with the activity;
- minimizing the costs of tourism development and ensuring that these are borne equitably among various interest groups at different geographical destinations;
- coordinating the development and marketing of tourism, including establishing and managing a strong tourism brand image;
- regulating markets to ensure consumer protection, as well as regulating particular aspects of tourist behaviour (e.g. gambling);
- providing public goods, such as street lighting, and merit goods, such as art galleries and museums;
- collecting the statistics required to monitor tourism activity and providing marketing intelligence.

Depending upon the extent of tourism's economic and political significance, national governments may or may not establish a dedicated ministry for the purposes of making and implementing tourism policy. Where tourism interests are highly influential in political and economic terms, such as is the case in many small island developing states, the sector has traditionally been put into its own ministry. In other cases, tourism policy tends to be developed within a more broad-based government department. In the UK, for example, the tourism sector has traditionally lacked political influence in spite of its considerable economic significance, and as a result has never been placed in its own specialist ministry. Indeed, tourism policy in the UK is currently located within the Department of Culture, Media and Sport, where tourism tends only to be a secondary focus of departmental policy-making.

Governments often establish National Tourism Organizations (NTOs) to execute their tourism policies. The NTO may either be situated within the ministerial department where tourism policy is made or it may take the form of a semi-independent government agency. A country's NTO is often situated at the apex of a pyramid-shaped organizational structure, with regional tourism organizations and then destination-level tourism organizations operating in tiers beneath the NTO. The remit of the organizations in the lower tiers will typically be to implement the policy measures developed by the NTO, often shaping and adapting them according to local conditions and contingencies. For example, the NTO for Wales, known as Visit Wales, has established four regional partnerships – Tourism Partnership Mid-Wales, Tourism Partnership North Wales, Tourism Partnership South West Wales and Capital Region Tourism – giving each devolved resources and a mandate to roll out Visit Wales national tourism development and marketing strategies in their particular regions. Various other organizations, including the Welsh local authorities and destination marketing organizations such as Visit Cardiff, are then required to respond to these policies at the destination level. Other countries have NTOs that are not formally part of the public sector but have developed as private organizations, usually funded by member subscription. Often known as convention and visitor bureaux, their membership typically comprises commercial tourism organizations and, in most cases, government representatives.

An increasingly important focus of tourism policy at the national level relates to the need to facilitate the sustainable development of tourism. Bramwell (2005) notes that there is a growing recognition among governments of the world that market forces are insufficient in themselves to bring about the transformation required. Government policy-making will therefore need to identify suitable policy instruments for this purpose. Bramwell (2005) argues that these tend to fall into four main groups:

1 Government encouragement of sustainable tourism through education, information and persuading the public to adopt more sustainable forms of behaviour. An example of this would be to introduce an eco-label or ratings system to inform potential tourists of the sustainability implications of their proposed holiday.
2 Government financial incentives, such as taxes, levies, subsidies or incentives, which serve to alter the market prices that decision-makers in the tourism system face. These will be designed to encourage behaviour that is consistent with sustainable tourism development and discourage behaviour that is not.

3 Direct government expenditure may be required to facilitate the sustainable development of tourism. This could range from public investment in more sustainable transport systems, such as railway networks, to the establishment of national parks or other nature conservation designations.

4 There are opportunities for governments to introduce regulations that either prohibit or proscribe particular actions, usually on the part of businesses and public-sector organizations. These range from setting environmental quality standards to introducing requirements about the publication of company environmental reports.

Tourism policy at the international level is largely expressed in terms of a country's international trade policy. Despite the historical significance of international tourism as a form of international trade, tourism has rarely been subject to international trade regimes or the subject of international trade negotiations. The main exceptions include the negotiation of bilateral air transport agreements and the provision of protection for foreign investment in a country's tourism industry. International tourism policies that aim to reduce or remove worldwide barriers to international trade in tourism have rarely even been considered by national governments, let alone implemented. Instead, national governments have tended to focus their attention on trying to promote their country as an attractive tourism destination in comparison to its main competitors.

Tourism flows are nevertheless heavily influenced by many of the measures introduced by countries as part of their foreign policies. Hall (1994) argues that, at its simplest, the presence of substantial tourist flows between countries may be evidence of a positive political relationship between them. Tourism trade flows encourage economic interdependence, which may be politically valuable for either or both of the countries involved. Indeed, perhaps nowhere is the ideological importance of international tourism greater than among the constituent member states of the European Union, where international tourism has been encouraged not so much for the economic benefits that are involved as for its value as a means of binding the member states together into a fully integrated political and economic union.

It is also common for countries to impose restrictions on international tourism flows. These can range from refusal to admit tourists from a particular country to setting limits on the amount of foreign currency that outbound tourists can take out of the country. The justification for doing so is usually based on one of the following four arguments:

1 First, restricting outbound tourism may help to retain foreign currency at time of economic crisis.
2 Outbound tourism represents an import in the country's balance of payments, while inbound tourism represents an export. Discouraging the former and encouraging the latter may thereby help to ease a country's adverse balance of payments situation.
3 A country may wish to restrict inbound tourism in order to protect indigenous natural resources and human cultures from the negative impacts of tourism.
4 Countries may restrict tourism flows as a response to national security issues.

A number of multinational organizations are involved in informing tourism policy at the international level. Prominent among these is the United Nations World Tourism Organization (UNWTO). Established in 1970 as the WTO, it serves as a global forum for tourism policy and a source of practical tourism know-how. One of its major functions is to conduct research and provide information on a range of issues relevant to tourism. The WTO became a specialized agency of the United Nations in 2005, changing its acronym to UNWTO. Other important multinational agencies include the International Civil Aviation Organization (ICAO), the International Air Transport Association (IATA), the United Nations Environment Programme (UNEP) and the Organization for Economic Co-operation and Development (OECD).

Tourism policy has also been shaped by various global policy summits. Perhaps the best known of these is the Earth Summit, which was held in Rio de Janeiro in 1992. Officially entitled the United Nations Conference on Environment and Development (UNCED), the purpose of the Earth Summit was to consider how the principles of sustainable development could best be applied by policy-makers. While the summit barely mentioned tourism, its implications have been significant for tourism policy. Indeed, the outcomes of the summit include the Rio Declaration on Environment and Development, which establishes 27 principles of sustainable development, including the right of nations to pursue development, the use of the precautionary principle, the importance of public participation in decision-making and the vital role of indigenous peoples. Another important policy document to arise from the Earth Summit was Agenda 21, a blueprint for action on sustainable development at the global, national and local levels. There has since been global policy summits focused entirely on tourism. A prominent example is the World Ecotourism Summit (WES), which took place during May 2002 in Québec City, Canada. Initiated by the UNWTO and UNEP, the summit was intended to bring together all of the stakeholders of ecotourism in order to encourage them to share their experiences and exchange ideas. The WES culminated in the agreement of the Québec Declaration on Ecotourism, a document that has been significant in shaping national policy on the development of ecotourism in many countries.

Further reading

Cooper, C., Fletcher, J., Fyall, A., Gilbert, D. and Wanhill, S. (2008) *Tourism: Principles and Practice*, 4th edition, Pearson Education Limited, Essex, UK

Stevenson, N., Airey, D. and Miller, G. (2008) 'Tourism policy making: The policymakers' perspective', *Annals of Tourism Research*, vol 35, no 3, pp732–750

Tyler, D. and Dinan, C. (2001) 'The role of interested groups in England's emerging tourism policy network', *Current Issues in Tourism*, vol 4, no 2–4, pp210–252

Dr. Brian Garrod

TOURISM STRATEGY

Tourism strategy is an outcome of a strategic decision-making process that involves external and internal analysis of a tourism organization's or destination's business environment, with a view to choosing the most suitable long-term direction for the organization or destination that creates and sustains its value, competitive advantage and superior performance through appropriate configuration of its resources while fulfilling its stakeholders' expectations. The choices made during the strategic decision-making process normally require significant resource commitments, are not easily reversible due to high investment costs and have significant impact upon the economic performance of the tourism organization or destination. An effective tourism strategy generates superior performance through blending the various resources, functions and activities of a tourism organization or destination in such a way that synergy can be achieved – which is a situation where the combined effect of the various resources, functions and activities is greater than their individual contribution.

Tourism strategy as a concept has much in common with military strategy, for the term 'strategy' originates from the Greek term *stratēgia*, meaning 'generalship'. Given that tourism strategy is considered a specific type of business strategy, a range of academic disciplines make important contribution to our understanding of the tourism strategy process. They include:

- economics (e.g. theory of firm's behaviour in competitive environment and profit maximizing/economic value theories);
- management science (e.g. use of scientific analytical tools and scenario planning);
- cognitive science (e.g. theories that help to understand the rationality of human decision-making);
- sociology (e.g. theories that provide insights into strategy formulation as a social process);
- psychology (e.g. theories that contribute to our understanding of leadership charisma); and
- political science (e.g. theories that help to understand public policy-making).

In terms of strategy process, general strategy literature recognizes that most strategies are a mix between purely deliberate strategies (i.e. strategies that are intended and planned as a means towards the end) and emergent strategies (i.e. strategies that evolve gradually over time in response to business needs and the opportunities presented by the business environment as and when they occur). These phenomena were first recognized and explained in strategy literature by Mintzberg and Waters (1985) in their influential article 'Of strategies, deliberate and emergent'. Further observation of business strategy processes by Mintzberg et al (1998) led these scholars to identifying ten different perspectives of strategy formation. While three of these perspectives (i.e. the design, planning and positioning perspectives) represent prescriptive schools of strategy formation (*strategy 'ought to'*), the remaining seven perspectives (i.e. the entrepreneurial, cognitive, learning, power, cultural, environmental, and configuration perspectives) represent descriptive schools of strategy formation (*strategy 'is'*). Mintzberg and Lampel (1999, p21) consider them to be both 'fundamentally different processes of strategy making [and] different *parts* of the same process'.

There are two major approaches to strategy formulation that general strategy literature recognizes: the environmental-led 'fit' approach and the resource-led 'stretch' approach. While the former approach is influenced by Ansoff's (1965) early work in strategy and mainly shaped by the seminal work of Michael Porter (1980, 1985, 1990, 1996), several scholars have contributed to the development of the latter approach (e.g. Wernerfelt, 1984; Prahalad and Hamel, 1990; Barney, 1991; Peteraf, 1993; Hamel and Prahalad, 1993, 1994). Unlike the fit (*outside-in*) approach to strategy formulation, which assumes that it is the industry's business environment and the organization's competitive positioning that determine the organization's strategy, the stretch (*inside-out*) approach assumes that it is the organization's resources and distinctive competences that constitute the starting point in strategy formulation. Consequently, while the fit approach encourages finding and defending a unique market position in attractive industries, concentrates on building a portfolio of products and/or businesses, and develops organizational structures based on functions, products and geographical areas, the stretch approach encourages creating market space and changing the rules of the game, concentrates on building a portfolio of distinctive competences, and develops organizational structures based on knowledge, skills and capabilities.

Generic strategic options that support the fit approach include Porter's cost leadership strategy and differentiation strategy that can both be applied to the broad and narrow market target and that are both derived from the microeconomic concept of profit. Similarly, Ansoff's growth-vector matrix offers four strategic options (market penetration, market development, product development and diversification) which can be seen as supporting the fit approach. In contrast, Hamel and Prahalad's resource leverage strategies (concentrating, accumulating, complementing, conserving and recovering resources) support the stretch approach. Although such generic strategic options provide a useful starting point in designing strategies, they are not ready-made strategies *per se*. Indeed, it is the strategic context – the set of circumstances within the business environment under which the strategic choices are made – that determines the strategic process and strategy content of an individual tourism destination or organization. A careful analysis of these differing contexts and strategic issues arising from them influences strategic thinking and results in formulating unique tourism strategies.

Early academic writing considers tourism strategy predominantly within the context of destination planning, with particular emphasis on community planning. For example, Haywood (1988) considers tourism strategies as an outcome of a community planning process and stresses the need for involving all stakeholders in this process. He proposes 'A sample community planning paradigm' (Haywood, 1988, p.114), which indicates the relationships among a range of contextual factors (i.e. tourism information, decision-making participants and objectives) that shape tourism strategies at the national, community and individual business levels. He recognizes that achieving and sustaining such a participative process that results in strategy formulation requires adequate leadership at the community level and rewarding the commitment of the participants. While Haywood mainly considers these issues from the theoretical perspective, Murphy (1988) provides examples of effective community planning in British Columbia, Canada. He argues that workshops that bring all stakeholders together are essential in developing synergistic community partnerships. Similarly, within the context of the Isle of Man, Cooper (1990) recognizes that collaboration between the public and private sectors as well as professional leadership are essential in choosing the most appropriate strategic option that resort managers could pursue with a view to 'rejuvenating' declining cold-water resorts.

A useful overview of early tourism strategy research was carried out by Athiyaman (1995), who found that the term strategy was mainly used in a casual way, that the majority (90 per cent) of articles were concerned with either analysing the business environment (51 per cent) or with strategy implementation (39 per cent), and that there was hardly any research work on the strategy processes of tourism organizations. Similar trends can be observed in more recent academic work on tourism strategy, most of which is concerned with the role of strategy in destination sustainable tourism development or with destination marketing strategies.

In practice, examples of tourism strategies can be found at various destination levels (national, regional and local strategies) and at various organizational levels (corporate, business and functional strategies).

Many countries develop national tourism strategies that are concerned with the overall purpose and direction for a country's tourism in relation to its socio-economic priorities. Most recent examples include UK's *Winning: A Tourism Strategy for 2012 and Beyond*, Jordan's *National Tourism Strategy 2011–2015* or South Africa's *National Tourism Sector Strategy 2011–2020*. At the regional level, tourism strategies attempt to contribute to the attainment of regional socio-economic goals. For example, Dumfries and Galloway's *Regional Tourism Strategy 2011–2016* attempts to make the region a world-class destination of superb quality with a view to maximizing the long-term economic and social impacts of tourism. Similarly, local tourism strategies tend to support local economies by maximizing the value of tourism. For example, *Tourism Strategy for the City of Yarra 2011–2016* recognizes the socio-economic value of tourism and attempts to realize its potentialities for the benefit of local stakeholders.

From the organizational viewpoint, tourism strategies are developed at corporate, business and functional levels. Corporate tourism strategies are concerned with the overall purpose and scope of the organization, which reflect stakeholders' views and indicate how value can be created through achieving organizational synergies. For example, Thomas Cook Group's corporate strategy developed in 2007 – following a merger between Thomas Cook AG and MyTravel Group plc – aims at strengthening the group's core businesses and investing for future growth. It creates value through mergers, acquisitions and partnerships. In contrast, business tourism strategies indicate choices made by an organization with regard to the ways in which the organization can successfully compete in particular markets. Strategic decisions made at this level concern issues such as differentiation, cost structure and innovation. For example, while both EasyJet and Ryanair pursue cost leadership strategies, they differ in their choices of growth strategies, with the former investing in penetrating the low-fare European market and the latter serving larger European airports while charging higher prices for such flights. At the functional level, strategies help in achieving operational efficiency of individual business functions, such as marketing, research and development, finance or production. For example, Accor's *Marketing and Brand Strategy* (2011) aims at creating one mega-brand (ibis) with three diversified but complementary brands (ibis budget hotels, ibis hotels and ibis styles hotels). Such an approach is likely to reduce overall marketing communication costs since it will generate economies of scale through fostering preference for the mega-brand and offering choices at various price levels which will contribute to improving the brand's image and awareness.

Designing effective strategies is a complex and difficult task for tourism managers because strategy is about an organization's or destination's behaviour in the future and the future cannot be fully predicted. Indeed, unpredictable events such as the outbreak of the foot-and-mouth disease in the UK in 2001, the terrorist attacks of 2001 or the closure of airspace in 2010 due to volcanic ash significantly affected the tourism industry and undermined some of the tourism strategies chosen by tourism organizations or destinations. However, as many of these events are of a temporary nature, some risks can be considered at the stage of strategy formulation. It is for this reason that effective strategies tend to demonstrate some degree of flexibility and/or develop contingency plans with a view to offsetting the consequences of unpredictable events and changes in the business environment.

Tourism strategy as a field of academic study and business practice is complex; but it is this complexity that provides a wide range of opportunities for in-depth studies and for engaging in creative thinking processes that may result in the designing of unique strategies. Future studies of tourism strategy processes and contextual factors that influence strategic choices and their effectiveness would further enhance our knowledge and understanding of this dynamic concept.

Further reading

Athiyaman, A. (1995) 'The interface of tourism and strategy research: An analysis', *Tourism Management*, vol 16, pp447–453

Evans, N., Campbell, N. and Stonehouse, G. (2003) *Strategic Management for Travel and Tourism*, Butterworth-Heinemann, Oxford, UK

Tribe, J. (2010b) *Strategy for Tourism*, Goodfellow Publishers, Woodeaton

Dr. Marcjanna M. Augustyn

TOURISM SUPPLY AND DEMAND

The **tourism system** helps to show the interactions between the supply side of tourism within a destination region and the demand side of tourism in the generating region and the transit route region. The model also helps to illustrate the demand for tourism (from the generating region) and the supply of tourism from the destination.

Tourism supply consists of visitor **attractions**, services/facilities (superstructure), infrastructure activities, **hospitality** and events for visitors to the destination. Services and facilities will help tourists to access attractions, and without an adequate superstructure a destination would struggle to compete with other regions.

Infrastructure describes all surface and underground developments, including the supply of water and electricity, sewage disposal, gas lines, drainage, roads, healthcare, communications and other public utilities. Infrastructure is not always well developed in some destinations, and local communities and visitors must both share the same lack of services. Tourism supply is affected by both price and non-price factors. These include the price of inputs, the level of technology, the number of sellers, the price of other products, profit expectations, future prices, weather, taxes and subsidies.

Tourism demand is defined as the total number of persons who travel or wish to travel to use tourist facilities and services at the place away from their work or residence. Effective or actual demand comprises the actual number of people who are travelling. This is the most common and easily measured form of demand. Demand for tourism is made up not only for those who participate, but those who want to travel but cannot for specific reasons. This is called suppressed demand, which can be distinguished as:

- Potential demand: a demand that could become effective if a change happens in an individual's circumstances, such as a change in purchasing power.
- Deferred demand: a demand that is postponed because of problems in the supply of tourism due to terrorist activity, or epidemics and health risks.

Finally, there will be always those who simply do not wish to travel, constituting a category of no demand.

Tourism demand describes the quantity of goods, services and attractions demanded by consumers within a destination. The level of demand has a major influence on the prices of tourism goods and services, as well as other social, cultural and political factors.

Demand in travel and tourism is very elastic and price sensitive and is measured in different ways. The most commonly used measure for demand includes:

- numbers of visitor arrivals or numbers of participants;
- tourism expenditure or receipts;
- length of stay or tourism nights spent at the destination site;
- travel propensity indices.

Factors that influence demand include the motivation of a person or group to travel (see **Motivation in tourism**) and their ability to travel, which is influenced by a broad range of factors found in both the generating region and destination region. Such factors can be called determinants of demand for tourism and could be divided into economic and non-economic factors

The economic determinants are the easiest to measure and are commonly employed in tourism demand studies. These include:

- *National income:* there is a direct relationship between the level of income in the originating county and the demand for tourism in its population. Countries with higher levels of income produce more tourists than other countries.
- *Personal income:* changes in consumers' income can cause changes in the demand for tourism goods and services. Tourism is a luxury product and the most useful measure of the ability to participate in tourism activities is discretionary income, which refers to a person's

income left after taxes, living expenses and other essential expenditure. As discretionary income rises, the tendency to engage in tourism and related activities will also increase, although research suggests that people try to save money for leisure (and tourism) activities even when there is less money available to meet the cost of living.

- *Employment:* the nature of employment not only influences income levels, but also has an effect upon holiday demand through the availability of holiday, holiday entitlements and the need to return to work at short notice during holiday periods (in some businesses), together with job security and other employment benefits.
- *Exchange rate:* tourism demand is expected to be affected by tourism prices in a destination relative to those in the country or region of origin. Countries in the developing world may be less expensive for international tourists to visit, which may result in increased international travel flow. Conversely, countries with strong economies may receive lower numbers of international tourists as prices relative to those in the originating country or region are much higher. Where economies are broadly similar, international travel tends to be an activity influenced by individual wealth and disposable income.
- *Substitute prices:* many travellers consider the price at the destination relative to the cost of living at home, which generates the substitution price effect.

Non-economic determinants are difficult to measure and to incorporate within economic demand models as some value has to be ascribed to them. These factors are usually examined in relation to travel decision-making and destination selections (Sirakaya et al, 1996) and are vital in any understanding of the market and its demand for tourism. Non-economic factors include:

- *Political factors:* the political atmosphere of the originating country can encourage or discourage the travel propensity of the population. On the other hand, the political situation within a destination and political relations between countries are also important considerations.
- *Social factors:* there are many social factors to consider, such as level of urbanization – in urbanized countries the distribution of the population will be greater in cities, and the city environment stimulates travel propensity.
- *Technological factors:* countries with greater technological advancements can better support inbound and outbound tourism. Technology

enables travel to become safer, easier and faster, and offers a greater range of information to the consumer.

- *Population:* origin population is expected to influence the level of tourism. An increase in population could result in an increased tourism demand.
- *Other factors:* the image of the destination, its seasonality and various pull factors also determine tourism demand.
- *Demographics and lifestyle:* age and gender – different age and gender groups can be distinguished with different types of demand and travel propensities.
- *Relationships and families:* relationships influence the type of tourism products and services that are chosen. Couples and families, for example, are more interested in safe destinations, while young single travellers are more likely to seek **adventure tourism** and older travellers may have more interest in **educated in tourism**. Family type and size is an important factor in determining travel propensity.
- *Retirements:* early retirement is creating a large, active and mobile group (Cooper et al, 2009) with greater wealth and higher standards; people see their retirement as an opportunity for personal development and fulfilment.
- *Education:* education broadens horizons and stimulates the desire to travel. The better educated the individual, the higher the awareness of travel opportunities.
- *Mobility:* a person's ability to be mobile can be referred to as 'mobility' and it has an important influence on travel propensity.
- *Price:* supply and demand have a major influence on the prices of touristic goods and services. Price equilibrium is found where supply and demand are equal. This is the point where both sellers and buyers are happy with the price and quantity. If supply is greater than demand, then prices will fall over time. In case of supply being equal to demand, prices will remain stable. When supply is lower than demand, then prices will rise.

Further reading

Goeldner, C. R. and Ritchie, J. R. B. (2006) *Tourism: Principles, Practices and Philosophies*, tenth edition, John Wiley and Sons Inc, New Jersey, pp327–370

Sinclair, M. T. and Stabler, M. (1997) *Economics of Tourism*, Routledge, London

Vanhove, N. (2011) *The Economics of Tourism Destinations*, second edition, Elsevier, London, pp61–108

Roya Rahimi

TOURISM SYSTEM

Drawing on the general system theorizing of Bertalanffy (1972) and Emery (1969), Leiper (1979, see also 1990) first modelled the tourism system, heuristically identifying basic system elements. These included the tourist, the generating and destination regions, and the tourism sector, as illustrated in Figure 10.

Leiper's model has been widely adopted in tourism (see Hall and Page, 2010) and draws on one of the key strengths of systems theorizing – that is, providing a holistic, transdisciplinary framework within which tourism can be theorized. The model is applicable to any scale of analysis, allows for the incorporation of different forms of tourism and ties together that which is of greatest import in tourism studies: the tourist and the destination (Cooper et al, 2005). Based on this model, various sub-themes can be perceived in systemic terms, focusing on the general components of the system. For example:

- the tourists, the companies and destinations;
- their interrelatedness through supply and demand;
- how their relations change over time;
- how various external political, economic, social, regulatory and technological factors affect the system, analysed through micro- and macro-environmental analysis (see micro- and macro-environments).

System theorizing has special appeal to tourism scholars as tourism is a multidisciplinary field of enquiry. The dynamic relations of a system can be interpreted through the lens of sociology, anthropology, geography, marketing, economics, environmental studies and more (Veal, 2006).

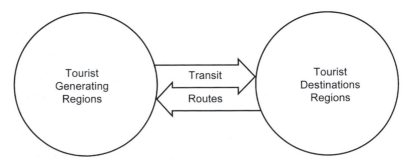

Figure 10 The tourism system (Source: Leiper, 1979, p397)

These relations can also be analysed at any scale. The grandest scale would apply to international global tourism, drawing on Marxian world systems theories (Wallerstein, 1984). Britton (1991, p455) postulates how tourism destinations are the product of what he terms 'tourism production systems' and thus the various 'commercial and public institutions designed to commodify and provide travel and touristic experiences'. Tourism is here seen as a set in the dynamic interplay between actors of capital accumulation, affecting both the materiality and social meaning of places. Two particular sub-themes of tourism systems thinking can be related to the scalar considerations of tourism. The first approach is based on commodity chain analysis. On the global scale, it focuses on how the flow of people and goods transgress state boundaries and is concerned with processes of globalization and dependencies (Gereffi and Korzeniewicz, 1994). Related approaches are value- and supply-chain analysis. The second approach deals with tourism innovation systems (Hjalager, 2010). Drawing on ideas from Lundvall (1992) and Nelson (1993), the tourism innovation system can be approached at a variety of geographic scales and sectorally – that is, how various external political, economic, social, regulatory and technological factors impact upon the tourism sector much like the aforementioned micro- and macro-environmental analysis. In either case the defined system elements are the institutions that function through processes of knowledge transfer, facilitating tourism innovation.

Scalar considerations, and often notions of production, lend themselves all too easily to epistemologies that are reliant on static notions of destinations, tourists and other elements of a system. This results in research that unpacks hierarchies, relations of dependencies, trickle-down economics and the dynamics of neo-liberal and other types of hegemonic frameworks, wherein each element exerts a defined and measurable impact upon other system components. Recent approaches in tourism respond to this. One is framed around the notion of mobilities (Sheller and Urry, 2004). In this perspective tourism does not occur without travel and the elements of the tourism system are seen as explicitly constructed from mobilities, making more sense of how they change (Saarinen, 2004). Mobilities tie in with the so-called complexity turn (Urry, 2003a), where tourism is recognized as a dynamic system, being socially, culturally and geographically complex. Through combining system and process thinking, tourism becomes emergent, with unpredictable outcomes and unforeseeable futures. Another way to approach tourism dynamic system analysis is Actor Network Theory (ANT), which elaborates upon tourism in terms of orderings (Ren et al, 2012). An exploration into the ontological ramifications of the fundamental irreducibility and exteriority of these ordering practices to their elemental terms (Deleuze, 2006) has not been carried out in tourism.

Blurring the elemental aspect of the system departs from Leiper's (1979) claim that he would provide a 'value-free approach to tourism policy'. Tourism policy depends upon the interplay between various actors. It follows that in order to understand the production of tourist places, it is necessary to trace their interplay in the material setting of a destination and how it also plays a role. The traces of tourism research most readily visible here are those of collaborative planning, sustainability and **community-based tourism.**

Further reading

Britton, S. (1991) 'Tourism, capital, and place: Towards a critical geography of tourism', *Environment and Planning D: Society and Space*, vol 9, pp451–478

Hall, M. C. and Page, S. (2010) 'The contribution of Neil Leiper to tourism studies', *Current Issues in Tourism*, vol 13, no 4, pp299–309

Leiper, N. (1979) 'The framework of tourism: Towards a definition of tourism, tourist, and the tourist industry', *Annals of Tourism Research*, vol VI, no 4, pp390-407

Ren, C., Jóhannesson, G. T. and van der Duim, R. (2012) *Actor Network Theory and Tourism: Ontologies, Methodologies and Performances*, Taylor and Francis, London

Sheller, M. and Urry, J. (2004) *Tourism Mobilities: Places to Play, Places in Play*, Routledge, London

Dr. Edward H. Hujibens

TOURIST EXPERIENCE

Tourist experience refers to an individual's inner state that is formed by the apprehension of a continual flow of blended events, situations, perceptions, thoughts and emotions that the tourist undergoes during the process of planning, engaging with and recollecting a specific tourist activity – for example, a short leisure break, a holiday or a business trip.

One of the earliest models that influenced some conceptualizations of the tourist experience was Clawson's (1963) linear five-phase recreation experience model. Both Killion (1992) and Craig-Smith and French (1994) adapted the model to represent the tourist experience. While Killion emphasized the need for demonstrating the likely iterative nature of the tourist experience and proposed a curvilinear model, Craig-Smith and French modified the original model into a three-phase linear model of the tourist experience which included anticipatory, experiential and reflective phases. Meanwhile, several independent tourist experience theories have been proposed. As Uriely (2005) noted, developments in theorizing on the tourist experience have been influenced by modernist and post-modernist thought in the social sciences.

In one of the first seminal works on the tourist experience, Cohen (1979) identified five phenomenologically distinct modes of the tourist experience:

1 the recreational mode, which is oriented towards enjoyment, entertainment, rejuvenation and recreation;
2 the diversionary mode, which is oriented towards escaping from the boredom and routine of everyday existence;
3 the experiential mode, which is oriented towards observing authenticity and searching for a new meaning within novel landscapes and cultures;
4 the experimental mode, which is oriented towards sampling new 'life-ways' with a view to discovering new meanings; and
5 the existential mode, which is oriented towards acceptance of the culture and society of the place visited and towards commitment to its authentic and real life.

Cohen (1979, p192) suggested that each mode is characterized by a clearly defined relation to the perceived 'centre' and that each mode is associated with specific motives for engaging with a specific tourist activity. These motives range from 'superficial ... desire for mere pleasure' to the most 'profound ... quest for meaning'. According to Cohen, more than one mode of the tourist experience may occur in a single tourist activity and these modes may also change throughout the lifetime of an individual tourist.

The complexity and overlapping nature of the subjective tourist experience have also been emphasized by Mannell and Iso-Ahola (1987), Urry (1990) and contributors to a pivotal volume entitled *The Tourist Experience: A New Introduction*, edited by Ryan (1997). While Mannell and Iso-Ahola discussed the complex psychological nature of the tourist experience, Urry and Ryan considered the various influences upon tourist experiences. Complementing Urry's view that tourist experiences may be affected by society, social groups and contexts, Ryan also stressed the importance of studying motivations and the diverse ways in which tourists express and satisfy their needs.

Furthermore, he identified a range of other factors that influence the tourist experience, all of which are encapsulated in his model of the tourist experience (Ryan, 1997, p54).

Although Ryan's model focuses on the holiday experience only, the generic variables included in this model (i.e. personal factors, travel experience, nature of destination, nature of personal interactions, responsive mechanisms) are also relevant to other types of the tourist experience. This has been demonstrated in the significant body of recent subject literature that includes Jennings and Nickerson's (2006) edited book *Quality Tourism Experiences*, Dallen's (2007) collection of critical essays on heritage tourist experience, and the most recent volume, *Tourist Experience*, edited by Sharpley and Stone (2011).

It is widely accepted among tourism researchers that the tourist experience contributes to overall tourist satisfaction, which may determine future tourist behaviour patterns. Studying such relationships is, however, challenging given that the tourist experience is inherently personal and subject to continual reconstruction and reinterpretation in relation to the specific external and internal influences (Jennings and Nickerson, 2006). Similarly, the diverse influences that form a unique tourist experience are largely beyond the control of a single tourism supplier. Consequently, it is difficult for tourism firms and destinations to manage experiences with a view to enhancing tourist satisfaction and generating favourable future purchase behaviours.

Nevertheless, some approaches to influencing such experiences have been proposed by, for example, several contributors to the special issue of *International Journal of Tourism Research* 'Extraordinary Experiences' (vol 11, issue 2, 2009). Within wider business literature, Pine and Gilmore (1998, p97) consider experiences as 'distinct economic offerings' which can be designed and promoted. Staging such experiences is, however, difficult in tourism due to the temporal, dynamic and subjective nature of the tourist experience. Indeed, the phenomenon of staged experiences (see **Authenticity**) has been extensively discussed in tourism literature following Boorstin's (1964) and Fussell's (1979) influential writing on pseudo-events. What emerges from this literature is that the quest for authentic tourist experiences (MacCannell, 1973; Pearce and Moscardo, 1986) may be in conflict with the offer of staged experiences in tourism. Furthermore, as tourists themselves are co-creators of their experiences, staging tourist experiences may have limited effect upon tourist satisfaction and future purchase behaviour. Indeed, it is ultimately the subjective tourist experience that determines the level of tourist satisfaction.

Tourist experience as a concept continues to be widely used by academics, practitioners and tourists alike. Further extensive research is therefore needed to enhance our understanding of the concept and our knowledge of the relationships between the tourist experience, tourist behaviour and the economic performance of tourism firms and destinations.

Further reading

Clawson, M. (1963) *Land and Water for Recreation: Opportunities, Problems and Policies*, Rand McNally, Chicago, IL
Cohen, E. (1979) 'A phenomenology of the tourist experiences', *Sociology*, vol 13, pp179–201
Pine, J. and Gilmore, J. (1998) 'Welcome to the experience economy', *Harvard Business Review*, vol 76, pp97–105
Ryan, C. (ed) (1997) *The Tourist Experience: A New Introduction*, Cassell, London

Dr. Marcjanna M. Augustyn

TOURIST GAZE

The tourist gaze is an important concept in tourism and has underpinned research into many other 'gazes'. Gaze describes the action of looking at and observing sights of interest and considered to be worth seeing. Urry (2002), who has carried out the principal research into *The Tourist Gaze*, suggests that it decides the need to gaze upon people, places and sights that are unusual. The concept originates from the idea that, on holiday, tourists constantly gaze on people, places or sights as a core element of tourist activity – for example, visiting New York to see the Statue of Liberty, or France to see the Eiffel Tower. It can also extend to activities that are unusual to the viewer – for example, people transporting goods to market using donkeys in Vietnam.

Central to the concept of the tourist gaze is the distinction between the ordinary and extraordinary. MacCannell (1973) explains that sites have to be marked as worth seeing and have, therefore, undergone a process of site sacralization, where the site is named, framed and elevated, enshrined, reproduced mechanically (as souvenirs) and socially, representing the importance of **semiotics** within the construction of the gaze. Where the gaze is only for a short period of time, however, it has been more recently referred to as the 'glance', a quick and temporal look, perhaps recorded through photographs as tourists seek to visit as many places as possible.

This type of gaze is defined as *the visual gaze*, and it is important to recognize that there are also other gazes to consider:

- *Romantic:* defined by solitude, privacy and personal relationships, and a suggested immersion in idealistic 'romantic' landscapes best exemplified by early tourists and their works of art and literature.
- *Collective:* defines the sharing of an experience with other people and is, therefore, a shared gaze. This is best exemplified by attendance at an event or festival.
- *Family:* defines the gaze when it is shared with family members, who may also be present in the images that are recorded of the site in question (Haldrup and Larsen, 2003).
- *Spectatorial:* also a shared activity, the spectatorial gaze is more akin to the 'glance', with many short stops at places of interest, where many souvenirs and photographs are collected.
- *Aerial:* defines the gaze when a site is viewed from the air and the viewer is perhaps offered a privileged view of areas that cannot usually be seen on the ground, a view which is offered by Google Earth.
- *Anthropological:* an individual study of specific places or cultures, this can be best described as a solitary traveller choosing to live with unfamiliar communities for a period of time.
- *Environmental:* similar to anthropological, but with a focus upon the environment, potentially involving active conservation.

The concept of the gaze has been criticized and developed since its inception two decades ago. The emphasis is overwhelmingly placed on the visuality of a site and does not consider interaction with the other senses, which may be equally or more important when tourists are, for example, experiencing wine tasting. The concept also ignores the second gaze, which looks beyond the immediately obvious and seeks the unseen aspects of the experience. Tourists rushing from place to place have also been criticized for glancing rather than gazing and therefore paying scant attention to the very sites they have chosen to visit.

Further reading

Haldrup, M. and Larsen, J. (2003) 'The family gaze', *Tourist Studies*, vol 3, no 1, pp23–46

Page, S. and Connell, J. (2009) *Tourism: A Modern Synthesis*, Cengage Learning, Hampshire

Strain, E. (2003) *Public Places, Private Journeys: Ethnography, Entertainment and the Tourist Gaze*, Rutgers University Press, New Brunswick, NJ

Urry, J. (2002) *The Tourist Gaze*, second edition, Sage Publications, London

Peter Robinson

TRANSPORT

Transport represents a multidimensional component of the tourism system (Page, 2005). At a more functional level, transport enables the flow of tourists, as well as related resources, between and within the tourist-generating region, transit route region and tourist destination region. Consequently, the oft-quoted axiom 'no transport, no tourism' is widely recognized as a fundamental tourism truism, although advocates of virtual tourism may challenge this in the future. Transport developments are directly related to tourism development in terms of nature, scope and scale. For example, the introduction of the wide-bodied jet aircraft enabled the growth of mass package tourism in the mid-twentieth century, while the emergence of low-cost airlines since the 1990s has opened up a wider range of destinations to tourism and led to a significant increase in short break holidays, especially to urban areas.

The modes of transport are essentially delineated as land (road and rail), water and air. Space represents a fourth dimension, although both supply of, and demand for, it are currently severely limited, especially due to cost. For tourism transport to function, three basic subcomponents are required: vehicles, ways and terminals. Therefore, any tourism development plan must acknowledge all three components; provision or shortage of any of these components will directly affect the flow of visitors. Terminals represent an increasingly complex and significant part of the transport mix. For example, Amsterdam Schiphol Airport in The Netherlands represents some or all of the following: a place for passengers to board and alight; an interchange with other modes of transport; a place to stay; a place to eat/drink; a place to shop; and a place to relax and recuperate. A more recent development at Schiphol – the 'Floating Dutchman' – also now means that air passengers can break their long-haul flight with a road- and water-way journey around Amsterdam via an amphibious bus, thus linking the three transport modes together.

The 'Floating Dutchman' example also emphasizes that transport also plays a sexier role within the tourism system. Lumsdon and Page

(2004) conceptualize the relationship between transport and tourism within their tourist transport continuum. At one end of the spectrum, transport plays a purely functional role, has low intrinsic value and is essentially seen as a means to an end. Examples of this form of transport include taxi and bus journeys, ski-lift rides and low-cost flights. As such, transport in this case simply represents a 'facilitator' (Holloway et al, 2009), which is arguably how the role of transport within tourism has historically been viewed. However, at the other end of the continuum, transport represents the *raison d'être* for tourism, and has a high intrinsic and experiential value; consequently, transport represents a 'motivator' for tourism (Holloway et al, 2009). Examples of this role include a wide range of transport forms and activities, including cruises, cycling holidays, adventure holidays including kayaking and ballooning, theme park rides, famous railway journeys such as the *Orient Express*, and events such as the Grand Prix. This experiential aspect of transport has started to receive more attention at both practical and academic levels. For example, it is increasingly recognized that transport components represent the first and last 'moments of truth' when visitors arrive at, and depart from, a destination, and can therefore make a significant impression upon the visitor experience. As such, it is no surprise that taxi drivers are targeted for customer service and language training by destination marketing organizations. Furthermore, transport brands such as Singapore and Emirate Airlines can promote the image of destinations, as well as act as significant revenue streams through their operational and strategic practices.

As well as providing access, vehicles, ways and terminals also provide attractions and amenities for a range of travellers, depending upon their needs and wants. In some cases, tourism has rejuvenated outmoded forms of transport. For example, Liverpool's Mersey Ferries in the UK – the theme of the 1960s classic song 'Ferry 'Cross the Mersey' – has reinvented itself via the development of a range of tourist services since the early 1990s, thus enabling the retention of a more functional transport service for local residents, as well as providing unique tourist experiences. Arguably, this transformation represents a case of 'no tourism, no transport'.

While transport contributes significantly to the development of tourism, and its numerous benefits, it also has one of the highest profiles in terms of negative tourism outcomes. This applies especially to environmental impacts. For example, transport providers and users, and related stakeholders such as governments and transport authorities, are coming under increasing pressure to reduce carbon footprints and behave in a more sustainable manner (Page, 2005). Furthermore, in other cases where transport itself may not be the direct cause of damage, the components of transport can open up otherwise sensitive areas with previously limited access and carrying capacities to larger numbers of tourists, thereby indirectly facilitating damage.

Transport, and its development, clearly does not exist in a vacuum. In addition to environmental pressures, it is also sensitive to political, economic, sociocultural, technological and legal forces. The terrorist attack on the Twin Towers in 2001 arguably affected air transport more than any other industry. While the airline industry has generally fought back successfully, the period since has seen a number of airlines go out of business and the introduction of major changes to airline and airport operations, with subsequent impacts upon its players, employees and customers.

To summarize, the notion of 'no transport, no tourism' emphasizes the symbiotic relationship that exists between transport and tourism. Far from being a simple relationship, it is one that is multidimensional and complex, functional and experiential, and positive and negative. As such, transport will remain at the forefront of any debate relating to tourism for the foreseeable future.

Further reading

Holloway, C., Davidson, R. and Humphreys, C. (2009) *The Business of Tourism*, FT Prentice Hall, Harlow

Lumsdon, L. and Page, S. J. (eds) (2004) *Tourism and Transport: Issues and Agenda for the New Millennium*, Elsevier, Oxford, UK

Page, S. (2005) *Transport and Tourism: Global Perspectives*, second edition, Pearson Education Ltd, Harlow

Dr. Paul Fallon

TRAVEL

Travel is one of the essential elements of tourism, alongside accommodation and the destination facilities. However, travel is increasingly being regarded as an industry in its own right. The two main developments driving this new phenomenon are communication technology and low-cost air travel. But before a consideration of these factors, it would be helpful to begin with an investigation into the factors that need to be present for travel to take place.

In its simplest form, travel must be considered against two criteria. The first is what makes travel possible, the *enabling factors*, and second is what persuades people to travel, the *motivating factors* (Holloway,

2006, p32). Only when both of these factors are present can travel take place. But for travel to occur at all, there are two essential prerequisites: time and money.

Enabling factors are many and varied, each with various levels of control exerted upon them by those on the supply side of the industry. Clearly, an infrastructure needs to be present if travel is to take place. Airlines cannot run a service to a destination without an airport in which to land; road travel needs a minimum standard of hard surface to allow travellers to reach their destination. Tourists need places to stay and may expect certain basic services such as freshwater and provision made for personal cleanliness. The standards of these may be variable depending upon the cost paid and the cultural experience required. It may be fine for someone to stay overnight in a room without air conditioning in a Kenyan safari lodge as mosquito nets may be part of the 'authentic' experience that matches the expectations of those who grew up in the 1950s watching wildlife films! But, generally speaking, such primitive provision would not be acceptable in Nairobi. It may be a novelty to use an earth closet in the outback; but in a hotel, most visitors would expect the 'luxury' of a WC!

Passports and visas would be other examples of enablers. The governments of several countries, including Russia, Tibet, Nigeria and Cuba, all severely restrict tourist numbers either by limiting annual numbers or making the process of getting the necessary papers difficult. Anyone wishing to travel from the UK to Nigeria, for example, may think they are able to speed the process up by initially going online. The reality is, however, that once done, one needs to travel to the Nigerian Embassy and queue for perhaps several days to get a visa because the demand is high and the opening hours restricted.

Motivation to travel itself is not a simple study area. It may come as the result of a latent desire that may have only just been realized for reasons such as financial ability, a medical need or a forthcoming event. Honeymoons are often taken at destinations where one or other partner wanted to go anyway; they may have been looking for a way of justifying the outlay! The motivation may have been triggered by an effective advertising campaign run by a destination or travel company. Invariably, TV holiday shows promote packages where the company has overcapacity and needs to increase sales to recoup some of their costs.

From one perspective, it could be argued accurately that the motivating factors are intrinsic, whereas enablers are extrinsic, and that the traveller needs the motivation to travel in order for travel to take place; but such a statement would be overly simplistic. A considerable amount of travel is done under the guise of business travel where the location may not be one of choice, rather of necessity. Indeed, the business event being attended may have come about as a result of a marketing campaign driven by the private sector, yet assisted by the public sector. A government may make a development grant available to a hotel chain to build in their location; the chain then targets business to come and utilize their facility. The government enables, but it is the event organizer who motivates, not the traveller.

Taking this train of thought a stage further, motivation for travel can and should be considered under two further headings: push-and-pull factors (Cooper et al, 2008a, p34). The intrinsic factors are pushing the resident into becoming a traveller – a seemingly endless list of working days, a monotonous routine or a desire for warmth and sun – anywhere! These pressures are within the individual, who needs to get away from the work or home environment for a short time. The destination is relatively unimportant to this urge to pack a bag and go. Effective advertising is often seen as being able to persuade the would-be traveller to be pulled to one specific location rather than another. A push factor may be to have some winter sunshine, whereas the pull factor draws the traveller to a particular sunny resort. Invariably, it is the blend of these two that will create the most enjoyable holiday, although issues such as cost, value for money, weather and fellow travellers may have a significant role to play here.

With these factors in mind, one must now consider two other issues: time and money. One in isolation is insufficient as both need to be available in equal measure. Having one without the other is not helpful to the travel industry. There is no benefit to the travel industry if an individual with ample financial resources cannot leave the desk. Conversely, unemployment provides many with the time to travel but without money; few can use this opportunity to the full. However, some 'time-rich' travellers do take the opportunity to travel on the strength of their redundancy package! For these reasons, historically, travelling and tourism was the preserve of the rich and famous, the pilgrimages to holy sites and the Grand Tour being two well-documented examples (Holloway, 2006, p26). In many, but not all, countries, this changed dramatically during the twentieth century.

During this period, the travel industry received assistance from an unlikely source: employment legislation. Throughout the nineteenth century and a third of the way through the next, all UK employees were only paid for every day that they worked and remained unpaid for any day that they did not. Such was the low hourly rate, the wage earner(s) needed to work all the daylight hours available in order to feed their families. Holidays were out of the question. Bank holidays were in existence; but then, as now, there was no legal requirement to pay for any time taken. In 1938, the Holiday with Pay Act marked the end of a struggle that began in 1918 to force employers to pay their staff to engage with leisure activities. This resultant legislation came six years after the 'Mass Trespass' on Kinder Scout on August Bank Holiday Monday 1932. Here, and on that day, thousands of walkers, demanding the 'Right to Roam' across the British countryside, engaged in one of the most famous acts of civil disobedience in history. Their action put pressure on the British government and its response was the National Parks and Access to the Countryside Act which entered the statute books in1949.

Here another key link can be made in the *evolution of travel*! Until the 1930s, the vast majority of citizens across the Western world depended upon the most reliable piece of travel capability on the planet – their feet. Private motor cars remained primarily the reserve of wealthy employers and public transport between towns and cities was unreliable and slow. As mass production techniques and technological advancements continued to be until the outbreak of war in 1939, rail, coach and private car travel jumpstarted the travel industry into life. However, wherever travel was being considered, it was invariably domestic travel: Germans travelling around Germany, Russians travelling around the Soviet Union and Americans around America. Indeed, the vast amount of Americans still take their vacations at home; less than 20 per cent of Americans hold a passport.

At least two of the outcomes of World War II assisted the growth of the travel and tourism industry; the two industries were inextricably entwined at that stage. The first was that there were a number of troop-carrying aircraft no longer needed for the movement of troops. The second was that the returning troops had been given a taste of air travel and distant destinations, some of which held good memories. Accordingly, there was a fleet of obsolete aircraft, an *army* of would-be passengers; all that was missing was an entrepreneurial spirit. It was found 'down under'. In 1952, Harold Bamberg bought and operated two Vickers Vikings from an airbase in New Zealand and began a local scheduled service. By 1956, he brought his idea to Europe and made air travel affordable for all. As is so often the case with entrepreneurs, business got in the way of the vision and big business finished the company, but not before glimpses of the future had been seen by others in the market. Married to Cunard, Eagle Airways moved almost effortlessly into transatlantic travel and virtually invented the intercontinental package tour sector singlehanded. Such was the size of the vision and potential rewards, the Cunard management made a secret betrothal to British Overseas Airways Corporation (BOAC) and quietly divorced their former partner. Within weeks, two of the faster Boeing 707 jets were bought with the dowry. Freddie Laker introduced his 'Sky-Train' in the 1970s, which, as the name suggests, was intended to run on a regular yet basic schedule between Britain and America – a low-cost strategy that sought to considerably reduce the cost of flying across the Atlantic, a plan that was to succumb to excessive pressures within the marketplace. And so began a 50-year battle between flag-bearers and low-cost airlines that remains to this day (see **Air transport**).

No one knows what would have happened if Harold Bamberg and Sir Freddie Laker had been trading in the twenty-first century. Certainly, those who have followed in their footsteps have not only benefitted from their vision, but have, with the help of technology, created what is essentially a new industry and turned aviation on its head. The travel industry is no longer simply a component part of the tourism amalgam; rather, it is self-supporting, self-sufficient and, in the case of low-cost air travel, continuing to evolve. Over the past years, most such flight providers have embedded within their website details of car hire, hotels and currency. For several years now, low-cost flyers have operated what is known as *yield management*. This has allowed them to maximize their loading by reducing the cost of a booked fare on a flight that has not sold at the expected rate and by increasing the fares on those that have. Without the Internet, such massaging of demand would be impossible. With the advent of the Internet, the traveller has been able to put together an itinerary – and has become the target for relationship marketing. Neither needs hotel managers or other accommodation providers. They don't have to wait to be contacted; they can be proactive with e-mails and text messaging, while taking full advantage of travel review sites such as *TripAdviser*. For their part, empowered travellers are no longer required to consult an agent to find out what package is available; rather, they make their own.

Further reading

Beaver, A. (2002) *A Dictionary of Travel and Tourism Terminology*, CABI, Wallingford, UK

Davidson, R. (2003) *Business Travel, Conference, Incentive Travel, Exhibitions, Corporate Travel*, Prentice Hall, Harlow

Firth, L. (2008) *Travel and Tourism Issues*, Independence, Cambridge

Hudson, L. (2003) *Geography of Travel*, Thomson, UK

Taylor, M. (1999) *World Travel Atlas*, Columbus, London

Geoff Shirt

URBAN TOURISM

Urban tourism encompasses the activities of international and domestic visitors, as well as local residents in urban areas, contextualized by built and natural landscapes, amenities and infrastructure. Urban areas such as towns and cities are sources of travellers, act as tourism destinations and are gateways to other places. Over 50 per cent of the world's population is urbanized; thus, the dynamics and features of urban tourism are important to understand as drivers of the global tourism economy. Urban tourism is inseparable from the social, spatial, economic and technological, as well as governance, issues of urbanization and local responses to globalization.

Case study approaches dominate the literature on urban tourism. Examples of research in this field encompass developmental and inner-city regeneration (Karski, 1990; Page, 1995), geographic (Pearce, 2001), recreation (Law, 1993, 2000), heritage (Chang et al, 1996; van der Borg et al, 1996) and events (Getz, 1991). Yet, as a field of study, urban tourism is challenged by vague demarcation and a lack of analytical frameworks (Page, 1995; Pearce, 2001; Edwards et al, 2008; Ashworth and Page, 2011). A broader social science view of urbanization processes, including investigations of social dynamics, the notion of world cities, re-globalization and re-scaling of cities (Ashworth and Page, 2011) and migration, might aid understanding of the scope and scale of urban tourism.

As large centres of population, cities are major generators of tourist traffic, in part caused by the desire to holiday away from crowds (UNWTO, 2002). Yet, the global options for travel destinations are extensive, meaning that cities compete alongside all others for visits longer than short break or single visits (Dwyer et al, 2009). As destinations, cities and towns are characterized by high densities of physical structures, people and functions, cultural and social heterogeneity, multifunctional economies and physical centrality within regional and inter-urban networks (Pearce, 2001). Tourism in urban environments can be addressed at micro-geographic neighbourhood levels of analysis and at a wider systems level (Page, 1995). The wider analysis encompasses flows across urban transportation, natural and built infrastructure. Tourism flows are driven by consumer demand and supply of tourism services mitigated by public- and private-sector management strategies, marketing, planning and development, and other factors.

The scale of urbanization and urban tourism ranges from megacities of more than 10 million inhabitants, to small cities and towns in both the developed and undeveloped worlds. Urban tourism is likely to follow geopolitical shifts from developed world cities to cities in the undeveloped world, in parallel with the development of megacities. In 1950, the globe had two megalopolises of more than 10 million people (UN, 2005), by 2000, 18 million, and in 2007, 19 million – the majority in the developing countries of Asia, Africa and Latin America. By 2050, over 27 million are anticipated, most likely to be in Asia, 2 million in Africa and 1 million in Europe (Smith, 2010); but none in North America. Global changes in age profiles, economic wealth and migration produced by political, climatic and economic shifts will continue to drive urban tourism trends.

In terms of scope, urban tourism encompasses site-specific, district, city-wide, national and international linkages (Pearce, 2001). Urban tourism is made up of:

- *primary elements*, such as visitor attractions with the ability to attract tourists and
- *secondary elements*, such as transportation used by tourists to travel to the destination or as services after arrival (Jansen-Verbeke, 1986).

Tourists visit cities for many purposes, but are largely economically and physically invisible (Ashworth and Page, 2011) since it is difficult to quantify discrete 'tourist' usage of infrastructures or amenity supply, as opposed to the use of the same amenities by residents (Page, 1995). Exceptions are small island cities in developing states where tourists may be more ethnically and functionally visible (Nunkoo and Ramkissoon, 2010b). Major tourism events such as the Olympics provide a legacy of infrastructure in urban settings, with facilities and processes created for visitors, but remaining for resident benefit after the events.

Paradoxically, little of the city has been created specifically for tourist use (Ashworth and Page, 2011). Tourism activities do not take place evenly across the cityscape but tend to be concentrated in the central city or dispersed across the city in clusters of arts, ethnic or natural activities, multipurpose events amenities and facility-specific locations. The city centre offers a wide variety of activities in a relatively compact environment (Kadri, 2007), offering ambiance, contrasts of contemporary and historical architecture, and a range of nightlife, shopping and other amenities (Erhlich and Dreier, 1999). The urban landscape also provides areas that attract visitors, such as creative arts precincts (Pappalepore et al, 2010), historic districts (Ashworth, 1990; Tunbridge and Ashworth, 1996; Jansen-Verbeke, 2010), ethnic migrant neighbourhoods (Conforti, 1996; Chang, 1997), and sacred spaces and entertainment destinations (Pearce, 2001). These factors are all significant, but so too are issues such as effective city management, transport infrastructures and traffic congestion (Hensher and Puckett, 2007).

The rural–urban fringe is often a locus for many recreational, leisure and tourism activities. Incorporation of open natural landscapes within city environments has become essential to urban tourism, linked to the idea that cities are for work and the 'country' is for pleasure (Tacoli, 1998). For instance, rural scenic areas (Xiao and Wall, 2009) and urban forests function as a main attractor for many visitors and complement other tourism attractions (i.e. historical sites) in the city (Deng et al, 2010). The city of Montreal in Canada links tourism in parklands and water with its urban environments (Timur and Getz, 2009).

Revitalization of marginalized economies or mature city destinations developed in the latter part of the twentieth century (Law, 2000) as a worldwide trend for urban regeneration, based around multiyear development strategies, the development of multifunctional entertainment venues, expos and hallmark events such as the Olympic Games (Getz, 1991).

There is asymmetry in the tourist–city relationship. A vibrant tourism industry needs the variety, accessibility and flexibility that cities can provide, but in terms of city planning and policy, tourism is only one element amongst many. While tourism has potential for economic benefits to cities, the greatest benefits are produced in cities that have a wide and varied economic base, yet are the least dependent upon tourism (Tunbridge and Ashworth, 1992; Pearce, 2001; Ashworth and Page, 2011).

Further reading

Ashworth, G. and Page, S. J. (2011) 'Urban tourism research: Recent progress and current paradoxes', *Tourism Management*, vol 32, no 1, pp1–16
Edwards, D., Griffin, T. and Hayllar, B. (2008) 'Urban tourism research: Developing an agenda', *Annals of Tourism Research*, vol 35, no 4, pp1032–1052
Law, C. M. (2000) 'Regenerating the city centre through leisure and tourism', *Built Environment*, vol 26, no 2, pp117–129

Dr. Lee Jolliffe and Dr. Jenny Cave

VIRTUAL TOURISM

The virtualization of tourism describes the change in the nature and dynamics of business (see also **e-tourism**) from businesses operating in a time-constrained (9am to 5pm) work pattern and relying on the telephone to plan and book activities in order to sell products online 24 hours a day, globally networked and able to communicate at low cost. While businesses benefit from this change through e-tourism and e-distribution, consumers are able to engage in many very different ways.

Virtual tourism offers tourists an opportunity to visit and experience a destination using a computer or other technologies. Such technologies provide travellers with an opportunity to view a destination before they visit, and is best exemplified through the multi-layered datasets provided through Google Earth which offers street-level navigation and images, also referred to as 3DVT (three-dimensional virtual tourism), where viewers may interact with a destination without actually travelling to it. This type of technology has already been adopted by a number of tourism destinations, including South Africa, Ireland and Nova Scotia, Canada, to act as a marketing tool.

This emerging area of tourism has been discussed since the 1990s, but only with faster Internet access and greater technological access has it become a reality, although this also means that there is currently little research in existence. Other theoretical perspectives are offered by Urry (2002) and Strain (2003); but research is limited and Urry's comments tend to only hint at the idea that the Internet opens up new social networks and allows individuals to engage in tourism or related activities at any time and in any location.

Further reading

Urry, J. (2002) *The Tourist Gaze*, second edition, Sage Publications, London

Peter Robinson

VISITOR ATTRACTIONS

Visitor attractions encompass a multiplicity of places, objects and activities that draw people from within and outside a given geographic region, as illustrated in the **tourism system**. The purpose for such visits may be to participate in or enjoy leisure, recreation, educational and religious activities or benefits. Pearce (1991, p46) defines an attraction as 'a named site with a specific human or natural feature which is the focus of visitor and management attention'.

Visitor attractions include the natural environment and the built environment, as well as cultural resources, services/products and festivals and events purposely developed and managed to provide an exciting, educational and enjoyable experience for the visitor (Page and Connell, 2009). Swarbrooke (1995) classifies attractions into four types:

1 natural;
2 man-made but not originally designed primarily to attract visitors;
3 man-made;
4 purpose built to attract visitors and special events.

The study of visitor attractions is inundated with academic and practice-based argument *vis-à-vis* definition, classification and even nomenclature. In the early stages of the development of tourism they are referred to as tourist attractions. It is suggested that terminology such as this fails to recognize that a wide range of people visit attractions for many different purposes (pilgrimage, research, on business or for enjoyment) and may not necessarily be tourists.

Definitions suggested by tourist boards (see Page and Connell, 2009) have been criticized for being too narrow in their scope. These definitions have been alleged to have the aim of enabling the harmonization of industry statistics in order to ascertain the volume and value of the sector, rather than providing an encompassing overview of these businesses. Definitions are mostly based on one or two features, such as size, permanency, management regime, aesthetic nature and appeal, and a host of other characteristics of visitor attractions. It is essential to note that no single definition has been found to describe the scope and structure of visitor attractions.

It has been argued in some quarters that an attraction, for example, may include some events and festivals, as well as business travel, and in some occasions may not necessarily be 'a named site' in a tourism context. There has been intense debate on the role of permanency in defining and classifying attractions.

It is a common knowledge that visitor attractions are central to tourism development and more often than not are the reasons why people travel to most destinations. It has been argued, rightly or wrongly, that attractions research has not been given much attention, unlike other areas of tourism such as tourism motivation, impacts of tourism and destination image, to mention just a few.

However, the growing interest in attraction competitiveness has no doubt brought about focus being directed towards the conceptualization of the attraction product, and how visitors consider its different components. The process by which a site, object or event is transformed into a visitor attraction is tourism's exceptional ability to turn natural or man-made resources into products that visitors must travel to consume. It is important to consider the core product's (the imagescape's) tangible features and augmented service. Location market and the core product have been found to be key factors in the development of an attraction.

Examples of attractions may include historic houses open to the public, museums, country parks, zoos, aquariums, theme parks, visitor centres, permanent and temporary exhibitions, galleries, events and festivals, sports activities, religious sites, viewing points and rural honeypots. It could be argued that some destinations, especially small tourism honeypots, are in fact attractions in their own right.

Further reading

Fyall, A., Garrod, B., Leask, A. and Wanhill, S. (eds) (2008) *Managing Visitor Attractions: New Direction*, second edition, Butterworth-Heinemann, Oxford, UK

Swarbrooke, J. (2002) *The Development and Management of Visitor Attractions*, second edition, Butterworth-Heinemann, Oxford, UK

Ade Oriade

VISITOR INTERPRETATION

Visitor interpretation is used by visitor attractions to tell a story about a site's significance and its context (physical, natural, social, aesthetic or spiritual). The purpose of visitor interpretation is informal education and first-hand participatory learning, often about heritage (Moscardo, 1996) or natural environments (Sharpe, 1982). But interpretation is also used to enhance knowledge of authenticity (McIntosh and Prentice, 1999; Firth, 2011), stimulate change in attitudes and behaviour (Armstrong and Weiler, 2002) and explain ideologies (Lia et al, 2010). Interpretation is complemented by visitor management tools such as information and directional signage and trail design (Hughes et al, 2009).

Interpretive devices mediate between the visitor and the site and can be used in any natural, cultural or built heritage setting. They range in style from unstructured immersive experiences to constructed, programmed interventions and variously described as hot and cold media (McCluhan, 1964) or social, cognitive and spatial interactive approaches (Goulding, 2000).

Moving at their own pace during the visit, the visitor is free to interact (or not) with interpretive devices that can include:

- *People:* first-person (personal) interpretation, which occurs as 'animation' when an actor adopts a period character and 'demonstration' when an actor is not in character, but talking about the historical period. Second-person (non-personal) interpretation is undertaken by an 'interpreter' when the person is a subject expert, but not in period costume (Widner Ward and Wilkinson, 2006). Interpretive personnel can include indigenous representatives, tour guides, tourism operators, docents, security guards and educators, curators or park rangers.

- *Media:* virtual environments, interactive devices, educational signage, graphics, sound, smell, exhibits (interactive and static).
- *Objects:* artefacts, buildings, animals (stuffed and alive), plants, rocks, models, figures, props.
- *Self-guiding tools:* maps, guidebooks, podcasts, interactive computers, dedicated radio stations, geographic information systems (GIS).
- *Built structures:* interpretation centres and interpretive signage, etc.

Visitor interpretation is often separated into natural and cultural styles (Ablett and Dyer, 2009), traceable to the beginning of nature guiding in the US during the later years of the 1800s and a late nineteenth-century Western dualism that separates nature from culture (Aldridge, 1989). Yet, Tilden (1957) developed a holistic set of six historio-cultural and natural interpretive principles which continue to influence contemporary practitioners (Beck and Cable, 1998). According to Tilden (1957): interpretation (1) must relate what is displayed to the experience of the visitor, (2) is revelation rather than information, (3) is a teachable art, (4) provoke rather than instruct, (5) relate parts to an underlying whole and that (6) children need a qualitatively different interpretive approach from adults:

> Interpretation is an educational activity which aims to reveal meanings and relationships through the use of original objects, by first hand experience, and by illustrative media rather than simply to communicate factual information. Interpretation is revelation of a larger truth that lies behind any statement of fact.
>
> (Tilden 1957)

However, since the 1970s, cognitive psychology, behaviourism (Hammitt, 1984) and communication theory have tended to dominate visitor interpretation in efforts to understand the cognitive processes embedded in the visitor experience and to positively influence its outcomes. Examples of analysis linked to the design of interpretive techniques include reasoned action (Ham and Krumpe, 1996) behaviourism (Hammitt, 1984) and reductionist communication (Ham,

1983). In many cases, attraction practitioners used evaluation to reshape the design of their interpretive tools in order to improve communication and demonstrate educational effectiveness (Loomis, 1987; Dewar, 1991). These developments were driven partly by the need to demonstrate social relevance and to justify public expenditure (Goulding, 2000).

During the late twentieth century, however, trends for democratization, closer relationships with schools and communities and a shift towards discovery and child-centred learning expanded the range of interpretive techniques used (Hooper-Greenhill, 2007) in multisensory visitor environments (Moscardo, 1999). More recently, awareness of the roles of power, morality and ethics in filtering visitor information, parallel worldviews (Stewart and Kirby, 1998; Cave, 2005) and absences of indigenous voice (James, 1999; Mason, 2008) have led to a resurgence in holistic interpretations of site, mediated by cultural meaning and visitor-centred experiences.

Further reading

Ablett, P. G. and Dyer, P. K. (2009) 'Heritage and hermeneutics: Towards a broader interpretation of interpretation', *Current Issues in Tourism*, vol 12, no 3, pp209–233

Ham, S. and Krumpe, E. (1996) 'Identifying audiences and messages for non-formal environmental education: A theoretical framework for interpreters', *Journal of Interpretation Research*, vol 1, no 1, pp11–23

Tilden, F. (1957) *Interpreting Our Heritage*, third edition, University of North Carolina Press, Chapel Hill

Dr. Lee Jolliffe and Dr. Jenny Cave

VOLUNTARY (THIRD) SECTOR

While scholars generally agree that the economy should be divided into three sectors for analytical purposes, and while there is no evident dissent that the first should be referred to as the public sector and the second as the private sector, there is almost no agreement about what the third sector should be called. The private sector is distinctive in that organizations working within it are motivated primarily (if not exclusively) by the goal of making profit, while the public sector is characterized by the production of goods and services by state-owned organizations. There is, however, a third sector of the economy, comprising organizations that are essentially neither government owned nor primarily profit motivated. A number of terms have been coined to denote this sector, including the 'voluntary sector', the 'community sector', the 'non-profit sector' and the 'not-for-profit sector'. Such terms are often taken to be synonymous with each other, but there are some important distinctions between them. For example, many people prefer not to use the term 'voluntary' sector, given the widespread tendency for organizations operating in it also to employ people on a paid basis. The term 'non-profit', meanwhile, does not cover the many co-operatives and mutual societies that are widely considered to be part of the sector, yet clearly operate in order to earn profits for their members. Such organizations would not fit any better into the public or private sectors, so are normally categorized as part of the third sector. Another frequently used term is the 'civic sector', linking in to the concept of civic society. However, this term, like the similar term 'community sector', does not seem to recognize the lack of community or civic involvement in many organizations that are included in the sector.

In view of the considerable problems of definition noted above, many people refer to the sector simply as the 'third sector'. Organizations operating in the third sector vary greatly in terms of their size, remit and *modus operandi*. Non-governmental organizations (NGOs) are third-sector organizations that receive their funding directly from donations by the public or from government grants. Many NGOs take the legal form of charities or trusts, while others call themselves associations or societies. There are also many agencies and partnerships in the third sector, many of which have been 'spun out' from central, regional or local government and often receive a substantial part of their funding directly from government sources. Organizations in the third sector have a wide range of concerns, including the natural environment, heritage, children and young people, public health and well-being, community, minority groups, poverty, and the promotion of particular beliefs, practices and activities.

The third sector is extremely important in the context of tourism for a number of reasons. One is that the sector has a significant involvement in the attractions sector. It is estimated, for example, that approximately 30 per cent of all paid-entry visitor attractions in Scotland are owned and managed by trusts, charities and societies (Garrod et al, 2006). Comparable estimates are 38 per cent for Australia, 37 per cent for Canada and 40 per cent for New Zealand, suggesting that the third sector has a considerable role to play in the provision of tourist attractions in various countries around the world.

Many such visitor attractions have established themselves as charities, trusts or societies in their own right. Registering as a charity opens up a number of advantages and opportunities to those who own and manage them. For example, in the UK:

- Registered charities are eligible to apply for a variety of different types of tax break.
- A large number of grant-making bodies and other types of funders, such as the Heritage Lottery Fund, only make grant awards to organizations that are registered as charities.
- Many other organizations are willing to provide information, advice and support to registered charities at preferential rates, sometimes even for free.
- There is an increased likelihood that individuals, groups and organizations will be interested and willing to offer their time and effort, and perhaps also their financial support, to an organization that has registered as a charity.

The terms of registration as a charity, trust or society often imply that the building, site or collection will need to be made accessible to the public. This can be done by opening it, for specific days and times of the year, as a visitor attraction. This is also true of places that have received funding from the third sector to help towards maintenance or conservation.

Other visitor attractions are part of the portfolio of national third-sector organizations, such as The National Trust in England and Wales and the National Trust for Scotland. The National Trust is one of the biggest landowners in England and Wales (National Trust, 2011a), with a substantial number of forests, woods, fens, beaches, farmland, downs, moorland, islands, archaeological remains, castles, nature reserves, villages, historic houses, gardens and ancient monuments that have either been donated to The National Trust or have been purchased for their natural or historic value and with potential to offer some public benefit. The National Trust was incorporated as the 'National Trust for Places of Historic Interest or Natural Beauty' in 1894 as an 'association not for profit' under English and Welsh law. It became a charitable organization under the Charities Act of 1993. The Trust was founded with the purpose of 'the preservation for the benefit of the Nation of lands and tenements (including buildings) of beauty or historic interest and, as regards lands, for the preservation of their natural aspect, features and animal and plant life [and] also the preservation of furniture, pictures and chattels of any description having national and historic or artistic interest'. The National Trust is also heavily involved in educating the public about the importance of the natural environment and of preserving the national heritage for the benefit of future generations.

The National Trust's income during 2009 to 2010 was over UK £400 million. Its largest source of income was private membership subscriptions (31 per cent), followed by direct property income (26 per cent), revenues from its commercial operations, such as tea rooms and gift shops at National Trust properties (13 per cent), and legacies (12 per cent). Individual membership subscription, which may be purchased on an annual or lifetime basis, allows the holder unlimited free entry to all of The National Trust's properties that are open to the public. In 2011, The National Trust had more than 350 properties open to the public and had a membership roll of over 3.6 million. In addition to visits by its members, The National Trust's portfolio of properties also attracted 14 million paid visits by non-members and an estimated 50 million visits to open-air, free-admission properties in 2009 to 2010 (National Trust, 2011b). The Trust's most-visited property in 2009 to 2010 was Wakehurst Place Garden in West Sussex, England. Administered by the Royal Botanic Gardens, Kew, the property received an estimated 439,627 visitors that year.

The third sector is also important in tourism terms because many such organizations are involved in the tourist accommodation sector. A prominent example in the UK is the Youth Hostel Association (YHA), which is a charitable organization established in 1930. The YHA covers England and Wales, with Scotland and Northern Ireland having their own separate associations. The YHA was established in order to 'help all, especially young people of limited means, to a greater knowledge, love and care of the countryside, particularly by providing hostels or other simple accommodation for them in their travels, and thus to promote their health, rest and education'. Its first hostel, opened that year, was Pennant Hall near Llanrwst in Wales.

The YHA today operates a network of more than 200 hostels around England and Wales (YHA, 2011). It is also part of Hostelling International, giving members a choice of more than 4000 hostels in 90 different countries. The product offered by the association has changed considerably since it began operation, largely in an attempt to widen its market by providing a product that will better suit modern tastes. Membership, previously aimed solely at young people, is now open to all. The accommodation, originally in single-sex dormitories, now incorporates a range of private rooms suitable for couples and families, an increasing number of which have en-suite facilities. The consumption of alcohol on YHA premises has been permitted since 1980. Guests are no longer required to perform chores such as washing dishes. Until the 1950s, guests were not permitted to bring their cars, the hostels being intended for walkers, cyclists and canoeists; but since 1984 car-parking at hostels has been allowed. Initially a network of hostels located exclusively in the more rural parts of England and Wales, the YHA now has a number of hostels in large cities, including London, Bristol and Liverpool.

In many other ways, the YHA has remained true to its original philosophies and practices. The association still provides basic but clean budget accommodation, with self-catering facilities for those who wish to prepare their own meals. Many also continue to offer a catering service for those who wish to purchase hot meals. Most hostels still offer drying rooms for those who have been walking and storage facilities for those who have brought bicycles. The YHA also has a tradition of sharing, encouraging people to mix with each other and to meet people from around the world. The association also maintains a commitment to encouraging hostellers to:

- grow in their skills, confidence, self-reliance and well-being;
- engage with diverse people and communities;
- explore wider horizons of culture and location, particularly for young people.

Further reading

Evers, A. and Laville, J.-L. (2004) *The Third Sector in Europe*, Edward Elgar, Cheltenham and Northampton

Dr. Brian Garrod

WILDLIFE TOURISM

Wildlife tourism as defined by the United Nations Environment Programme (UNEP) is travel to destinations with the main purpose of watching animals in their natural habitats. This therefore implies that wildlife tourism includes other niche markets, such as bird-watching and the exploration of marine life (e.g. whale-watching in Sydney) (UNEP, 2006).

Africa is the market leader and accounts for around one half of all wildlife tourism trips worldwide. The traditional wildlife destinations of Kenya, South Africa, Botswana, Namibia and Tanzania receive the greatest volume of visitors. In East Africa, wildlife watching is one of the attractions for international tourists, and the basis for the majority of their national income from tourism (UNEP, 2006). According to the Ministry of Tourism, Kenya received 2,385,000 visitors to its parks and reserves in 2009.

Wildlife tourism overlaps with many other typologies, including **nature tourism** and **ecotourism**, but is most commonly recognized within defined consumer products, including safaris and wildlife-based scuba diving. Equally, there are many tourists who engage in wildlife watching, swimming with dolphins and shark baiting as part of a series of holiday activities that focus on adventure in wild places (**adventure tourism**), and for whom engaging with wildlife is an added attraction rather than a primary motivation. Wildlife tourism can also include appropriately operated mass tourism activities. One example is the viewing of the annual migration of 1.5 million wildebeest from the Serengeti Plains to the Masai Mara in Kenya. Another example given by UNEP (2006) is the 'Penguin Parade' on Phillip Island, close to Melbourne in Australia, where over 425,000 visitors a year watch penguins come up the beach each evening to their nesting sites on the island. Ultimately, wildlife watching has links to a wide range of different types of tourism, and tourists participate in these activities for many different reasons (see Table 16).

Animal communities (for example, gorillas in Rwanda) may be protected from visitors as part of conservation and breeding programmes. The challenges with management include a lack of willingness to pay for community benefits by tourists. This is because the percentage of park revenues used to enhance local community development within the national park does not have a significant effect on tourism demand. There needs to be more education of

Table 16 Popular wildlife tourism destinations

Wildlife	Destination region
Big Five (lion, elephant, rhinoceros, buffalo and leopard)	East Africa, South Africa, Asia
Cheetahs	Asia, Africa
Tigers	Africa, Asia
Gorillas	Central Africa
Sharks	Caribbean, Africa, Pacific
Snakes	Asia
Birds	Asia, Europe, South America
Polar bears	North America
Dolphins	Australia

tourists about the human dimension of conservation in order to emphasize the conceptual link between the local population needs and biodiversity conservation. Developing the assets that partners need in order to maximize their opportunities for entering productive partnerships should be a fundamental part of plans to widen (and deepen) participation (Nielsen and Spenceley, 2010).

Increasingly, tour operators are emphasizing that tourism needs to be sustainable, and are developing and marketing tourism products that are 'wildlife friendly', as well as carbon neutral, and which ensure that a fair share of tourist income goes to local people. In some places, such as East Africa, the Seychelles or the Galapagos Islands, wildlife has been the foundation upon which their tourism has developed. In others, wildlife watching is a newer attraction that is helping to diversify tourism and to promote community development in remote areas. The lands outside the parks are crucial to wildlife since they serve as dispersal areas. These areas are threatened with increasing 'land sub-division, agricultural expansion and unplanned development of tourist accommodation, thus increasing human-wildlife conflicts' (Republic of Kenya, 1997, p88; Sindiga, 1999, p107). Wildlife in many protected areas is under threat from human encroachment, 'insularization', hunting, poaching for commercial or subsistence purposes, habitat degradation, through incompatible land uses, loss of migration and dispersal areas, and ever-contested values of different stakeholders and native wildlife. In determining hunting policies, perhaps it is important to have a clear distinction between where hunting is allowed and where hunting is prohibited. In a scenario where wildlife-induced damages to human property and life are neither controlled nor compensated, negative local attitudes towards conservation and wildlife resources become entrenched (Okello and Wishitemi, 2006, p90; Okech, 2010). This is made worse when local communities do not benefit from wildlife resources and are alienated from wildlife-related economic enterprises, such as lucrative tourism activities. When local communities feel that both governments and conservation stakeholders value wildlife more than their lives, livelihoods or their aspirations, retaliation and opposition to conservation initiatives can be swift and uncompromising.

Further reading

Lovelock, B. (ed) (2007) *Tourism and the Consumption of Wildlife: Hunting, Shooting and Sport Fishing*, Routledge, Oxon, UK

Newsome, D., Dowling, R. K. and Moore, S. A. (2005) *Wildlife Tourism – Aspects of Tourism*, Channel View Publications, Clevedon, UK

Nielsen, H. and Spenceley, A. (2010) *The Success of Tourism in Rwanda: Gorillas and More*, Joint paper of the World Bank and SNV (The Netherlands Development Organization)

Okech, R. N. (2010) 'Wildlife–community conflicts in conservation areas in Kenya', *African Journal of Conflict Resolution*, vol 10, no 2, pp65–80

Okello, M. M and Wishitemi, B. E. L. (2006) 'Principles for the establishment of community wildlife sanctuaries for ecotourism: Lessons from Maasai Group Ranches, Kenya', *African Journal of Business and Economics*, vol 1, no 1, pp90–109

UNEP (2006) *Wildlife Watching and Tourism: A Study of Benefits and Risks of a Fast-Growing Tourism Activity and Its Impacts on Species*, UNEP, Nairobi

Dr. Roselyne N. Okech

WINE TOURISM

As a form of special interest tourism, wine tourism is becoming increasingly popular. It is argued that, alongside the attraction of the wine itself, the attributes of a wine region, such as scenery, provide an additional incentive to visit the region (Hall et al, 2000). This winescape is 'characterised by three main elements: the presence of vineyards, the winemaking activity and the wineries where the wine is produced and stored (Telfer, 2001, cited in Sparks, 2007, p1181). The notion of winescape thus encompasses 'more of the feeling of region, which is a culmination of all of its physical and cultural parts' (Sparks, 2007, p1181).

Motivations for wine tourists may therefore be considered to include education benefits (i.e. an increased awareness and understanding of wine and its production, perceived destination attractiveness, enhanced cultural and lifestyle awareness, the opportunities for social interaction offered by participation in wine tastings, an opportunity to purchase wine, and possibly even health reasons) (Charters and Ali-Knight, 2002; Sparks, 2007).

According to Stewart et al (2008, p310), wine tourists 'tend to be more educated and experienced travellers'. Stewart et al (2008) also argue that they are therefore more demanding in terms of service and product quality. In the case of the Niagara region in Ontario, Canada, located in close proximity to the US border, cross-border collabora-tion through the development of wine routes, enhanced service and improved quality of information for wine tourists are all initiatives which serve to grow the target customer base. Such initiatives may also be adopted by wine regions globally.

According to Sparks (2007, p1180), 'wine tourism is defined as visits to a wine region for recreational purposes'. Wine tourism may therefore be defined as travel away from home for the purpose of enhancing awareness and understanding of wine through consumption and education. Wine tourism may be the sole purpose for the visit to a destination, or an activity pursued as part of a destination experience, either intentionally or spontaneously. Charters and Ali-Knight (2002, p311) refer to wine tourism as 'form of consumer behaviour in which wine lovers and those interested in wine regions travel to preferred destinations'.

Getz and Brown (2006) consider wine tourism in broader terms, proposing that most definitions of wine tourism relate to consumer motivation and experience rather than the wider perspectives on the subject, such as wine tourism being part of a destination's development and marketing strategy, a form of **consumer behaviour** 'and a marketing opportunity for wineries to educate, and to sell their products, directly to consumers' (Getz and Brown, 2006, p147).

'The wine product has been a fundamental part of hospitality and the hospitality industry for centuries' (Alonso and Liu, 2010, p247). This complementary nature of wine and **hospitality** has combined to provide a tourism product which is increasingly important globally. Wine is often identified by its geographical place of origin (Hall, 2005) – for example, Champagne, Burgundy, Bordeaux and Rioja.

Many wine regions were in existence long before tourism made them an attraction in their own right and 'wine is an environmentally dependent resource' (Hall, 2005, p157). Increasingly, 'wine exports play an important role in commercial terms for so-called "New World" wine countries including Argentina, Australia, Chile, and South Africa' (Alonso and Liu, 2010, p245).

Hall (2005), Stewart et al (2008) and Alonso and Liu (2010) explore the role of food, wine and tourism in regional development, highlighting their importance in rural areas: wine tourism is an important element in local economic development strategies due to the relationship between sectors and the potential for enhancement of the multiplier effect (see **Multiplier and Leakage**) – that is, prolonged circulation of income within local economies, resulting in reduction of economic leakage. According to Hall (2005, p149), 'rural areas have sought to innovate and diversify their agricultural bases through tourism-related consumption and production'.

The growth of wine tourism during recent years has allowed rural communities the opportunity 'to diversify and stimulate development, and for travellers to enjoy an activity that brings together educational and gastronomic experiences' (Alonso and Liu, 2010, p245). For many rural areas, wine tourism has brought significant benefits, growing from a relatively minor agricultural industry to dominating the landscape in some areas (Hall, 2005). Referring to the growth and development of wine tourism in New Zealand, Hall (2005, p157) indicates that 'This growth can be charted not only in terms of number of wineries and the area under vine but also in the substantial export returns that have developed.'

The relationship between wineries and the wider tourism and hospitality industries is explored by Alonso and Liu (2010) and Sparks (2007), who conclude that it is vital for tourism authorities, organizations and wineries to understand the attributes of wine tourism that attract consumers. This understanding serves to inform marketing strategies and product and service development, enabling a match with 'intentions to engage in consumptive behaviours' (Sparks, 2007, pp1180–1181). Sparks also refers to the importance of ascertaining 'the fundamental drivers of the desire to engage in wine tourism'.

Wine tourism, according to Charters and Ali-Knight (2002, p318), 'is rarely a discrete activity, but will probably be undertaken in conjunction with some or all of rural, eco-cultural or adventure tourism, and its participants are unlikely to separate the various tourism forms'.

Much research into wine tourism has been carried out at wineries and focuses on consumer satisfaction and the decision-making process (Getz and Brown, 2006). There remains scope for further research into consumer motivation, potentially conducted away from the winery in the tourism generating region in order to further ascertain consumer preferences.

Further reading

Charters, S. and Ali-Knight, J. (2002) 'Who is the wine tourist?', *Tourism Management*, vol 23, pp311–319
Getz, D. and Brown, G. (2006) 'Critical success factors for wine tourism regions: A demand analysis', *Tourism Management*, vol 27, pp146–158
Hall, C. M., Sharples, L., Cambourne, B. and Macionis, N. (eds) (2000) *Wine Tourism around the World*, Butterworth-Heinemann, Oxford, UK

Carol Southall

BIBLIOGRAPHY

Ablett, P. G. and Dyer, P. K. (2009) 'Heritage and hermeneutics: Towards a broader interpretation of interpretation', *Current Issues in Tourism*, vol 12, no 3, pp209–233

Accor (2011) *Accors Marketing and Brand Strategy*, http://www.accor.com/fileadmin/user_upload/Contenus_Accor/Finance/Documentation/2011/EN/Presentation_va_part01.pdf, accessed 19 November 2011

Adams, W. M. and Hutton, J. (2007) 'People, parks and poverty: Political ecology and biodiversity conservation', *Journal of Conservation and Society*, vol 5, issue 2, pp147–183

Adler, J. (1985) 'Youth on the road: Reflections on the history of tramping', *Annals of Tourism Research*, vol 12, pp335–354

Agarwal, S. (1997) 'The resort life cycle and seaside tourism', *Tourism Management*, vol 18, no 2, pp65–73

Agarwal, S. and Shaw, G. (eds) (2007) *Managing Coastal Tourism: A Global Perspective*, Channel View Publications, Clevedon, UK

Airey, D. and Tribe, J. (2005) *An International Handbook of Tourism Education (Advances in Tourism Research)*, Elsevier Science, Oxford, UK

Aldridge, D. (1989) 'How the ship of interpretation was blown off course in the tempest: Some philosophical thoughts', in D. Uzzell (ed) *Heritage Interpretation: The Natural and Built Environment*, vol 1, Belhaven, London and New York, pp64–87

Ali-Knight, J. and Robertson, M. M. (2003) 'Introduction to arts, culture and leisure', in I. Yeoman (ed) *Festivals and Events Management: An International Arts and Culture Perspective*, Butterworth-Heinemann Ltd, Jordan Hill, UK, pp3–28

Allen, J., O'Toole, W., Harris, R. and McDonnell, I. (2008) *Festival and Special Event Management*, fourth edition, Wiley and Sons, Milton, UK

Alonso, D. and Liu, Y. (2010) 'Changing visitor perceptions of a capital city: The case of Wellington, New Zealand', in B. W. Ritchie and R. Maitland (eds) *City Tourism: National Capital Perspectives*, CABI, Wallingford, UK, pp110–245

Alrouf, A. A. (2010) 'Regenerating urban traditions in Bahrain: Learning from Bab-Al-Bahrain: The authentic fake', *Journal of Tourism and Cultural Change*, vol 8, no 1–2, pp50–68

Altinay, L., Altinay, M. and Bicak, H. A. (2002) 'Political scenarios: The future of the North Cyprus tourism industry', *International Journal of Contemporary Hospitality Management*, vol 14, issue 4, pp176–182

Altobelli, R. D. and Kirstges, T. (2008) 'Mass tourism', in M. Lueck (ed) *Encyclopedia of Tourism and Recreation in Marine Environments*, CABI, Wallingford, UK

Andsager, J. L. and Drzewiecka, J. A. (2002) 'Desirability of differences in destinations', *Annals of Tourism Research*, vol 29, pp401–421

Ansoff, I. (1965) *Corporate Strategy*, McGraw-Hill, New York, NY

Archer, B. (1978) 'Domestic tourism as a development factor', *Annals of Tourism Research*, vol 5, no 1, pp126–141

Archer, B. H. (1995) 'Importance of tourism for the economy of Bermuda', *Annals of Tourism Research*, vol 22, no 4, pp918–930

Archer, B. H. and Fletcher, J. (1996) 'The economic impact of tourism in the Seychelles', *Annals of Tourism Research*, vol 23, no 1, pp32–47

Arellano, A. B. R. de (2011) 'Medical tourism in the Caribbean', *Signs*, vol 36, no 2, pp289–297

Armstrong, E. K. and Weiler, B. (2002) 'Getting the message across: An analysis of messages delivered by tour operators in protected areas', *Journal of Ecotourism*, vol 1, no 2/3, pp104–121

Ashley, C., Goodwin, H. and Roe, D. (2001) *Pro-Poor Tourism Strategies: Expanding Opportunities for the Poor*, UK Department for International Development (DFID), London

Ashworth, G. (1990) 'The historic cities of Groningen: Which is sold to whom?', in G. Ashworth and B. Goodall (eds) *Marketing Tourism Places*, Routledge, London, pp138–155

Ashworth, G. and Page, S. J. (2011) 'Urban tourism research: Recent progress and current paradoxes', *Tourism Management*, vol 32, no 1, pp1–16

Ashworth, G. and Tunbridge, J. E. (1992) 'Is there an urban tourism?', *Tourism Recreation Research*, vol 17, no 2, pp3–8

Ateljevic, I., Pritchard, A. and Morgan, N. (2005) *The Critical Turn in Tourism Studies: Innovative Research Methodologies*, Advances in Tourism Research Series, Elsevier, The Netherlands

Athiyaman, A. (1995) 'The interface of tourism and strategy research: An analysis', *Tourism Management*, vol 16, pp447–453

Ball, S. and Taleb, M. A. (2011) 'Benchmarking waste disposal in the Egyptian hotel industry', *Tourism and Hospitality Research*, vol 11, no 1, pp1–18

Baloglu, S. and McCleary, K. W. (1999) 'A model of destination image formation', *Annals of Tourism Research*, vol 26, no 4, pp868–897

Barnett, C., Cafaro, P. and Newholm, T. (2005) 'Philosophy and ethical consumption', in R. Harrison, T. Newholm and D. Shaw (eds) *The Ethical Consumer*, Sage Publications, London, pp11–24

Barney, J. B. (1991) 'Firm resources and sustained competitive advantage', *Journal of Management*, vol 17, pp99–120

Barthes, R. (1982) *Empire of Signs* (translated by R. Howard), Jonathan Cape, London

Battisti, G. and Stoneman, P. (2003) 'Inter- and intra-firm effects in the diffusion of new process technology', *Research Policy*, vol 32, no 9, pp1641–1655

Baudrillard, J. (1988) 'Simulacra and simulations', in M. Poster (ed) *Jean Baudrillard: Selected Writings*, Blackwell, Cambridge, USA

Baudrillard, J. (1993) *The Transparency of Evil*, Verso, London

Baum, T. (2006) *Human Resource Management for Tourism, Hospitality and Leisure: An International Perspective*, Thomson Learning, London

Beaver, A. (2002) *A Dictionary of Travel and Tourism Terminology*, CABI, Wallingford, UK

Beck, L. and Cable, T. (1998) *Interpretation for the 21st Century: Fifteen Guiding Principles for Interpreting Nature and Culture*, Sagamore Publishing, Champaign, IL

Beech, J. and Chadwick, S. (eds) (2006) *The Business of Tourism Management*, FT Prentice Hall, Harlow

Beedie, P. and Hudson, S. (2003) 'Emergence of mountain-based adventure tourism', *Annals of Tourism Research*, vol 30, no 3, pp625–643

Beer, S. (2008) 'Authenticity and food experience – commercial and academic perspectives', *Journal of Foodservice*, vol 19, no 3, pp153–163

Beerli, A. and Martin, J. D. (2004) 'Factors influencing destination image', *Annals of Tourism Research*, vol 31, no 3, pp657–681

Beeton, S. (2005) *Film-Induced Tourism*, Channel View Publications, Clevedon, UK

Beeton, S. (2006) 'Rural tourism communities', in *Community Development through Tourism*, Landlinks Press, Collingwood, UK

Beeton, S. (2012) *Tourism and the Moving Image*, Channel View Publications, Clevedon, UK

Behaire, T. and Elliot White, M. (1999) 'The application of geographical information systems (GIS) in sustainable tourism planning: A review', *Journal of Sustainable Tourism*, vol 7, no 2, pp159–174

Bell, S. (2005) *Design for Outdoor Recreation*, Spon Press-Taylor and Francis e-print Library, London

Bell, S. (2008) *Design for Outdoor Recreation*, second edition, Taylor and Francis, Abingdon, Oxon, UK

Bennett, P. D. (ed) (1995) *Dictionary of Marketing Terms*, second edition, American Marketing Association and NTC Business Books, Chicago, IL

Bertalanffy, L. V. (1972) *The History and Status of General Systems Theory*, John Wiley and Sons, New York, NY

Bird, K. and Hughes, D. R. (1997) 'Ethical consumerism: The case of fairly-traded coffee', *Business Ethics: A European Review*, vol 6, no 3, pp159–167

Blackstock, K. (2005) 'A critical look at community based tourism', *Community Development Journal*, vol 40, no 1, pp39–49

Bohdanowicz, P. and Martinac, I. (2007) 'Determinants and benchmarking of resource consumption in hotels – case study of Hilton International and Scandic in Europe', *Energy and Buildings*, vol 39, pp82–95

Bohdanowicz, P. and Zientara, P. (2009) 'Hotel companies' contribution to improving the quality of life of local communities and the well-being of their employees', *Tourism and Hospitality Research*, vol 9, no 2, pp147–158

Boorstin, D. J. (1961) *The Image: or What Happened to the American Dream*, Atheneum, New York, NY

Boorstin, D. (1962) *The Image*, Weidenfeld and Nicolson, London

Boorstin, D. J. (1964) *The Image: A Guide to Pseudo-Events in America*, Harper, New York, NY

Born, K. (2004) 'Die besondere Bedeutung des operativen Geschäfts im Touristikkonzern' ['The specific importance of operations at the integrated tourism corporation'], in H. Bastian and K. Born (eds) *Der integrierte Touristikkonzern* [*The Integrated Tourism Corporation*], Oldenbourg, München, Germany, pp195–212

Botterill, D. (2001) 'The epistemology of a set of tourism studies', *Leisure Studies*, vol 20, no 3, pp199–214

Bowdin, G., Allen, J., O'Toole, W., Harris, R. and McDonnell, I. (2006) *Events Management*, second edition, Elsevier, Oxford, UK

Bramwell, B. (2005) 'Interventions and policy instruments for sustainable tourism', in W. F. Theobald (ed) *Global Tourism*, third edition, Elsevier, Burlington, VT

Branch, M. C. (1985) *Comprehensive City Planning: Introduction and Explanation*, American Planning Association, Planners Press, Washington, DC

Britton, S. (1991) 'Tourism, capital, and place: Towards a critical geography of tourism', *Environment and Planning D: Society and Space*, vol 9, pp451–478

Brocaglia, J. (2011) 'The importance of human capital', *Tourism Management*, vol 29, pp967–979

Bronner, F. and de Hoog, R. (2008) 'Agreement and disagreement in family decision-making', *Tourism Management*, vol 29, pp967–979

Brotherton, B. (2003) *The International Hospitality Industry: Structure, Characteristics and Issues*, Butterworth-Heinemann, Oxford, UK

Brotherton, B. (2006) 'Some thoughts on a general theory of hospitality', *Tourism Today*, issue 6, autumn, pp8–19

Buckland, B. S. (2007) 'Eating authenticity: M. F. K. Fisher and American visions of France', *Petits Propos Culinaire*, vol 83, pp81–91

Buckley, R. (2006a) *Adventure Tourism*, CABI, Wallingford, UK

Buckley, R. (2006b) 'Adventure tourism products: Price, duration, size, skill, remoteness', *Tourism Management*, vol 28, no 6, pp1428–1433

Buckley, R., Pickering, C. and Weaver, D. B. (eds) (2003) *Nature-Based Tourism, Environment and Land Management*, CABI, Wallingford, UK

Buhalis, D. (2000) 'Marketing the competitive destination of the future', *Tourism Management*, vol 21, no 1, pp97–116

Buhalis, D. (2003a) *eTourism – Information Management*, Prentice Hall, Harlow, UK

Buhalis, D. (2003b) *eTourism: Information Technology for Strategic Tourism Management*, Pearson (Financial Times/Prentice Hall), London

Buhalis, D. and Law, R. (2008) 'Progress in information technology and tourism management: 20 years on and 10 years after the internet – the state of eTourism research', *Tourism Management*, vol 29, no 4, pp609–623

Buhalis, D. and Main, H. (1998) 'Information technology in peripheral small and medium hospitality enterprises: Strategic analysis and critical factors', *International Journal of Contemporary Hospitality Management*, vol 10, no 5, pp198–202

Burkart, A. J. and Medlik, S. (1981) *Tourism: Past, Present and Future*, second edition, Heinemann, London

Burke, R. (2006) *Project Management: Planning and Control Techniques*, Wiley and Sons, Chichester, UK

Burns, P., Lester, J.A. and Bibbings, L. (2010) *Tourism and Visual Culture*, CABI, Wallingford, UK

Bushell, R. and Sheldon, P. (eds) (2009) *Wellness and Tourism: Mind, Body, Spirit and Place*, Cognizant Communication, Elmsford, NY

Business Tourism Partnership (2007) *Value of Britain's Business Tourism Grows to £22 Billion*, Business Tourism Partnership Press Release, 14 March, UK

Butler, R. R. W. (1975) 'Tourism as an agent of social change', in F. Helleiner (ed) *Tourism as a Factor in National and Regional Development*, Department of Geography, Occasional Paper No 4, Trent University, Peterborough, Ontario, pp85–90

Butler, R. W. (1980) 'The concept of the tourism area cycle of evolution', *Canadian Geographer*, vol 24, no 1, pp5–12

Butler, R. W. (2006) *The Tourism Area Life Cycle*, two volumes, Channel View Publications, Clevedon, UK

Butler, R., Hall, C. and Jenkins, J. (1998) 'Introduction', in R. Butler, C. Hall and J. Jenkins (eds) *Tourism and Recreation in Rural Areas*, John Wiley and Sons, New York, NY, pp3–16

Carl, D., Kindon, S. and Smith, K. (2007) '"Tourists" experiences of film locations: New Zealand as "Middle-Earth"', *Tourism Geographies*, vol 9, no 1, pp49–63

Carpenter, I., Decker, D. and Lipscomb, J. (2000) 'Stakeholder acceptance of capacity in wildlife management', *Human Dimensions of Wildlife*, vol 5, no 3, pp5–19

Carroll, A. B. (1979) 'A three dimensional conceptual model of corporate social performance', *Academy of Management Review*, vol 4, no 4, pp497–505

Carroll, A. B. (1991) 'The pyramid of corporate social responsibility: Toward the moral management of organizational stakeholders', *Business Horizons*, July–August, pp39–48

Carroll, A. B. (1999) 'Corporate social responsibility: Evolution of a definitional construct', *Business and Society*, vol 38, no 3, September, pp268–295

Carroll, A. B. and Shabana, K. M. (2010) 'The business case for corporate social responsibility: A review of concepts, research and practice', *International Journal of Management Reviews*, vol 12, no 1, March, pp85–105

Cartwright, R. and Baird, C. (1999) *The Development and Growth of the Cruise Industry*, Butterworth-Heinemann, Oxford, UK

Casson, M., Yeung, B., Basu, A. and Wadeson, N. (eds) (2006) *The Oxford Handbook of Entrepreneurship*, Oxford University Press, Oxford, UK

Cave, J. (2005) 'Conceptualising Otherness as a management framework for tourism enterprise', in C. Ryan and M. Aicken (eds) *Indigenous Tourism: The Commodification and Management of Culture*, Pergamon, Oxford, pp315–334

Cerina, F., Markandya, A. and McAleer, M. (2010) *Economics of Sustainable Tourism*, Routledge, Oxon, UK

Chadwick, G. (1971) *A Systems View of Planning*, Pergamon, Oxford, UK

Chalkiti, K. and Sigala, M. (2010) 'Staff turnover in the Greek tourism industry: A comparison between insular and peninsular regions', *International Journal of Contemporary Hospitality Management*, vol 22, no 3, pp333–359

Chambers Dictionary (2008) 'Environment' in Chambers Dictionary, 11th edition, Chambers Harrap Publishers Ltd., Edinburgh, Scotland

Chandran, D., Kang, K. S. and Leveaux, R. (2001) 'Internet culture in developing countries with special reference to e-commerce', in *Proceedings of the 5th Pacific Asia Conference on Information Systems (PACIS): Information Technology for Estrategy*, Seoul, pp656–664

Chang, T. C. (1997) 'From instant Asia to multi-faceted jewel: Urban imaging strategies and tourism development in Singapore', *Urban Geography*, vol 18, pp542–562

Chang, T. C., Milne, S., Fallon, D. and Pohlmann, C. (1996) 'Urban heritage tourism: The global–local nexus', *Annals of Tourism Research*, vol 23, pp284–305

Charters, S. and Ali-Knight, J. (2002) 'Who is the wine tourist?', *Tourism Management*, vol 23, pp311–319

Chase, R. B., Jacobs, F. R. and Aquilano, N. J. (2007) *Operations Management for Competitive Advantage*, 11th edition, McGraw-Hill, New York, NY

Chaudhary, M. (2008) *Tourism Marketing*, Oxford University Press, Oxford, UK

Chin, C. (2008) *Cruising in the Global Economy: Profits, Pleasure and Work at Sea*, Ashgate Publishing Limited, Hampshire, UK

Chon, K. and Edgell, D. L. (2006) *Managing Sustainable Tourism: A Legacy for the Future*, Routledge, Oxon, UK

Church Tourism Association (2007) *About the Churches Tourism Association*, www.churchestourismasscoiation.info, accessed 19 November 2011

Clark, C. (2001) 'The future of leisure time', in A. Lockwood and S. Medlik (eds) *Tourism and Hospitality in the 21st Century*, Butterworth-Heinemann, Oxford, pp71–81

Clark, G. and Johnston, R. (2000) *Service Operations Management*, FT Prentice Hall, London

Clarke, J. (1997) 'A framework of approaches to sustainable tourism', *Journal of Sustainable Tourism*, vol 5, no 3, pp224–233

Clawson, M. (1963) *Land and Water for Recreation: Opportunities, Problems and Policies*, Rand McNally, Chicago, IL

CLIA (Cruise Lines International Association Inc.) (2010) *The Overview: 2010 CLIA Cruise Market Overview*, http://www.cruising.org, accessed 29 October 2011

Clift, S., Luongo, M. and Callister, C. (eds) (2002) *Gay Tourism: Culture, Identity and Sex*, Continuum, London

Coccossis, H. (1996) 'Tourism and sustainability: Perspectives and implications', in G. K. Priestley, J. A. Edwards and H. Coccossis (eds) *Sustainable Tourism? European Experiences*, CABI, Wallingford, UK, pp1–21

Cohen, E. (1972) 'Towards a sociology of international tourism', *Social Research*, vol 39, no 1, pp64–82

Cohen, E. (1973) 'Nomads from affluence: Notes on the phenomenon of drifter-tourism', *International Journal of Comparative Sociology*, vol 14, pp89–102

Cohen, E. (1979) 'A phenomenology of the tourist experiences', *Sociology*, vol 13, pp179–201

Cohen, E. (1984) 'The sociology of tourism: Approaches, issues, and findings', *Annual Review of Sociology*, vol 10, pp373–392

Cohen, E. (1987) 'Alternative tourism: A critique', *Tourism Recreation Research*, vol 12, no 2, pp13–18

Cohen, E. (1988) 'Authenticity and commoditisation in tourism', *Annals of Tourism Research*, vol 15, no 3, pp371–386

Cohen, E. (2003) 'Backpacking: Diversity and change', *Journal of Tourism and Cultural Change*, vol 1, no 2, pp95–110

Cohen, E. (2004) 'Backpacking: Diversity and change', in G. Richards and J. Wilson (eds) *The Global Nomad: Backpacker Travel in Theory and Practice*, Channel View Publications, Clevedon, UK, pp43–59

Cohen, E. and Avieli, N. (2004) 'Food in tourism: Attraction and impediment', *Annals of Tourism Research*, vol 31, no 4, pp755–778

Cohen, M. and Bodeker, G. (eds) (2008) *Understanding the Global Spa Industry*, Butterworth-Heinemann, Oxford, UK

Cohen, S. B. (2003) *Geopolitics of the World System*, Rowman and Littlefield, London

Community Marketing Inc. (2011) *15th Annual Gay and Lesbian Tourism Report: Exploring Tourism and Hospitality Opportunities in the Gay and Lesbian Marketplace, 2010–2011*, Community Marketing, Inc., San Francisco, CA

Conforti, J. (1996) 'Ghettos as tourism attractions', *Annals of Tourism Research*, vol 23, pp830–842

Connell, J. (2005) 'Toddlers, tourism and Tobermory: Destination marketing issues and television-induced tourism', *Tourism Management*, vol 26, pp763–776

Connell, J. (2006) 'Medical tourism: sea, sun, sand ... surgery', *Tourism Management*, vol 27, pp1093–1100

Connell, J. and Meyer, D. (2009) 'Balamory revisited: An evaluation of the screen tourism destination-tourist nexus', *Tourism Management*, vol 30, pp194–207

Constanti, P. and Gibbs, P. (2005) 'Emotional labour and surplus value: The case of holiday reps', *The Service Industries Journal*, vol 25, no 1, pp103–116

Cook, R. A., Yale, L. J. and Marqua, J. J. (2010) *Tourism: The Business of Travel*, fourth edition, Prentice Hall, Upper Saddle River, NJ

Cooper, C. (1990) 'Resorts in decline – the management response', *Tourism Management*, vol 11, pp63–67

Cooper, C. and Hall, C. M. (2008) *Contemporary Tourism: An International Approach*, Butterworth-Heinemann, Oxford, UK

Cooper, C. P., Fletcher, J., Gilbert, D. and Wanhill, S. (2000) *Tourism Principles and Practice*, second edition, Pitman Publishing, London

Cooper, C., Fletcher, J., Gilbert, D., Fyall, A. and Wanhill, S. (2005) *Tourism: Principles and Practice*, third edition, Longman, London

Cooper, C., Fletcher, J., Fyall, A., Gilbert, D. and Wanhill, S. (2008a) 'Interrelationships and classifications', in C. Cooper, J. Fletcher, A. Fyall, D. Gilbert and S. Wanhill (eds) *Tourism: Principles and Practice*, fourth edition, Prentice Hall, Pearson Education Limited, Harlow, UK

Cooper, C., Fletcher, J., Fyall, A., Gilbert, D. and Wanhill, S. (2008b) *Tourism: Principles and Practice*, fourth edition, Pearson Education Limited, Harlow, UK

Cooper, P. E. and Malcolm, C. (2009) *Health and Wellness Tourism: Spas and Hot Springs*, Channel View Publications, Bristol, UK

Cooper-Martin, E. and Holbrook, M. B. (1993) 'Ethical consumption experiences and ethical space', *Advances in Consumer Research*, vol 20, pp113–118

Corcoran, L. M., Gillmor, D. A. and Killen, J. E. (1996) 'An analysis of summer sun tourists – outbound package holidays from Dublin Airport', *Irish Geography*, vol 29, no 2, pp106–115

Cowe, R. and Williams, S. (2011) *Who Are the Ethical Consumers?*, http://www.caseplace.org/pdfs/All-Cooperative%20Bank-2000-Who%20are%20the%20ethical%20consumers%20pt.%201.pdf, accessed 21 August 2011

Cox Innal Communications (1996) *Cultivating Rural Tourism*, Cox Innal Communications Pty Ltd, Canberra, Australia

Cracow Tours (2011) *About Us*, http://www.cracowtours.pl/, accessed 19 November 2011

Craig-Smith, S. and French, C. (1994) *Learning to Live with Tourism*, Pitman, Melbourne, Australia

Crebbin-Bailey, J., Harcup, J. and Harrington, J. (2005) *The Spa Book: The Official Guide to Spa Therapy*, Thomson, London

Crick, A. (2000) *A Preliminary Investigation into the Delivery of Sustained Personalized Service: The Case of All-Inclusive Entertainment Coordinators*, PhD thesis, State University of New Jersey, Rutgers, New Brunswick, NJ

Crick, M. (1989) 'Representations of international tourism in the social sciences: Sun, sex, sights, savings, and servility', *Annual Review of Anthropology*, vol 18, pp307–344

Crompton, J. (1979) 'Motivations for pleasure vacation', *Annals of Tourism Research*, vol 6, no 4, pp408–424

Crook, C. (2005) 'The good company – a survey of corporate social responsibility', *The Economist*, 20 January 2005, pp3–18

Crouch, D. and Lubbren, N. (2003) *Visual Culture and Tourism*, Berg, London

Cruise Industry News (2008) 'Focus: Meeting crew needs', *Cruise Industry News Quarterly*, winter 2008/2009

Culler, J. (1981) 'Semiotics of tourism', *American Journal of Semiotics*, vol 1, pp127–158

D'Angelo, J. M. (2010) *Spa Business Strategy: A Plan for Success*, second edition, Cengage Learning, New York, NY

Dahlsrud, A. (2006) 'How corporate social responsibility is defined: An analysis of 37 definitions', *Corporate Social Responsibility and Environmental Management*, vol 15, issue 1, January/February, pp1–13

Dallen, J. T. (ed) (2007) *The Heritage Tourist Experience: Critical Essays, Volume Two*, Ashgate, Farnham

Dallen, J. T. and Boyd, S. W. (2003) *Heritage Tourism*, Pearson Education Limited, Harlow, UK

Dann, G. (1977) 'Anomie, ego-enhancement and tourism', *Annals of Tourism Research*, vol 4, no 4, pp184–194

Dann, G. and Cohen, E. (1991) 'Sociology and tourism', *Annals of Tourism Research*, vol 18, pp155–169

David, J., Grabski, S. and Kasavana, M. (1996) 'The productivity paradox of hotel–industry technology', *Cornell Hotel and Restaurant Administration Quarterly*, vol 37, no 2, pp64–70

Davidson, R. (2003) *Business Travel, Conference, Incentive Travel, Exhibitions, Corporate Travel*, Prentice Hall, Harlow, UK

Davidson, R. and Cope, B. (2003) *Business Travel: Conferences, Incentive Travel, Exhibitions, Corporate Hospitality and Corporate Travel*, Prentice Hall, Harlow, UK

DCMS (2007) *Winning: A tourism Strategy for 2012 and Beyond*, http://www.visitbritain.org/Images/DCMS-Tourism2012Strategy_fullreport_tcm29-14543.pdf, accessed 23 August 2011

De Bakker, F. G. A., Groenewegen, P. and Den Hond, F. (2005) 'A bibliometric analysis of 30 years of research and theory on corporate social responsibility and corporate social performance', *Business and Society*, vol 44, no 3, September, pp283–317

Debord, G. (1995) *Society of the Spectacle*, Zone Books, New York, NY

Decrop, A. and Snelders, D. (2005) 'A grounded typology of vacation decision-making', *Tourism Management*, vol 26, pp121–132

Deleuze, G. (2006) *Dialogues II*, Continuum, London

Deng, J. Y., Arano, K. G., Pierskalla, C. and McNeel, J. (2010) 'Linking urban forests and urban tourism: A case of Savannah, Georgia', *Tourism Analysis*, vol 15, no 2, pp167–181

Deutsches Jugendherbergswerk (2011) *1909: Geburtsjahr des Deutschen Jugendherbergswerk*, http://www.jugendherberge.de/de/ueberuns/1909bisheute/1909/index.jsp, accessed 4 August 2011

Devesa, M., Laguna, M. and Palacios, A. (2009) 'The role of motivation in visitor satisfaction: Empirical evidence in rural tourism', *Tourism Management*, vol 31 (2010), pp547–552

Devlin, E. S. (2006) *Crisis Management Planning and Execution*, Auerbach Publications, New York, NY

Dewar, K. (1991) 'Evaluation of sender competencies in personal service interpretive programs', Paper presented at the Heritage Interpretation International Joining Hands for Quality Tourism: Interpretation, Preservation and the Travel Industry, 3–8 November, Honolulu, Hawaii

Dickinson, B. and Vladimir, A. (2007) *Selling the Sea: An Inside Look at the Cruise Industry*, John Wiley and Sons, Hoboken, NJ

Dickinson, J. and Lumsden, L. (2010) *Slow Travel and Tourism*, Earthscan, London

Douglas, N., Douglas, N. and Derrett, R. (eds) (2002) *Special Interest Tourism*, John Wiley and Sons, Chichester, UK

Dowling, R. K. and Newsome, D. (2006) *Geotourism*, Elsevier–Butterworth-Heinemann, Oxford, UK

Doxey, G.V. (1975) 'A causation theory of resident visitor irritants', in *The Sixth Annual Conference Proceedings of the Travel Research Association*, pp195–198

Doxey, G. V. (1976) 'When enough's enough: The natives are restless in Old Niagara', *Heritage Canada*, vol 2, pp26–27

Dredge, D. (2006) 'Networks, conflict and collaborative communities', *Journal of Sustainable Tourism*, vol 14, no 6, pp562–581

Dredge, D. and Jenkins, J. (2007) *Tourism Policy and Planning*, John Wiley and Sons, Brisbane, Australia

Dredge, D. and Jenkins, J. (eds) (2011) *Stories of Practice: Tourism Policy and Planning*, Ashgate, Surrey, UK

Driver, F. (1999) 'Imaginative geographies', in N. J. Clifford et al (eds) *Key Concepts in Geography*, Sage Publications, Oxford

Dror, Y. (1973) 'The planning process: A facet design', in A. Faludi (ed) *A Reader in Planning Theory*, Pergamon Press, Oxford, pp323–343

Drucker, P. F. (2007) *Innovation and Entrepreneurship: Practice and Principles*, Butterworth-Heinemann, Oxford, UK

Duffy, R. (2002) *A Trip too Far: Ecotourism, Politics and Exploitation*, Earthscan, London

Duggan, E. (1997) 'Tourism, cultural authenticity and the native crafts cooperative: The Eastern Cherokee experience', in E. J. Chambers (ed) *Tourism and Culture: An Applied Perspective*, State University of New York Press, Albany, NY

Duval, D. T. (2007) *Tourism and Transport: Modes, Networks and Flows*, Channel View Publications, Clevedon, UK

Dwivedi, M., Yadav, A. and Patel, V. R. (2009) 'The online destination image of Goa', *Worldwide Hospitality and Tourism Themes*, vol 1, no 1, pp25–39

Dwyer, L., Edwards, D., Mistilis, N., Roman, C. and Scott, N. (2009) 'Destination and enterprise management for a tourism future', *Tourism Management*, vol 30, no 1, pp63–74

Eco, U. (1986) *Faith in Fakes*, Vintage, New York, NY

Eco, U. (1990) *Travels in Hyperreality*, Harvest Books, New York, NY

Edelheit, J. (2009) 'Opportunities in medical tourism and understanding the US marketplace', Paper presented at the Service Summit, Guatemala City, 10–12 September 2009

Edwards, D., Griffin, T. and Hayllar, B. (2008) 'Urban tourism research: Developing an agenda', *Annals of Tourism Research*, vol 35, no 4, pp1032–1052

Egger, R. and Buhalis, D. (eds) (2008) *eTourism Case Studies: Management and Marketing Issues in eTourism*, Butterworth-Heinemann, Oxford, UK

EIU (2008) *Global Business Barometer Survey*, http://www.economist.com/media/pdf/20080116CSRResults.pdf, accessed 25 July 2011

Emery, F. E. (1969) *Systems Thinking*, Penguin Modern Management, Harmondsworth, UK

Engel, J. F., Kollat, D., and Blackwell, R. D. (1968) *Consumer Behaviour*, New York: Holt Rinehart and Winston

Engel, J. F., Blackwell, R. D. and Miniard, P. W. (1995) *Consumer Behavior*, eighth edition, Dryden Press, Fort Worth, TX

England, J. (2010) *What is Ethical Tourism*, http://www.sustainablestuff.co.uk/what-ethical-tourism.html, accessed 25 August 2011

Epstein, A. and Meyers, K. (2009) 'Captivating medical tourism: Understanding and underwriting the risks', Paper presented at the Bermuda Captive Conference, 21–24 June 2009

Erfurt-Cooper, P. and Cooper, M. (2009) *Health and Wellness Tourism: Spas and Hot Springs*, Channel View Publications, Clevedon, UK

Erhlich, B. and Dreier, P. (1999) 'The new Boston discovers the old: Tourism and the struggle for a livable city', in D. R. Judd and S. S. Fainstein (eds) *The Tourist City*, Yale University Press, New Haven, Connecticut, CT, pp155–178

Euromonitor International (2011a) *City Travel Briefing: London and the Olympic Games Global Briefing*, London

Euromonitor International (2011b) *How Hard Times Are Altering Consumer Mindsets*, London, April

European Geoparks (2011) *Home Page*, http://www.europeangeoparks.org/isite/page/2,1,0.asp?mu=1andcmu=7andthID=0, accessed 19 November 2011

Evans, N., Campbell, N. and Stonehouse, G. (2003) *Strategic Management for Travel and Tourism*, Butterworth-Heinemann, Oxford, UK

Evers, A. and Laville, J.-L. (2004) *The Third Sector in Europe*, Edward Elgar, Cheltenham and Northampton

Farley, J. V. and Ring, L. W. (1970) 'An empirical test of the Howard-Sheth Model of Buyer Behavior', *Journal of Marketing Research*, vol 7, pp427–438

Fawcett, C. and Cormack, P. (2001) 'Guarding authenticity at literary tourism sites', *Annals of Tourism Research*, vol 28, no 3, pp686–704

Fearn-Banks, K. (2011) *Crisis Communications: A Casebook Approach*, fourth edition, Routledge, Oxon, UK

Fennell, D. (2008) *Ecotourism: An Introduction*, third edition, Routledge, Abingdon, Oxon, UK

Fennell, D. A. and Malloy, D. C. (2007) 'Codes of ethics in tourism: Practice, theory, synthesis', in *Codes of Ethics in Tourism: Practice, Theory, Synthesis*, Channel View Publications, Clevedon, UK

Filby, M. P. (1992) 'The figures, the personality and the bums: Service work and sexuality', *Work Employment and Society*, March, vol 6, no 1, pp23–42

Firth, L. (2008) *Travel and Tourism Issues*, Independence, Cambridge

Firth, T. F. (2011) 'Tourism as a means to industrial heritage conservation: Achilles heel or saving grace?', *Journal of Heritage Tourism*, vol 6, no 1, pp45–62

Fitzsimmons, J. A. and Fitzsimmons, M. J. (2008) *Service Management: Operations, Strategy, Information Technology*, sixth edition, McGraw-Hill, New York, NY

Fletcher, J. and Archer, B. H. (1991) 'The development and application of multiplier analysis', in C. P. Cooper and A. Lockwood (eds) *Progress in Tourism, Recreation and Hospitality Management: Volume 3*, Belhaven Press, London, pp28–47

Florida-Caribbean Cruise Association (2011) *Cruise Industry Overview – 2010*, Florida-Caribbean Cruise Association, Florida

Font, X. and Cochrane, J. (2005) *Integrating Sustainability into Business: A Management Guide for Responsible Tour Operations*, United Nations Publications, Blue Ridge Summit, PA

Franklin, A. (2003a) *Tourism: An Introduction*, Sage Publications Ltd, London

Franklin, A. (2003b) 'The tourist syndrome: An interview with Zigmunt Bauman', *Tourist Studies*, vol 3, no 2, pp205–217

Franklin, A. and Crang, M. (2001) 'The trouble with tourism and travel theory?', *Tourist Studies*, vol 1, no 1, pp5–22

Frederick, W. C. (1994) 'From CSR1 to CSR2', *Business and Society*, vol 33, no 2, pp150–164

Freyer, W. (2006) *Tourismus: Einführung in die Fremdenverkehrsökonomie [Tourism: Introduction to Tourism Economics]*, eighth edition, Oldenbourg, München, Germany

Frost, W. (2006) *From Diggers to Baristas: Tourist Shopping Villages in the Victorian Goldfields*, Thomson Gale

Fussell, P. (1979) 'The stationary tourist', *Harpers*, April, pp31–38

Fyall, A. (2011a) 'Destination management: Challenges and opportunities', in Y. Wang and A. Pizam (eds) *Destination Marketing and Management: Theories and Applications*, CABI, Oxford, UK, pp340–357

Fyall, A. (2011b) 'The partnership challenge', in N. Morgan, A. Pritchard and R. Pride (eds) *Destination Brands: Managing Place Reputation*, third edition, Elsevier, Oxford, UK, pp91–103

Fyall, A., Garrod, B., Leask, A. and Wanhill, S. (eds) (2008) *Managing Visitor Attractions: New Direction*, second edition, Butterworth-Heinemann, Oxford, UK

Fyall, A., Fletcher, J. and Spyriadis, T. (2010) 'Diversity, devolution and disorder: The management of tourism', in M. Kozak, J. Gnoth and L. Andreu (eds) *Advances in Tourism Destination Marketing: Managing Networks*, Routledge, Oxford, UK, pp15–26

Galdini, R. (2007) *Tourism and the City: Opportunity for Regeneration*, MPRA Munich Personal RePEc Archive, MPRA Paper No 6370, December, http://mpra.ub.uni-muenchen.de/6370

Gale, T. (2005) 'Modernism, post-modernism and the decline of British seaside resorts as long holiday destinations: A case study of Rhyl, north Wales', *Tourism Geographies*, vol 7, no1, February, pp86–112

Gale, T. and Botterill, D. (2005) 'A realist agenda for tourist studies or why destination areas really rise and fall in popularity', *Tourist Studies*, vol 5, no 2, pp151–174

Gallarza, M. G., Gil Saura, I. and Calderon-Garcia, H. (2002) 'Destination image: Towards a conceptual framework', *Annals of Tourism Research*, vol 29, no 1, pp56–78

Garrigós, F., Simón Narangajavana, Y. and Palacios Marqués, D. (2004) 'Carrying capacity in the tourism industry: A case study of Hengistbury Head', *Tourism Management*, vol 25, issue 2, April, pp275–288

Garrod, B., Fyall, A. and Leask, A. (2006) 'Managing visitor impacts at visitor attractions: An international assessment', *Current Issues in Tourism*, vol 9, no 2, pp125–151

Gartner, W. C. (1993) 'Image formation process', *Journal of Travel and Tourism Marketing*, vol 2, no 2/3, pp191–215

Gee, C. Y. (1996) *Resort Development and Management*, Lansing, MI

Gee, C. Y., Makens, J. C. and Choy, D. J. L. (1997) *The Travel Industry*, third edition, John Wiley and Sons, New York, NY

Geertz, C. (1973) 'Deep play: Notes on the Balinese cockfight', in C. Geertz (ed) *The Interpretation of Cultures*, Fontana Press, New York, NY

George, E., Mair, H. and Reid, D. (2009) *Rural Tourism Development: Localism and Cultural Change*, Channel View Publications, Bristol, UK

George Washington University School of Business, Adventure Travel Trade Association and Xola Consulting (2010) *Adventure Tourism Market Report*, August 2010, http://www.adventuretravel.biz/wp-content/uploads/2010/09/adventure_travel_market082610.pdf, accessed 29 March 2012

Gereffi, G. and Korzeniewicz, M. (1994) *Commodity Chains and Global Capitalism*, Praeger, Westport, CT

Getz, D. (1987) 'Tourism planning and research: Traditions, models and futures', Paper presented at the Australian Travel Research Workshop, Bunbury, Western Australia, 5–6 November 1987

Getz, D. (1991) *Festivals, Special Events and Tourism*, Van Nostrand Reinhold, New York, NY

Getz, D. (1992) 'Tourism planning and destination life cycle', *Annals of Tourism Research*, vol 19, no 4, pp752–770

Getz, D. (1993) 'Tourist shopping villages: Development and planning strategies', *Tourism Management*, vol 14, no 1, pp15–26

Getz, D. (2005) *Event Management and Event Tourism*, Cognizant Communication Corporation, New York, NY

Getz, D. and Brown, G. (2006) 'Critical success factors for wine tourism regions: A demand analysis', *Tourism Management*, vol 27, pp146–158

Gezici, F. and Kerimoglu, E. (2010) 'Culture, tourism and regeneration process in Istanbul', *International Journal of Culture, Tourism and Hospitality Research*, vol 4, no 3, pp252–265

Gibbs, J. L. and Kraemer, K. L. (2004) 'A cross-country investigation of the determinants of scope of e-commerce use: an institutional approach', *Electronic Markets*, vol 14, no 2, pp124–137

Gilbert, D. C. (1992) 'Touristic development of a viticultural region of Spain', *International Journal of Wine Marketing*, vol 4, issue 2, pp25–32

Gilbert, D. C. (1998) 'Tourism marketing – its emergence and establishment', in C. P. Cooper (ed) *Progress in Tourism, Recreation and Hospitality Management*, CBS Publishers, New Delhi, pp77–90

Global Spa Summit (2011) *Wellness Tourism and Medical Tourism: Where Do Spas Fit?*, May 2011

Godfrey, J. L. (2011) *The Motivations of Backpackers in New Zealand*, Industry report prepared for the Tourism Strategy Group of the New Zealand Ministry for Economic Development as part of the requirements of a 2010 Tourism Research Scholarship, http://www.tourismresearch.govt.nz/Documents/Scholarships/TSG%20Jane%20Godfrey%20Tourism%20research%20scholarship%20industry%20report%20final.pdf, accessed 9 August 2011

Goeldner, C. R. and Ritchie, J. R. B. (2006) *Tourism: Principles, Practices and Philosophies*, tenth edition, John Wiley and Sons Inc, New Jersey

Goldblatt, J. (2002) *Special Events: Global Event Management in the 21st Century*, The Wiley Event Management Series, John Wiley and Sons, London

Goodrich, J. N. and Goodrich, G. E. (1991) 'Health-care tourism', in S. Medlik (ed) *Managing Tourism*, Butterworth-Heinemann, Oxford, UK, pp107–114

Goodwin, H. and Francis, J. (2003) 'Ethical and responsible tourism: Consumer trends in the UK', *Journal of Vacation Marketing*, vol 9, no 3, pp271–284

Gordon, B. (1986) 'The souvenir: messenger of the extraordinary', *Journal of Popular Culture*, vol 20, pp135–146

Gordon, G. (2001) (ed) *Tourism: Putting Ethics into Practice*, Tearfund, Dublin

Goulding, C. (1999) 'Interpretation and presentation', in A. Leask and I. Yeoman (eds) *Heritage Visitor Attractions*, Cassell, London, pp54–67

Goulding, C. (2000) 'The museum environment and the visitor experience', *European Journal of Marketing*, vol 34, no 3/4, pp261–278

Graham, M. (2002) 'Challenges from the margins: Gay tourism as cultural critique', in S. Clift, M. Luongo and C. Callister (eds) (2002) *Gay Tourism: Culture, Identity and Sex*, Continuum, London, Chapter 1, pp17–41

Gray, H. P. (1970) *International Travel: International Trade*, Heath, Lexington

Greasley, A. (2006) *Operations Management*, John Wiley and Sons, Chichester, UK

Gross, S. (2011). *Tourismus und Verkehr: Grundlagen, Marktanalysen und Strategien von Verkehrsunternehmen*, Oldenbourg, Munich, Germany

Gross, S. and Schroeder, A. (eds) (2007) *Handbook of Low Cost Airlines: Strategies, Business Processes and Market Environment*, Erich Schmidt Verlag, Goettingen, Germany

Guerrier, Y. (1999) *Organizational Behaviour in Hotels and Restaurants: An International Perspective*, John Wiley and Sons, Wiley, New York, NY

Guerrier, Y. and Adib, A. (2000) 'No, we don't provide that service: The harassment of hotel employees by customers', *Work, Employment and Society*, vol 14, no 4, pp689–705

Gunn, C. A. (1972) *Vacationscape: Designing Tourist Regions*, University of Texas, Austin, TX

Gunn, C. (1994) *Tourism Planning*, third edition, Taylor and Francis, New York, NY

Gunn, C. A. and Var, T. (2002) *Tourism Planning*, fourth edition, Routledge, New York, NY

Haldrup, M. and Larsen, J. (2003) 'The family gaze', *Tourist Studies*, vol 3, no 1, pp23–46

Hall, C. M. (1994) *Tourism and Politics: Policy, Power and Place*, John Wiley and Sons, Chichester, UK

Hall, C. M. (2000) *Tourism Planning, Policies, Processes and Relationships*, Prentice Hall, Harlow

Hall, C. M. (2003) 'Spa and health tourism', in S. Hudson (ed) *Sport and Adventure Tourism*, Haworth Press, Binghampton, NY, pp273–292

Hall, C. (2005) *Tourism: Rethinking the Social Science of Mobility*, Pearson Education, Harlow

Hall, C. M. (2007a) *Introduction to Tourism in Australia: Development, Issues and Change*, Pearson Education Australia, Frenchs Forest

Hall, C. M. (2007b) *Pro-Poor Tourism: Who Benefits? Perspectives on Tourism and Poverty Reduction*, Channel View Publications, Bristol, UK

Hall, C. M. (2008) *Tourism Planning: Policies, Processes and Relationships*, Pearson Education, Harlow

Hall, C. M. (2010) 'Spatial analysis: A critical tool for tourism geographies', in J. Wilson (ed) *Space, Place and Tourism: New Perspectives in Tourism Geographies*, Routledge, London

Hall, C. M. and Boyd, S. (eds) (2005) *Nature Based Tourism in Peripheral Areas: Development or Disaster?*, Channel View Publications, Clevedon, UK

Hall, C. M. and Lew, A. (1998) *Sustainable Tourism*, Prentice Hall, Harlow

Hall, C. M. and Page, S. J. (2006) *The Geography of Tourism and Recreation: Environment, Place and Space*, Routledge, London

Hall, C. M. and Page, S. J. (2008) 'Progress in tourism management: From the geography of tourism to the geographies of tourism – a review', *Journal of Tourism Management*, xxx, pp1–14

Hall, C. M. and Page, S. (2010) 'The contribution of Neil Leiper to tourism studies', *Current Issues in Tourism*, vol 13, no 4, pp299–309

Hall, C. M. and Tucker, H. (2004) *Tourism and Post-Colonialism*, Routledge, Abingdon, Oxon, UK

Hall, C. M., Sharples, L., Cambourne, B. and Macionis, N. (eds) (2000) *Wine Tourism around the World*, Butterworth-Heinemann, Oxford, UK

Hall, D., Kirkpatrick, I. and Mitchell, M. (2005a) *Rural Tourism and Sustainable Business*, Channel View Publications, Clevedon, UK

Hall, D., Mitchell, M. and Roberts, R. (2005b) 'Tourism and countryside: Dynamic relationship', in D. Hall, L. Roberts and M. Mitchell (eds) *New Directions in Rural Tourism*, Ashgate, Surrey, UK

Hall, M. C. (2006) 'Introduction: Culinary tourism and regional development – from slow food to slow tourism?', *Tourism Review International*, vol 9, no 4, pp303–305

Haller, R. and Baer, S. (1994) *From Wasteland to Paradise: The Breath-Taking Success Story of a Unique Ecological Experiment on the Kenya Coast*, Koshany Verlag, Mombassa, Kenya

Ham, S. (1983) 'Cognitive psychology and interpretation: Synthesis and application', *Journal of Interpretation*, vol 8, no 1, pp11–28

Ham, S. and Krumpe, E. (1996) 'Identifying audiences and messages for non-formal environmental education: A theoretical framework for interpreters', *Journal of Interpretation Research*, vol 1, no 1, pp11–23

Hamel, G. and Prahalad, C. K. (1993) 'Strategy as stretch and leverage', *Harvard Business Review*, March–April, pp75–84

Hamel, G. and Prahalad, C. K. (1994) *Competing for the Future*, Harvard Business School Press, Boston, MA

Hammitt, W. (1984) 'Cognitive processes involved in environmental interpretation', *Journal of Environmental Education*, vol 15, no 4, pp11–15

Hanlon, P. (1999) *Global Airlines*, second edition, Butterworth-Heinemann, Oxford, UK

Hannam, K. (2006) 'Heritage tourism and development III: Performances, performativities and mobilities', *Progress in Development Studies*, vol 6, no 3, pp243–249

Hannam, K. and Ateljevic, I. (eds) (2007) *Backpacker Tourism: Concepts and Profiles*, Channel View Publications, Clevedon, UK

Hannam, K. and Diekmann, A. (eds) (2010) *Beyond Backpacker Tourism*, Channel View Publications, Clevedon, UK

Hannam, K. and Knox, D. (2010) *Understanding Tourism: A Critical Introduction*, Sage Publications Ltd, London

Hannerz, U. (1998) *Transnational Connections: Culture, People, Places*, Routledge, London

Harrison, J. S. and Enz, C. A. (2005) *Hospitality Strategic Management: Concepts and Cases*, John Wiley and Sons, New Jersey

Haslinda, A. (2009) 'Evolving terms of human resource management and development', *The Journal of International Social Research*, vol 2, no 9, pp180–186

Hassan, J. (2003) *The Seaside, Health and the Environment in England and Wales since 1800*, Ashgate, Farnham

Hawthorn, J. (1994) *A Concise Glossary of Contemporary Literary Theory*, Hodder Education Publishers, London

Haywood, K. (1988) 'Responsible and responsive tourism planning in the community', *Tourism Management*, vol 9, no 2, pp105–118

Heitmann, S. (2011) 'Authenticity in tourism', in P. Robinson, S. Heitmann and P. Dieke (eds) *Research Themes for Tourism*, CABI, Wallingford, UK

Heitmann, S. and Robinson, P. (2009) 'Slow cities – the Emperor's new clothes or (another) solution for sustainable tourism management?', Paper presented at the BAM Conference, Brighton, UK, 15–17 September 2009

Heitmann, S., Robinson, P. and Povey, G. (2011) 'Slow tourism', in P. Robinson, S. Heitmann and P. Dieke (2011) *Research Themes for Tourism*, CABI, Wallingford, UK

Heizer, J. and Render, B. (2006) *Principles of Operations Management*, sixth edition, Prentice Hall, New Jersey

Henderson, J. C. (2010) 'New visitor attractions in Singapore and sustainable destination development', *Worldwide Hospitality and Tourism Themes*, vol 2, no 3, pp251–261

Hensher, D. and Puckett, S. (2007) 'Congestion and variable user charging as an effective travel demand management instrument', *Transportation Research Part A: Policy and Practice*, vol 41, no 7, pp615–626

Herbert, D. (2001) 'Literary places, tourism and the heritage experience', *Annals of Tourism Research*, vol 28, no 2, pp312–333

Higgins-Desbiolles, F., Schmiechen, J. and Trevorrow, G. (2010) *A Case Study in the Development of an Aboriginal Tourism Enterprise: The Coorong Wilderness Lodge of South Australia – An Emic Perspective*, CRC for Sustainable Tourism Pty Ltd, Australia

Higham, J. and Lück, M. (2002) 'Urban ecotourism: A contradiction in terms', *Journal of Ecotourism*, vol 1, no 1, pp36–51

Hill, T. (2005) *Operations Management*, second edition, Palgrave Macmillan, Basingstoke, UK

Hjalager, A.-M. (2010) 'Regional innovation systems: The case of angling tourism', *Tourism Geographies*, vol 12, no 2, pp192–216

Holden, A. (2005) *Tourism Studies and the Social Sciences*, Routledge, Abingdon, UK

Hollinshead, K. and Jamal, T. B. (2007) 'Tourism and the third ear: Further prospects for qualitative inquiry', *Tourism Analysis*, vol 12, pp85–129

Holloway, C., Davidson, R. and Humphreys, C. (2009) *The Business of Tourism*, FT Prentice Hall, Harlow

Holloway, J. C. (2006) *The Business of Tourism*, seventh edition, Prentice Hall, Harlow

Holloway, J. C. (2009) *The Business of Tourism*, eighth edition, Prentice Hall, Harlow

Holloway, J. T. and Plant, R. V. (1992) *Marketing for Tourism*, Pitman, London

Honey, M. (2008) *Ecotourism and Sustainable Development: Who Owns Paradise?*, second edition, Island Press, Washington, DC

Hooper-Greenhill, E. (2007) *Museums and Education: Purpose, Pedagogy, Performance*, Taylor and Francis, Oxford, UK

Hospitalitynet (2011) *MKG World Hotel Group Ranking 2009*, Hospitalitynet

Hotel Rooms (2011) *Hotel Ratings and Categories*, http://www.hotelrooms.com/categories.html, accessed 22 July 2011

Howe, G. (1996) 'An untapped heritage resource: The British public house', *International Journal of Wine Marketing*, vol 8, no 1, pp41–52

Howell, D. W., Ellison, R. A., Bateman Ellison, M. and Wright, D. (2003) *Passport: An Introduction to the Tourism Industry*, third edition, Nelson, Toronto, Ontario

Howitt, B. and Julian, R. (2002) *Heinemann Society and Culture*, Heinemann, Port Melbourne, Australia

HRGuide (2011) *Compensation: Outline and Definitions*, http://www.hr-guide.com/data/G400.htm

Huang, L. (2008) 'Bed and breakfast industry adopting e-commerce strategies in e-service', *The Service Industries Journal*, vol 28, no 5, pp633–648

Hudson, A. (2008). *Tourism and Hospitality Marketing: A Global Perspective*, Sage Publications Ltd, London

Hudson, L. (2003) *Geography of Travel*, Thomson, UK

Hudson, S. (ed) (2003) *Sport and Adventure Tourism*, Haworth Hospitality Press, London

Hughes, G. (1992) 'Changing approaches to domestic tourism', *Tourism Management*, vol 13, no 1, pp85–90

Hughes, H. (2000) *Arts, Entertainment and Tourism*, Butterworth-Heinemann, Oxford, UK

Hughes, H. L. (2002) 'Marketing gay tourism in Manchester: New market for urban tourism or destruction of gay space?', *Journal of Vacation Marketing*, vol 9, no 2, pp152–163

Hughes, H. L. (2004) 'A gay tourism market: Reality or illusion, benefit or burden?', *Journal of Quality Assurance in Hospitality and Tourism*, vol 5, no 2/3/4, pp57–74

Hughes, H. (2006) *Pink Tourism: Holidays of Gay Men and Lesbians*, CABI, Wallingford, UK

Hughes, M., Ham, S. H. and Brown, T. (2009) 'Influencing park visitor behaviour: A belief-based approach', *Journal of Park and Recreation Administration*, vol 27, no 4, pp38–53

Hultsman, J. (1995) 'Just tourism', *Annals of Tourism Research*, vol 22, no 3, pp553–567

Hunziker, W. and Krapf, K. (1942) *Grundriß der Allgemeinen Fremdenverkehrslehre*, Polygr. Verlag, Zurich

Hurd, A. R., Barcelona, R. J. and Meldrum, J. T. (2008) *Leisure Services Management*, Human Kinetics, Champaign

IATA (International Air Transport Association) (2011) International Air Transport Association, http://www.iata.org/Pages/default.aspx, accessed 17 August 2011

ICAO (International Civil Aviation Organization) (2011) International Civil Aviation Organization, http://www.icao.org/, accessed 17 August 2011

Ignatov, E. and Smith, S. (2006) 'Segmenting Canadian culinary tourists', *Current Issues in Tourism*, vol 9, no 3, pp235–255

Imber, J. and Toffler, B. A. (2008) *Dictionary of Marketing Terms*, fourth edition, Barrons Business Guides, China

Inkpen, G. (1998) *Information Technology for Travel and Tourism*, Addison Wesley Longman, Essex, UK

Inskeep, E. (1991) *Tourism Planning: An Integrated and Sustainable Development Approach*, John Wiley and Sons, New York, NY

Ioannides, D. and Apostolopolous, Y. (1999) 'Political instability, war, and tourism in Cyprus: Effects, management, and prospects for recovery', *Journal of Travel Research*, August, vol 38, no 1, pp51–56

Iso-Ahola, S. (1982) 'Toward a social psychological theory of tourism motivation: A rejoinder', *Annals of Tourism Research*, vol 9, no 2, pp256–262

Jafari, J. (1986) 'On domestic tourism', *Annals of Tourism Research*, vol 13, no 3, pp491–496

Jafari, J. (ed) (2000) *Encyclopedia of Tourism*, Routledge, London and New York

Jago, L. K. and Shaw, R. N. (1998) 'A conceptual and differential framework', *Festival Management and Event Tourism*, vol 5, no 1/2, pp21–32

Jamal, T. (2004) 'Virtue ethics and sustainable tourism pedagogy: Phronesis, principles and practice', *Journal of Sustainable Tourism*, vol 12, no 6, pp530–545

James, J. (1999) 'Interpreting Umeewarra mission', *International Journal of Heritage Studies*, vol 5, no 3/4, pp203–212

Jansen-Verbeke, M. (1986) 'Inner city tourism: Resources, tourists, promoters', *Annals of Tourism Research*, vol 13, no 1, pp79–100

Jansen-Verbeke, M. (2010) 'Transformation from historic cityscapes to urban tourismscapes', *Rivisata di Scienze del Turismo*, vol 2, pp31–49

Jansen-Verbeke, M. and Diekmann, A. (2008) *The Future of Historic Spa Towns: Spa Symposium Workbook*, Castermans, Belgium

Jayawardena, C., Patterson, D. J., Choi, C. and Brain, R. (2008) 'Sustainable tourism development in Niagara: Discussions, theories, projects and insights', *International Journal of Contemporary Hospitality Management*, vol 20, no 3, pp258–277

Jenkins, O. H. (1999) 'Understanding and measuring tourist destination images', *International Journal of Tourism Research*, vol 1, no 1, pp1–15

Jenkins, O. (2003) 'Photography and travel brochures: The circle of representation', *Tourism Geographies*, vol 5, no 3, pp305–328

Jennings, G. (ed) (2007) *Water-Based Tourism, Sport, Leisure, and Recreation Experiences*, Elsevier, Burlington, MA

Jennings, G. and Nickerson, N. (eds) (2006) *Quality Tourism Experiences*, Elsevier, Burlington, VT

Jepson, P and Whittaker, R. J. (2002) 'Histories of protected areas: Internationalisation of conservationist values and their adoption in the Netherlands Indies (Indonesia)', *Environment and History*, vol 8, pp129–172

Johnson, G. and Scholes, K. (2002) *Exploring Corporate Strategy*, sixth edition, Pearson Education, Harlow

Jonckers, P. (2005) 'General trends and skill needs in the tourism sector in Europe', in O. Strietska-Ilina and M. Tessaring (eds) *Trends and Skill Needs in Tourism*, Cedefop Panorama Series, Office for Official Publications of the European Communities, Luxembourg

Jones, D. G. B. and Shaw, E. H. (2002) 'A history of marketing thought', in A. W. Barton and R. Wenslet (eds) *Handbook of Marketing*, Sage Publications, London, pp39–65

Jones, I. (2000) 'A model of serious leisure identification: The case of football fandom', *Leisure Studies*, vol 19, no 4, pp283–298

Jones, P. (1999) 'Operational issues and trends in the hospitality industry', *International Journal of Hospitality Management*, vol 18, no 4, pp427–442

Jones, P. (2011) *Ethical Tourism*, http://www.roughguide-betterworld.com/?page_id=28, accessed 25 August 2011

Joppe, M. (2010) 'One country's transformation to spa destination: The case of Canada', *Journal of Hospitality and Tourism Management*, vol 17, pp117–126

Josiam, B. M., Mattson, M. and Sullivan, P. (2004) 'The historaunt: Heritage tourism at Mickeys Dining Car', *Tourism Management*, vol 25, pp453–461

Journal of Sustainable Tourism (1994) *Special Issue: Rural Tourism and Sustainable Tourism Development*, vol 2, pp1–2

Kadri, B. (2007) 'The city and tourism: An ancient relationship, new complexity and a conceptual challenge, Téoros', *Revue de Recherche en Tourisme*, vol 26, no 3, pp76–79

Kandampully, J., Mok, C. and Sparks, B. (eds) (2001) *Service Quality Management in Hospitality, Tourism and Leisure*, Haworth Hospitality Press, Binghamton, NY

Kane, M. J. and Zink, R. (2004) 'Package adventure tours: Markets in serious leisure careers', *Leisure Studies*, vol 23, no 4, pp329–345

Kang, S. K. and Hsu, C. H. C. (2005) 'Dyadic consensus on family vacation destination selection', *Tourism Management*, vol 26, pp571–582

Karadag, E., Cobanoglu, C. and Dickinson, C. (2009) 'The characteristics of IT investment decisions and method used in the US lodging industry', *International Journal of Contemporary Hospitality Management*, vol 21, no 1, pp52–68

Karski, A. (1990) 'Urban tourism: A key to urban regeneration', *The Planner*, 6 April, pp15–17

Kasim, A. (2004) 'BESR in the hotel sector: A look at tourists' propensity towards environmentally and socially friendly hotel attributes in Pulau Pinang, Malaysia', *International Journal of Hospitality and Tourism Administration*, vol 5, no 2, pp61–83

Kauffman, R. J. and Kumar, A. (2005) *A Critical Assessment of the Capabilities of Five Measures for ICT Development*, Working paper, MIS Research Centre, University of Minnesota, Minneapolis, MN

Kaur J. H. G., Sundar, D. V. and Bhargava, S. (2007) 'Health tourism in India: Growth and opportunities', Paper presented to the International Marketing Conference on Marketing and Society, 8–10 April 2007, IIMK

Kaur Puar, J. (ed) (2002) 'Circuits of queer mobility: Tourism, travel and globalization', *Journal of Lesbian and Gay Studies*, vol 8, no 1–2, pp101–137

Kelly, I. and Nankervis, T. (2001) *Visitor Destinations*, John Wiley and Sons, Milton, UK

Kennedy, V. (2000) *Edward Said: A Critical Introduction*, Polity Press, Cambridge

Keyser, H. (2002) *Tourism Development*, Oxford University Press, Cape Town, South Africa

Kibicho, W. (2004) 'Tourism and the sex trade: Roles male sex workers play in Malindi, Kenya', *Tourism Review International*, vol 7, no 3 and 4, pp129–141

Kibicho, W. (2005) 'Tourism and the sex trade in Kenya's coastal region', *Journal of Sustainable Tourism*, vol 13, no 3, pp256–280

Killion, G. L. (1992) *Understanding Tourism: Study Guide*, Central Queensland University, Rockhampton, Australia

Killon, L. (2001) 'Rural tourism', in N. Douglas, N. Douglas and R. Derret (eds) *Special Interest Tourism: Context and Cases*, John Wiley and Sons, Australia, pp164–184

Kim, D., Lehto, X. Y. and Morrison, A. M. (2007a) 'Gender differences in online travel information search: Implications for marketing communications on the internet', *Tourism Management*, vol 28, no 2, pp423–433

Kim, S. S., Argusa, J., Lee, H. and Chon, K. (2007b) 'Effects of Korean television dramas on the flow of Japanese tourists', *Tourism Management*, vol 28, no 5, pp1340–1353

Kitha, J. and Lyth, A. (2011) 'Urban wildscapes and green spaces in Mombassa and their potential contribution to climate change adaptation and mitigation', *Environment and Urbanization*, vol 23, no 1, pp251–265

Kivela, J. and Crotts, J. C. (2006) 'Gastronomy tourism: A meaningful travel market segment', *Journal of Culinary Science and Technology*, vol 4, no 2, pp39–55

Knox, P. (2005) 'Creating ordinary places: Slow cities in a fast world', *Journal of Urban Design*, vol 10, no 1, pp1–11

Ko, D. W. and Stewart, W. P. (2002) 'A structural model for residents' attitude for tourism development', *Tourism Management*, vol 23, pp521–530

Koncept Analytics (2010) *Analysis of the Global Cruise Market*, Koncept Analytics

Kotler, P. and Lee, N. (2005) *Corporate Social Responsibility: Doing the Most Good for Your Company and Your Cause*, John Wiley and Sons, Hoboken, NJ

Kotler, P., Bowen, J. T. and Makens, J. (2006) *Marketing for Hospitality and Tourism*, fourth edition, Prentice Hall, New York, NY

Kotler, P., Bowen, J. and Makens, J. (2010) *Marketing for Tourism and Hospitality*, fifth edition, Prentice Hall, New York, NY

Kozak, M. (2010) 'Holiday taking decisions – the role of spouses', *Tourism Management*, vol 31, pp489–494

Kozak, M., Gnoth, J. and Andreu, L. (2009) *Advances in Tourism Destination Marketing: Managing Networks*, Routledge, Oxford, UK

Krippendorf, J. (1987) *The Holiday Makers: Understanding the Impact of Leisure and Travel*, Heinemann, Oxford

Laffoley, D. (1991) *Use of Coastal Land and Water Space: Recreation, Marine Conservation Handbook*, second edition, English Nature, UK

Lagiewski, R. M. (2006) 'The application of the TALC model', in R. W. Butler (ed) *The Tourism Area Life Cycle: Volume 1*, Channel View Publications, Clevedon, UK, pp27–50

Lam, C. C., du Cros, H. and Vong, T. N. (2011) 'Macao's potential for developing regional Chinese medical tourism', *Tourism Review*, vol 66, no ½, pp68–82

Lane, B. (1994) 'What is rural tourism?', *Journal of Sustainable Tourism*, vol 2, no 1–2, pp7–21

Lash, S. and Urry, J. (1994) 'Mobility, modernity and place', in S. Lash and J. Urry (eds) *Economies of Signs and Space*, Sage Publications, London, pp252–278

Law, C. M. (1993) *Urban Tourism: Attracting Visitors to Large Cities, Tourism, Leisure and Recreation*, Mansell, New York, NY

Law, C. M. (2000) 'Regenerating the city centre through leisure and tourism', *Built Environment*, vol 26, no 2, pp117–129

Laws, E., Richins, H., Agrusa, J. F. and Scott, N. (2011) *Tourist Destination Governance: Practice, Theory and Issues*, CABI, Oxford, UK

Lee, G., Morrison, A. A., Lheto, X. Y., Webb, J. and Reid, J. (2005) 'VFR: Is it really marginal? A financial consideration of French overseas travellers', *Journal of Vacation Marketing*, vol 11, no 4, pp340–356

Lee, S. Y., Petrick, J. F. and Crompton, J. (2007) 'The roles of quality and intermediary constructs in determining festival attendees' behavioural intensions', *Journal of Travel Research*, vol 45, pp402–412

LeHew, S. C. and Wesley, M. L. A. (2007) 'Tourist shoppers' satisfaction with regional shopping mall experiences', *International Journal of Culture, Tourism and Hospitality*, vol 1, no 1, pp82–96

Leiper, N. (1979) 'The framework of tourism: Towards a definition of tourism, tourist, and the tourist industry', *Annals of Tourism Research*, vol VI, no 4, pp390–407

Leiper, N. (1990) *Tourism Systems: An Interdisciplinary Perspective*, Massey University, Palmerston North

Leiper, N. (1995) *Tourism Management*, RMIT Press, Melbourne, Australia

Leitner, M. J. and Leitner, S. F. (1996) *Leisure in Later Life*, Haworth Press, New York, NY

Leitner, M. J. and Leitner, S. F. et al (2004) *Leisure Enhancement*, third edition, Haworth Press, Binghamton

Lennon, J. and Foley, M. (2000) *Dark Tourism: The Attraction of Death and Disaster*, Continuum, London

Letzner, V. (2010) *Tourismusökonomie [Tourism Economics]*, Oldenbourg, München, Germany

Lew, A. A. (2008) 'Long tail tourism: New geographies for marketing niche tourism products', *Journal of Travel and Tourism Marketing*, vol 25, no 3–4, pp409–419

Li, J., Li, K. and Zhang, Y. (2003) 'Crisis accidents and its management in tourism', *Human Geography*, 2003-06

Li, X. and Petrick, J. F. (2008) 'Tourism marketing in an era of paradigm shift', *Journal of Travel Research*, vol 46, pp235–244

Lia, L., Hu, Z. Y. and Zhang, C. Z. (2010) 'Red tourism: Sustaining communist identity in a rapidly changing China', *Journal of Tourism and Cultural Change*, vol 8, no 1–2, pp101–119

Liburd, J. and Edwards, D. (2010) *Understanding the Sustainable Development of Tourism*, Goodfellow, Oxford, UK

Lindberg, K. (1991) *Policies for Maximising Nature Tourisms Ecological and Economic Benefits*, World Resources Institute, Washington, DC

Lindberg, K. (1992) 'International issues in ecotourism management with applications to Kenya', in C. G. Gakahu and B. E. Goode (eds) *Ecotourism and Sustainable Development in Kenya*, Wildlife Conservation International, Kenya, pp1–13

Lindberg, K. (2001) 'Economic impacts', in D. B. Weaver (ed) *The Encyclopedia of Ecotourism*, CABI, Wallingford, UK, pp363–377

Linquist, J. D. and Sirgy, M. J. (2003) *Shopper, Buyer, and Consumer Behaviour: Theory, Marketing Applications, and Public Policy Implications*, Atomic Dog Publishing, Ohio

Littlewood, I. (2001) *Sultry Climates: Travel and Sex*, John Murray Publishers Limited, London

Littrell, M. S. et al (1994) 'Souvenirs and tourism styles', *Journal of Travel Research*, vol 33, no 1, pp3–11

Loker-Murphy, L. and Pearce, P. (1995) 'Young budget travelers: Backpackers in Australia', *Annals of Tourism Research*, vol 22, pp819–843

Lomine, L. and Edmunds, J. (2007) *Key Concepts in Tourism*, Palgrave Macmillan, Basingstoke, UK

Loomis, R. (1987) *Museum Visitor Evaluation: New Tool for Management*, American Association for State and Local History, Nashville, Tennessee

Lovat, T. (ed) (2000) *New Society and Culture,* second edition, Social Sciences Press, Katoomba

Lovelock, B. (ed) (2007) *Tourism and the Consumption of Wildlife: Hunting, Shooting and Sport Fishing*, Routledge, Oxon, UK

Lowe, R. and Marriott, S. (2006) *Enterprise: Entrepreneurship and Innovation: Concepts, Contexts and Commercialization*, Butterworth Heinemann, Oxford, UK

Lozanski, K. (2007) *Violence in Independent Travel to India: Unpacking Patriarchy and Neo-Colonialism, Tourist Studies*, Sage, London

Luck, M. (2007) *Nautical Tourism: Concepts and Issues*, Cognizant Communication, Elmsford, NY

Luengo-Jones, S. (2001) *All-To-On: The Winning Model for Marketing in the Post-Internet Economy*, McGraw-Hill, London

Lumsdon, L. and Page, S. J. (eds) (2004) *Tourism and Transport: Issues and Agenda for the New Millennium*, Elsevier, Oxford, UK

Lundvall, B. Å. (1992) *National Systems of Innovation*, Pinter, London

MacCannell, D. (1973) 'Staged authenticity: arrangement of social space in tourist settings', *American Journal of Sociology*, vol 79, no 3, pp589–603

MacCannell, D. (1976) *The Tourist: A New Theory of the Leisure Class*, Schocken Books, New York, NY

MacCannell, D. (1999) *The Tourist: A New Theory of the Leisure Class*, second edition, University of California Press, Berkeley, CA

MacCannell, D. (2011) *The Ethics of Sightseeing*, University of California Press, Berkeley and Los Angeles

MacKenzie, J. (2005) 'Empires of travel', in J. K. Walton (ed) *Histories of Tourism: Representation, Identity and Conflict* (Tourism and Cultural Change), Channel View Publications, Clevedon, UK, pp19–38

Macleod, D. V. L. (2003) 'Culture and the construction of a niche market destination', in D. V. L. Macleod (ed) *Niche Tourism in Question*, University of Glasgow Chrichton Publications, Dumfries, Scotland, pp30–44

Maitland, R. (2007) 'Culture, city users and creation of new tourism areas', in M. K. Smith (ed) *Cities: Tourism, Culture and Regeneration*, CABI, Wallingford, UK

Mak, J. (2004) *Tourism and the Economy: Understanding the Economics of Tourism*, University of Hawaii Press, Hawaii

Maldonado, E. and Montagnini, F. (2005) 'Carrying capacity of La Tigra National Park, Honduras: Can the park be self-sustainable?', *Journal of Sustainable Forestry*, vol 19, no 4, pp29–48

Malinowski, B. (1922) *Argonauts of the Western Pacific: An Account of Native Enterprise and Adventure in the Archipelagoes of Melanesian New Guinea*, Routledge, London

Manacap-Johnson, M. (2011) 'The many faces of the spa consumer', *Pulse*, October, pp33–40

Mannell, R. C. and Iso-Ahola, S. E. (1987) 'Psychological nature of leisure and tourism experience', *Annals of Tourism Research*, vol 14, pp314–331

Manyara, G. and Jones, E. (2007) 'Community-based tourism enterprises development in Kenya: An exploration of their potential as avenues of poverty reduction', *Journal of Sustainable Tourism*, vol 15, no 6, pp628–644

March, R. (1994) 'Tourism marketing myopia', *Tourism Management*, vol 15, no 6, pp411–415

Marcus, G. E. (1998) 'Ethnography in/of the World System: The emergence of multi-sited ethnography', in G. E. Marcus (ed) *Ethnography through Thick and Thin*, Princeton University Press, Princeton, NJ

Markwick, M. (2001) 'Postcards from Malta: Image, consumption, context', *Annals of Tourism Research*, vol 28, no 2, pp417–438

Maslow, A. (1943) 'A theory of human motivation', *Psychological Review*, vol 50, pp370–396

Mason, P. (2003) *Tourism Impacts, Planning and Management*, Elsevier Butterworth-Heinemann, Oxford and Burlington

Mason, P. (2008) *Tourism Impacts, Planning and Management*, second edition, Butterworth-Heinemann, London

Mathieson, A. and Wall, G. (1982) *Tourism: Economic, Social and Environmental Impacts*, Longman, London

Mayer, H. and Knox, P. (2006) 'Slow cities – sustainable places in a fast world', *Journal of Urban Affairs*, vol 28, no 4, pp321–334

Mayhew, L. H. (1968) 'Society', in *International Encyclopedia of the Social Sciences*, vol 14, Macmillan and Free Press, pp577–586

McCluhan, M. (1964) *Understanding Media: The Extensions of Man*, McGraw Hill, New York, NY

McCool, S. F. and Patterson, R. N. (2000) *Tourism, Recreation, and Sustainability: Linking Culture and the Environment*, CABI, Wallingford, UK

McIntosh, A. and Prentice, R. (1999) 'Affirming authenticity: Consuming cultural heritage', *Annals of Tourism Research*, vol 26, no 3, pp589–612

McIntosh, R. W., Goeldner, C. R. and Ritchie, J. R. B. (1990) *Tourism: Principles, Practices and Philosophies*, second edition, John Wiley and Sons, Chichester and New York

McKercher, B. and Chan, A. (2005) 'How special is "special interest tourism"?', *Journal of Travel Research*, vol 44, no 1, pp21–31

McKercher, B. and du Cros, H. (2002) *Cultural Tourism: The Partnership Between Tourism and Cultural Heritage Management*, Haworth Press, New York, NY

Mclean, D. D., Hurd, A. R. and Rogers, N. B. (2008) *Kraus Recreation and Leisure in Modern Society*, eighth edition, Jones and Barlett Publishers, Sudbury

McMahon, U. and Yeoman, I. (2004) *Sport and Leisure Operations Management*, Thomson, London

McNeil, K. R. and Ragins, R. J. (2005) 'Staying in the spa marketing game: Trends, challenges, strategies and techniques', *Journal of Vacation Marketing*, vol 11, no 1, pp31–39

McWilliams, A. and Siegel, D. (2001) 'Corporate social responsibility: A theory of the firm perspective', *Academy of Management Review*, vol 26, no 1, pp117–127

Medlik, S. and Middleton, V. T. C. (1973) 'Products formulation in tourism', in *Tourism and Marketing*, AIEST, Berne

Meethan, K. (2001) *Tourism in Global Society: Place, Culture, Consumption*, Palgrave, Basingstoke, UK

Mensah, I. (2007) 'Environmental management and sustainable tourism development: The case of hotels in Greater Accra Region (GAR) of Ghana', *Journal of Retail and Leisure Property*, vol 6, no 1, pp15–22

Messerli, H. R. and Oyama, Y. (2004) 'Global health and wellness tourism', *Travel and Tourism Analyst*, August, pp1– 54

Middleton, V. T. C. (1988) *Marketing in Travel and Tourism*, Butterworth-Heinemann, Oxford

Middleton, V. T. C., Fyall, A., Morgan, M. with Ranchhod, A. (2009) *Marketing in Travel and Tourism*, fourth edition, Butterworth Heinemann, Oxford, UK

Mintel (2007) 'Spa tourism international', *Travel and Tourism Analyst*, June, pp1–65

Mintel (2009) *Health and Wellness Holidays, UK*, Mintel Oxygen Reports Platform, http://academic.mintel.com, accessed 10 October 2011

Mintzberg, H. and Lampel, J. (1999) 'Reflecting on the strategy process', *Sloan Management Review*, vol 40, pp21–30

Mintzberg, H. and Waters, J. A. (1985) 'Of strategies, deliberate and emergent', *Strategic Management Journal*, vol 6, pp257–272

Mintzberg, H., Ahlstrand, B. and Lampel, J. (1998) *Strategy Safari*, The Free Press, New York, NY

Moncarz, E., Zhao, J. and Kay, C. (2009) 'An exploratory study of US lodging properties organisational practices on employee turnover and retention', *International Journal of Contemporary Hospitality Management*, vol 21, no 4, pp437–458

Morgan, M., Hemmington, N. and Edwards, J. S. A. (2008) 'From foodservice to food experience? Introduction to the topical focus papers: extraordinary experiences in foodservice', *Journal of Foodservice*, vol 19, pp151–152

Morgan, M., Elbe, J. and de Esteban Curiel, J. (2009) 'Has the experience economy arrived? The views of destination managers in three visitor-dependent areas', *International Journal of Tourism Research*, vol 11, no 2, pp201–216

Morgan, N., Pritchard, A. and Pride, R. (2011) *Destination Brands: Managing Place Reputation*, third edition, Elsevier, Oxford, UK

Moscardo, G. (1996) 'Mindful visitors: Heritage and tourism', *Annals of Tourism Research*, vol 23, no 2, pp376–397

Moscardo, G. (1999) *Making Visitors Mindful: Principles for Creating Quality Sustainable Visitor Experiences through Effective Communication*, Sagamore Publishing, Champaign, IL

Mougayar, W. (1998) *Opening Digital Markets: Battle Plans and Business Strategies for Internet Commerce*, McGraw-Hill, New York, NY

Moulin, C. (1995) 'Concepts of community cultural tourism', *Revue de Tourisme – The Tourist Review – Zeitschrift für Fremdenverkehr*, vol 4, pp35–39

Moutinho, L. (1987) 'Consumer behaviour in tourism', *European Journal of Marketing*, vol 21, no 10, pp5–44

Mowforth, M. and Munt, I. (2009) *Tourism and Sustainability: Development, Globalisation and New Tourism in the Third World*, third edition, Routledge, Abingdon, Oxon, UK

Mueller, H. and Kaufmann, E. L. (2001) 'Wellness tourism: Market analysis of a special health tourism segment and implications for the hotel industry', *Journal of Vacation Marketing*, January, vol 7, no 1, pp5–17

Mukerji, C. (1978) 'Bullshitting: Road lore among hitchhikers', *Social Problems*, vol 25, pp241–252

Muresan, A. and Smith, K. A. (1998) 'Dracula's castle in Transylvania: Conflicting heritage marketing strategies', *International Journal of Heritage Studies*, vol 4, no 2, pp73–85

Murphy, P. E. (1985) *Tourism: A Community Approach*, Methuen, London

Murphy P. E. (1988) 'Community driven tourism planning', *Tourism Management*, vol 9, pp96–104

National Trust (2011a) *Annual Reports, 2010/2011*, http://www.national-trust.org.uk/main/w-estate01.pdf, accessed 15 December 2011

National Trust (2011b) *The Charity*, http://www.nationaltrust.org.uk/main/w-trust/w-thecharity.htm, accessed 15 December 2011

Needle, D. (2000) *Business in Context* (3rd ed), Thomson Learning London

Neirotti, L. D. (2003) 'An introduction to sport and adventure tourism', in S. Hudson (ed) *Sport and Adventure Tourism*, Haworth Hospitality Press, London

Nelson, R. (1993) *National Systems of Innovation: A Comparative Study*, Oxford University Press, Oxford

Neumann, R. P. (1996) 'Dukes, earls, and *ersatz* Edens: Aristocratic nature preservationists in colonial Africa', *Environment and Planning: Society and Space*, vol 14, no 1, pp79–98

Neveling, P. and Wergin, C. (2009) 'Projects of scale-making: New perspectives for the anthropology of tourism', *Etnografica*, vol 13, no 2, pp315–342

New York Area Bisexual Network (2010) A *Brief Trip Thru Bisexual NYCs History*, http://www.nyabn.org/Pages/WhoWeR/OurHistory.html, accessed 26 August 2011

Newsome, D., Dowling, R. K. and Moore S. A. (2005) *Wildlife Tourism – Aspects of Tourism*, Channel View Publications, Clevedon, UK

Newsome, D. Moore, S. A. and Dowling, R. K. (2007) *Aspects of Tourism 4: Natural Area Tourism-Ecology, Impacts and Management*, Channel View Publications, Clevedon, UK

Nichols, C. M. and Snepenger, D. J. (1999) 'Family decision making and tourism behaviors and attitudes', in A. Pizam and Y. Mansfield (eds) (1999) *Consumer Behaviour in Travel and Tourism*, Haworth Hospitality Press, New York, NY

Nickerson, N. and Jurowski, C. (2001) 'The influence of children on vacation travel patterns', *Journal of Vacation Marketing*, vol 7, no 1, pp19–30

Nielsen, H. and Spenceley, A. (2010) *The Success of Tourism in Rwanda: Gorillas and More*, Joint paper of the World Bank and SNV (The Netherlands Development Organization)

Nilsson, J. H., Svard, A. C., Widarsson, A. and Wirell, T. (2007) 'Slow destination marketing in small Italian towns', Paper presented to the 16th Nordic Symposium in Tourism and Hospitality Research, Helsingborg, 2007

Nkrumah, K. (1969), *Neo-Colonialism, The Last Stage of Imperialism*, Thomas Nelson and Sons, Ltd., London

Norzaidi, M. D., Chong, S. C., Murali, R. and Intan Salwani, M. (2007) 'Intranet usage and managers' performance in the port industry', *Industrial Management and Data Systems*, vol 107, no 8, pp1227–1250

Novelli, M. (ed) (2005) *Niche Tourism: Contemporary Issues, Trends and Cases*, Elsevier, Oxford, UK

Nunkoo, R. and Ramkissoon, H. (2010a) 'Residents' satisfaction with community attributes and support for tourism', *Journal of Hospitality and Tourism Research*, vol 35, no 2, pp171–190

Nunkoo, R. and Ramkissoon, H. (2010b) 'Small island urban tourism: A resident's perspective', *Current Issues in Tourism*, vol 13, no 1, pp37–60

Nykiel, R. A. (2005) *Hospitality Management Strategies*, Pearson/Prentice Hall, New Jersey

O'Connor, D. (2006) 'Toward a new interpretation of hospitality', *International Journal of Contemporary Hospitality Management*, vol 17, no 3, pp267–271

O'Reilly, C. C. (2006) 'From drifter to gap year tourist: Mainstreaming backpacker travel', *Annals of Tourism Research*, vol 33, no 4, pp998–1017

O'Sullivan, E. (2006) 'Power, premise, potential, and possibilities of parks, recreation and leisure', in G. Kassing et al (eds) *Introduction to Recreation and Leisure*, Human Kinetics, Champaign, IL

Oh, K., Jeong, Y., Lee, D., Lee, W. and Choi, J. (2003) 'Determining development density using the urban carrying capacity assessment system', *Landscape and Urban Planning*, vol 73, issue 1, pp1–15

Okech, R. N (2007) 'Sex tourism and its effect on women: Case study of the coastal region in Kenya', *International Journal for Women and Gender Research*, vol 1, no 1, pp75–83

Okech, R. N. (2010) 'Wildlife–community conflicts in conservation areas in Kenya', *African Journal of Conflict Resolution*, vol 10, no 2, pp65–80

Okech, R. N (2011) 'Ecotourism development and challenges: A Kenyan experience', *Special Issue: Tourism Analysis: An Interdisciplinary Journal* (forthcoming)

Okello, M. M and Wishitemi, B. E. L. (2006) 'Principles for the establishment of community wildlife sanctuaries for ecotourism: Lessons from Maasai Group Ranches, Kenya', *African Journal of Business and Economics*, vol 1, no 1, pp90–109

Okumus, B., Okumus, F. and McKercher, B. (2007) 'Incorporating local and international cuisines in the marketing of tourism destinations: The cases of Hong Kong and Turkey', *Tourism Management*, vol 28, pp253–261

ONS (Office for National Statistics) (2009) *Social Trends Report*, ONS, London

ONS (2011) *Households and families*, ONS, London

Oppermann, M. and Chon, K.-S. (1997) *Tourism in Developing Countries*, Thomson, London

Orams, M. (1999) *Marine Tourism: Developments, Impacts and Management*, Routledge, Abingdon, Oxon

Orams, M. B. (2001) 'Types of ecotourism', in D. Weaver (ed) *The Encyclopedia of Ecotourism*, CABI, Wallingford, UK

Ottenbacher, M., Harrington, R. and Parsa, H. (2009) 'Defining the hospitality discipline: A discussion of pedagogical and research implications', *Journal of Hospitality and Tourism Research*, vol 33, no 3, pp263–283

Otto, J. E. and Ritchie, J. R. B. (1996) 'The service experience in tourism', *Tourism Management*, vol 17, no 3, pp165–174

Page, S. J. (1995) *Urban Tourism*, Routledge, London

Page, S. J. (ed) (2004) *Tourism and Transport: Issues and Agenda for the New Millennium*, Elsevier, Amsterdam, The Netherlands

Page, S. (2005) *Transport and Tourism: Global Perspectives*, second edition, Pearson Education Ltd, Harlow

Page, S. J. (2007) *Tourism Management: Managing for Change*, second edition, Butterworth-Heinemann, Oxford and Burlington

Page, S. J. (2009) *Transport and Tourism: Global Perspectives*, 3rd edition, Pearson Prentice Hall, Harlow, UK

Page, S. and Connell, J. (2009) *Tourism: A Modern Synthesis*, Cengage Learning, Hampshire

Page, S. and Getz, D. (1997) *The Business of Rural Tourism: International Perspectives*, International Thomson Business Press, Oxford, UK

Page, S. and Swarbrooke, J. (2001) *The Development and Management of Visitor Attractions*, Butterworth-Heinemann, Oxford, UK

Pappalepore, I., Maitland, R., Smith, A., Kay, P. and Polonsky, M. (2010) 'Exploring urban creativity: Visitor experiences of Spitalfields, London', *Tourism Culture and Communication*, vol 10, no 3, pp217–230

Parasuraman, A., Zeithaml, V. A. and Berry, L. L. (1985) 'A conceptual model of service quality and its implications for future research', *Journal of Marketing*, vol 49 (fall), pp41–50

Paris, C. M. (2009) 'The virtualization of backpacker culture', in W. Höpken, U. Gretzel and R. Law (eds) *Information and Communication Technologies in Tourism*, Proceedings of the International Conference in Amsterdam, The Netherlands, Springer Verlag, Wien, pp25–35

Patullo, P. (1996) *Last Resorts: The Cost of Tourism in the Caribbean*, Ian Randle Publishers, Kingston

Pearce, D. (1981) *Tourist Development*, Longman: London

Pearce, D. (1987) *Tourism Today: A Geographical Analysis*, Longman Scientific and Technical Publishers, New York, NY

Pearce, D. G. (2001) 'An integrative framework for urban tourism research', *Annals of Tourism Research*, vol 28, no 4, pp926–946

Pearce, D. G. and Butler, R. W. (1993) *Tourism Research: Critiques and Challenges*, Routledge, London

Pearce, P. (1988) *The Ulysses Factor: Evaluating Visitors in Tourist Settings*, Springer Verlag, New York, NY

Pearce, P. (1990) *The Backpacker Phenomenon: Preliminary Answers to Basic Questions*, James Cook University of North Queensland, Townsville

Pearce, P. L. (1991) 'Analysing tourist attractions', *Journal of Tourism Studies*, vol 2, no 1, pp46–55

Pearce, P. L. and Moscardo, G. M. (1986) 'The concept of authenticity in tourist experiences', *Journal of Sociology*, vol 22, pp121–132

Pearce, P. L., Moscardo, G. and Ross, G. F. (1996) *Tourism Community Relationships*, Pergamon Press, Oxford

Pearce, P. L., Murphy, L. and Brymer, E. (2009) *Evolution of the Backpacker Market and the Potential for Australian Tourism*, CRC for Sustainable Tourism, Australia, http://www.crctourism.com.au/wms/upload/Resources/110017%20EvolBackpackerMarket%20WEB.pdf

Pender, L. and Sharpley, R. (eds) (2005) *The Management of Tourism*, Sage Publications, London

People 1st (2011) *Our Industries*, Uxbridge, http://www.people1st.co.uk/about-us/who-we-are/our-industries, accessed 18 July 2011

Peteraf, M. (1993) 'The cornerstones of competitive advantage: A resource-based view', *Strategic Management Journal*, vol 14, pp179–191

Peterson, C. A. and McCarthy, C. (2000) 'Locational enhancements of cultural tourism destinations', *The Tourist Review*, vol 55, no 4, pp14–22

Phua, K. H. (2011) 'Cross-border medical tourism: A typology and implications for the public and private medical care sectors in the South-East Asian region', Lecture notes, School of Medical and Health Sciences, Monash University (Sunway Campus), www.pitt.edu/~super4/33011-34001/33501.ppt

Phua, K. H. and Chew, A. H. (2002) 'Towards a comparative analysis of health system reforms in the Asia-Pacific region', *Asia Pacific Journal of Public Health*, vol 14, no 1, pp9–16

Pigram, J. (1995) 'Alternative tourism: Tourism and sustainable resource management', in V. L. Smith and W. R. Eadington (eds) *Tourism Alternatives*, John Wiley and Sons, Chichester, UK

Pigram, J. J. and Jenkins, J. M. (1999) *Outdoor Recreation Management*, Routledge, London

Pike, S. (2004) *Destination Marketing Organisations*, Elsevier, Oxford, UK

Pine, J. and Gilmore, J. (1998) 'Welcome to the experience economy', *Harvard Business Review*, vol 76, pp97–105

Pirnar, I. (1994) *Kriz Pazarlamasi ve Yonetimi, Isletme ve Finans Dergisi*, 11/126, Eylul Ankara, pp54–60

Pirnar, I. (2007) 'Saglik turizmi, ozellikleri ve Izmir icin potansiyel', V. Ulusal Turizm Sempozyumu: EXPO 2015 icin bir Isik: Saglik Turizmi, Dokuz Eylul University- BIMER, 25–26 Ekim 2007, İzmir, Bildiriler Kitabi, Beta Basin Yayim Dagitim, pp31–41

Pirnar, I. and İçöz, O. (2010) 'Health tourism in Izmir: Potential, strategies and suggestions', in TTRA (ed) *Health, Wellness and Tourism: Healthy Tourists, Healthy Business?*, 1–3 September 2010, Budapest, Hungary, pp32–33, http://pc.parnu.ee/~htooman/Proceedingnyomdanak.pdf

Pitts, B. G. (1999) 'Sports tourism and niche markets: Identification and analysis of the growing lesbian and gay sports tourism industry', *Journal of Vacation Marketing*, vol 5, no 1, pp31–50

Pizam, A. and Mansfeld, Y. (eds) (1999) *Consumer Behavior in Travel and Tourism*, Haworth Hospitality Press, New York, NY

Pizam, A. and Shani, A. (2009) 'The nature of the hospitality industry: Present and future managers' perspectives, Anatolia', *International Journal of Tourism and Hospitality Research*, vol 20, no 1, pp134–150

Plog, S. (1973) 'Why destination areas rise and fall in popularity', *Cornell Hotel and Restaurant Administration Quarterly*, vol 14, no 3, pp13–16

Pocock, N. S. and Phua, K. H. (2011) 'Medical tourism and policy implications for health systems: A conceptual framework from a comparative study of Thailand, Singapore and Malaysia', *Globalization and Health*, vol 7, p12

Poon, A. (1993) *Tourism, Technology and Competitive Strategies*, CAB International, Wallingford, UK

Porter, M. (1980) *Competitive Strategy: Techniques for Analyzing Industries and Competitors*, Free Press, New York, NY

Porter, M. E. (1985) *Competitive Advantage*, Free Press, New York, NY

Porter, M. E. (1990) *The Competitive Advantage of Nations*, Free Press, New York, NY

Porter, M. E. (1996) 'What is strategy?', *Harvard Business Review*, November–December, pp61–78

Povey, G. (2006) 'Factors influencing the identity of regional food products: a grounded theory approach', *Cyprus Journal of Sciences*, vol 4, pp145–157

Prahalad, C. K. and Hamel, G. (1990) 'The core competence of the corporation', *Harvard Business Review*, May–June, pp79–91

Pritchard, A., Morgan, N., Sedgley, D., Khan, E. and Jenkins, A. (2000) 'Sexuality and holiday choices: Conversations with gay and lesbian tourists', *Leisure Studies*, vol 19, pp267–282

Pro-Poor Tourism Partnership (2011) *PPT Definition*, http://www.propoor tourism.org.uk/info_sheets/1%20info%20sheet.pdf, accessed 28 October 2011

Puczko, L. and Bacharov, M. (2006) 'Spa, bath, thermae: What's behind the labels?', *Journal of Tourism Recreation Research*, vol 31, no 1, pp83–91

Quan, S. and Wang, N. (2004) 'Towards a structural model of the tourist experience: An illustration from food experiences in tourism', *Tourism Management*, vol 25, pp297–305

Quinn, B. (2010) 'Arts festivals, urban tourism and cultural policy', *Journal of Policy Research in Tourism, Leisure and Events*, vol 2, issue 3, pp264–279

Racheria, P. and Hu, C. (2009) 'A framework for knowledge-based crisis management in the hospitality and tourism industry', *Cornell Hospitality Quarterly*, November, vol 50, pp561–577

Reijnders, S. (2011) *Places of the Imagination: Media, Tourism, Culture*, Ashgate Publishing, Surrey, UK

Reisinger, Y. (2009) *International Tourism: Cultures and Behaviours*, Butterworth Heinemann, Oxford, UK

Reisinger, Y. and Steiner, C. J. (2006) 'Reconceptualising object authenticity', *Annals of Tourism Research*, vol 33, no 1, pp65–86

Ren, C., Jóhannesson, G. T. and van der Duim, R. (2012) *Actor Network Theory and Tourism: Ontologies, Methodologies and Performances*, Taylor and Francis, London

Republic of Kenya (1997) *The Eighth National Development Plan for the Period 1997 to 2001*, Government Printer, Nairobi

Richards, G. (2001) 'The experience of industry and the creation of attractions', in G. Richards (ed) *Cultural Attractions and European Tourism*, CABI, Wallingford, UK, pp55–69

Richards, G. (1996) 'Introduction: Cultural tourism in Europe', in G. Richards (ed) *Cultural Tourism in Europe*, CABI, Wallingford, UK

Richards, G. and Wilson, J. (eds) (2004) *The Global Nomad: Backpacker Travel in Theory and Practice*, Channel View Publications, Clevedon, UK

Riley, P. (1988) 'Road culture of international long-term budget travelers', *Annals of Tourism Research*, vol 15, pp313–328

Ritchie, B. W. (2003) *Managing Educational Tourism*, Channel View Publications, Clevedon, UK

Ritchie, J. R. B. and Crouch, G. I. (2003) *The Competitive Destination: A Sustainable Tourism Perspective*, CABI, Oxford, UK

Roberts, C. (2011) 'Sport and adventure tourism', in P. Robinson, S. Heitmann and P. U. C. Dieke (eds) *Research Themes for Tourism*, CABI, London, pp146–159

Roberts, K. (1978) *Contemporary Society and the Growth of Leisure*, Longman, London

Roberts, L. and Hall, D. (2001) *Rural Tourism and Recreation: Principles to Practice,* CABI Publishing, Wallingford, UK

Robinson, L. (2004) *Managing Public Support and Leisure Services*, Routledge, Oxford

Robinson, P. (ed) (2009) *Operations Management in the Travel Industry*, CABI, Wallingford, UK

Robinson, P., Lueck. M. and Smith, S. (2012) *Tourism*, CABI, Wallingford, UK

Robinson, P., Wale, D. and Dickson, G. (eds) (2010) *Event Management*, CABI, Wallingford, UK

Robinson P., Lueck, M. and Smith, S. (2012) *Tourism*, CABI, Wallingford, UK

Robinson, S. and Kenyon, A. J. (2009) *Ethics in the Alcohol Industry*, Palgrave, London

Roesch, S. (2009) *The Experiences of Film Location Tourists*, Channel View Publications, Clevedon, UK

Rogers, E. M. (1969) *Diffusion of Innovations*, Free Press, New York, NY

Rojek, C. (1993) *Ways of Escape: Modern Transformations in Leisure and Travel*, Macmillan, London

Rojek, C. (2010) *The Labour of Leisure*, Sage Publications, London

Rojek, C. and Urry, J. (1997) *Touring Cultures: Transformations of Travel and Theory*, Routledge, London

Rose, G. (2001) *Visual Methodologies*, Sage Publications, London

Ryan, C. (ed) (1997) *The Tourist Experience: A New Introduction*, Cassell, London

Ryan, C. (2002) *The Tourist Experience*, Continuum, London

Ryan, C. and Hall, C. M. (2001) *Sex Tourism: Marginal People and Liminalities*, Routledge, Oxon, UK

Saarinen, J. (2004) 'Destinations in change: The transformation process of tourist destinations', *Tourist Studies*, vol 4, pp161–179

Sacks, J. (2002) *The Money Trail: Measuring Your Impact on the Local Economy Using LM3*, New Economics Foundation and the Countryside Agency, London

Saeed, S. (1998) 'Environmental impact management in the tourism industry of Maldives', in K. Sawkar, L. Noronha, A. Mascarenhas and O. S. Chauhan (eds) *Tourism and the Environment*, Economic Development Institute of the World Bank, Washington, DC

Said, E. (1978) *Orientalism: Western Conceptions of the Orient*, Routledge and Kegan Paul, London

Santos, C. A. and Yan, G. (2010) 'Genealogical tourism: A phenomenological examination', *Journal of Travel Research*, vol 49, no 1, pp56–57

Sassen, S. (2000) *Cities in a World Economy*, second edition, Pine Forge Press, Thousand Oaks, CA

Sawkar, K., Noronha, L., Mascarenhas, A., Chauhan, O. S. and Saeed, S. (1998) *Tourism and the Environment: Case studies on Goa, India and the Maldives*, Economic Development Institute of the World Bank, Washington, DC

Scheyvens, R. (2000) 'Promoting women's empowerment through involvement in ecotourism: Experiences from the third world', *Journal of Sustainable Tourism*, vol 8, no 3, pp232–249

Schmoll, G. A. (1977) *Tourism Promotion: Marketing Background, Promotion Techniques and Promotion Planning Methods*, Tourism International Press, London

Schwartz, K., Tapper, R. and Font, X. (2008) 'A sustainable supply chain management framework for tour operators', *Journal of Sustainable Tourism*, vol 16, no 3, pp298–314

Scott Morton, M. S. (1991) *The Corporation of the 1990s: Information Technology and Organisational Transformation*, Oxford University Press, Oxford

Seaton, A. V. (1999) 'Book towns as tourism developments in peripheral areas', *International Journal of Tourism Research*, vol 1, no 4, pp389–399

Seaton, A. (2000) 'Thanatourism', in J. Jafari (ed) *Encyclopedia of Tourism*, Routledge, London and New York, p578

Seaton, A. (2010) 'Thanatourism and its discontents: An appraisal of a decade's work with some future issues and directions', in T. Jamal and M. Robinson (eds) *The Sage Handbook of Tourism Studies*, Sage Publications, London, pp521–542

Seaton, A. and Lennon, J. (2004) 'Thanatourism in the early 21st century: Moral panics, ulterior motives and alterior desires', in T. V. Singh (ed) *New Horizons in Tourism – Strange Experiences and Stranger Practices*, CABI, Wallingford, UK, pp63–82

Seaton, T. (2009) 'Purposeful Otherness: Approaches to the management of thanatourism', in R. Sharpley and P. R. Stone (eds) *The Darker Side of Tourism: The Theory and Practice of Dark Tourism*, Channel View Publications, Bristol, UK, pp75–108

Shackley, M. (2001) *Managing Sacred Sites: Service Provision and Visitor Experience*, Continuum, London

Shaffer, M, (2001) *See America First: Tourism and National Identity 1880–1940*, Smithsonian Books, US

Shamir, B. (1980) 'Between service and servility: Role conflict in subordinate service roles', *Human Relations*, vol 33, no 10, pp741–756

Sharma, K. K. (2005) *Tourism and Development*, Sarup and Sons, New Delhi

Sharpe, G. W. (1982) *Interpreting the Environment*, John Wiley and Sons, New York, NY

Sharpley, R. (2005) 'Travels to the edge of darkness: Towards a typology of dark tourism', in C. Ryan, S. Page and M. Aicken (eds) *Taking Tourism to the Limit: Issues, Concepts and Managerial Perspectives*, Elsevier, London, pp215–226

Sharpley, R (2006) *Travel and Tourism*, Sage Publications Ltd, London

Sharpley, R. (2008) *Tourism, Tourists and Society*, fourth edition, Elm Publications, Huntingdon

Sharpley, R. and Sharpley, J. (1997) *Rural Tourism: An Introduction*, Thomson Publishing Inc., Oxford, UK

Sharpley, R. and Stone, P. R. (eds) (2009) *The Darker Side of Travel: The Theory and Practice of Dark Tourism*, Aspect of Tourism Series, Channel View Publications, Bristol, UK

Sharpley, R. and Stone, P. R. (eds) (2011) *Tourist Experience: Contemporary Perspectives*, Routledge, Abingdon, Oxford, UK

Sharpley, R. and Telfer, D. J. (2002) *Tourism and Development: Concepts and Issues*, Channel View Publications, Clevedon, UK

Shaw, E. H. and Jones, D. G. B. (2005) 'A history of schools of marketing thought', *Marketing Theory*, vol 5, no 3, pp239–281

Shaw, G. and Williams, A. M. (1994) *Critical Issues in Tourism: A Geographical Perspective*, Blackwell, Oxford, UK

Shaw, G. and Williams, A. (eds) (1997) *The Rise and Fall of British Coastal Resorts*, Pinter, London

Shaw, G. and Williams, A. M. (2002) *Critical Issues in Tourism: A Geographical Perspective*, second edition, Blackwell, Oxford, UK

Shaw, G. and Williams, A. (2004) *Tourism and Tourism Spaces*, Sage Publications, London

Shekkar, M. (2009) 'Crisis management – a case study on Mumbai terrorist attack', *European Journal of Scientific Research*, vol 27, no 3, pp358–371

Sheldon, P. (1997) *Tourism Information Technology*, CAB International, Wallingford, UK, and New York, US

Sheldon, P. J. and Park, S.-Y. (2011) 'An exploratory study of corporate social responsibility in the U.S. travel industry', *Journal of Travel Research*, vol 50, no 4, pp392–407

Sheller, M. and Urry, J. (2004) *Tourism Mobilities: Places to Play, Places in Play*, Routledge, London

Sheth, J. N., Gardner, D. M. and Garrett, D. E. (1988) *Marketing Theory: Evolution and Evaluation*, John Wiley and Sons, New York, NY

Shirt, G. (2011) 'Culture and access', in P. Robinson, S. Heitmann and P. U. Dieke (eds) *Research Themes for Tourism*, CABI, Wallingford, UK

Shmyrov, V. (2001) 'The Gulag Museum', *Museum International*, vol 53, no 1

Sigala, M., Lockwood, A. and Jones, P. (2001) 'Strategic implementation and IT: Gaining competitive advantage from the hotel reservations process', *International Journal of Contemporary Hospitality Management*, vol 13, no 7, pp364–371

Siguaw, A., Enz, A. and Namasivayam, K. (2000) 'Adoption of information technology in US hotels: Strategically driven objectives', *Journal of Travel Research*, vol 39, no 2, pp192–201

Sikich, G. W. (2008) *All Hazards Crisis Management Planning*, www.cool. conservation-us.org/byauth/sikich/allhz.html

Sims, R. (2009) 'Food, place and authenticity: Local food and the sustainable tourism experience', *Journal of Sustainable Tourism*, vol 17, no 3, pp321–336

Sinclair, M. T. and Stabler, M. (1997) *Economics of Tourism*, Routledge, London

Sindiga, I. (1999) *Tourism and African Development: Change and Challenge of Tourism in Kenya*, African Studies Centre Research Series, Kenya

Sirakaya, E., Mclellan, R. W. and Uysal, M. (1996) 'Modelling vacation destination decisions behavioural approach relationship marketing consumer markets: Antecedents and consequences', *Journal of Travel and Tourism Marketing*, vol 5, no 1/2, pp52–75

Sirirak, S., Islam, N. and Khang, D. B. (2011) 'Does ICT adoption enhance hotel performance?', *Journal of Hospitality and Tourism Technology*, vol 2, no 1, pp34–49

Slack, N., Chamber, S. and Johnston, R. (2007) *Operations Management*, fifth edition, Prentice Hall, Harlow

Slow Food (2011) *About Us*, http://www.slowfood.com/international/1/about-us?-session=query_session:519F46FF1b527200AFhU1B137160, accessed 19 November 2011

Smith, A. (2005) 'Conceptualizing city image change: The reimaging of Barcelona', *Tourism Geographies*, vol 7, no 4, pp398–423

Smith, K. A. (2003) 'Literary enthusiasts as visitors and volunteers', *International Journal of Tourism*, vol 5, no 2, pp83–95

Smith, L. C. (2010) *The World in 2050: Four Forces Shaping Civilisations Northern Future*, Dutton (Penguin Group), New York, NY

Smith, M. (2003) *Issues in Cultural Tourism Studies*, Routledge, London

Smith, M. (2006) *Tourism, Culture and Regeneration*, CABI, Wallingford, UK

Smith, M. K. (2009) *Issues in Cultural Studies*, Taylor and Francis, Oxon, London

Smith, M. and Puczko, L. (2009) *Health and Wellness Tourism*, Butterworth-Heinemann, Oxford, UK

Smith, M., Macleod, N. and Robinson, M. H. (2010a) *Key Concepts in Tourist Studies*, Sage Publications, Oxford, UK

Smith, M., Derry, M. and Puczko, L. (2010b) 'The role of health, wellness and tourism for destination development', *Journal of Hospitality and Tourism Management*, vol 17, no 1, pp94–95

Smith, S. and Costello, C. (2009) 'Segmenting visitors to a culinary event: Motivations, travel behavior, and expenditures', *Journal of Hospitality Marketing and Management*, vol 18, pp44–67

Smith, V. L. (1978) *Hosts and Guests: The Anthropology of Tourism*, University of Pennsylvania Press, Philadelphia, PA

Smith, V. L. (1989) *Hosts and Guests: The Anthropology of Tourism*, second edition, University of Pennsylvania Press, Philadelphia, PA

Sonmez, S., Apostolopoulos, Y. and Tarlow, P. (1999) 'Tourism in crisis: Managing the effects of terrorism', *Journal of Travel Research*, August, vol 38, no 1, pp13–18

Sørensen, A. (2003) 'Backpacker ethnography', *Annals of Tourism Research*, vol 30, pp847–867

Southall, C. and Fallon, P. (2011) 'LGBT tourism', in P. Robinson, S. Heitmann and P. U. C. Dieke (eds) (2011) *Research Themes for Tourism*, CABI, Wallingford, UK, pp218–232

Sparks, B. (2007) 'Planning a wine tourism vacation? Factors that help to predict tourist behavioural intentions', *Tourism Management*, vol 28, no 5, pp1180–1192

Spenceley, A. (2008) *Responsible Tourism: Critical Issues for Conservation and Development*, Earthscan, London

Squire, S. J. (1996) 'Literary tourism and sustainable tourism: Promoting *Anne of Green Gables* in Prince Edward Island', *Journal of Sustainable Tourism*, vol 4, no 3, pp119–134

SRI International (2010) *Global Spa Summit, Spas and the Global Wellness Markets*, SRI International

Stabler, M. (1997) *Environmental Standards for Sustainable Tourism in Tourism and Sustainability: Principles to Practice*, CABI, Wallingford, UK

Stebbins, R. A. (1982) 'Serious leisure: A conceptual statement', *Pacific Sociological Review*, vol 25, no 2, pp251–272

Stebbins, R. A. (1992) *Amateurs, Professionals, and Serious Leisure*, McGill–Queens University Press, Montreal, Quebec

Stebbins, R. A. and Graham, M. (2004) *Volunteering as Leisure: Leisure as Volunteering – An International Assessment*, CABI, Wallingford and Cambridge

Stevenson, N., Airey, D. and Miller, G. (2008) 'Tourism policy making: The policymakers' perspective', *Annals of Tourism Research*, vol 35, no 3, pp732–750

Stewart, E. and Kirby, V. (1998) 'Interpretive evaluation: Towards a place approach', *International Journal of Heritage Studies*, vol 4, no 1, pp30–44

Stewart, J. W., Bramble, L. and Ziraldo, D. (2008) 'Key challenges in wine and culinary tourism with practical recommendations', *International Journal of Contemporary Hospitality Management*, vol 20, no 3, pp302–312

Stockdale, J. (1985) *What Is Leisure? An Empirical Analysis of the Concept of Leisure and the Role of Leisure in People's Lives*, The Sports Council and ESRC, London

Stone, P. R. (2005) 'Consuming dark tourism: A call for research', *eReview of Tourism Research*, vol 3, no 5, pp10–117, http://ertr.tamu.ed/appliedresearch.cfm?articleid=90

Stone, P. R. (2006) 'A dark tourism spectrum: Towards a typology of death and macabre related tourist sites, attractions and exhibitions', *Tourism: An Interdisciplinary International Journal*, vol 54, no 2, pp145–160

Stone, P. R. and Sharpley, R. (2008) 'Consuming dark tourism: A thanatological perspective', *Annals of Tourism Research*, vol 35, no 2, pp574–595

Strain, E. (2003) *Public Places, Private Journeys: Ethnography, Entertainment and the Tourist Gaze*, Rutgers University Press, New Brunswick, NJ

Supapol, A. B. and Barrows, D. (2007) 'Canadian health and wellness tourism: Obstacles impeding international competitiveness', *The Innovation Journal: The Public Sector Innovation Journal*, vol 12, no 3, pp2–18

Swarbrooke, J. (1995) *The Development and Management of Visitor Attractions*, Butterworth-Heinemann, Oxford

Swarbrooke, J. (1997) *Sustainable Tourism Management*, CABI, Wallingford, UK

Swarbrooke, J. (2002) *The Development and Management of Visitor Attractions*, second edition, Butterworth-Heinemann, Oxford, UK

Swarbrooke, J. (2007) *Mass Tourism*, Keynote address at the First Meeting of ATLAS Mass tourism SIG, Coventry, 14 May 2007

Swarbrooke, J. and Horner, S. (2001) *Business Travel and Tourism*, Butterworth-Heinemann, Oxford and Woburn

Swinglehurst, E. (1974) *The Romantic Journey: The Story of Thomas Cook and Victorian Travel*, Harper and Row, New York, NY

Tabacchi, M. (2008) 'American and European spas', in M. Cohen and G. Bodeker (eds) *Understanding the Global Spa Industry*, Butterworth-Heinemann, Oxford, pp26–40

Tacoli, C. (1998) 'Rural–urban interactions: A guide to the literature', *Environment and Urbanization*, vol 10, no 1, pp147–166

Tae, G. K., Jae, H. L. and Rob, L. (2008) 'An empirical examination of the acceptance behavior of hotel front office systems: An extended technology acceptance model', *Tourism Management*, vol 29, no 3, pp500–513

Tan, K. S., Chong, S. C. and Lin, B. (2009) 'Internet-based ICT adoption among small and medium enterprises: Malaysia's perspective', *Industrial Management and Data Systems*, vol 109, no 2, pp224–244

Tangeland, T. and Aas, O. (2011) 'Household composition and the importance of experience attributes of nature based tourism activity products: A Norwegian case study of outdoor recreationists', *Tourism Management*, vol 32, pp822–832

Tavmergen (Pirnar), I. and Ozdemir, P. M. (2001) 'Turizm sektorunde kriz pazarlamasi ve yonetimi', *Uluslararasi Turizm Arastirmalari Dergisi*, T.C. Maltepe Universitesi, pp111–120

Taylor, M. (1999) *World Travel Atlas*, Columbus, London

Taylor Nelson Sofres Research International Travel and Tourism (2010) *The UK Tourist – Statistics 2009*, Visit Scotland, Northern Ireland Tourist Board, Visit Wales and Visit England, Edinburgh

TC Saglik Bakanligi (2010) *Medikal Turizm Araştırması, Birinci bolum*, Ekim – Aralik 2010, Ankara, http://tuyev.org/yayinlarimiz/SB.pdf

Teas, J. (1974) 'I'm studying monkeys: What do you? Youthful travelers in Nepal', Paper presented at the Symposium on Tourism and Culture, Annual Meeting of the American Anthropological Association

Telfer, J. and Sharpley, R. (2008) *Tourism and Development in the Developing World*, Routledge, Oxford, UK

Teo, P. and Leong, S. (2006) 'A postcolonial analysis of backpacking', *Annals of Tourism Research*, vol 33, no 1, pp109–131

Terkenli, T. S. (2002) 'Landscapes of tourism: Towards a global cultural economy of space?', *Tourism Geographies*, vol 4, no 3, pp227–254

Thorp, J. (1998) *The Information Paradox: Realizing the Business Benefits of Information Technology*, McGraw-Hill Ryerson, Toronto, Ontario

Tilden, F. (1957) *Interpreting Our Heritage*, third edition, University of North Carolina Press, Chapel Hill

Timothy, D. J. (2005) *Shopping Tourism, Retailing and Leisure*, Channel View Publications, Clevedon, UK

Timothy, D. J. and Boyd, S. W. (2003) *Heritage Tourism*, Pearson Education, Harlow

Timothy, D. J. and Boyd, S. W. (2006) 'Heritage tourism in the 21st century: Valued traditions and new perspectives', *Journal of Heritage Tourism*, vol 1, no 1, pp1–16

Timothy, D. J. and Butler, R. W. (1995) 'Cross- border shopping: A North American perspective', *Annals of Tourism Research*, vol 22, no 1, pp16–34

Timothy, D. and Nyaupane, G. (2009) *Cultural Heritage and Tourism in the Developing World*, Routledge, Oxford, UK

Timothy, D. J. and Olsen, D. H. (2006) *Tourism, Religion and Spiritual Journeys*, Routledge, London

Timur, S. and Getz, D. (2009) 'Sustainable tourism development: How do destination stakeholders perceive sustainable urban tourism?', *Sustainable Development*, vol 17, no 4, pp220–232

Toomaney, J. (2010) *Place-Based Approaches to Regional Development: Global Trends and Australian Implications*, Australian Business Foundation, Sydney

Torkildsen, G. (2005) *Leisure and Recreation Management*, fifth edition, Routledge, Oxford, UK

Tourism Alliance (2010) *Tourism: The Opportunity for Employment and Economic Growth*, www.tourismalliance.com

Tourism New South Wales (2011) *Backpacker Tourism*, Tourism New South Wales Corporate website, http://corporate.tourism.nsw.gov.au/Backpacker_Tourism_p726.aspx, accessed 5 August 2011

Tourism Research Australia (2010) *Snapshots 2009: Backpacker Accommodation in Australia*, Department of Resources, Energy and Tourism, Australia

Towner, J. (1985) 'The Grand Tour: A key phase in the history of tourism', *Annals of Tourism Research*, vol 12, pp297–326

Towner, J. (1991) 'Approaches to tourism history', *Annals of Tourism Research*, vol 15, issue 1, pp47–62

Towner, J. (1995) 'What is tourism's history?', *Tourism Management*, vol 16, issue 5, pp339–343

Towner, J. (1996) *An Historical Geography of Recreation and Tourism in the Western World 1540–1940*, John Wiley and Sons, Chichester, UK

Towner, J. and Wall, G. (1991) 'History and tourism', *Annals of Tourism Research*, vol 18, no 1, pp71–84

Tracey, S. (2000) 'Becoming a character for commerce: Emotion labour, self-subordination and discursive construction of identity in a total institution', *Management Communication Quarterly*, vol 14, no 1, pp90–128

Tracey, W. R. (2004) *Human Resources Glossary: The Complete Desk Reference for HR Executives, Managers, and Practitioners*, third edition, Saint Lucie Press, Boca Raton, FL

Traucer, B. (2006) 'Conceptualising special interest tourism: Frameworks for analysis', *Tourism Management*, vol 27, no 2, pp183–200

Tresidder, R. (2011) 'The semiotics of tourism', in P. Robinson, S. Heitmann and P. Dieke (eds) (2011) *Research Themes for Tourism*, CABI, Wallingford, UK

Tribe, J. (2002) 'Research trends and imperatives in tourism education', *Acta Turistica*, vol 14, no 1, pp61–81

Tribe, J. (2004) 'Knowing about tourism: Epistemological issues', in J. Phillimore and L. Goodson (eds) *Qualitative Research in Tourism: Ontologies, Epistemologies, and Methodologies*, Routledge, London, pp46–62

Tribe, J. (2010a) 'Territories and networks in the tourism academy', *Annals of Tourism Research*, vol 37, no 1, pp7–33

Tribe, J. (2010b) *Strategy for Tourism*, Goodfellow Publishers, Woodeaton

Tribe, J., Font, X., Griffiths, N., Vickery, R. and Yale, K. (2000) *Environmental Management for Rural Tourism and Recreation*, Cassell, London

Tsaur, S. H., Yen, C. and Chen, C. L. (2010) 'Independent tourist knowledge and skills', *Annals of Tourism Research*, vol 37, no 4, pp1035–1054

Tsing, A. (2000) 'The global situation', *Cultural Anthropology*, vol 15, pp327–360

Turkeli, S., Olmez, F. and Saatcioglu, B. (2011) *Analysis of Turkey's Current Medical Tourism Strategy*, 9th Health Management Congress, Cyprus

Tunbridge, J. E. and Ashworth, G. J. (1996) *Dissonant Heritage: The Management of the Past as a Resource in Conflict*, John Wiley and Sons, Chichester, UK

Tyler, D. and Dinan, C. (2001) 'The role of interested groups in England's emerging tourism policy network', *Current Issues in Tourism*, vol 4, no 2–4, pp210–252

Tyler, M. and Abbott P (1998) *Chocs Away: Weight Watching in the Contemporary Airline Industry*. Sociology, August 1998, 32 (3), 433–450

UNEP (United Nations Environment Programme) (2003) *Tourism and the Local Agenda 21: The Role of Local Authorities in Sustainable Tourism*, UNEP, Paris

UNEP (2005) *Making Tourism Sustainable: A Guide for Policy Making*, UNEP, Paris

UNEP (2006) *Wildlife Watching and Tourism: A Study of Benefits and Risks of a Fast-Growing Tourism Activity and Its Impacts on Species*, UNEP, Nairobi

UNESCO (1976) 'The effects of tourism on socio-cultural values', *Annals of Tourism Research*, vol 4, pp74–105

UNESCO (2010) *World Heritage List*, http://whc.unesco.org/en/list

UN (United Nations) (2005) *World Urbanization Prospects: The 2005 Revision*, Department of Economic and Social Affairs, Population Division, United Nations, New York, NY

UNWTO (United Nations World Tourism Organization) (1995) *Concepts, Definitions and Classifications for Tourism Statics: Technical Manual No 1*, UNWTO, Madrid

UNWTO (1999) *Global Code of Ethics for Tourism*, http://www.unep.org/bpsp/Tourism/WTO%20Code%20 of %20Conduct.pdf, accessed 25 August 2011

UNWTO (2002) *Vision Global Forecasts and Profiles of Market Segments, Volume 7*, UNWTO, Madrid

UNWTO (2005) *Making Tourism More Sustainable: A Guide for Policy Makers*, UNWTO, Madrid

UNWTO (2010a) *Cruise Tourism: Current Situation and Trends*, UNWTO, Madrid

UNWTO (2010b) *Facts and Figures: Information, Analysis and Know How. Tourism 2020 Vision*, UNWTO, Madrid

UNWTO (2011a) *UNWTO World Tourism Barometer January 2011*, UNWTO, Madrid

UNWTO (2011b) *Facts and Figures: Information, Analysis and Know How. Tourism 2020 Vision*, UNWTO, Madrid

UNWTO (2011c) *Tourism Highlights 2010*, http://unwto.org/facts/eng/pdf/highlights/UNWTO_Highlights10_en_HR.pdf, accessed 18 August 201

Upchurch, R. S. (1998) 'A conceptual foundation for ethical decision making: A stakeholder perspective in the lodging industry (U.S.A.)', *Journal of Business Ethics*, vol 17, no 3, pp1349–1361

Uriely, N. (1997) 'Theories of modern and post-modern tourism', *Annals of Tourism Research*, vol 24, no 4, pp982–984

Uriely, N. (2005) 'The tourist experience: Conceptual developments', *Annals of Tourism Research*, vol 32, pp199–216

Uriely, N., Yonay, Y. and Simchai, D. (2002) 'Backpacking experiences: A type and form analysis', *Annals of Tourism Research*, vol 29, no 2, pp520–538

Urry, J (1990) *The Tourist Gaze: Leisure and Travel in Contemporary Society*, Sage Publications, London

Urry, J. (2001) *The Tourist Gaze: Leisure and Travel in Contemporary Society*, TCS, London

Urry, J. (2002) *The Tourist Gaze*, second edition, Sage Publications, London

Urry, J. (2003a) *Global Complexity*, Polity Press, Cambridge

Urry, J. (2003b) 'The sociology of tourism', in C. Cooper (ed) *Classic Reviews in Tourism*, Channel View Publications, Clevedon, UK

Urry, J. (2007) *Mobilities*, Polity Press, Cambridge

Urry, J. and Larsen, J. (2011) *The Tourist Gaze 3.0*, Sage Publications, London

Van de Merwe, M. and Wöcke, A. (2007) 'An investigation into responsible tourism practices in the South African hotel industry', *South African Journal of Business Management*, vol 28, no 2

van der Borg, J., Costa, P. and Gotti, G. (1996) 'Tourism in European heritage cities', *Annals of Tourism Research*, vol 23, no 2, pp306–321 van Westering, J. (1999) 'Heritage and gastronomy: The pursuits of the new tourist', *International Journal of Heritage Studies*, vol 5, no 2, pp75–81

Vanhove, N. (2011) *The Economics of Tourism Destinations*, second edition, Elsevier, London, pp61–108

Veal, A. J. (1992) *Research Methods for Leisure and Tourism*, Longman, Harlow

Veal, A. J. (2002) *Leisure and Tourism Policy*, second edition, CABI, Oxford

Veal, A. J. (2006) *Research Methods for Leisure and Tourism*, Prentice Hall, Sydney

Veek, A. (2010) 'Encounters with extreme foods: Neophilic/neophobic tendencies and novel foods', *Journal of Food Products Marketing*, vol 16, pp246–260

Verbole, P. (2005) 'The role of education in the management of rural tourism and leisure', in D. Hall, L. Roberts and M. Mitchell (eds) *New Directions in Rural Tourism*, Ashgate Publishing Limited, Hampshire, UK, pp183–189

Vespestad, M. K. and Lindberg, F. (2010) 'Understanding nature-based tourist experiences: An ontological analysis', *Current Issues in Tourism*, 10 September

Visit Wales (2011) *About Visit Wales*, www.visitwales.com, accessed 19 November 2011

Vogt, J. (1976) 'Wandering: Youth, and travel behavior', *Annals of Tourism Research*, vol 4, pp25–41

Voigt, C., Laing, J., Wray, M., Brown, G., Howat, G., Weiler, B. and Trembath, R. (2010) *Health Tourism in Australia: Supply, Demand and Opportunities*, CRC for Sustainable Tourism Pty Ltd, Australia

Walbeek, V. B. (2004) *Crisis Management: Could You Cope if the Unthinkable Happened, Hotel Online Special Report*, http://www.hotel-online.com/News/PR2003_2nd/Jun03_CrisisMgmt.html, accessed 19 November 2011

Walker, M. (2010) 'From the dunghill of England to the Jewel of the Commonwealth: Using the concept of tourism image to explore identity in tourism in 19th century and early 20th century Tasmania', in P. M. Burns, J. A. Lester and L. Bibbings (eds) *Tourism and Visual Culture: Methods and Cases*, CABI, Wallingford, UK, pp135–145

Wallace, J. (2010) 'Art off the grid', *Saltscapes*, vol 11, no 5, pp44–47

Wallerstein, I. (1984) *The Politics of the World-Economy*, Cambridge University Press, Cambridge

Walter, T. (1984) 'Death as recreation: Armchair mountaineering', *Leisure Studies*, vol 3, no 1, pp67–76

Walton, J. K. (1997) 'Taking the history of tourism seriously', *European History Quarterly*, vol 27, no 4, pp563–571

Walton, J. K. (2000) *The British Seaside, Holidays and Resorts in the Twentieth Century Manchester Studies in Popular Culture*, Manchester University Press, Manchester, UK

Walton, J. K. (ed) (2005) *Histories of Tourism: Representation, Identity and Conflict* (Tourism and Cultural Change), Channel View Publications, Clevedon, UK

Walton, J. K. (2009) 'Tourism histories', in T. Jamal and M. Robinson (eds) *Sage Handbook of Tourism Studies*, Sage Publications, London, pp115–129

Wang, T. and Zan, L. (2011) 'Management and presentation of Chinese sites for UNESCO World Heritage List (UWHL)', *Facilities*, vol 29, no 7/8, pp313–325

Wang, Y. (2008) 'Collaborative destination marketing: Understanding the dynamic process', *Journal of Travel Research*, vol 47, no 2, pp151–166

Wang, Y. (2012) *Tourism Destination Marketing: Collaborative Strategies*, CABI, Oxford, UK

Wang, Y. and Pizam, A. (2011) *Destination Marketing and Management: Theories and Applications*, CABI, Oxford, UK

Warraq, I. (2007) *Defending the West: A Critique of Edward Said's Orientalism*, Prometheus Books, Amherst, NY

Wassler, P. (2010) *An Interpretive Approach to the Host–Guest Relations in Lazise/Italy*, MA thesis, Tourism Destination Management Masters Programme, NHTV University of Applied Sciences, Breda

WCED (World Commission on Environment and Development) (1987) *Our Common Future*, Oxford University Press, Oxford

Wearing, S. (2001) 'Exploring socio-cultural impacts on local communities', in D. B. Weaver (ed) *The Encyclopedia of Ecotourism*, CABI, Wallingford, UK, pp395–410

Weaver, D. B. (1999) 'Magnitude of ecotourism in Costa Rica and Kenya', *Annals of Tourism Research*, vol 26, no 4, pp792–816

Weaver, D. B. (ed) (2001) *The Encyclopedia of Ecotourism*, CABI, Wallingford, UK

Weaver, D. (2006). *Sustainable Tourism: Theory and Practice*, Elsevier Ltd, Oxford

Weaver, D. (2008) *Ecotourism*, second edition, John Wiley, Australia

Weaver, D. and Fennell, D. (1997) 'Rural tourism in Canada: The Saskatchewan vacation farm operator as entrepreneur', in S. Page and D. Getz (1997) *Business of Rural Tourism: International Perspectives*, Series in Tourism and Hospitality Management, Cengage Learning EMEA, Andover

Weaver, D. and Lawton, L. (2010) *Tourism Management*, fourth edition, John Wiley and Sons, Milton, Qld, Australia

Weed, M. (2006) 'Sports tourism', in J. Beech. and S. Chadwick (eds) (2006) *The Business of Tourism Management*, Pearson Education Limited, Harlow

Weeden, C. (2001) 'Ethical tourism: An opportunity for competitive advantage?', *Journal of Vacation Marketing*, vol 8, no 2, pp141–153

Weiermair, K. and Mathies, C. (2004) *The Tourism and Leisure Industry: Shaping the Future*, Haworth Hospitality Press, Binghamton

Weiler, B. and Hall, C. M. (1992) *Special-Interest Tourism*, Belhaven, London

Welk, P. (2004) 'The beaten track: Anti-tourism as an element of backpacker identity construction', in G. Richards and J. Wilson (eds) The *Global Nomad: Backpacker Travel in Theory and Practice*, Channel View Publications, Clevedon, UK, pp77–92

Welsh Assembly Government (2011) *About Visit Wales*, Wales

Wernerfelt, B. (1984) 'A resource-based view of the firm', *Strategic Management Journal*, vol 5, pp171–180

Werthner, H. and Klein, S. (1999) *Information Technology and Tourism: A Challenging Relationship*, Springer, Wien and New York

Wheat, S. (1999) *Ethical Tourism: Tourism Concern*, http://www.ecotourism.org.hk/other%20files/Ethical%20Tourism.doc, accessed 20 August 2011

Whetton, D. A., Rands, G. and Godfrey, P. (2002) 'What are responsibilities of business to society?', in A. Pettigrew, H. Thomas and R. Whittington (eds) *Handbook of Strategy and Management*, Sage Publications, London

Widner Ward, C. and Wilkinson, A. E. (2006) *Conducting Meaningful Interpretation: A Field Guide for Success*, Fulcrum Publishing, Colorado

Williams, C. and Buswell, J. (2003) *Service Quality in Leisure and Tourism*, CABI, Oxford, UK

Williams, R. Y. and Williams, S. (2011) 'Medical tourism: A continuing public health concern?', *International Medical Travel Journal*, http://www.imtj.com/articles/2011/medical-tourism-a-continuing-public-health-concern-30108/

Williams, S. (1998) *Tourism Geography*, Routledge, London

Witt, S. F. (1987) 'Economic impact of tourism on Wales', *Tourism Management*, vol 8, no 4, pp306–316

Wood, R. E. (2004) 'Cruise ships: Deterritorialized destinations', in L. Lumsdon and S. Page (eds) *Tourism and Transport: Issues and Agenda for the New Millennium*, Elsevier, Oxford, pp133–145

Wood, R. and Brotherton, B. (eds) (2008) *The Sage Handbook of Hospitality Management*, Sage Publications Ltd, London

Woodward, S. (2004) 'Faith and tourism: Planning tourism in relation to places of worship', *Tourism and Hospitality Planning and Development*, vol 1, no 2, pp173–186

World Leisure Organization (2011) *Charter for Leisure*, http://www.worldleisure.org/userfiles/file/charter.pdf, accessed 14 August 2011

WTO (World Trade Organization) (2000) *Ethical Conducts in Tourism*, http://search.wto.org/search?q=ethical+tourism, accessed 22 August 2011

WTTC (World Travel and Tourism Council) (2002) *Corporate Social Leadership in Travel and Tourism*, WTTC, Paris

WTTC and WTO (1996) *Agenda 21 for the Travel and Tourism Industry towards Environmentally Sustainable Development*, WTTO, London

WWF-UK and IBLF (2005) *Why Environmental Benchmarking Will Help Your Hotel*, WWF-UK and International Business Leaders Forum, London

Xiao, G.-R. and Wall, G. (2009) 'Urban tourism in Dalian, China', *Anatolia*, vol 20, no 1, pp178–195

Yachts of Seabourn (2010) *Home Page*, www.seabourn.com/, accessed 1 November 2011

Yasumura, K. (1987) 'Toward a scientific foundation of sociology: Lessons from the epistemologies of Cassirer and Lewin', *Journal of Applied Sociology*, vol 28, pp397–417

Yasumura, K. (1994) *The Sociological Sphere of Tourism as a Social Phenomenon*, Revised version of a draft for the Workshop on Tourism Studies of the Department of Tourism, Hokkai Gakuen University of Kitami, http://yasumura.info/files/02-01.pdf, accessed 19 November 2011

Yildirim, O. (2005) *Termal turizm isletmelerinde musteri sadakati ve bir arastirma*, Yayinlanmamis Yuksek Lisans Tezi, T.C. Balikesir Universitesi, Sosyal Bilimler Enstitüsü, Turizm Isletmeciligi ve Otelcilik Ana Bilim Dali, Balikesir

York, D. (2008) 'Medical tourism: The trend toward outsourcing medical procedures to foreign countries', *Journal of Continuing Education in the Health Professions*, vol 28, no 2, pp99–102

Youell, R. (1995) *Leisure and Tourism*, Longman, London

Young, G. (1973) *Tourism, Blessing or Plight?*, Penguin Books Ltd, Harmondsworth

Youth Hostels Association (2011) *About YHA*, http://www.yha.org.uk/about-yha, accessed 15 December 2011

Zavala, I. (2000) 'The retroaction of the postcolonial: The answer of the real and the Caribbean as thing: An essay on critical fiction', *Interventions*, vol 2, no 3, pp364–378

Zelenka, J. (2009) 'Information and communication technologies in tourism: Influence, dynamics, trends', *EpM Ekonomie a Management*, vol 12, no 1, pp123–132

Zeppel, H. and Hall, C. M. (1992) 'Arts and heritage tourism', in B. Weiler and C. M. Hall (eds) *Special-Interest Tourism*, Belhaven, London

INDEX